Blind Goddess

Blind Goddess

A Reader on Race and Justice

EDITED BY
ALEXANDER PAPACHRISTOU

THE NEW PRESS

NEW YORK
LONDON

Requests for permission to reproduce selections from
this book should be mailed to: Permissions Department,
The New Press, 38 Greene Street, New York, NY 10013.

Pages 349–50 constitute an extension of this copyright page.

Published in the United States by The New Press, New York, 2011
Distributed by Perseus Distribution

LIBRARY OF CONGRESS CATALOGING-IN-PUBLICATION DATA

Blind goddess : a reader on race and justice / edited by Alexander Papachristou.
p.   cm.
Includes bibliographical references.
ISBN 978-1-59558-699-5 (pbk.: alk. paper)
1. Race discrimination—Law and legislation—United States.   2. Criminal
justice, Administration of—United States.   3. United States—Race
relations.   I. Papachristou, Alexander.
KF4755.B55 2011
305.896'073—dc23   2011031207

The New Press was established in 1990 as a not-for-profit alternative to the
large, commercial publishing houses currently dominating the book publishing
industry. The New Press operates in the public interest rather than for private
gain, and is committed to publishing, in innovative ways, works of educational,
cultural, and community value that are often deemed insufficiently profitable.

www.thenewpress.com

Composition by dix!
This book was set in ITC New Baskerville

Printed in the United States of America

2   4   6   8   10   9   7   5   3   1

Contents

Foreword   *Patricia J. Williams*   viii

Preface   *Alexander Papachristou*   xiii

PART I: SETTING THE STAGE: IS JUSTICE REALLY SO BLACK AND WHITE?   1

1. The New Jim Crow   *Michelle Alexander*   3

2. Race, Incarceration, and American Values   *Glenn C. Loury*   21

3. Class, Race & Hyperincarceration in Revanchist America
   Loïc Wacquant   30

PART II: POLICING: WHERE ARE THE COPS WHEN YOU NEED THEM?   47

4. Profiling Unmasked: From Criminal Profiling to
   Racial Profiling   *David A. Harris*   49

5. Stop-Question-Frisk Analyses   *Center for Constitutional Rights*   57

6. The Shame of New York City   *Bob Herbert*   62

PART III: THE WAR ON DRUGS: WHO IS THE REAL ENEMY?   65

7. The War on Drugs and the African American Community
   Marc Mauer   67

8. Decades of Disparity: Drug Arrests and Race in the
   United States   *Human Rights Watch*   80

PART IV: LAWYERING: WHOM ARE THE LAWYERS REALLY REPRESENTING?   85

9. Should Good People Be Prosecutors?   *Paul Butler*   87

10. "What's a Defense?"   *Amy Bach*   100

PART V: THE JURY:
WHO ARE YOUR PEERS AND WHO ARE MINE?   115

11. Judgment and Discrimination   *David Cole*   117

12. Illegal Racial Discrimination in Jury Selection:
    A Continuing Legacy   *Equal Justice Initiative*   139

PART VI: SENTENCING:
DOES TIME COME IN DIFFERENT COLORS?   157

13. No Exit: The Expanding Use of Life Sentences in
    America   *Ashley Nellis and Ryan S. King*   159

14. New Political and Cultural Meanings   *David Garland*   171

PART VII: PRISON: WHAT ARE THE WALLS HIDING?   187

15. Texas Tough   *Robert Perkinson*   190

16. Prisoners of the Census in New York:
    Democracy on the March!   *Eric Lotke*   212

PART VIII: COLLATERAL CONSEQUENCES:
COULD IT GET ANY WORSE?   215

17. Incarceration and Social Inequality   *Bruce Western
    and Becky Pettit*   218

18. Death by a Thousand Little Cuts: Studies of the Impact
    of Incarceration   *Todd R. Clear*   224

PART IX: SOLUTIONS: CAN ANYTHING BE DONE
ABOUT THIS?   247

19. Doing Less Harm   *Michael Tonry*   251

20. The Fire This Time   *Michelle Alexander*   264

21. From Racial Profiling to Racial Literacy   *Lani Guinier* 293

Notes   297
Bibliography   343
Permissions   349

Justice

That Justice is a blind goddess
Is a thing to which we blacks are wise:
Her bandage hides two festering sores
That once perhaps were eyes.

—L<small>ANGSTON</small> H<small>UGHES</small>

Foreword

Patricia J. Williams

In 2000, I read an article in the *New York Post* titled "Tired? Pop Your Pal's Ritalin." The story featured interviews with students at New York University who were taking attention-deficit drugs like Ritalin and Adderall without prescription. "Students say the two drugs are far more effective than non-prescription stimulants . . . and it's easier to bum a Ritalin from a roommate than to head to a Starbucks." The piece went on to specify how much the going rate was in the dorms (about $2 for a single pill) and to cite a study at the University of Wisconsin concluding that misuse of prescription drugs was "pretty much a part of student culture."[1]

By 2005, the phenomenon had become so common that one article in *Science Daily* was headlined "The Ritalin Generation Goes to College." The typical user, it concluded, was "white, male and well focused."[2] The typical motivation was reportedly "tied to the need to achieve." Coverage in the *New York Times* also drove home this latter point, citing Dr. Robert Herman, a psychiatrist at the University of Maryland: "Students tell me it's really changed their lives for the better, that they are so much more focused and organized." While advising his patients not to "share" medication, Dr. Herman also observed, "I can't exactly go into their dorm room and count their pills."[3]

By 2008, experts were no longer describing these drugs as remedies for attention deficit disorder, but rather as "cognitive-enhancing." The esteemed journal *Nature* published a forum of scientists and ethicists who endorsed the idea that healthy individuals might profit from their giving a "boost" to memory and concentration.[4] And by 2011, almost all articles on the topic of Ritalin and other stimulants on campus cited Stanford Law School professor Henry Greely's opinion that "concentration aids" should be freely available because they are no more "cheating" than having a tutor or getting extra sleep before a test. Indeed, Brittanie Walker Reid, a residence coordinator at the University of Ottawa, stated that "too often students who turn to study drugs are seen as a problem, not the victim of a more significant issue of academic expectations."[5]

I carry on at some length about this because it illustrates a trajectory of thought embodying the species of blind justice to which Langston Hughes refers in his poem, as well as the separate-but-not-at-all-equal ethical systems that demarcate the lives of those privileged by race and class from less fortunate others. From the first time I heard of "the Ritalin generation," I was struck by the very different discourses used to describe the mostly white young people enrolled at NYU, for example, as opposed to those describing black and Latino youth dwelling a few miles north in Harlem and the South Bronx. It is very hard to find journalism that speaks of selling or "bumming" pills in university dorms as anything like the moral equivalent of "drug trafficking." With regard to this population, it is nearly impossible to find mention of the Rockefeller drug laws or harsh determinate sentencing or the punitiveness of life imprisonment based on three-strikes-and-you're-out.

Indeed, when poor minority young people are arrested—as they are, at a rate of about eight times that of whites—one never hears about the stresses they're under or the "student culture" of self-medication, or why they feel it might be easier to ingest illicit stimulants than a vente frappuccino at Starbucks. For impoverished kids, particularly black kids, drug use is never tied to the struggle to compete in an unforgiving world; rarely is there any hesitation to break into their rooms or cars or backpacks in order to take stock of potential contraband. Rather, "pathology of failure" is the favored narrative. There are no "study drugs" or "concentration aids" in this world, just plain old amphetamines, methamphetamines, and degraded, dangerously dosed concoctions like "crack" or "crank." For the bottom rungs of our society, in other words, there is no "Ecstasy," no "party" or "velvet-rope club" intoxicants—only "street" or "ghetto" or "trailer trash" drugs.

This perspectival divide sets us up for the sort of cognitive dissonance that allows many Americans to remain impervious to huge disparities in punitive outcomes for those who are subordinate in social status. Our incarceration rate, so racially skewed that some have called it eugenic, is somehow invisible to the majority of American citizens. Our incarceration rate, so class-marked as to refute the very notion of American social mobility, is tolerated with little dissent. And that incarceration rate, which "disappears" and disenfranchises men at significantly disproportionate rates (and is unkind to women as well), is justified as crime control rather than sheer human waste.

Such willful invisibility is challenged by the kinds of empirical analyses gathered in this volume—by historical data showing that the present-day population of prisoners exceeds all those who were enslaved before the Civil War or subjected to Jim Crow. Similarly, lateral data show the United States as first on the planet in terms of per-capita inmate populations. The essays herein focus a laser beam of attention to the incoherence of public policy regarding swelling investments in prisons, policing, and profiling, compared with budget cuts in funding for education, health, and social benefits.

As Marc Mauer explains in chapter 7, the phenomenon of mass incarceration stems most directly from practices associated with the proclaimed war on drugs. That national effort, like Prohibition before it, has been plagued with corruption, violently exuberant gunplay, and open hypocrisy. The unconscionable legal distinction between powdered and "crack" forms of cocaine is perhaps the most glaring icon of the drug war's iniquities; although chemically identical, crack cocaine is sold mostly in black communities, while powdered cocaine is used mostly by wealthier whites. But possession for powder still carries a vastly lesser sentence than for crack cocaine.

Sometimes the inconsistency is most visible by comparisons among media accounts. Take, for example, the overdoses that led to the demises of Ol' Dirty Bastard and Heath Ledger, both so talented yet so extremely mentally unstable; one black, one white; one universally demonized as willfully profligate, the other depicted as victimized by pathos and depression. Even beyond the categories of race and class, the awarding of criminal agency is complicated, contradictory territory: Charlie Sheen, so clearly in the grip of bipolar disease or similar mental illness, is relentlessly mocked as concertedly, premeditatedly clownish. And those deemed clowns, particularly celebrity clowns, rarely go to jail for their manic misbehavior, even where, as with Sheen, that misbehavior allegedly involves assault, battery, adultery, addiction, trespass, and endangerment of the welfare of minors.

At the other end of the class, race, and gender spectrum from Sheen, one might invoke the case of sisters Jamie and Gladys Scott, who each served sixteen years of life sentences for a robbery whose yield was estimated to be about $11. Despite thin evidence and their consistent assertions of innocence, their fate as African American citizens in the state of Mississippi, despite extraordinary global publicity, still consigns them to long-term struggle. In 2011, the sisters were released, but not pardoned, by Governor Haley Barbour, on the condition that Gladys donate a kidney to Jamie, who is on dialysis—in the absence of any proof that one is a match for the other, that either is in good enough health for such intervention, or that they have funds for such surgery. Not coincidentally, the cost of the dialysis treatments in question had begun to creep upward of $200,000 a year. Governor Barbour explained his gracious intervention in the following terms: "Jamie Scott's medical condition creates a substantial cost

to the State of Mississippi."⁶ In the concluding chapter, Harvard law professor Lani Guinier writes eloquently in the context of racial profiling of
the historical and contemporary realities that permit and perpetuate such
polarized experiences.

Political consensus about whom to punish or imprison versus whom
to help or forgive is too often held captive by freighted and disastrously
predictable scripts—the false neutrality of "process" driving means, the
means defeating ends. The empirical findings in this book reveal fallacies,
new and old, by which the bitter metrics of those teetering scales of justice
are ultimately negotiated. The contributors to this volume represent the
very best of scholarship and advocacy on how justice really works in America today and what it means for millions of Americans, particularly those
who are poor and of color.

A prosecutor's duty is to represent a collective state interest in all evidence, including exculpatory evidence, as summoned by the government's
broad police power over specific individuals. As law professor and former
federal prosecutor Paul Butler depicts in chapter 9, this is a precious discretion that is completely countermanded by careless profiling practices
and the kinds of open trawling for "types" that have so fed our exploding
dockets. Similarly, a defense attorney's duty is not only to articulate the
interests of defendants in the technical language of law, but also first and
foremost to push for and assure that the state lives up to its very high burden of proof—a task rendered nearly impossible against a social backdrop
where the mere sight of a black face fosters fear and presumes guilt. The
law then forecloses challenges to sentencing based on claims of discrimination absent direct evidence, which is nearly impossible to obtain.

The book takes us all the way through the criminal justice labyrinth,
from investigation to imprisonment and through post-conviction collateral consequences. We see that race distorts the law's purported purity of
process at every turn. Constitutional protections become booby traps, as
police, prosecutors, jury clerks, and prison wardens exercise the discretion that the law allows to infiltrate a system meant to focus on fact-finding
and individual acts. Instead we judge people based on group affiliation
and can't stop using race as the handiest of groupings, packaged so
conveniently with historical and current stereotypes.

Sometimes there are surprises, even if they often function as the exceptions that prove the rule. In 2010, five white students at Columbia University were arrested on drug dealing charges. The students' defense was that
they were merely trying to put themselves through a school whose tuition,
before room and board, was then in excess of $55,000 a year (and now
costs even more). The police, on the other hand, cited sales of "$11,000

for 31 purchases of LSD, marijuana, cocaine, Ecstasy, and prescription stimulants." As New York City police commissioner Raymond Kelly put it, "This is no way to work your way through college."[7]

Indeed, given the imbalanced statistics so endemic in our criminal law, it is understandable that some might see the arrest of those five relatively privileged Columbia students as an overdue counterweight to the careless scooping up of easier marks, those poor minority kids whose parents cannot afford lawyers, to say nothing of suits and ties with which to confront a jury of their peers. Yet if—as the excerpts in this anthology underscore—a large factor in the United States' over-incarceration has to do with the over-criminalization of drugs, it is well past time we analyzed our voracious all-American appetite for uppers, downers, and pain-killers on a national scale and as part of an overall crisis in health and welfare, rather than sorting our responses according to glaringly divisive and documented prejudices. In the absence of real commitment to actual equity, we will remain forever split by narratives of thrill-seeking wastrels on the one hand versus pathetically self-medicating victims of stressful circumstance on the other. We will be left with the searing injustice of our darkly burgeoning body count, utterly unable to decipher the deep puzzlements of violence and volition, fear and freedom, fairness and foul play.

Preface

Alexander Papachristou

The irony within Langston Hughes's poem "Justice" hints at a basic discrepancy in the American notion of justice. On the one hand, we expect our institutions of government to follow the law "without fear or favor"; we believe that justice should disregard—be blind to—circumstances that somehow don't matter, such as an accused person's wealth or race.

On the other hand, we believe in justice as fundamental fairness, producing outcomes that naturally accommodate individual needs, human foibles, and shortcomings. We expect that the law will make sense of chaos, produce order, and somehow appease everyone, more or less. In this sense, justice is not only process, it is the desired result. What Hughes tells us poetically is that the process does not always, if ever, produce this result, but rather leads to blinding unfairness, especially for black Americans.

This discrepancy—between relying on processes that treat all people the same and expecting results fair to each person—underlies much of the controversy over race that has afflicted the United States in recent years. As we have overcome egregious race-based oppression—slavery, Jim Crow, "separate but equal" treatment—we have stiffened in our resistance to recognizing residual, but no less real, racial inequality. Affirmative action thus seems to be a process that unfairly benefits individuals who may not have suffered past discrimination themselves. Likewise, school busing and the sanctions of the Voting Rights Act punish individuals who did not necessarily participate in the practices being remedied. In a cockeyed version of Langston Hughes's irony, the election of Barack Obama seemed to some people to be an individual achievement that provided mass redemption and entry into a post-racial era.

America's continuous contortion around race has produced various means of mediating confrontation even while postponing resolution. Our system of laws has been central to this mediation, with its inspirational, though not always enforceable, principles and its convenient emphasis on process as the guarantor of fairness. As it developed, the law has incorporated and reinforced the American ideal of individualism, itself key to mediating racial conflict. Thus, historical injustice is no excuse for personal responsibility or qualification for special advantage, especially when the injustice cannot be linked directly to the person seeking redress. Even one's own dysfunctional upbringing, underfunded education, thwarted employability, or social subordination does not constitute a defense from criminal liability.

Criminal justice is where the law bares its teeth and bites most meaningfully. Thus, its procedural protections are predictably the most intricate, even while its substantive proscriptions are definite and inflexible. The Bill of Rights requires that police have reasonable suspicion before stopping someone on the street; that judges issue search warrants; that interrogations be voluntary; that lawyers be appointed; that incrimination not be self-inflicted; that juries of peers indict and convict; that prosecutors prove guilt beyond a reasonable doubt; and that, throughout it all, no one should consider the race, age, gender, employment, wealth, or anything else about the alleged criminal other than whether he or she "did it."

Here again, in the juxtaposition of manifold measures of "due process"—the defendant is innocent until proven guilty—and the restrictive substantive focus on the facts of the case—the defendant did it or didn't do it—is the irony of the blind goddess. However, in our day, this is irony masking tragedy of epic proportions. In the United States today, more black Americans are incarcerated than ever were enslaved at one time. They outnumber black students enrolled in colleges and universities across the country. They constitute nearly half of all the nation's prisoners, even while black Americans overall make up less than 13 percent of the U.S. population.

Such racial imbalance in the harsh accounting of criminal justice would be tragic regardless of the underlying circumstances; however, further analysis reveals even greater inequity. Over the thirty-odd years that so many more black Americans (and more—but not so many more— white Americans) have been sent to prison, crime was not worsening, and black Americans were not committing so many more crimes. Indeed, they were committing arguably fewer crimes. Moreover, crime rates did not seem to decrease as a result of this prison population explosion, at least not substantially. Adding insult to injury, it is *poor* black Americans who have borne the brunt of this iron-barred thresher. The greatest contributing factor to unabated incarceration has been the nation's indisputably failed and superfunded war on drugs, which focuses on crimes for which victims—at least direct victims—are not easily identified.

At an enormous expense, the United States has become the world's leader in imprisoning its own citizens over the last thirty years, a phenomenon that has little if any relation to crime trends and largely targets poor black and Latino Americans for drug crimes that almost always result in low-level sale or possession charges. Needless to say, this has wreaked havoc on the lives of not only those incarcerated or threatened with incarceration, but also their families and communities. Over this same period of time, government programs to support poor communities tightened eligibility requirements and suffered severely reduced funding. The war on drugs seems to be part of a broader war on the poor.

This book confronts how such a wasteful and harmful eventuality could transpire within a legal system that so many in the world, particularly Americans themselves, so greatly admire. We must examine and try to understand how our laws, by our own application, have brought about this enormous injustice. For the mass and skewed incarceration of poor black Americans has been official, legal, and judicial, not in any way outside of the law, but—as the expression goes—fully within the color of law.

It is not an exaggeration to say that American criminal justice has become thoroughly colorized. At all stages of due process, we find racial skewing: starting with police profiling and continuing through the exercise of prosecutorial discretion and judicial sentencing. The result is an ever-widening disproportionality of alleged criminality. The so-called funnel effect has poor black Americans suspected more; of those suspected, more are arrested; of those arrested, more are prosecuted; of those prosecuted, more are convicted; and of those convicted, more are imprisoned, producing such disparities as the fact that blacks are ten times as likely as whites who use illegal drugs to end up in prison. With this level of failure of the system's procedural protections at every stage, the restricted focus on the substantive outcome—whether the accused did or did not commit the crime—thus ends up ratifying the bias in the procedures, rather than excluding supposedly inappropriate factors like the defendant's race, age, or wealth.

We know instinctively that the law's attempt to separate who someone is from what someone did is artificial and tricky. Just as we insist on knowing what a model prisoner is "in for," we yearn to understand personal circumstances before judging a fellow human being's conduct. We also know instinctively that we use convenient data to "know" someone; we form quick assessments from appearance, accent, and incidental behavior. Race may seem to be a most handy tool; however, it is not a convenience but a distortion. It is taking a general concept and turning it into an individual attribute. Stereotyping replaces the actual particular facts about an individual with ideas about groups to which the individual is assumed to belong. These ideas belong to the observer, the one making the judgment, not to the observed and the judged. They come from unrelated personal experiences, cultural and ideological influences, and even unacknowledged emotions.

When the criminal justice system allows racial stereotypes or any other prejudice to enter the calculations of law enforcement, there is a double failure. We are not meant to consider any personal circumstances in deciding whether to arrest or prosecute someone. Then, when we consider whether to imprison someone, we are meant to consider only those personal circumstances for which the individual can be considered responsible. That today so many poor black Americans sit in prisons and jails at rates hugely disproportionate not only to white Americans, but also to crime rates, trends, and the apparent criminality of black Americans themselves, is an inescapable indictment of the U.S. legal system; based on all evidence, it is guilty of succumbing to rampant if unintended racial bias.

This collection is organized according to the stages of due process that the law provides to protect the innocent and punish the guilty. After setting the stage with depictions of how we have ended up with a racially skewed criminal justice system, the book examines police conduct, the role of lawyers, jury selection, judicial sentencing, and incarceration. Along the way, it focuses specifically on the War on Drugs, which over the last thirty years has exemplified and intensified the system's imbalance. The final selections explore the consequences of this imbalance for black Americans and their communities and present efforts to redress the racial disparities of the legal system.

The selections within these pages are drawn from the most compelling recent writing on race and justice.* They represent a range of media sources: books, scholarly journals, law reviews, news media, and issue-based research reports. Similarly, the authors come from many disciplines: political science, sociology, the teaching and practice of law, and various fields of advocacy. The variety offered is intended to correspond to the collaboration of law, politics, and socioeconomics in maintaining a system that singles out some for different treatment, while purporting to be blind to difference.

Some have contended that race is America's special feature.[1] We might go so far as to say that it is our own invention, crucial to our definition of ourselves.[2] The concept of race (as opposed to ethnicity or country of origin) has served to set some of us apart from others, even among those who share a common nationality or citizenship.[3] All of this has had significant political and economic consequences throughout U.S. history.

Today, there are signs that race is beginning to mean less, or perhaps signify something more complex than it did a generation ago. Americans increasingly identify themselves as "of mixed race," although their parentage is not diversifying as much as their self-reporting.[4] Thus, while Barack

---

*Space constraints required omitting many worthy selections. Some of these are noted in the introductory text as "Further Reading."

Obama defined himself as "black" in the 2010 census, despite having valid options that could have accounted for his mother's race,[5] what remains precedent-setting about him is his race, as both he and others define it—rather than, for example, his being the first first-generation American president (excluding the Founding Fathers).

Yes, race still matters, and it is the overriding feature of our system of criminal justice. That we so disproportionately arrest, prosecute, convict, and imprison black Americans is an inescapable and inexcusable fact. That these are predominantly poor fellow citizens of ours does not explain this fact but only compounds the heinousness of it. After all, we do not outlaw poverty; indeed, we try, or at least pretend to try, to combat it. While a degree of poverty surely does encourage some lawlessness, our over-criminalization of poor black Americans does not result, either exclusively or even significantly, from extra lawbreaking.

We assign our black fellow citizens criminality because of our historical and current instincts and interests. We are getting something we want or need out of this, presumably more than what is obvious. It costs too much, financially and morally, to be holdover or happenstance, and appears to be complicated and concealed both within ourselves and our society. We need to find it, face it, and overcome it. Then—and only then—can justice choose to wear a blindfold, rather than have her eyes burned shut from the pain and shame of it all.

My thanks go, as it turns out, to many women: at The New Press, to Diane Wachtell for envisioning and entrusting to me this project and to Tara Grove and Sarah Fan for shepherding me through it so deftly; to Nina, Lucy, and Clara, for giving me cause for hope of a better future; to Judy, for giving me what wisdom I have; to Anne, for giving me perspective, empathy, and joy of companionship; and to one man, Tician, for the lessons of finding one's way all over the world, loving language, and caring so very much.

I dedicate this book to Judge Myron H. Thompson, whose intellect and character provide trenchant, enduring insight to justice.

Part I

Setting the Stage: Is Justice Really So Black and White?

Tracking what goes on in the criminal justice system is daunting. Most activity is spread out at the state and even county levels, although federal law enforcement agencies may also participate, especially in drug cases, whether or not they end up in federal or state courts. The volume is huge: while 2.3 million people are incarcerated at any one time, nearly 14 million are arrested, over 13 million enter prison or jail over the course of one year, and another 5 million are kept under so-called criminal justice supervision, which includes probation and parole.

Statistics are easy to come by, since the system is intensely bureaucratic. Making sense of the numbers, and the reality that underlies them, is another matter altogether. Trends over the last three decades show explosive growth in all categories. These require further parsing to reveal significantly disparate phenomena for different people. Lo and behold, race turns out to be a factor that defines enormous incongruity in how criminal laws affect Americans.

The three selections in this part serve to set the stage for our analysis of U.S. justice and its particular impact on black Americans. In addition to presenting the history and the statistics, the selections identify shifts in the theories justifying penological policy and offer analyses of how these shifts correlate with ever-increasing racial skewing. How such imbalance could come about and then persist is a conundrum that these authors tackle head-on.

The New Jim Crow: Mass Incarceration in the Age of Colorblindness is the first book by Michelle Alexander, a former ACLU staffer and law professor. As its title suggests, the book contends that mass incarceration is today's version of structural racism, serving to keep black Americans, particularly

1

young males, in a permanent underclass. She contends that this is a caste, a manifestation of social control that permanently restricts opportunity and has community-wide consequences. As Alexander explains, structural racism, previously manifest in slavery and Jim Crow, operates without need of hatred or even conscious bias. It is the accumulation of policies and practices that appear neutral but have a devastatingly disparate impact.

Race, Incarceration, and American Values is based on Glenn C. Loury's 2007 Tanner Lecture on Human Values at Stanford University. Loury, a Brown University professor and the author of *The Anatomy of Racial Inequality*, describes the new punitiveness that characterizes American criminal justice today: an increased likelihood that arrest will lead to incarceration, longer sentences, and an end to even a pretense of rehabilitation. He ties this to the racially skewed nature of incarceration, arguing that the system has become tougher as it has focused so much more on black Americans. To Loury, it is vital that we confront mass incarceration as a choice that we have made as a society, and that we try to align it with our fundamental values.

In a 2010 issue of *Dædalus* (the journal of the American Academy of Arts and Sciences) devoted entirely to the subject of mass incarceration, Loïc Wacquant challenges this nomenclature for the racial skewing of justice. He bases his alternative term, "hyperincarceration," on specific aspects of this phenomenon. For example, contrary to expectations, college-educated black Americans are less likely to be incarcerated now than they were in the past. It is poverty, race, and an incomplete high school education that combine to characterize those overrepresented in prison populations. Wacquant, a prolific sociologist at the University of California, Berkeley, focuses on historical segregation in ghettos and the reduction of antipoverty programs as crucial features of hyperincarceration.

1

The New Jim Crow

Michelle Alexander

It was no ordinary Sunday morning when presidential candidate Barack Obama stepped to the podium at the Apostolic Church of God in Chicago. It was Father's Day. Hundreds of enthusiastic congregants packed the pews at the overwhelmingly black church eager to hear what the first black Democratic nominee for president of the United States had to say.

The message was a familiar one: black men should be better fathers. Too many are absent from their homes. For those in the audience, Obama's speech was an old tune sung by an exciting new performer. His message of personal responsibility, particularly as it relates to fatherhood, was anything but new; it had been delivered countless times by black ministers in churches across America. The message had also been delivered on a national stage by celebrities such as Bill Cosby and Sidney Poitier. And the message had been delivered with great passion by Louis Farrakhan, who more than a decade earlier summoned one million black men to Washington, D.C., for a day of "atonement" and recommitment to their families and communities.

The mainstream media, however, treated the event as big news, and many pundits seemed surprised that the black congregants actually applauded the message. For them, it was remarkable that black people nodded in approval when Obama said: "If we are honest with ourselves, we'll admit that too many fathers are missing—missing from too many lives and too many homes. Too many fathers are MIA. Too many fathers are AWOL. They have abandoned their responsibilities. They're acting like boys instead of men. And the foundations of our families are weaker because of it. You and I know this is true everywhere, but nowhere is this more true than in the African American community."

From *The New Jim Crow: Mass Incarceration in the Age of Colorblindness* (New York: The New Press, 2010), 173–76, 180–95.

The media did not ask—and Obama did not tell—where the missing fathers might be found.

The following day, social critic and sociologist Michael Eric Dyson published a critique of Obama's speech in *Time* magazine. He pointed out that the stereotype of black men being poor fathers may well be false. Research by Boston College social psychologist Rebekah Levine Coley found that black fathers not living at home are more likely to keep in contact with their children than fathers of any other ethnic or racial group. Dyson chided Obama for evoking a black stereotype for political gain, pointing out that "Obama's words may have been spoken to black folk, but they were aimed at those whites still on the fence about whom to send to the White House."[1] Dyson's critique was a fair one, but like other media commentators, he remained silent about where all the absent black fathers could be found. He identified numerous social problems plaguing black families, such as high levels of unemployment, discriminatory mortgage practices, and the gutting of early-childhood learning programs. Not a word was said about prisons.

The public discourse regarding "missing black fathers" closely parallels the debate about the lack of eligible black men for marriage. The majority of black women are unmarried today, including 70 percent of professional black women.[2] "Where have all the black men gone?" is a common refrain heard among black women frustrated in their efforts to find life partners.

The sense that black men have disappeared is rooted in reality. The U.S. Census Bureau reported in 2002 that there are nearly 3 million more black adult women than men in black communities across the United States, a gender gap of 26 percent.[3] In many urban areas, the gap is far worse, rising to more than 37 percent in places like New York City. The comparable disparity for whites in the United States is 8 percent.[4] Although a million black men can be found in prisons and jails, public acknowledgment of the role of the criminal justice system in "disappearing" black men is surprisingly rare. Even in the black media—which is generally more willing to raise and tackle issues related to criminal justice—an eerie silence can often be found.[5]

Ebony magazine, for example, ran an article in December 2006 entitled "Where Have the Black Men Gone?" The author posed the popular question but never answered it.[6] He suggested we will find our black men when we rediscover God, family, and self-respect. A more cynical approach was taken by Tyra Banks, the popular talk show host, who devoted a show in May 2008 to the recurring question, "Where Have All the Good Black Men Gone?" She wondered aloud whether black women are unable to find "good black men" because too many of them are gay or dating white women. No mention was made of the War on Drugs or mass incarceration.

The fact that Barack Obama can give a speech on Father's Day dedicated to the subject of fathers who are "AWOL" without ever acknowledging that the majority of young black men in large urban areas are currently under the control of the criminal justice system is disturbing, to say the least. What is more problematic, though, is that hardly anyone in the mainstream media noticed the oversight. One might not expect serious analysis from Tyra Banks, but shouldn't we expect a bit more from the *New York Times* and CNN? Hundreds of thousands of black men are unable to be good fathers for their children, not because of a lack of commitment or desire but because they are warehoused in prisons, locked in cages. They did not walk out on their families voluntarily; they were taken away in handcuffs, often due to a massive federal program known as the War on Drugs.

More African Americans are under correctional control today—in prison or jail, on probation or parole—than were enslaved in 1850, a decade before the Civil War began.[7] The mass incarceration of people of color is a big part of the reason that a black child born today is less likely to be raised by both parents than a black child born during slavery.[8] The absence of black fathers from families across America is not simply a function of laziness, immaturity, or too much time watching *SportsCenter*. Thousands of black men have disappeared into prisons and jails, locked away for drug crimes that are largely ignored when committed by whites.

The clock has been turned back on racial progress in America, though scarcely anyone seems to notice. All eyes are fixed on people like Barack Obama and Oprah Winfrey, who have defied the odds and risen to power, fame, and fortune. For those left behind, especially those within prison walls, the celebration of racial triumph in America must seem a tad premature. More black men are imprisoned today than at any other moment in our nation's history. More are disenfranchised today than in 1870, the year the Fifteenth Amendment was ratified prohibiting laws that explicitly deny the right to vote on the basis of race.[9] Young black men today may be just as likely to suffer discrimination in employment, housing, public benefits, and jury service as a black man in the Jim Crow era—discrimination that is perfectly legal, because it is based on one's criminal record.

This is the new normal, the new racial equilibrium.

The launching of the War on Drugs and the initial construction of the new system required the expenditure of tremendous political initiative and resources. Media campaigns were waged; politicians blasted "soft" judges and enacted harsh sentencing laws; poor people of color were vilified. The system now, however, requires very little maintenance or justification. In fact, if you are white and middle class, you might not even realize the drug war is still going on. Most high school and college students today have no recollection of the political and media frenzy surrounding the drug war in the early years. They were young children when the war was declared, or not even born yet. Crack is out; terrorism is in.

Today, the political fanfare and the vehement, racialized rhetoric regarding crime and drugs are no longer necessary. Mass incarceration has been normalized, and all of the racial stereotypes and assumptions that gave rise to the system are now embraced (or at least internalized) by people of all colors, from all walks of life, and in every major political party. We may wonder aloud "where have the black men gone?" but deep down we already know. It is simply taken for granted that, in cities like Baltimore and Chicago, the vast majority of young black men are currently under the control of the criminal justice system or branded criminals for life. This extraordinary circumstance—unheard of in the rest of the world—is treated here in America as a basic fact of life, as normal as separate water fountains were just a half century ago. [. . .]

How It Works

Precisely how the system of mass incarceration works to trap African Americans in a virtual (and literal) cage can best be understood by viewing the system as a whole. In earlier chapters, we considered various wires of the cage in isolation; here, we put the pieces together, step back, and view the cage in its entirety. Only when we view the cage from a distance can we disengage from the maze of rationalizations that are offered for each wire and see how the entire apparatus operates to keep African Americans perpetually trapped.

This, in brief, is how the system works: The War on Drugs is the vehicle through which extraordinary numbers of black men are forced into the cage. The entrapment occurs in three distinct phases, each of which has been explored earlier, but a brief review is useful here. The first stage is the roundup. Vast numbers of people are swept into the criminal justice system by the police, who conduct drug operations primarily in poor communities of color. They are rewarded in cash—through drug forfeiture laws and federal grant programs—for rounding up as many people as possible, and they operate unconstrained by constitutional rules of procedure that once were considered inviolate. Police can stop, interrogate, and search anyone they choose for drug investigations, provided they get "consent." Because there is no meaningful check on the exercise of police discretion, racial biases are granted free rein. In fact, police are allowed to rely on race as a factor in selecting whom to stop and search (even though people of color are no more likely to be guilty of drug crimes than whites)—effectively guaranteeing that those who are swept into the system are primarily black and brown.

The conviction marks the beginning of the second phase: the period of formal control. Once arrested, defendants are generally denied meaningful legal representation and pressured to plead guilty whether they are or not. Prosecutors are free to "load up" defendants with extra charges, and their decisions cannot be challenged for racial bias. Once convicted, due to the drug war's harsh sentencing laws, drug offenders in the United States spend more time under the criminal justice system's formal control—in jail or prison, on probation or parole—than drug offenders anywhere else in the world. While under formal control, virtually every aspect of one's life is regulated and monitored by the system, and any form of resistance or disobedience is subject to swift sanction. This period of control may last a lifetime, even for those convicted of extremely minor, nonviolent offenses, but the vast majority of those swept into the system are eventually released. They are transferred from their prison cells to a much larger, invisible cage.

The final stage has been dubbed by some advocates as the period of invisible punishment.[10] This term, first coined by Jeremy Travis, is meant to describe the unique set of criminal sanctions that are imposed on individuals after they step outside the prison gates, a form of punishment that operates largely outside of public view and takes effect outside the traditional sentencing framework. These sanctions are imposed by operation of law rather than decisions of a sentencing judge, yet they often have a greater impact on one's life course than the months or years one actually spends behind bars. These laws operate collectively to ensure that the vast majority of convicted offenders will never integrate into mainstream, white society. They will be discriminated against, legally, for the rest of their lives—denied employment, housing, education, and public benefits. Unable to surmount these obstacles, most will eventually return to prison and then be released again, caught in a closed circuit of perpetual marginality.

In recent years, advocates and politicians have called for greater resources devoted to the problem of "prisoner re-entry," in view of the unprecedented numbers of people who are released from prison and returned to their communities every year. While the terminology is well intentioned, it utterly fails to convey the gravity of the situation facing prisoners upon their release. People who have been convicted of felonies almost never truly reenter the society they inhabited prior to their conviction. Instead, they enter a separate society, a world hidden from public view, governed by a set of oppressive and discriminatory rules and laws that do not apply to everyone else. They become members of an undercaste—an enormous population of predominantly black and brown people who, because of the drug war, are denied basic rights and privileges of American citizenship and are permanently relegated to an inferior status. This is the final phase, and there is no going back.

Nothing New?

Some might argue that as disturbing as this system appears to be, there is nothing particularly new about mass incarceration; it is merely a continuation of past drug wars and biased law enforcement practices. Racial bias in our criminal justice system is simply an old problem that has gotten worse, and the social excommunication of "criminals" has a long history; it is not a recent invention. There is some merit to this argument.

Race has always influenced the administration of justice in the United States. Since the day the first prison opened, people of color have been disproportionately represented behind bars. In fact, the very first person admitted to a U.S. penitentiary was a "light skinned Negro in excellent health," described by an observer as "one who was born of a degraded and depressed race, and had never experienced anything but indifference and harshness."[11] Biased police practices are also nothing new, a recurring theme of African American experience since blacks were targeted by the police as suspected runaway slaves. And every drug war that has ever been waged in the United States—including alcohol prohibition—has been tainted or driven by racial bias.[12] Even postconviction penalties have a long history. The American colonies passed laws barring criminal offenders from a wide variety of jobs and benefits, automatically dissolving their marriages and denying them the right to enter contracts. These legislatures were following a long tradition, dating back to ancient Greece, of treating criminals as less than full citizens. Although many collateral sanctions were repealed by the late 1970s, arguably the drug war simply revived and expanded a tradition that has ancient roots, a tradition independent of the legacy of American slavery.

In view of this history and considering the lack of originality in many of the tactics and practices employed in the era of mass incarceration, there is good reason to believe that the latest drug war is just another drug war corrupted by racial and ethnic bias. But this view is correct only to a point.

In the past, the criminal justice system, as punitive as it may have been during various wars on crime and drugs, affected only a relatively small percentage of the population. Because civil penalties and sanctions imposed on ex-offenders applied only to a few, they never operated as a comprehensive system of control over any racially or ethnically defined population. Racial minorities were always overrepresented among current and ex-offenders, but as sociologists have noted, until the mid-1980s, the criminal justice system was marginal to communities of color. While young minority men with little schooling have always had relatively high rates of incarceration, "before the 1980s the penal system was not a dominant presence in the disadvantaged neighborhoods."[13]

Today, the War on Drugs has given birth to a system of mass incarceration that governs not just a small fraction of a racial or ethnic minority but entire communities of color. In ghetto communities, nearly everyone is either directly or indirectly subject to the new caste system. The system serves to redefine the terms of the relationship of poor people of color and their communities to mainstream, white society, ensuring their subordinate and marginal status. The criminal and civil sanctions that were once reserved for a tiny minority are now used to control and oppress a racially defined majority in many communities, and the systematic manner in which the control is achieved reflects not just a difference in scale. The nature of the criminal justice system has changed. It is no longer concerned primarily with the prevention and punishment of crime, but rather with the management and control of the dispossessed. Prior drug wars were ancillary to the prevailing caste system. This time the drug war *is* the system of control.

If you doubt that this is the case, consider the effect of the war on the ground, in specific locales. Take Chicago, Illinois, for example. Chicago is widely considered to be one of America's most diverse and vibrant cities. It has boasted black mayors, black police chiefs, black legislators, and is home to the nation's first black president. It has a thriving economy, a growing Latino community, and a substantial black middle class. Yet as the Chicago Urban League reported in 2002, there is another story to be told.[14]

If Martin Luther King Jr. were to return miraculously to Chicago, some forty years after bringing his Freedom Movement to the city, he would be saddened to discover that the same issues on which he originally focused still produce stark patterns of racial inequality, segregation, and poverty. He would also be struck by the dramatically elevated significance of one particular institutional force in the perpetuation and deepening of those patterns: the criminal justice system. In the few short decades since King's death, a new regime of racially disparate mass incarceration has emerged in Chicago and become the primary mechanism for racial oppression and the denial of equal opportunity.

In Chicago, like the rest of the country, the War on Drugs is the engine of mass incarceration, as well as the primary cause of gross racial disparities in the criminal justice system and in the ex-offender population. About

90 percent of those sentenced to prison for a drug offense in Illinois are African American.[15] White drug offenders are rarely arrested, and when they are, they are treated more favorably at every stage of the criminal justice process, including plea bargaining and sentencing.[16] Whites are consistently more likely to avoid prison and felony charges, even when they are repeat offenders.[17] Black offenders, by contrast, are routinely labeled felons and released into a permanent racial undercaste.

The total population of black males in Chicago with a felony record (including both current and ex-felons) is equivalent to 55 percent of the black adult male population and an astonishing 80 percent of the adult black male workforce in the Chicago area.[18] This stunning development reflects the dramatic increase in the number and race of those sent to prison for drug crimes. From the Chicago region alone, the number of those annually sent to prison for drug crimes increased almost 2,000 percent, from 469 in 1985 to 8,755 in 2005.[19]

When people are released from Illinois prisons, they are given as little as $10 in "gate money" and a bus ticket to anywhere in the United States. Most return to impoverished neighborhoods in the Chicago area, bringing few resources and bearing the stigma of their prison record.[20] In Chicago, as in most cities across the country, ex-offenders are banned or severely restricted from employment in a large number of professions, job categories, and fields by professional licensing statutes, rules, and practices that discriminate against potential employees with felony records. According to a study conducted by the DePaul University College of Law in 2000, of the then ninety-eight occupations requiring licenses in Illinois, fifty-seven placed stipulations and/or restrictions on applicants with a criminal record.[21] Even when not barred by law from holding specific jobs, ex-offenders in Chicago find it extraordinarily difficult to find employers who will hire them, regardless of the nature of their conviction. They are also routinely denied public housing and welfare benefits, and they find it increasingly difficult to obtain education, especially now that funding for public education has been hard hit, due to exploding prison budgets.

The impact of the new caste system is most tragically felt among the young. In Chicago (as in other cities across the United States), young black men are more likely to go to prison than to college.[22] As of June 2001, there were nearly 20,000 more black men in the Illinois state prison system than enrolled in the state's public universities.[23] In fact, there were more black men in the state's correctional facilities that year *just on drug charges* than the total number of black men enrolled in undergraduate degree programs in state universities.[24] To put the crisis in even sharper focus, consider this: just 992 black men received a bachelor's degree from Illinois state universities in 1999, while roughly 7,000 black men were released from the state prison system the following year just for drug offenses.[25] The young men who go to prison rather than college face a lifetime of closed doors, discrimination, and ostracism. Their plight is not what we hear about on the evening news, however. Sadly, like the racial caste systems that preceded it, the system of mass incarceration now seems normal and natural to most, a regrettable necessity.

Mapping the Parallels

Those cycling in and out of Illinois prisons today are members of America's new racial undercaste. The United States has almost always had a racial undercaste—a group defined wholly or largely by race that is permanently locked out of mainstream, white society by law, custom, and practice. The reasons and justifications change over time, as each new caste system reflects and adapts to changes in the social, political, and economic context. What is most striking about the design of the current caste system, though, is how closely it resembles its predecessor. There are important differences between mass incarceration and Jim Crow, to be sure—many of which will be discussed later—but when we step back and view the system as a whole, there is a profound sense of déjà vu. There is a familiar stigma and shame. There is an elaborate system of control, complete with political disenfranchisement and legalized discrimination in every major realm of economic and social life. And there is the production of racial meaning and racial boundaries.

Many of these parallels have been discussed at some length in earlier chapters; others have yet to be explored. Listed below are several of the most obvious similarities between Jim Crow and mass incarceration, followed by a discussion of a few parallels that have not been discussed so far. Let's begin with the historical parallels.

Historical parallels. Jim Crow and mass incarceration have similar political origins. As described in chapter 1, both caste systems were born, in part, due to a desire among white elites to exploit the resentments, vulnerabilities, and racial biases of poor and working-class whites for political or economic gain. Segregation laws were proposed as part of a deliberate and strategic effort to deflect anger and hostility that had been brewing against the white elite away from them and toward African Americans. The birth of mass incarceration can be traced to a similar political dynamic. Conservatives in the 1970s and 1980s sought to appeal to the racial biases and economic vulnerabilities of poor and working-class whites through racially coded rhetoric on crime and welfare. In both cases, the racial opportunists offered few, if any, economic reforms to address the legitimate economic anxieties of poor and working-class whites, proposing instead a crackdown on the racially defined "others." In the early years of Jim Crow, conservative white elites competed with each other by passing ever more stringent and oppressive Jim Crow legislation. A century later, politicians in the early years of the drug war competed with each other to prove who could be tougher on crime by passing ever harsher drug laws—a thinly veiled effort to appeal to poor and working-class whites who, once again, proved they were willing to forgo economic and structural reform in exchange for an apparent effort to put blacks back "in their place."[26]

Legalized discrimination. The most obvious parallel between Jim Crow and mass incarceration is legalized discrimination. During Black History Month, Americans congratulate themselves for having put an end to discrimination against African Americans in employment, housing, public benefits, and public accommodations. Schoolchildren wonder out loud how discrimination could ever have been legal in this great land of ours. Rarely are they told that it is *still* legal. Many of the forms of discrimination that relegated African Americans to an inferior caste during Jim Crow continue to apply to huge segments of the black population today—provided they are first labeled felons. If they are branded felons by the time they reach the age of twenty-one (as many of them are), they are subject to legalized discrimination for their entire adult lives. The forms of discrimination that apply to ex-drug offenders mean that, once prisoners are released, they enter a parallel social universe—much like Jim Crow—in which discrimination in nearly every aspect of social, political, and economic life is perfectly legal. Large majorities of black men in cities across the United States are once again subject to legalized discrimination effectively barring them from full integration into mainstream, white society. Mass incarceration has nullified many of the gains of the Civil Rights Movement, putting millions of black men back in a position reminiscent of Jim Crow.

Political disenfranchisement. During the Jim Crow era, African Americans were denied the right to vote through poll taxes, literacy tests, grandfather clauses, and felon disenfranchisement laws, even though the Fifteenth Amendment to the U.S. Constitution specifically provides that "the right of citizens of the United States to vote shall not be denied . . . on account of race, color, or previous condition of servitude." Formally race-neutral devices were adopted to achieve the goal of an all-white electorate without violating the terms of the Fifteenth Amendment. The devices worked quite well. Because African Americans were poor, they frequently could not pay poll taxes. And because they had been denied access to education, they could not pass literacy tests. Grandfather clauses allowed whites to vote even if they couldn't meet the requirements, as long as their ancestors had been able to vote. Finally, because blacks were disproportionately charged with felonies—in fact, some crimes were specifically defined as felonies with the goal of eliminating blacks from the electorate—felony disenfranchisement laws effectively suppressed the black vote as well.[27]

Following the collapse of Jim Crow, all of the race-neutral devices for excluding blacks from the electorate were eliminated through litigation or legislation, except felon disenfranchisement laws. Some courts have found that these laws have "lost their discriminatory taint" because they have been amended since the collapse of Jim Crow; others courts have allowed the laws to stand because overt racial bias is absent from the legislative record.[28] The failure of our legal system to eradicate all of the tactics adopted during the Jim Crow era to suppress the black vote has major implications today. Felon disenfranchisement laws have been more effective in eliminating black voters in the age of mass incarceration than they were during Jim Crow. Less than two decades after the War on Drugs began, one in seven black men nationally had lost the right to vote, and as many as one in four in those states with the highest African American disenfranchisement rate.[29] These figures may understate the impact of felony disenfranchisement, because they do not take into account the millions of ex-felons who cannot vote in states that require ex-felons to pay fines or fees before their voting rights can be restored—the new poll tax. As legal scholar Pamela Karlan has observed, "felony disenfranchisement has decimated the potential black electorate."[30]

It is worthy of note, however, that the exclusion of black voters from polling booths is not the only way in which black political power has been suppressed. Another dimension of disenfranchisement echoes not so much Jim Crow as slavery. Under the usual-residence rule, the Census Bureau counts imprisoned individuals as residents of the jurisdiction in which they are incarcerated. Because most new prison construction occurs in predominantly white, rural areas, white communities benefit from inflated population totals at the expense of the urban, overwhelmingly minority communities from which the prisoners come.[31] This has enormous consequences for the redistricting process. White rural communities that house prisons wind up with more people in state legislatures representing them, while poor communities of color lose representatives because it appears their population has declined. This policy is disturbingly reminiscent of the three-fifths clause in the original Constitution, which enhanced the political clout of slaveholding states by including 60 percent of slaves in the population base for calculating Congressional seats and electoral votes, even though they could not vote.

Exclusion from juries. Another clear parallel between mass incarceration and Jim Crow is the systematic exclusion of blacks from juries. One hallmark of the Jim Crow era was all-white juries trying black defendants in the South. Although the exclusion of jurors on the basis of race has been illegal since 1880, as a practical matter, the removal of prospective black jurors through race-based peremptory strikes was sanctioned by the Supreme Court until 1985, when the Court ruled in *Batson v. Kentucky* that racially biased strikes violate the equal protection clause of the Fourteenth Amendment.[32] Today defendants face a situation highly similar to the one they faced a century ago. A formal prohibition against race-based peremptory strikes does exist; as a practical matter, however, the Court has tolerated the systematic exclusion of blacks from juries by allowing lower courts to accept "silly" and even "superstitious" reasons for striking black jurors.[33] To make matters worse, a large percentage of black men (about 30 percent) are automatically excluded from jury service because they have been labeled felons.[34] The combined effect of race-based peremptory strikes and the automatic exclusion of felons from juries has put black defendants in a familiar place—in a courtroom in shackles, facing an all-white jury.

Closing the courthouse doors. The parallels between mass incarceration and Jim Crow extend all the way to the U.S. Supreme Court. Over the years, the Supreme Court has followed a fairly consistent pattern in responding to racial caste systems, first protecting them and then, after dramatic shifts in the political and social climate, dismantling these systems of control and some of their vestiges. In *Dred Scott v. Sandford*, the Supreme Court immunized the institution of slavery from legal challenge on the grounds that African Americans were not citizens, and in *Plessy v. Ferguson*, the Court established the doctrine of "separate but equal"—a legal fiction that protected the Jim Crow system from judicial scrutiny for racial bias.

Currently, *McCleskey v. Kemp* and its progeny serve much the same function as *Dred Scott* and *Plessy*. In *McCleskey*, the Supreme Court demonstrated that it is once again in protection mode—firmly committed to the prevailing system of control. The Court has closed the courthouse doors to claims of racial bias at every stage of the criminal justice process, from stops and searches to plea bargaining and sentencing. Mass incarceration is now off-limits to challenges on the grounds of racial bias, much as its predecessors were in their time. The new racial caste system operates unimpeded by the Fourteenth Amendment and federal civil rights legislation—laws designed to topple earlier systems of control. The Supreme Court's famous proclamation in 1857—"[the black man] has no rights which the white man is bound to respect"—remains true to a significant degree today, so long as the black man has been labeled a felon.[35]

Racial segregation. Although the parallels listed above should be enough to give anyone pause, there are a number of other, less obvious, similarities between mass incarceration and Jim Crow that have not been explored in earlier chapters. The creation and maintenance of racial segregation is one example. As we know, Jim Crow laws mandated residential segregation, and blacks were relegated to the worst parts of town. Roads literally stopped at the border of many black neighborhoods, shifting from pavement to dirt. Water, sewer systems, and other public services that supported the white areas of town frequently did not extend to the black areas. The extreme poverty that plagued blacks due to their legally sanctioned inferior status was largely invisible to whites—so long as whites remained in their own neighborhoods, which they were inclined to do. Racial segregation rendered black experience largely invisible to whites, making it easier for whites to maintain racial stereotypes about black values and culture. It also made it easier to deny or ignore their suffering.

Mass incarceration functions similarly. It achieves racial segregation by segregating prisoners—the majority of whom are black and brown—from mainstream society. Prisoners are kept behind bars, typically more than a hundred miles from home.[36] Even prisons—the actual buildings—are a rare sight for many Americans, as they are often located far from population centers. Although rural counties contain only 20 percent of the U.S. population, 60 percent of new prison construction occurs there.[37] Prisoners are thus hidden from public view—out of sight, out of mind. In a sense, incarceration is a far more extreme form of physical and residential segregation than Jim Crow segregation. Rather than merely shunting black people to the other side of town or corralling them in ghettos, mass incarceration locks them in cages. Bars and walls keep hundreds of thousands of black and brown people away from mainstream society—a form of apartheid unlike any the world has ever seen.

Prisons, however, are not the only vehicle for racial segregation. Segregation is also created and perpetuated by the flood of prisoners who return to ghetto communities each year. Because the drug war has been waged almost exclusively in poor communities of color, when drug offenders are released, they are generally returned to racially segregated ghetto communities—the places they call home. In many cities, the reentry phenomenon is highly concentrated in a small number of neighborhoods. According to one study, during a twelve-year period, the number of prisoners returning home to "core counties"—those counties that contain the inner city of a metropolitan area—tripled.[38] The effects are felt throughout the United States. In interviews with one hundred residents of two Tallahassee, Florida, communities, researchers found that nearly every one of them had experienced or expected to experience the return of a family member from prison.[39] Similarly, a survey of families living in the Robert Taylor Homes in Chicago found that the majority of residents either had a family member in prison or expected one to return within the next two years.[40] Fully 70 percent of men between the ages of eighteen and forty-five in the impoverished and overwhelmingly black North Lawndale neighborhood on Chicago's West Side are ex-offenders, saddled for life with a criminal record.[41] The majority (60 percent) were incarcerated for drug offenses.[42] These neighborhoods are a minefield for parolees, for a standard condition of parole is a promise not to associate with felons. As Paula Wolff, a senior executive at Chicago Metropolis 2020 observes, in these ghetto neighborhoods, "It is hard for a parolee to walk to the corner store to get a carton of milk without being subject to a parole violation."[43]

By contrast, whites—even poor whites—are far less likely to be imprisoned for drug offenses. And when they are released from prison, they rarely find themselves in the ghetto. The white poor have a vastly different experience in America than do poor people of color. Because whites do not suffer racial segregation, the white poor are not relegated to racially defined areas of intense poverty. In New York City, one study found that 70 percent of the city's poor black and Latino residents live in high-poverty neighborhoods, whereas 70 percent of the city's poor whites live in non-poverty neighborhoods—communities that have significant resources, including jobs, schools, banks, and grocery stores.[44] Nationwide, nearly seven out of eight people living in high-poverty urban areas are members of a minority group.[45]

Mass incarceration thus perpetuates and deepens pre-existing patterns of racial segregation and isolation, not just by removing people of color from society and putting them in prisons, but by dumping them back into ghettos upon their release. Youth of color who might have escaped their ghetto communities—or helped to transform them—if they had been given a fair shot in life and not been labeled felons, instead find themselves trapped in a closed circuit of perpetual marginality, circulating between ghetto and prison.[46]

The racially segregated, poverty-stricken ghettos that exist in inner-city communities across America would not exist today but for racially biased government policies for which there has never been meaningful redress.[47] Yet every year, hundreds of thousands of poor people of color who have been targeted by the War on Drugs are forced to return to these racially segregated communities—neighborhoods still crippled by the legacy of an earlier system of control. As a practical matter, they have no other choice. In this way, mass incarceration, like its predecessor Jim Crow, creates and maintains racial segregation.

Symbolic production of race. Arguably the most important parallel between mass incarceration and Jim Crow is that both have served to define the meaning and significance of race in America. Indeed, a primary function of any racial caste system is to define the meaning of race in its time. Slavery defined what it meant to be black (a slave), and Jim Crow defined what it meant to be black (a second-class citizen). Today mass incarceration defines the meaning of blackness in America: black people, especially black men, are criminals. That is what it means to be black.

The temptation is to insist that black men "choose" to be criminals; the system does not make them criminals, at least not in the way that slavery made blacks slaves or Jim Crow made them second-class citizens. The myth of choice here is seductive, but it should be resisted. African Americans are not significantly more likely to use or sell prohibited drugs than whites, but they are *made* criminals at drastically higher rates for precisely the same conduct. In fact, studies suggest that white professionals may be the most likely of any group to have engaged in illegal drug activity in their lifetime, yet they are the least likely to be made criminals.[48] The prevalence of illegal drug activity among all racial and ethnic groups creates a situation in which, due to limited law enforcement resources and political constraints, some people are made criminals while others are not. Black people have been made criminals by the War on Drugs to a degree that dwarfs its effect on other racial and ethnic groups, especially whites. And the process of making them criminals has produced racial stigma.

Every racial caste system in the United States has produced racial stigma. Mass incarceration is no exception. Racial stigma is produced by defining negatively what it means to be black. The stigma of race was once the shame of the slave; then it was the shame of the second-class citizen; today the stigma of race is the shame of the criminal. Many ex-offenders describe an existential angst associated with their pariah status, an angst that casts a shadow over every aspect of their identity and social experience. The shame and stigma is not limited to the individual; it extends to family members and friends—even whole communities are stigmatized by the presence of those labeled criminals. Those stigmatized often adopt coping strategies African Americans once employed during the Jim Crow era, including lying about their own criminal history or the status of their family members in an attempt to "pass" as someone who will be welcomed by mainstream society.

The critical point here is that, for black men, the stigma of being a "criminal" in the era of mass incarceration is fundamentally a *racial* stigma. This is not to say stigma is absent for white criminals; it is present and powerful. Rather, the point is that the stigma of criminality for white offenders is different—it is a nonracial stigma.

An experiment may help to illustrate how and why this is the case. Say the following to nearly anyone and watch the reaction: "We really need to do something about the problem of white crime." Laughter is a likely response. The term *white crime* is nonsensical in the era of mass incarceration, unless one is really referring to white-collar crime, in which case the term is understood to mean the types of crimes that seemingly respectable white people commit in the comfort of fancy offices. Because the term *white crime* lacks social meaning, the term *white criminal* is also perplexing. In that formulation, *white* seems to qualify the term *criminal*—as if to say, "he's a criminal but not *that* kind of criminal." Or, he's not a *real* criminal—i.e., not what we mean by *criminal* today.

In the era of mass incarceration, what it means to be a criminal in our collective consciousness has become conflated with what it means to be black, so the term *white criminal* is confounding, while the term *black criminal* is nearly redundant. Recall the study discussed in chapter 3 that revealed that when survey respondents were asked to picture a drug criminal, nearly everyone pictured someone who was black. This phenomenon helps to explain why studies indicate that white ex-offenders may actually have an easier time gaining employment than African Americans *without* a criminal record.[49] To be a black man is to be thought of as a criminal, and to be a black criminal is to be despicable—a social pariah. To be a white criminal is not easy, by any means, but as a white criminal you are not a *racial* outcast, though you may face many forms of social and economic exclusion. Whiteness mitigates crime, whereas blackness defines the criminal.

As we have seen in earlier chapters, the conflation of blackness with crime did not happen organically; rather, it was constructed by political and media elites as part of the broad project known as the War on Drugs. This conflation served to provide a legitimate outlet to the expression of antiblack resentment and animus—a convenient release valve now that explicit forms of racial bias are strictly condemned. In the era of color-blindness, it is no longer permissible to hate blacks, but we can hate criminals. Indeed, we are encouraged to do so. As writer John Edgar Wideman points out, "It's respectable to tar and feather criminals, to advocate locking them up and throwing away the key. It's not racist to be against crime, even though the archetypal criminal in the media and the public imagination almost always wears Willie Horton's face."[50]

It is precisely because our criminal justice system provides a vehicle for the expression of conscious and unconscious antiblack sentiment that the prison label is experienced as a racial stigma. The stigma exists whether or not one has been formally branded a criminal, yet another parallel to Jim Crow. Just as African Americans in the North were stigmatized by the Jim Crow system even if they were not subject to its formal control, black men today are stigmatized by mass incarceration—and the social construction of the "criminalblackman"—whether they have ever been to prison or not. For those who have been branded, the branding serves to intensify and deepen the racial stigma, as they are constantly reminded in virtually every contact they have with public agencies, as well as with private employers and landlords, that they are the new "untouchables."

In this way, the stigma of race has become the stigma of criminality. Throughout the criminal justice system, as well as in our schools and public spaces, young + black + male is equated with reasonable suspicion, justifying the arrest, interrogation, search, and detention of thousands of African Americans every year, as well as their exclusion from employment and housing and the denial of educational opportunity. Because black youth are viewed as criminals, they face severe employment discrimination and are also "pushed out" of schools through racially biased school discipline policies.[51]

For black youth, the experience of being "made black" often begins with the first police stop, interrogation, search, or arrest. The experience carries social meaning—*this is what it means to be black*. The story of one's "first time" may be repeated to family or friends, but for ghetto youth, almost no one imagines that the first time will be the last. The experience is understood to define the terms of one's relationship not only to the state but to society at large. This reality can be frustrating for those who strive to help ghetto youth "turn their lives around." James Forman Jr., the cofounder of the See Forever charter school for juvenile offenders in Washington, D.C., made this point when describing how random and degrading stops and searches of ghetto youth "tell kids that they are pariahs, that no matter how hard they study, they will remain potential suspects." One student complained to him, "We can be perfect, perfect, doing everything right and still they treat us like dogs. No, worse than dogs, because criminals are treated worse than dogs." Another student asked him pointedly, "How can you tell us we can be anything when they treat us like we're nothing?"[52]

The process of marking black youth *as* black criminals is essential to the functioning of mass incarceration as a racial caste system. For the system to succeed—that is, for it to achieve the political goals described in chapter 1—black people must be labeled criminals before they are formally subject to control. The criminal label is essential, for forms of explicit racial exclusion are not only prohibited but widely condemned. Thus black youth must be made—labeled—criminals. This process of being made a criminal is, to a large extent, the process of "becoming" black. As Wideman explains, when "to be a man of color of a certain economic class and milieu is equivalent in the public eye to being a criminal," being processed by the criminal justice system is tantamount to being made black, and "doing time" behind bars is at the same time "marking race."[53] At its core, then, mass incarceration, like Jim Crow, is a "race-making institution." It serves to define the meaning and significance of race in America.

2

Race, Incarceration, and American Values

Glenn C. Loury

The early 1990s were the age of drive-by shootings, drug deals gone bad, crack cocaine, and gangsta rap. Between 1960 and 1990, the annual number of murders in New Haven rose from 6 to 31, the number of rapes from 4 to 168, the number of robberies from 16 to 1,784—all this while the city's population declined by 14 percent. Crime was concentrated in central cities: in 1990, two-fifths of Pennsylvania's violent crimes were committed in Philadelphia, home to one-seventh of the state's population. The subject of crime dominated American domestic-policy debates.

Most observers at the time expected things to get worse. Consulting demographic tables and extrapolating trends, scholars and pundits warned the public to prepare for an onslaught, and for a new kind of criminal— the anomic, vicious, irreligious, amoral, juvenile "super predator." In 1996, one academic commentator predicted a "bloodbath" of juvenile homicides in 2005.

And so we prepared. Stoked by fear and political opportunism, but also by the need to address a very real social problem, we threw lots of people in jail, and when the old prisons were filled we built new ones.

But the onslaught never came. Crime rates peaked in 1992 and have dropped sharply since. Even as crime rates fell, however, imprisonment rates remained high and continued their upward march. The result, the current American prison system, is a leviathan unmatched in human history.

According to a 2005 report of the International Centre for Prison Studies in London, the United States—with 5 percent of the world's

From *Race, Incarceration, and American Values* (Cambridge, MA: MIT Press, 2008), 3–28.

population—houses 25 percent of the world's inmates. Our incarceration rate (714 per 100,000 residents) is almost 40 percent greater than those of our nearest competitors (the Bahamas, Belarus, and Russia). Other industrial democracies, even those with significant crime problems of their own, are much less punitive: our incarceration rate is 6.2 times that of Canada, 7.8 times that of France, and 12.3 times that of Japan. We have a corrections sector that employs more Americans than the combined work forces of General Motors, Ford, and Wal-Mart, the three largest corporate employers in the country, and we are spending some $200 billion annually on law enforcement and corrections at all levels of government, a fourfold increase (in constant dollars) over the past quarter century.

Never before has a supposedly free country denied basic liberty to so many of its citizens. In December 2006, some 2.25 million persons were being held in the nearly 5,000 prisons and jails that are scattered across America's urban and rural landscapes. One-third of inmates in state prisons are violent criminals, convicted of homicide, rape, or robbery. But the other two-thirds consist mainly of property and drug offenders. Inmates are disproportionately drawn from the most disadvantaged parts of society. On average, state inmates have fewer than eleven years of schooling. They are also vastly disproportionately black and brown.

How did it come to this? One argument is that the massive increase in incarceration reflects the success of a rational public policy: faced with a compelling social problem, we responded by imprisoning people and succeeded in lowering crime rates. This argument is not entirely misguided. Increased incarceration does appear to have reduced crime somewhat. But by how much? Estimates of the share of the 1990s reduction in violent crime that can be attributed to the prison boom range from 5 percent to 25 percent. Whatever the number, analysts of all political stripes now agree that we long ago entered the zone of diminishing returns. The conservative scholar John Dilulio, who coined the term "super predator" in the early 1990s, was by the end of that decade declaring in *The Wall Street Journal*, "Two Million Prisoners Are Enough." But there was no political movement for getting America out of the mass-incarceration business. The throttle was stuck.

A more convincing argument is that imprisonment rates have continued to rise while crime rates have fallen because we have become progressively more punitive: not because crime has continued to explode (it hasn't), not because we made a smart policy choice, but because we have made a collective decision to increase the rate of punishment.

One simple measure of punitiveness is the likelihood that a person who is arrested will be subsequently incarcerated. Between 1980 and 2001, there was no real change in the chances of being arrested in response to a complaint: the rate was just under 50 percent. But the likelihood that an arrest would result in imprisonment more than doubled, from 13 to 28 percent. And because the amount of time served and the rate of prison admission both increased, the incarceration rate for violent crime almost tripled, despite the decline in the level of violence. The incarceration rate for nonviolent and drug offenses increased at an even faster pace: between 1980 and 1997 the number of people incarcerated for nonviolent offenses tripled, and the number of people incarcerated for drug offenses increased by a factor of eleven. Indeed, the criminal-justice researcher Alfred Blumstein has argued that none of the growth in incarceration between 1980 and 1996 can be attributed to more crime.

The growth was entirely attributable to a growth in punitiveness, about equally to growth in prison commitments per arrest (an indication of tougher prosecution or judicial sentencing) and to longer time served (an indication of longer sentences, elimination of parole or later parole release, or greater readiness to recommit parolees to prison for either technical violations or new crimes).

This growth in punitiveness was accompanied by a shift in thinking about the basic purpose of criminal justice. In the 1970s, the sociologist David Garland argues, the corrections system was commonly seen as a way to prepare offenders to rejoin society. Since then, the focus has shifted from rehabilitation to punishment and stayed there. Felons are no longer persons to be supported, but risks to be dealt with. And the way to deal with the risks is to keep them locked up. As of 2000, thirty-three states had abolished limited parole (up from seventeen in 1980), twenty-four states had introduced three-strikes laws (up from zero), and forty states had introduced truth-in-sentencing laws (up from three). The vast majority of these changes occurred in the 1990s, as crime rates fell.

This new system of punitive ideas is aided by a new relationship between the media, the politicians, and the public. A handful of cases—in which a predator does an awful thing to an innocent—get excessive media attention and engender public outrage. This attention typically bears no relation to the frequency of the particular type of crime, yet laws—such as three-strikes laws that give mandatory life sentences to nonviolent drug offenders—and political careers are made on the basis of the public's reaction to the media coverage of such crimes.

Despite a sharp national decline in crime, American criminal justice has become crueler and less caring than it has been at any other time in our modern history. Why?

The question has no simple answer, but the racial composition of prisons is a good place to start. The punitive turn in the nation's social policy—intimately connected with public rhetoric about responsibility, dependency, social hygiene, and the reclamation of public order—can be fully grasped only when viewed against the backdrop of America's often ugly and violent racial history: there is a reason why our inclination toward forgiveness and the extension of a second chance to those who have violated our behavioral strictures is so stunted, and why our mainstream political discourses are so bereft of self-examination and searching social criticism. This historical resonance between the stigma of race and the stigma of imprisonment serves to keep alive in our public culture the subordinating social meanings that have always been associated with blackness. Race helps to explain why the United States is exceptional among the democratic industrial societies in the severity and extent of its punitive policy and in the paucity of its social-welfare institutions.

Slavery ended a long time ago, but the institution of chattel slavery and the ideology of racial subordination that accompanied it have cast a long shadow. I speak here of the history of lynching throughout the country; the racially biased policing and judging in the South under Jim Crow and in the cities of the Northeast, Midwest, and West to which blacks migrated after the First and Second World Wars; and the history of racial apartheid that ended only as a matter of law with the civil rights movement. It should come as no surprise that in the post–civil rights era, race, far from being peripheral, has been central to the evolution of American social policy.

The political scientist Vesla Mae Weaver, in a recently completed dissertation, examines policy history, public opinion, and media processes in an attempt to understand the role of race in this historic transformation of criminal justice. She argues—persuasively, I think—that the punitive turn represented a political response to the success of the civil rights movement. Weaver describes a process of "frontlash" in which opponents of the civil rights revolution sought to regain the upper hand by shifting to a new issue. Rather than reacting directly to civil rights developments, and thus continuing to fight a battle they had lost, those opponents—consider George Wallace's campaigns for the presidency, which drew so much support in states like Michigan and Wisconsin—shifted attention to a seemingly race-neutral concern over crime:

> Once the clutch of Jim Crow had loosened, opponents of civil rights shifted the "locus of attack" by injecting crime onto the agenda. Through the process of frontlash, rivals of civil rights progress defined racial discord as criminal and argued that crime legislation would be a panacea to racial unrest. This strategy both imbued crime with race and depoliticized racial struggle, a formula which foreclosed earlier "root causes" alternatives. Fusing anxiety

about crime to anxiety over racial change and riots, civil rights and racial disorder—initially defined as a problem of minority disenfranchisement—were defined as a crime problem, which helped shift debate from social reform to punishment.

Of course, this argument—for which Weaver adduces considerable circumstantial evidence—is speculative. But something interesting seems to have been going on in the late 1960s regarding the relationship between attitudes on race and social policy.

Before 1965, public attitudes on the welfare state and on race, as measured by the annually administered General Social Survey, varied from year to year independently of one another: you could not predict much about a person's attitudes on welfare politics by knowing his or her attitudes about race. After 1965, the attitudes moved in tandem, as welfare came to be seen as a race issue. The year-to-year correlation between an index measuring liberalism of racial attitudes and attitudes toward the welfare state over the interval 1950–1965 was 0.03. These same two series had a correlation of 0.68 over the period 1966–1996. The association in the American mind of race with welfare, and of race with crime, was achieved at a common historical moment. Crime-control institutions are part of a larger social-policy complex—they relate to and interact with the labor market, family-welfare efforts, and health and social-work activities. Indeed, Garland argues that the ideological approaches to welfare and crime control have marched rightward to a common beat: "The institutional and cultural changes that have occurred in the crime control field are analogous to those that have occurred in the welfare state more generally." Just as the welfare state came to be seen as a race issue, so, too, crime came to be seen as a race issue, and policies have been shaped by this perception.

Consider the tortured racial history of the War on Drugs. Blacks were twice as likely as whites to be arrested for a drug offense in 1975 but four times as likely by 1989. Throughout the 1990s, drug-arrest rates remained at historically unprecedented levels. Yet according to the National Survey on Drug Abuse, drug use among adults fell from 20 percent in 1979 to 11 percent in 2000. A similar trend occurred among adolescents. In the age groups 12–17 and 18–25, use of marijuana, cocaine, and heroin all peaked in the late 1970s and began a steady decline thereafter. Thus, a decline in drug use across the board had begun a decade before the draconian anti-drug efforts of the 1990s were initiated.

Of course, most drug arrests are for trafficking, not possession, so usage rates and arrest rates needn't be expected to be identical. Still, we do well to bear in mind that the social problem of illicit drug use is endemic to our whole society. Significantly, throughout the period 1979–2000, white high school seniors reported using drugs at a significantly higher rate than black high school seniors. High drug-usage rates in white, middle-class American communities in the early 1980s accounts for the urgency many citizens felt to mount a national attack on the problem. But how successful has the effort been, and at what cost?

Think of the cost this way: to save middle-class kids from the threat of a drug epidemic that might not have even existed by the time drug offense–fueled incarceration began its rapid increase in the 1980s, we criminalized underclass kids. Arrests went up, but drug prices have fallen sharply over the past 20 years—suggesting that the ratcheting up of enforcement has not made drugs harder to get on the street. The strategy clearly wasn't keeping drugs away from those who sought them. Not only are prices down, but the data show that drug-related visits to emergency rooms also rose steadily throughout the 1980s and 1990s.

An interesting case in point is New York City. Analyzing arrests by residential neighborhood and police precinct, the criminologist Jeffrey Fagan and his colleagues Valerie West and Jan Holland found that incarceration was highest in the city's poorest neighborhoods, though these were often not the neighborhoods in which crime rates were the highest. Moreover, they discovered a perverse effect of incarceration on crime: higher incarceration in a given neighborhood in one year seemed to predict higher crime rates in that same neighborhood one year later. This growth and persistence of incarceration over time, the authors concluded, was due primarily to the drug enforcement practices of police and to sentencing laws that require imprisonment for repeat felons. Police scrutiny was more intensive and less forgiving in high-incarceration neighborhoods, and parolees returning to such neighborhoods were more closely monitored. Thus, discretionary and spatially discriminatory police behavior led to a high and increasing rate of repeat prison admissions in the designated neighborhoods, even as crime rates fell.

Fagan, West, and Holland explain the effects of spatially concentrated urban anti-drug-law enforcement in the contemporary American metropolis. Buyers may come from any neighborhood and any social stratum. But the sellers—at least the ones who can be readily found hawking their wares on street corners and in public vestibules—come predominantly from the poorest, most nonwhite parts of the city. The police, with arrest quotas to meet, know precisely where to find them. The researchers conclude:

> Incarceration begets more incarceration, and incarceration also begets more crime, which in turn invites more aggressive enforcement,

which then re-supplies incarceration ... three mechanisms ... contribute to and reinforce incarceration in neighborhoods: the declining economic fortunes of former inmates and the effects on neighborhoods where they tend to reside, resource and relationship strains on families of prisoners that weaken the family's ability to supervise children, and voter disenfranchisement that weakens the political economy of neighborhoods.

The effects of imprisonment on life chances are profound. For incarcerated black men, hourly wages are 10 percent lower after prison than before. For all incarcerated men, the number of weeks worked per year falls by at least a third after their release.

So consider the nearly 60 percent of black male high school dropouts born in the late 1960s who are imprisoned before their fortieth year. While locked up, these felons are stigmatized—they are regarded as fit subjects for shaming. Their links to family are disrupted; their opportunities for work are diminished; their voting rights may be permanently revoked. They suffer civic excommunication. Our zeal for social discipline consigns these men to a permanent nether caste. And yet, since these men—whatever their shortcomings—have emotional and sexual and family needs, including the need to be fathers and lovers and husbands, we are creating a situation in which the children of this nether caste are likely to join a new generation of untouchables. This cycle will continue so long as incarceration is viewed as the primary path to social hygiene.

I have been exploring the issue of causes: of why we took the punitive turn that has resulted in mass incarceration. But even if the racial argument about causes is inconclusive, the racial consequences are clear. To be sure, in the United States, as in any society, public order is maintained by the threat and use of force. We enjoy our good lives only because we are shielded by the forces of law and order, which keep the unruly at bay. Yet in this society, to a degree virtually unmatched in any other, those bearing the brunt of order enforcement belong in vastly disproportionate numbers to historically marginalized racial groups. Crime and punishment in America have a color.

In his fine 2006 study *Punishment and Inequality in America*, the Princeton University sociologist Bruce Western powerfully describes the scope, nature, and consequences of contemporary imprisonment. He finds that the extent of racial disparity in imprisonment rates is greater than in any other major arena of American social life: at eight to one, the black-white ratio of incarceration rates dwarfs the two-to-one ratio of unemployment rates, the three-to-one ratio of non-marital childbearing, the two-to-one ratio of infant-mortality rates and one-to-five ratio of net worth. While 3 out of 200 young whites were incarcerated in 2000, the rate for young blacks was 1 in 9. A black male resident of the state of California is more likely to go to a state prison than a state college.

The scandalous truth is that the police and penal apparatus are now the primary contact between adult black American men and the American state. Among black male high school dropouts aged twenty to forty, a third were locked up on any given day in 2000, fewer than 3 percent belonged to a union, and less than one-quarter were enrolled in any kind of social program. For these young men, government means, most saliently, coercion. Western estimates that nearly 60 percent of black male dropouts born between 1965 and 1969 were sent to prison on a felony conviction at least once before they reached the age of thirty-five.

One cannot reckon the world-historic American prison buildup over the past thirty-five years without calculating the enormous costs imposed upon the persons imprisoned, their families, and their communities. (Of course, this has not stopped many social scientists from pronouncing on the net benefits of incarceration without doing so.) Deciding on the weight to give to a "thug's" well-being—or to that of his wife or daughter or son—is a question of social morality, not social science. Nor can social science tell us how much additional cost borne by the offending class is justified in order to obtain a given increment of security or property or peace of mind for the rest of us. These are questions about the nature of the American state and its relationship to its people that transcend the categories of benefits and costs.

Yet the discourse surrounding punishment policy invariably discounts the humanity of the thieves, drug sellers, prostitutes, rapists, and, yes, those whom we put to death. It gives insufficient weight to the welfare, to the humanity, of those who are knitted together with offenders in webs of social and psychic affiliation. What is more, institutional arrangements for dealing with criminal offenders in the United States have evolved to serve expressive as well as instrumental ends. We have wanted to "send a message," and we have done so with a vengeance. In the process, we have created facts. We have answered the question, "Who is to blame for the domestic maladies that beset us?" We have constructed a national narrative. We have created scapegoats, indulged our need to feel virtuous, and assuaged our fears. We have met the enemy, and the enemy is them.

Incarceration keeps them away from us. Thus Garland writes, "The prison is used today as a kind of reservation, a quarantine zone in which purportedly dangerous individuals are segregated in the name of public safety." The boundary between prison and community is heavily patrolled and carefully monitored to prevent risks leaking out from one to the other. Those offenders who are released 'into the community' are subject to much tighter control than previously, and frequently find themselves returned to custody for failure to comply with the conditions that continue to restrict their freedom. For many of these parolees and ex-convicts, the 'community' into which they are released is actually a closely monitored terrain, a supervised space, lacking much of the liberty that one associates with 'normal life.'

Deciding how citizens of varied social rank within a common polity ought to relate to one another is a more fundamental consideration than deciding which crime-control policy is most efficient. The question of relationship, of solidarity, of who belongs to the body politic and who deserves exclusion—these are philosophical concerns of the highest order. A decent society will on occasion resist the efficient course of action, for the simple reason that to follow it would be to act as though we were not the people we have determined ourselves to be: a people conceived in liberty and dedicated to the proposition that we all are created equal. Assessing the propriety of creating a racially defined pariah class in the middle of our great cities at the start of the twenty-first century presents us with just such a case.

My recitation of the brutal facts about punishment in today's America may sound to some like a primal scream at this monstrous social machine that is grinding poor black communities to dust. And I confess that these brutal facts do at times leave me inclined to cry out in despair. But my argument is analytical, not existential. Its principal thesis is this: we law-abiding, middle-class Americans have made decisions about social policy and incarceration, and we benefit from those decisions, and that means from a system of suffering, rooted in state violence, meted out at our request. We had choices and we decided to be more punitive. Our society—the society we have made—creates criminogenic conditions in our sprawling urban ghettos, and then acts our rituals of punishment against them as some awful form of human sacrifice.

This situation raises a moral problem that we cannot avoid. We cannot pretend that there are more important problems in our society, or that this circumstance is the necessary solution to other, more pressing problems—unless we are also prepared to say that we have turned our backs on the ideal of equality for all citizens and abandoned the principles of justice. We ought to ask ourselves two questions: Just what manner of people are we Americans? And in light of this, what are our obligations to our fellow citizens—even those who break our laws?

3

Class, Race & Hyperincarceration in Revanchist America

Loïc Wacquant

The single greatest *political* transformation of the post–civil rights era in America is the joint rolling back of the stingy social state and rolling out of the gargantuan penal state that have remade the country's stratification, cities, and civic culture, and are recasting the very character of "blackness" itself. Together, these two concurrent and convergent thrusts have effectively redrawn the perimeter, mission, and modalities of action of public authority when it comes to managing the deprived and stigmatized populations stuck at the bottom of the class, ethnic, and urban hierarchy. The concomitant downsizing of the welfare wing and upsizing of the criminal justice wing of the American state have not been driven by raw trends in poverty and crime, but fueled by a politics of resentment toward categories deemed undeserving and unruly. Chief among those stigmatized populations are the public-aid recipients and the street criminals framed as the two demonic figureheads of the "black underclass" that came to dominate the journalistic, scholarly, and policy debate on the plight of urban America[1] in the revanchist decades that digested the civil disorders of the 1960s and the stagflation of the 1970s, and then witnessed the biggest carceral boom in world history.[2]

In this article, I show that the stupendous expansion and intensification of the activities of the American police, criminal courts, and prison over the past thirty years have been finely targeted, first by class, second by race, and third by place, leading not to *mass* incarceration but to the *hyper*incarceration of (sub)proletarian African American men from the imploding ghetto. This triple selectivity reveals that the building of the hyperactive and hypertrophic penal state that has made the United

From "Class, Race & Hyperincarceration in Revanchist America," *Dædalus*, Summer 2010, 74–90.

States world champion in incarceration is at once a delayed reaction to the civil rights movement and the ghetto riots of the mid-1960s[3] and a disciplinary instrument unfurled to foster the neoliberal revolution by helping to impose insecure labor as the normal horizon of work for the unskilled fractions of the postindustrial laboring class.[4] The double coupling of the prison with the dilapidated hyperghetto, on the one side, and with supervisory workfare, on the other, is not a moral dilemma—as recently argued by Glenn Loury in his Tanner Lecture[5]—but a political quandary calling for an expanded analysis of the nexus of class inequality, ethnic stigma, and the state in the age of social insecurity. Reversing the racialized penalization of poverty in the crumbling inner city requires a different policy response than mass incarceration would and calls for an analysis of the political obstacles to this response, which must go beyond "trickle-down" penal reform to encompass the multifaceted role of the state in producing and entrenching marginality.

The tale of the unexpected and exponential growth of jails and prisons over the past three decades in America after a half-century of carceral stability has often been told. But the raw increase of the population behind bars—from about 380,000 in 1975 to 2 million in 2000 and some 2.4 million today (counting juveniles and persons held in police lockups, who are not registered by official correctional statistics)—is only part of the story of the multisided expansion of the penal state.[6] Four distinctive yet submerged dimensions of America's punitive turn after the close of the Fordist era form the backdrop to my analysis of the deployment of the disciplinary tentacles of the state toward the poor.

First, this phenomenal increase is remarkable for having been fueled, not by the lengthening of the average sentence as in previous periods of carceral inflation, but primarily by the *surge in jail and prison admissions*. Thus the number of people committed to state and federal penitentiaries by the courts ballooned from 159,000 in 1980 to 665,000 in 1997 (accounting for more than 80 percent of inmate growth during that period) before stabilizing at about a half-million annually after 2002. This surge sharply differentiates the United States from Western European countries, most of which have also witnessed a steady, if comparatively modest, rise in incarceration over the past two decades, but one where growing stock is not due to increases in flow.[7] A major contributor to this "vertical" growth of the carceral system in America is the steep escalation in the volume of persons arrested by the police and the vastly enlarged role assumed by jails as frontline dams of social disorders in the city. This police hyperactivism has been disproportionate to and disjoined from trends in

crime. One example: in New York City, under the campaign of "zero tolerance" promoted by then-mayor Rudolph Giuliani, the number of arrests
increased by 40 percent between 1993 and 1998 to top 376,000 while
crime decreased by 54 percent to reach 323,000, meaning that the police
arrested more persons than it recorded offenses by the end of that period,
compared to half as many at the start. Even though a growing share of
these arrests were abusive and did not lead to charges, admissions to jail
rose by one-fourth, causing rampant congestion and daily pandemonium
in the city's custodial facilities.[8]

As a result of intensified policing coupled with a rising propensity to
confine miscreants, American jails have become gargantuan operations
processing a dozen million bodies each year nationwide, as well as huge
drains on the budgets of counties and pivotal institutions in the lives of
the (sub)proletariat of the big cities.[9] Indeed, because they treat vastly
more people than do prisons, under conditions that are more chaotic due
to high turnover, endemic overcrowding, population heterogeneity, and
the administrative shift to bare-bones managerialism (the two top priorities of jail wardens are to minimize violent incidents and to hold down
staff overtime), jails create more social disruption and family turmoil at
the bottom of the urban order than do prisons. Yet they have remained
largely under the radar of researchers and policy analysts alike.[10]

Second, the vertical rise of the penal system has been exceeded by its
"horizontal" spread: the ranks of those *kept in the long shadow of the prison via
probation and parole* have swelled even more than the population under lock,
to about 4 million and 1 million, respectively. As a result, the total population under criminal justice supervision bloated from 1.8 million in 1980 to
6.4 million by 2000 and 7.4 million in 2007. Probation and parole should
be incorporated into the debate on the penal state, not only because they
concern a much larger population than that of convicts (in 1998, eleven
states each held in excess of 100,000 probationers under their heel, more
than France did, with 87,000), but also because both are more likely to
lead (back) to imprisonment than not: two in five probationers and six in
ten parolees who exited this status in 1997 were returned to custody within
three years, either because they had committed a new offense or because
they had violated one or another administrative condition of their release
(failing an alcohol test or losing a job, missing an appointment with their
parole officer, or traveling outside of their county of assignment without
permission, for example). The purpose and functioning of parole have
changed drastically over the past thirty years, from spring toward rehabilitation to penal trap, so that parole is now properly construed as an *extension*
of the custodial system, rather than an *alternative* to it.[11]

The reach of penal authorities has also been dramatically enlarged beyond probation and parole by the exponential growth in the size, scope,
and uses of criminal justice databases that, as of 2000, contained roughly
sixty million files on an estimated thirty-five million individuals. Novel
panoptic measures include the diffusion of official "rap sheets" through
the Internet, the routinization of "background checks" by employers and
realtors, the spread of public notification statutes (and related laws seeking to expurgate specific categories of convicts, such as sex offenders,
from the social body), and the shift from old-style fingerprints and mug
shots to DNA prints coordinated by the FBI.[12] These institutional tentacles,
and the routine practices of profiling, surveillance, and enclosure at a distance that they permit, severely curtail the life chances of former convicts
and their families by stretching the effects of judicial stigma on the labor,
housing, and marital markets as well as into daily life.[13] Legislators have
further amplified these sanctions by adding a raft of restrictions on the
access of ex-felons to public services, privileges, and benefits, from public
housing and public employment to college scholarships, parenting, and
voting rights.[14]

Third, the advent of penal "big government" was made possible by astonishing increases in funding and personnel. Prison and jail expenditures in America jumped from $7 billion in 1980 to $57 billion in 2000
and exceeded $70 billion in 2007, even as crime first stagnated and then
declined steadily after 1993. (Meanwhile, criminal justice expenditures
grew sevenfold, from $33 billion to $216 billion.) This budgetary boom
of 660 percent—amounting to a veritable *carceral Marshall Plan* during
a period when successive administrations proclaimed to rein in public
spending—financed the infusion of an additional one million criminal
justice staff, which has made corrections the third largest employer in the
nation, behind only Manpower Inc. and Wal-Mart, with a monthly payroll
of $2.4 billion.

The upsizing of the carceral function of government has been rigorously proportional to the downsizing of its welfare role. In 1980, the
country spent three times as much on its two main assistance programs
($11 billion for Aid to Families with Dependent Children [AFDC] and
$10 billion for food stamps) than on corrections ($7 billion). By 1996,
when "welfare reform" replaced the right to public assistance by the obligation to accept insecure employment as a condition of support, the carceral
budget came to double the sums allocated to either AFDC or food stamps
($54 billion compared to $20 billion and $27 billion, respectively). Simi-
larly, during the 1990s alone, Washington cut funding for public housing by $17 billion (a reduction of 61 percent) and boosted corrections by

$19 billion (an increase of 171 percent), effectively making the construction of prisons the nation's main housing program for the poor.

Fourth, the building of America's gigantic penal state is a *nationwide endeavor and a bipartisan achievement*. Many scholars have rightly stressed that the United States does not have a criminal justice system so much as a loose patchwork of independent jurisdictions beset by administrative fragmentation and policy dispersal bordering on incoherence.[15] In light of wide regional and state variations, others have highlighted the role of "local political culture" and modes of "civic engagement" in determining the mix and intensity of penal sanctions.[16] Still others have reported that Republican governors, a large African American urban population, and "a state's religious and political culture" exert a significant influence on incarceration rates.[17] Yet for all these and other geographic disparities and peculiarities, it remains that, over the past thirty-odd years, penal escalation has left no corner of the country untouched and has brought about de facto unification in the aggressive deployment of punishment. Aside from Maine and Kansas, all states saw their correctional counts grow by more than 50 percent between 1985 and 1995, at the peak of the carceral boom. Everywhere the ideal of rehabilitation has been abandoned or drastically downgraded, making retribution and neutralization the main practical rationale for confinement.

Increases in the civic salience of crime and distrust in government have pushed all jurisdictions toward greater punitiveness.[18] Moreover, policy control over criminal justice has migrated to the federal level, where it has grown steadily more symbolic and less substantive since the 1970s.[19] Indeed, this national slant is one of the distinctive causes of the severity of the punitive turn, as it strikes at impoverished minority districts in the city.[20] This national trajectory has been uninterrupted by changes in political majority in statehouses, Congress, and the White House, as both parties have reflexively supported penal activism and expanded incarceration.[21] Republicans will claim that they are "tougher on crime," but Democratic majorities have run up the carceral tab in California, Illinois, Michigan, and New York. It was a Democratic president, Jimmy Carter (former governor of Georgia, one of the country's most repressive states), who jump-started America's great "carceral leap forward." And another Democratic president (and former governor of another superpunitive state, Arkansas), Bill Clinton, who pushed for the most costly crime bill in world history (the Violent Crime Control and Law Enforcement Act of 1994), oversaw the single largest expansion of incarceration in the annals of democratic societies: Clinton tallied an increase of 465,000 convicts for an added $15 billion, compared to 288,000 convicts for a boost of $8 billion for Ronald Reagan.

. . .

The foregoing indicates that the *footprint of the penal state on the national body is much broader and heavier* than usually depicted. At the same time, it is also considerably more *pointed* than conveyed by the current debate. It has become conventional among justice activists, journalists, and analysts of the U.S. carceral scene to designate the unprecedented and unparalleled expansion of the American correctional system at the close of the twentieth century as "mass incarceration."[22] The term was (re)introduced in the national prison debate in the late 1990s (until then, it had been used to refer to the internment of Japanese Americans in concentration camps during World War II) and was soon codified by David Garland at the interdisciplinary conference on "Mass Incarceration: Social Causes and Consequences," held at New York University in 2000, which boosted research on the topic.[23] The designation of mass incarceration is intuitively appealing because it helps spotlight the outlier status of the United States on the world scene, dramatize the condition at hand, and thus draw scholarly and public attention to it. But, much as it has been useful in terms of mobilizing intellectual and civic resources, the notion obscures signal features of the phenomenon.

Mass incarceration is a mischaracterization of what is better termed *hyperincarceration*. This is not a mere terminological quibble, for the change in wording points to a different depiction of the punitive turn, which leads to a different causal model and thence to different policy prescriptions. *Mass* incarceration suggests that confinement concerns large swaths of the citizenry (as with the mass media, mass culture, and mass unemployment), implying that the penal net has been flung far and wide across social and physical space. This is triply inaccurate. First, the prevalence of penal confinement in the United States, while extreme by international standards, can hardly be said to concern the masses. Indeed, a rate of 0.75 percent compares quite favorably with the incidence of such woes as latent tuberculosis infection (estimated at 4.2 percent) and severe alcohol dependency (3.81 percent), ailments which no one would seriously contend have reached mass proportions in the United States.[24] Next, the expansion and intensification of the activities of the police, courts, and prison over the past quarter-century have been anything but broad and indiscriminate.[25] They have been *finely targeted*, first by class, second by that disguised brand of ethnicity called race, and third by place. This cumulative targeting has led to the *hyper*incarceration of one particular category, *lower-class African American men trapped in the crumbling ghetto*, while leaving the rest of society—including, most remarkably, middle- and upper-class African Americans—practically untouched. Third, and more important still, this *triple selectivity is a constitutive property of the phenomenon*: had the

penal state been rolled out indiscriminately by policies resulting in the
capture of vast numbers of whites and well-to-do citizens, capsizing their
families and decimating their neighborhoods as it has for inner-city African Americans, its growth would have been speedily derailed and eventually stopped by political counteraction. "Mass" incarceration is socially
tolerable and therefore workable as public policy only *so long as it does not
reach the masses*: it is a figure of speech, which hides the multiple filters that
operate to point the penal dagger.[26]

Class, not race, is the first filter of selection for incarceration. The welcome focus on race, crime, and punishment that has dominated discussions of the prison boom has obliterated the fact that inmates are *first
and foremost poor people*. Indeed, this monotonic class recruitment is a
constant of penal history since the invention of houses of correction in
the late sixteenth century[27] and a fact confirmed by the annals of U.S.
incarceration.[28] Consider the social profile of the clientele of the nation's
jails—the gateway into America's carceral archipelago. This clientele is
drawn overwhelmingly from the most precarious fractions of the urban
working class[29]: fewer than half of inmates held a full-time job at the time
of arraignment and two-thirds issue from households with an annual income coming to less than *half* the "poverty line"; only 13 percent have
some postsecondary education (compared to a national rate above one-
half); 60 percent did not grow up with both parents, including 14 percent raised in foster homes or orphanages; and every other detainee has
had a member of his family behind bars. The regular clients of America's
jails suffer from acute material insecurity, cultural deprivation, and social
denudement—only 16 percent of them are married, compared to 58 percent for men of their age bracket nationwide. They also include disproportionate numbers of the homeless, the mentally ill, the alcohol- and
drug-addicted, and the severely handicapped: nearly one in four suffers
from a physical, psychic, or emotional ailment serious enough to hamper
his or her ability to work. And they come mostly from deprived and stigmatized neighborhoods that have been devastated by the double retrenchment of the formal labor market and the welfare state from the urban
core.[30] Conversely, very few members of the middle and upper classes ever
sojourn at the "Graybar hotel," especially for committing the minor to
middling crimes that account for the bulk of prison convictions. (In 1997,
11 percent of new court commitments to state penitentiaries were for public order offenses, 30 percent for narcotics convictions, and 28 percent for
property crimes.) Martha Stewart and Bernie Madoff are but spectacular
exceptions that spotlight this stringent class rule.

Race comes second. But the ethnic transformation of America's prison
has been at once more dramatic and more puzzling than generally

recognized. To start, the ethnoracial makeup of convicts has completely *flip-flopped* in four decades, turning over from 70 percent white and 30 percent "others" at the close of World War II to 70 percent African American and Latino versus 30 percent white by century's end. This inversion, which accelerated after the mid-1970s, is all the more stunning when the criminal population has both shrunk and become *whiter* during that period: the share of African Americans among individuals arrested by the police for the four most serious violent offenses (murder, rape, robbery, and aggravated assault) dropped from 51 percent in 1973 to 43 percent in 1996,[31] and it continued to decline steadily for each of those four crimes until at least 2006.[32]

Next, the rapid "blackening" of the prison population even as serious crime "whitened" is due *exclusively* to the astronomical increase in the incarceration rates of *lower-class* African Americans. In his book *Punishment and Inequality in America*, sociologist Bruce Western produces a stunning statistic: whereas the cumulative risk of imprisonment for African American males without a high-school diploma tripled between 1979 and 1999, to reach the astonishing rate of 59 percent, the lifetime chance of serving time for African American men with some college education *decreased* from 6 percent to 5 percent.[33] Here again, the media melodrama around the arrest of Harvard University star professor Henry Louis Gates in Summer 2009 has hidden the fact that middle- and upper-class African Americans are *better off* under the present penal regime than they were thirty years ago. It has played to the national obsession for the black-white duality, which obfuscates the fact that *class disproportionality inside each ethnic category is greater than the racial disproportionality between them*: African American men are eight times more likely to sojourn behind bars than European American men (7.9 percent versus 1.0 percent in 2000), but the lifetime probability of serving time in prison for African American males who did not complete their secondary education is twelve times that for African American males who went to college (58.9 percent versus 4.9 percent), whereas that class gap among white men stands at sixteen to one (11.2 percent versus 0.7 percent).[34] The fact that these ratios were considerably lower two decades ago for both African Americans and European Americans (of the order of one to three and one to eight, respectively) confirms that enlarged imprisonment has struck very selectively by class inside of race, which again refutes the diagnosis of a "mass" phenomenon.

How was such double, nested selectivity achieved? How is it possible that criminal laws ostensibly written to avoid class and color bias would lead to throwing so many (sub)proletarian African American men under lock, and not other African American men?[35] The class gradient in racialized imprisonment was obtained by targeting one particular place: the *remnants of the dark ghetto*. I insist here on the word *remnants*, because the ghetto of old, which held in its grip a unified, if stratified, African American community, is no more. The communal Black Belt of the Fordist era, described by a long lineage of distinguished African American sociologists, from W.E.B. Du Bois and E. Franklin Frazier to Drake and Cayton to Kenneth Clark, imploded in the 1960s, to be replaced by a dual and decentered structure of seclusion composed of a degraded *hyperghetto* doubly segregated by race and class, on the one hand, and the *satellite African American middle-class districts* that mushroomed in the adjacent areas vacated by the mass exodus of whites to the suburbs, on the other.[36]

But to detect the tightening linkage between the decaying ghetto and the booming prison requires that one effects two analytic moves. First, one must break out of the narrow ambit of the "crime and punishment" paradigm that continues to hamstring the scholarly and policy debate, in spite of its increasingly glaring inadequacy. A simple ratio suffices to demonstrate that crime cannot be the cause behind carceral hyperinflation: the number of clients of state and federal prisons boomed from 21 convicts per thousand "index crimes" in 1975 to 125 per thousand in 2005. In other words, holding the crime rate constant shows that the American penal state is six times more punitive today than it was three decades ago.[37] Instead of getting sidetracked into investigations of the crime-punishment (dis)connection, one must recognize that the prison is not a mere technical implement of government designed to stem offending, but a core state capacity devoted to *managing dispossessed and dishonored populations*. Returning to the early history of the prison in the long sixteenth century readily discloses that penal bondage developed, not to fight crime, but to dramatize the authority of rulers, and to repress idleness and enforce morality among vagrants, beggars, and assorted categories cast adrift by the advent of capitalism.[38] The rise of the prison was part and parcel of the building of the early modern state to discipline the nascent urban proletariat and to stage sovereignty for the benefit of the emerging citizenry. The same is true four centuries later in the dualizing metropolis of neoliberal capitalism.[39]

A second analytic shift is needed to ferret out the causal connection between hyperghettoization and hyperincarceration: to realize that the ghetto is not a segregated quarter, a poor neighborhood, or an urban district marred by housing dilapidation, violence, vice, or disrepute, but an *instrument of ethnoracial control* in the city. Another return to social history demonstrates that a ghetto is a sociospatial contraption through which a dominant ethnic category secludes a subordinate group and restricts its life chances in order to both exploit and exclude it from the life-sphere

of the dominant. Like the Jewish ghetto in Renaissance Europe, the
Black Belt of the American metropolis in the Fordist age combined four
elements—stigma, constraint, spatial confinement, and institutional
encasement—to permit the economic extraction and social ostracization
of a population deemed congenitally inferior, defiled and defiling by virtue of its lineal connection to bondage. Succeeding chattel slavery and Jim
Crow, the ghetto was the third "peculiar institution" entrusted with defining, confining, and controlling African Americans in the urban industrial
order.[40]

Penal expansion after the mid-1970s is a political response to the collapse of the ghetto. But why did the ghetto collapse? Three causal series
converged to undercut the "black city within the white" that hemmed in
African Americans from the 1920s to the 1960s. The first is the postindustrial economic transition that shifted employment from manufacturing to
services, from central city to suburb, and from the Rustbelt to the Sunbelt
and low-wage foreign countries. Together with renewed immigration, this
shift made African American workers redundant and undercut the role of
the ghetto as a reservoir of unskilled labor. The second cause is the political displacement provoked by the Great White Migration to the suburbs:
from the 1950s to the 1970s, millions of white families fled the metropolis
in reaction to the influx of African Americans from the rural South. This
demographic upheaval, subsidized by the federal government and bolstered by the courts, weakened cities in the national electoral system and
reduced the political pull of African Americans. The third force behind
the breakdown of the ghetto as ethnoracial container is African American protest, fostered by the accumulation of social and symbolic capital
correlative of ghettoization, culminating with the civil rights legislation,
the budding of Black Power activism, and the eruption of urban riots that
rocked the country between 1964 and 1968.

Unlike Jim Crow, then, the ghetto was not dismantled by forceful government action. It was left to crumble onto itself, trapping lower-class African Americans in a vortex of unemployment, poverty, and crime abetted
by the joint withdrawal of the wage-labor market and the welfare state,
while the growing African American middle class achieved limited social
and spatial separation by colonizing the districts adjacent to the historic
Black Belt.[41] As the ghetto lost its economic function of labor extraction
and proved unable to ensure ethnoracial closure, the prison was called
on to help contain a dishonored population widely viewed as deviant,
destitute, and dangerous. This coupling occurred because, as previously
suggested, ghetto and prison belong to the same organizational genus,
namely, *institutions of forced confinement*: the ghetto is a sort of "ethnoracial
prison" in the city, while the prison functions in the manner of a "judicial

ghetto" at large. Both are charged with enfolding a stigmatized category
so as to defuse the material and/or symbolic threat it poses for the broader
society from which it has been extruded.

To be sure, the structural homology and functional surrogacy of ghetto
and prison do not mandate that the former be replaced by or coupled with
the latter. For that to happen, specific policy choices had to be made, implemented, and supported. This support sprang from the fearful reaction
of whites to the urban riots and related racial upheavals of the 1960s and
from the rising political resentment generated by government powerless-
ness in the face of the stagflation of 1970s and the subsequent spread of
social insecurity along three tacks. First, middle-class whites accelerated
their exodus out of the capsizing cities, which enabled the federal government to dismantle programs essential to the succor of inner-city residents. Second, working-class whites joined their middle-class brethren in
turning against the welfare state to demand that public aid be curtailed—
leading to the "end of welfare as we know it" in 1996. Third, whites across
the class spectrum allied to offer ardent political backing for the "law
and order" measures that primed the penal pump and harnessed it to
the hyperghetto. The meeting ground and theater of these three political
thrusts was the "revanchist city"[42] in which increasing inequality, diffus-
ing social precariousness, and festering marginality fed citizens' rancor
over the alleged excessive generosity of welfare and leniency of criminal
justice toward poor African Americans.

Two trains of converging changes then bolstered the knitting of the
hyperghetto and the prison into a carceral mesh ensnaring a population
of lower-class African Americans rejected by the deregulated labor market and the dereliction of public institutions in the inner city.[43] On the
one side, *the ghetto was "prisonized"* as its class composition became monot-
onously poor, its internal social relations grew stamped by distrust and
fear, and its indigenous organizations waned to be replaced by the social
control institutions of the state. On the other side, *the prison was "ghettoized"*
as rigid racial partition came to pervade custodial facilities; the predatory
culture of the street supplanted the "convict code" that had traditionally
organized the "inmate society"[44]; rehabilitation was abandoned in favor
of neutralization; and the stigma of criminal conviction was deepened
and diffused in ways that make it akin to racial dishonor. The resulting
symbiosis between hyperghetto and prison not only perpetuates the socioeconomic marginality and symbolic taint of the African American sub-
proletariat, feeding the runaway growth of the carceral system. It also
plays a key role in the revamping of "race" by associating blackness with
devious violence and dangerousness,[45] the redefinition of the citizenry via
the production of a racialized public culture of vilification of criminals,

and the construction of a post-Keynesian state that replaces the social-welfare treatment of poverty with its punitive containment.

Yet the tightening nexus between the hyperghetto and the prison does not tell the whole story of the frenetic growth of the penal institution in America after the civil rights revolution. In *Punishing the Poor,* I show that the unleashing of a voracious prison apparatus after the mid-1970s partakes of a broader restructuring of the state tending to criminalize poverty and its consequences so as to impress insecure, underpaid jobs as the modal employment situation of the unskilled segments of the postindustrial proletariat. The sudden hypertrophy of the penal state was thus matched and complemented by the planned atrophy of the social state, culminating with the 1996 law on Personal Responsibility and Work Opportunity, which replaced the right to "welfare" with the obligation of "workfare." Each in its fashion, workfare and prisonfare respond, not just to the crisis of the ghetto as a device for the sociospatial seclusion of African Americans, but to the repudiation of the Fordist wage-work compact and of the Keynesian social compromise of the postwar decades. Together, they ensnare the marginal populations of the metropolis in a *carceral-assistential net* designed to steer them toward deregulated employment through moral retraining and material suasion and, if they prove too recalcitrant and disruptive, to warehouse them in the devastated core of the urban Black Belt and in the penitentiaries that have become its distant yet direct satellites.

The workfare revolution and the penal explosion are the two sides of the same historical coin, two facets of the reengineering and masculinizing of the state on the way to the establishment of a novel political regime that may be characterized as *liberal-paternalist*: it practices laissez-faire at the top, toward corporations and the privileged, but it is intrusive and disciplinary at the bottom, when it comes to dealing with the consquences of social disinvestment and economic deregulation for the lower class and its territories. And, just as racial stigma was pivotal to the junction of hyperghetto and prison, the taint of "blackness" was epicentral to the restrictive and punitive overhaul of social welfare at century's end. In the wake of the ghetto mutinies of the 1960s, the diffusion of blackened images of crime fueled rising hostility toward criminals and fostered (white) demands for *expansive* prison policies narrowly aimed at retribution and neutralization.[46] During the same years, the spread of blackened images of urban destitution and dependency similarly fostered mounting resentment toward public aid, bolstering (white) support for *restrictive* welfare measures centered on deterrence and compulsion.[47] Race turns out to be the symbolic linchpin that coordinated the synergistic transformation of these two sectors of public policy toward the poor.[48]

Again, like the joining of hyperghetto and prison, this second institutional pairing feeding carceral growth can be better understood by paying attention to the structural, functional, and cultural similarities between workfare and prisonfare as "people-processing organizations"[49] targeted on problem populations and neighborhoods. It was tightened by the transformation of welfare in a punitive direction and by the expansion of the penal system to "treat" more and more of the traditional clientele of welfare. Both programs of state action are narrowly directed at the bottom of the class and ethnic hierarchy; both effectively assume that their recipients are "guilty until proven innocent" and that their conduct must be closely supervised as well as rectified by restrictive and coercive measures; and both use deterrence and stigma to achieve behavioral modification.

In the era of hypermobile capital and fragmented wage-work, the monitoring of the precarious segments of the working class is no longer handled solely by the maternal social arm of the welfare state, as portrayed by Frances Fox Piven and Richard Cloward in their classic 1971 study *Regulating the Poor*.[50] It entails a *double regulation* through the virile and controlling arms of *workfare and prisonfare acting in unison*. This dynamic coupling of social and penal policy at the bottom of the class and ethnic structure operates through a familiar division of labor between the sexes: the public aid bureaucracy, reconverted into an administrative springboard to subpoverty employment, takes up the task of inculcating the duty of working for work's sake to poor women (and indirectly to their children), while the penal quartet formed by the police, the court, the prison, and the probation or parole officer shoulders the mission of taming their men—that is, the boyfriends or husbands, brothers, and sons of these poor women. Welfare provision and criminal justice are animated by the same punitive and paternalist philosophy that stresses the "individual responsibility" of the "client"; they both rely on case supervision and bureaucratic surveillance, deterrence and stigma, and graduated sanctions aimed at modifying behavior to enforce compliance with work and civility; and they reach publics of roughly comparable size. In 2001, 2.1 million households received Temporary Assistance to Needy Families, for a total of some 6 million beneficiaries, while the carceral population topped 2.1 million and the stock under criminal justice supervision surpassed 6.5 million.

In addition, welfare recipients and inmates have nearly identical social profiles and extensive mutual ties of descent and alliance confirming that they are the two gendered components of the same population. Both categories live below 50 percent of the federal poverty line (for one-half and two-thirds of them, respectively); both are disproportionately African American and Hispanic (37 percent and 18 percent versus 41 percent and 19 percent); the majority did not finish high school; and many suffer from serious physical and mental disabilities limiting their workforce participation (44 percent of AFDC mothers as against 37 percent of jail inmates). And they are closely bound to one another by kin and marital and social bonds, reside overwhelmingly in the same impoverished households and barren neighborhoods, and face the same bleak life horizon at the bottom of the class and ethnic structure. This intertwinement indicates that we cannot hope to untie the knot of class, race, and imprisonment, and thus explain hyperincarceration, if we do not relink prisonfare and workfare, which in turn implies that we must bring the social wing of the state and its transformations into our analytic and policy purview.

Revanchism as public policy toward the dispossessed has thrust the country into a historical cul-de-sac, as the double coupling of hyperghettoization and hyperincarceration, on the one hand, and workfare and prisonfare, on the other, damages both society and the state. For society, the spiral of penal escalation has become self-reinforcing as well as self-defeating: the carceral Moloch actively destabilizes the precarious fractions of the postindustrial proletariat it strikes with special zeal, truncates the life options of its members, and further despoils inner-city neighborhoods, thereby reproducing the very social disorders, material insecurity, and symbolic stain it is supposed to alleviate. As a result, the population behind bars has kept on growing even as the overall crime rate dropped precipitously for some fifteen years, yielding a paradoxical pattern of *carceral levitation*. For the state, the penalization of poverty turns out to be financially ruinous, as it competes with, and eventually consumes, the funds and staff needed to sustain essential public services such as schooling, health, transportation, and social protection.[51] Moreover, the punitive and panoptic logic that propels criminal justice seeps into and erodes the shielding capacities of the welfare sector, for instance by inflecting the practices of child protective services in ways that turn them into adjuncts of the penal apparatus.[52] It similarly undercuts the educational springboard, as depleted inner-city schools serving a clientele roiled by mass unemployment and penal disruption come to prioritize and manage issues of student discipline through a prism of crime control.[53] Lastly, the law-and-order guignol diverts the attention of elected officials and saps the energy of bureaucratic managers charged with handling the problem populations and territories of the dualizing city.

If the diagnosis of the rise of the penal state in America sketched here is correct, and hyperincarceration proceeding along steep gradients of class, race, and space—rather than mass incarceration—is the offshoot of a novel government of social insecurity installed to absorb the shock of the crash of the ghetto and normalize precarious wage labor, then policies aimed at shrinking the carceral state must effectively *reverse revanchism*. They must go well beyond criminal justice reform to encompass the gamut of government programs that collectively set the life chances of the poor, and whose concurrent turnaround toward restriction and discipline after the mid-1970s have boosted the incidence, intensity, and duration of marginality at the bottom of the class and ethnic order.[54]

A variety of cogent proposals for reducing America's overreliance on confinement to check the reverberations of urban dispossession and dishonor have been put forward on the penal front over the past decade.[55] These proposals range from the renewal of intermediate sanctions, the diversion of low-level drug offenders, the abolition of mandatory sentencing, and the generalized reduction of the length of prison terms, to the reform of parole revocation, the incorporation of fiscal and social impacts into judicial proceedings, and the promotion of restorative justice. Whatever the technical means chosen, achieving sustained carceral deflation will require insulating judicial and correctional professionals from the converging pressures of the media and politicians, and rehabilitating rehabilitation through a public campaign debunking the neoconservative myth that "nothing works" when it comes to reforming offenders.[56]

Deep and broad justice reform is urgently needed to reduce the astronomical financial costs, skewed social and administrative burdens, and rippling criminogenic effects of continued hyperincarceration. But generic measures to diminish the size and reach of the prison across the board will leave largely untouched the sprouting epicenter of carceral growth—that is, the urban wastelands where race, class, and the penal state meet and mesh—unless they are combined with a concerted attack on labor degradation and social desolation in the decaying hyperghetto. For that to happen, the downsizing of the penal wing must be accompanied by the reconstruction of the economic and social capacities of the state and by their active deployment in and around the devastated districts of the segregated metropolis. The programmed dereliction of public institutions in the inner city must be remedied through massive investment in schools, social services, health care, and unfettered access to drug and alcohol rehabilitation. A Works Progress Administration–style public works program aimed at the vestiges of the historic Black Belt would help at once to rebuild its decrepit infrastructure, to improve housing conditions, and to offer economic sustenance and civic incorporation to local residents.[57]

In sum, the diagnosis of hyperincarceration implies that puncturing America's bloated and voracious penal state will take more than a full-bore political commitment to fighting social inequality and ethnic marginality through progressive and inclusive government programs on the economic, social, and justice fronts. It will necessitate also a spatially targeted policy to break the noxious nexus now binding hyperghettoiza-tion, restrictive workfare, and expansive prisonfare in the racialized urban core.

Part II

Policing: Where Are the Cops When You Need Them?

Everyone breaks the law sometimes, and many transgressions and even crimes go unnoticed, unreported, or unpunished. What we do not always recognize is that this reality means that there is a lot of discretion in law enforcement, especially at the start of the process.

The police decide not only whom to suspect and investigate at the outset, but also what crimes to prioritize and, when it comes to victimless crimes like drug possession, what neighborhoods and even what people to target. By the time a jury is involved, the only concern is whether the person arrested committed the crime charged; all the other people who might have done wrong got away a long time ago.

Discretion is inherently subjective and thus invites wide, but not necessarily appropriate, considerations. Much of what the law is meant to do is to restrict discretion, often with the handy if ineffable qualifier "reasonable." Thus the police may stop someone on the street for questioning or frisking if they have a "reasonable articulable suspicion" that he or she is on the verge or in the aftermath of committing a crime. As the U.S. Supreme Court has interpreted this basic concept, it has become permissible for the police to include someone's race as a factor in their suspicion, as long as it is not the only factor.[1]

This is racial profiling. The classic case has the police officer suspecting someone of criminality *because* he is black or Latino—or, in the post-9/11 era, someone who "looks Muslim" (whatever that may mean). This suspicion can arise from the officer's own hunch or from the use of an official policy detailing defined characteristics of criminals. Such profiling represents the conflating of race with unlawfulness that pervades not just the criminal justice process, but also television police dramas and

47

law-and-order political campaigning. Art and life mimic each other in a
mutually reinforcing cycle of stereotyping.

Racial profiling is more than an individual exercise of discretion. Police officials set strategies targeting high-crime areas that happen to be
inhabited mostly by black Americans. They design formal profiles of those
they expect to be drug couriers on highways and trains. Here, too, profiling is self-fulfilling: it does catch in its arbitrarily cast net low-level criminals, especially drug dealers and buyers, who happen to be black. What we
never get to know is what would happen if similar targeting were focused
on predominantly white neighborhoods, where drugs are sold mostly in-
doors rather than on the street. Discretion in law enforcement all too often means unaccountability.

The selections in this part provide the nuts and bolts of racial profiling, along with an analysis of what it means for law enforcement. David A.
Harris, a University of Pittsburgh law professor and a respected specialist
in these matters, is the author of *Profiles in Injustice: Why Racial Profiling
Cannot Work*. This book describes the origins of profiling as a law enforcement technique to identify criminals, and explains how race has infected
this technique. It surveys studies conducted by law enforcement officials
and social scientists to determine the efficacy and costs of racial profiling.
In the chapter excerpted here, Harris focuses on several states, notably
New Jersey and Maryland, where lawyers made pioneering challenges to
police profiling based on exhaustive data collection and analysis of highway stops.

The remaining selections highlight New York City's infamous stop-and-
frisk policy. For many years, the New York Police Department has sent officers to targeted locations in specific neighborhoods to stop, question,
and, if appropriate, frisk people in public spaces. While these people
are meant to meet certain criteria *before the stop*, such as resemblance to
criminal suspects or appearance of having weapons, they all too often are
young black men who, the police then report, made "furtive movements"
or otherwise reacted to the presence of police. Increasing numbers of people are stopped year after year, with consistently disproportionate percentages being black or Latino youth. However, few are arrested, and hardly
any of these have weapons that the policy purports to target. Civil rights
lawyers have sued, and their explanations of this litigation are included
here, along with newspaper commentary on this currently controversial
example of racial profiling.

4

Profiling Unmasked: From Criminal Profiling to Racial Profiling

David A. Harris

New Jersey

In the late 1980s and early 1990s, African Americans complained that state troopers on the New Jersey Turnpike made a regular practice of stopping and searching them. This had happened to many of them several times. One man—an African American dentist who drove a gold BMW—said that he had been stopped approximately fifty times, was never given a ticket, and was always asked whether he had drugs or guns in the car.[1] Such plentiful anecdotal evidence led observers to suspect strongly that troopers targeted and stopped blacks in numbers far out of proportion to their presence on the road. Criminal defense lawyers had long observed the effects of these tactics as they defended case after case based on these traffic stops. They saw firsthand that "a strikingly high proportion of cases arising from stops and searches on the New Jersey Turnpike involved black persons."[2] In 1990, a group of these lawyers mounted a challenge to this practice. The case, *State* v. *Pedro Soto*,[3] transformed the idea of criminal profiling by showing how it became racial profiling.

From the start, the state fought the allegations in *Soto* with a sharp-edged bitterness, denying at every turn the existence of any racial profiling. William Buckman, one of the attorneys who represented the defendants claiming profiling, remembers the constant, scathing denials, both in court proceedings and in the press. "Certainly in the courts, the state's response was a complete denial of any wrongdoing," Buckman says. Proceedings in the case began in November 1994, before the Honorable Robert Francis of the New Jersey Superior Court. Both sides presented

From *Profiles in Injustice: Why Racial Profiling Cannot Work* (New York: The New Press, 2002), 53–62.

49

statistical experts, but it was the analysis of Dr. John Lamberth of Temple University that mattered most.[4]

Lamberth, who was retained by the defendants as an expert to study the problem, set out to measure whether, in fact, New Jersey State Troopers were stopping and investigating African Americans in numbers significantly higher than the number of blacks in the traveling population on the turnpike.[5] To do this, Lamberth used a research methodology designed to determine two things: first, the rate at which troopers stopped, ticketed, and arrested blacks on the relevant portion of the highway and, second, the percentage of blacks among all travelers on the same stretch of road. Data concerning the rate at which blacks were stopped, ticketed, and arrested came from reports of all arrests resulting from stops on the turnpike from April 1988 through May 1991, patrol activity logs from randomly selected days from 1988 through 1991, and police radio logs from randomly selected days from 1988 through 1991.[6] Lamberth then measured the racial composition of the population of drivers on the road with a roadway census—direct observation by teams of researchers in randomly distributed blocks of time on different days. He also conducted a violator census—a rolling survey in which teams of observers in cars driving down the turnpike observed all the cars that passed them violating the speed limit, and noted the race of the drivers. Lamberth's surveys of the driving and violating population of the turnpike included observations of more than forty-two thousand cars.[7]

Lamberth's analysis of the data began by addressing an alternative hypothesis: even if blacks do get stopped by police in higher percentages, perhaps this happens because blacks violate the traffic laws at higher rates. In other words, maybe police stop more black drivers not because of their skin color but because of their driving behavior. The violator survey Lamberth performed yielded a direct answer: absolutely not. The data showed unequivocally that blacks and whites violate some aspect of the traffic laws at almost exactly the same, very high rate. There was no statistical difference in driving behavior between the two groups.[8] The testimony of several New Jersey State Police supervisors and troopers bolstered Lamberth's conclusion. All of them testified in the *Soto* case that they had never observed any difference in black and white driving behavior.[9] Gil Gallegos, the national president of the Fraternal Order of Police and a veteran police officer, put it this way: "I think [all racial and ethnic groups] drive the same. Terrible." Most people commit traffic violations every time they drive, he says, "including police officers in their driving."[10] Gallegos confirms what police officers everywhere say: no driver anywhere can drive for more than a few blocks without committing some type of traffic offense. Both the violator census results and the police testimony dovetail perfectly with what police officers everywhere have said for years: everyone breaks one or more traffic laws during any drive.

Lamberth's analysis then moved on to the key question of whether the New Jersey State Police had targeted blacks for disproportionate enforcement. To obtain the answer, Lamberth compared data on state police stops, citations, and arrests to the black driving population. He found that although blacks made up 73.2 percent of those arrested, only 13.5 percent of the cars on the turnpike had a black occupant—a difference Lamberth described as "statistically vast." [11] To understand how large the difference is, it is useful to consider the statistical measuring tool known as standard deviation. Statisticians calculate the standard deviation to decide whether a difference between two numbers is real—statistically significant—or is the result of pure chance. Statisticians agree that a difference is real—not the result of chance—at approximately two standard deviations. According to Lamberth, there were 54.27 standard deviations in the comparison between the arrest figure for blacks and the turnpike's population of blacks. According to Lamberth, this meant that the probability that the difference between these two numbers is the result of chance is "infinitesimally small." [12] Records of stops in state police radio and patrol logs were also quite different than the percentage of blacks on the highway. Blacks were approximately 35 percent of those stopped, and 13.5 percent of those on the road—19.45 standard deviations. Taking into account all the records of police activity and observations in the data, the chance that 35 percent of the cars of those who were stopped, ticketed, and arrested would have black occupants is, in Lamberth's words, "substantially less than one in one billion." [13] Lamberth concluded that, all in all, the data allowed a dispassionate observer to come to only one possible explanation:

> Absent some other explanation for the dramatically disproportionate number of stops of blacks, it would appear that the race of the occupants and/or drivers of the cars is a decisive factor or a factor with great explanatory power. I can say to a reasonable degree of statistical probability that the disparity outlined here is strongly consistent with the existence of a discriminatory policy, official or de facto, of targeting blacks for stops and investigation . . . Put bluntly, the statistics demonstrate that in a population of blacks and whites which is (legally) virtually universally subject to police stops for traffic law violation (cf. the turnpike violator census), blacks in general are several times more likely to be stopped than non-blacks. [14]

Judge Francis evaluated both Lamberth's analysis and the statistical work of the state's expert and came to the devastating conclusion in his

1996 decision that the state police had, indeed, been targeting African Americans on the turnpike for years. No other explanation, the judge said, could account for the large disparities between whom police stopped, ticketed, and arrested and the much smaller population of black drivers on the road. Lamberth's data were simply too powerful to ignore. His analysis showed that, contrary to the assertions of the state officials, blacks and other minorities had not been imagining things or exhibiting some kind of group persecution complex. Racial profiling was real.

Lamberth's statistics alone would have been enough to prove the case, but Judge Francis did not stop there. He based his decision not only on the data, but also on a completely independent source—evidence that the state police hierarchy, from the superintendent on down, had long known about these practices but at best failed to do anything about them and at worst even condoned them. Troopers at every level got the message in myriad ways: keep on doing what you're doing, and we'll take the heat and back you up.[15] Looked at together, Judge Francis said, the statistics and the actions of the state police showed beyond a doubt that African Americans and other minorities had been right all along.

The New Jersey Attorney General's Office, which defended the state police in court, appealed Judge Francis's decision, denying that there had been any racial profiling. But documents released in late 2000 reveal that officials within both the attorney general's office and the state police seem to have known at least since 1996 that there was, in fact, clear evidence of racial profiling. Internal state police documents show that officials at the highest level had evidence that a problem of racial targeting existed. In a memorandum dated October 4, 1996, Captain Ron Touw, Bureau Chief of State Police Internal Affairs, says that an examination of data from the Moorestown station showed that "the percentage of minorities stopped by both minority and nonminority troopers was dramatically higher than the 'expert' testified to in [the Soto case]." In other words, the situation was even worse than John Lamberth had said. Another memorandum, this one from Sergeant Thomas Gilbert to Carl Williams, who was then superintendent of the state police, examines numbers from the Moorestown and Cranbury stations from 1994 and 1996. These were the same two state police stations than had been at the center of the allegations of profiling in the Soto case. The memorandum reports that the motorists searched by troopers were overwhelmingly minorities, most of them black. Records of some of the individual troopers showed that they searched mostly minority citizens; some of them searched no one else. Sergeant Gilbert concluded from this that "at this point, we are in a very bad spot . . . the [U.S.] Justice Department"—which was by then beginning its investigation into the New Jersey State Police—"has a very good understanding of how we operate and what type of numbers they can get their hands on to prove their position."[16]

An event in the spring of 1998 eventually became the catalyst for real public attention to the issue of racial profiling. Two troopers on the New Jersey Turnpike stopped a van carrying four young black men. According to the troopers, the van attempted to back into them after the stop, and they reacted with a volley of gunshots. The van ended up in a ditch, and so did the four occupants, three of them bleeding from gunshot wounds. Miraculously, none of the men died. The men said later that police refused to allow them to have medical attention until the police had pulled apart their clothes and searched them. Investigations into the shootings began, and it quickly emerged that the young men had been headed to a basketball tryout at North Carolina Central University. No weapons or drugs—only basketball equipment and a Bible—were found in the van.

The controversy continued to bubble, with a U.S. Justice Department investigation into the shooting intertwining with the department's existing investigation into the allegations of profiling. On February 10, 1999, the Newark *Star-Ledger*, the state's largest circulation daily, said that police records indicated that 75 percent of those arrested on the turnpike were minorities.[17] As tensions continued to mount, New Jersey Attorney General Peter Verniero appointed a task force to put together a comprehensive report on the state police, including the issue of profiling. On February 26, Governor Christie Whitman nominated Verniero—who, as attorney general, had ultimate official responsibility for the state police—to a seat on the New Jersey Supreme Court. Then, on February 28, 1999, another article in the *Star-Ledger* brought the ongoing profiling controversy to a fever pitch: Carl Williams, the superintendent of the state police, told the newspaper that minorities perpetrated most of the drug and drug-trafficking in his state. "The drug problem is mostly cocaine and marijuana. It is most likely a minority group that's involved with that." When the president of the United States wanted to discuss international drug trafficking, Williams said, he went to Mexico, not Ireland or England.[18] William's comments seemed to confirm the worst suspicions about the state police. They also seemed likely to imperil Verniero's nomination. Whitman fired Williams the next day, but she still refused to admit that the problem existed.[19]

Shortly afterward, the attorney general's task force issued its report. Few expected anything like what it contained. Despite numerous strong statements to the contrary by state officials over the years, the report said that the evidence left little room for doubt that "minority motorists have been treated differently than non-minority motorists in the course of traffic stops on the New Jersey Turnpike. . . . [T]he problem of disparate treatment is real—not imagined."[20] Examining statistics on traffic stops from 1997 and 1998, a period that *followed* the damning verdict in *Soto* as well as intense media coverage of the allegations of profiling by the state police, the task force reported that more than 40 percent of all traffic stops involved a racial minority, and that blacks made up more than one in four of all persons stopped.[21] All of this was "consistent with the data developed during the course of the Soto litigation."[22]

Data on searches of drivers—drawn from a larger stretch of time than the data on stops—showed even larger biases: almost 80 percent of these searches involved either a black or Hispanic driver.[23] With remarkable understatement, the report said this meant that "race and ethnicity may have influenced the exercise of discretion by some officers" performing searches. The report also broke down citations issued by type of enforcement unit. Radar units, which used radar to track speed, exercised relatively little discretion in whom they stopped. Tactical patrol units focused on vehicle law enforcement with particular objectives in particular locations—they exercised somewhat more discretion. General patrol units exercised the most discretion. The more discretion a unit exercised, the task force reported, the greater the proportion of its tickets went to African American drivers: radar, 18 percent; tactical patrol, 23.8 percent; and general patrol, 34.2 percent. For tickets issued south of turnpike exit 3 the disproportion was even greater, with the general patrol unit issuing 43.8 percent of its tickets to African Americans. This meant that "officers who had more time to devote to drug interdiction may have been more likely to rely upon racial or ethnic stereotypes" than others.[24] All of this, the report said, generated fear, anger, and resentment among minorities; made law enforcement's job more difficult by eroding public confidence in police; and divided black and white citizens on questions of race, criminal justice, and public safety. For all of these reasons, the report concluded, the New Jersey State Police had to make a number of crucial changes, including the way in which they conducted traffic stops and their techniques of supervision, training, discipline, and information management.

The New Jersey Task Force report represents one of the most far-reaching statements on profiling and traffic stops any government at any level has ever made. New Jersey's struggle with profiling illustrates many of the problems found in the use of traffic stops as a high-discretion enforcement tool: lack of accountability, denial, a failure to face facts, defensiveness, and an utter disregard for the implications of policing policies, no matter how loudly some members of the public cry out.

Maryland

Recall the story of Robert Wilkins, the African American Harvard law graduate whose rental car was stopped and searched as he and his family were returning to the Washington, D.C., area from a family funeral in Chicago. Civil rights lawyers sometimes say that despite the volume of complaints they receive about racially biased traffic stops, victims usually feel reluctant to come forward and sue. Some may fear retaliation. Others may not want to get involved in complex, politically charged, protracted, and very public litigation charging a police department with racial bias. To get involved in a case like this, one must have an absolutely squeaky clean personal history, the knowledge and personal resources to access the legal system, and the moxie to take on the task. Most people would simply rather forget these unpleasant experiences.[25]

As an attorney with substantial experience in search and seizure law, Robert Wilkins knew exactly what his rights were and how the Maryland State Police had violated them. And he was unafraid of the legal system—working within it was his daily bread and butter. Wilkins and his family members contacted the American Civil Liberties Union (ACLU), which filed suit on behalf of the four of them and all other motorists whom police had treated the same way. The suit alleged that the police had violated civil rights laws and other statutes by illegally stopping and detaining them on the basis of a racial profile.[26] The state police vigorously denied Wilkins's allegations. A spokesman said the practice of stopping a disproportionate number of blacks represented not racism but "an unfortunate byproduct of sound police policies."[27] Despite this and other race-neutral explanations, the turning point in the lawsuit came when a document entitled "Criminal Intelligence Report" came to light. This document contained an explicit profile targeting African Americans and was dated just days before the state police stopped Wilkins and his family. A settlement followed soon after. Wilkins and his family received small amounts of monetary damages, and the state police agreed to change their policies, practices, and training. But the real meat of the agreement was the settlement's requirement that the state police keep data on every traffic stop that resulted in a search, and submit the data to the court for a period of three years so that it could monitor whether the state police had in fact changed their ways.[28]

It was these data that emerged as the key contribution of Wilkins's suit. When they became available, the ACLU retained John Lamberth to perform the same kind of analysis he had done in the New Jersey case. Lamberth took the data from the state police concerning the number of stops broken down by race, and he compared these data to road population surveys and violator surveys he and his research associates conducted on I-95, the main location of Maryland State Police drug interdiction.[29] What he found was that blacks and whites drove no differently; every racial and ethnic group violated the traffic laws at the same very high rate.[30] But more important, he found that although 17 percent of the driving population on that road was black, African Americans were a full 72 *percent* of all those stopped and searched.[31] In more than 80 percent of the cases, the person stopped and searched was a member of a racial minority.[32] The numbers were also broken down by individual officer: half of the officers stopped more than 80 percent African Americans, one officer stopped more than 95 percent African Americans; and two officers stopped *only* African Americans.[33] The disparity between 17 percent (the black driving population) and 72 percent (percentage of drivers stopped and searched who were black) includes 34.6 standard deviations, a level of statistical significance that Lamberth described as "literally off the charts."[34] In careful, temperate language, Lamberth came to a devastating conclusion:

> While no one can know the motivation of each individual trooper in conducting a traffic stop, the statistics presented herein, representing a broad and detailed sample of highly appropriate data, show without question a racially discriminatory impact on blacks. . . . The disparities are sufficiently great that taken as a whole, they are consistent and strongly support the assertion that the state police targeted the community of black motorists for stop, detention and investigation within the Interstate 95 corridor.[35]

5

Stop-Question-Frisk Analyses

The Center for Constitutional Rights

*F*loyd, et al. v. City of New York, et al. is a federal class action lawsuit filed in 2008 against the New York City Police Department that charges the NYPD with engaging in racial profiling and suspicion-less stop-and-frisks of law-abiding New York City residents. According to Center for Constitutional Rights attorneys, the named plaintiffs in CCR's case—David Floyd, David Ourlicht, Lalit Clarkson, and Deon Dennis—represent the thousands of New Yorkers who have been stopped without any cause on the way to work, in front of their house, or just walking down the street. CCR and the plaintiffs allege that the NYPD unlawfully stopped these individuals because they are men of color.

The *Floyd* case stems from CCR's landmark racial profiling case, *Daniels, et al. v. City of New York, et al.*, which led to the disbanding of the infamous Street Crime Unit and a settlement with the city in 2003. The *Daniels* settlement agreement required the NYPD to maintain a written racial profiling policy that complies with the U.S. and New York State Constitutions and to provide stop-and-frisk data to CCR on a quarterly basis from the last quarter of 2003 through the first quarter of 2007. However, an analysis of the data revealed that the NYPD has continued to engage in suspicion-less and racially pretextual stop-and-frisks. The 2003 settlement agreement from *Daniels* also required the NYPD to audit officers who engage in stop-and-frisks and their supervisors to determine whether and to what extent the stop-and-frisks are based on reasonable suspicion and whether and to what extent the stop-and-frisks are being documented.

The Center for Constitutional Rights (CCR) is dedicated to advancing and protecting the rights guaranteed by the U.S. Constitution and the Universal Declaration of Human Rights. Founded in 1966 by attorneys who represented civil rights movements in the South, CCR is a nonprofit legal and educational organization committed to the creative use of law as a positive force for social change.

After significant noncompliance with the *Daniels* settlement and after new information released publicly by the city showed a remarkable increase in stop-and-frisks from 2002 to 2006, CCR decided to file a new lawsuit challenging the NYPD's racial profiling and stop-and-frisk policy.

Floyd focuses not only on the lack of any reasonable suspicion to make these stops, a violation of the Fourth Amendment, but also on the obvious racial disparities in who gets stopped and searched by the NYPD—more than 80 percent of those stopped are black and Latino, even though these two groups make up only around 50 percent of the city's population— which constitute a violation of the Equal Protection Clause of the Fourteenth Amendment.

Under court order, the city was required to turn over to CCR all the previous stop-and-frisk data from 1998 to the present, and to continue to do so on a quarterly basis until the conclusion of the litigation.

On October 26, 2010, CCR released an expert report for its New York Police Department (NYPD) stop-and-frisk case, *Floyd v. City of New York*. The report includes key findings in the following three areas:

Race (Equal Protection, Fourteenth Amendment)

- This report analyzes six years of the NYPD's own data using controls for multiple factors. The findings demonstrate that *the NYPD's stop-and-frisk program is about race, not crime.*
- The NYPD has engaged in a pattern of unconstitutional stops that disproportionately affect black and Latino New Yorkers.
- Most stops occur in black and Latino neighborhoods, and even after adjustments for other factors including crime rates, social conditions, and allocation of police resources in those neighborhoods, race is the main factor determining NYPD stops.
- Blacks and Hispanics are more likely to be stopped than whites even in areas with low crime rates, where populations are mixed or mostly white.

Unreasonable Search and Seizure (Fourth Amendment)

- Nearly 150,000 stops over the last six years are facially unconstitutional and lack any legal justification. Another 544,252 stops may be unconstitutional but were not documented sufficiently to determine this. All together, 30 percent of all stops are either illegal or of questionable legality, underlining a severe lack of adequate officer oversight in the NYPD.

- Nearly half of all documented stops are justified by citing the vague category "furtive movements," in stark contrast to the only 15 percent of stops citing "fits relevant description." In more than half of all stops, NYPD officers cite "high crime area" as an "additional circumstance" even in precincts with *lower* than average crime rates. The Supreme Court has found it specifically unconstitutional to stop and frisk a person simply because they are in a so-called high-crime neighborhood.

- Arrests take place in less than 6 percent of all stops, a "hit rate" that is lower than the rates of arrests and seizures at random checkpoints. If NYPD officers stopped people based on reasonable suspicion, the department would have higher rates of lawful arrests and seizures than what is achieved through completely random stops, clearly demonstrating that stop-and-frisk is neither an efficient nor effective police practice.

- Black and Latino suspects are treated more harshly in instances in which police officers make the determination that a crime has occurred. Black and Latino suspects are more likely to be arrested rather than issued a summons when compared to white suspects who are accused of the same crimes. Black and Latino suspects are more likely to have force used against them.

- The rate of gun seizures is nearly zero—0.15 out of a hundred stops— a disturbingly low return for a law enforcement tactic the NYPD itself claims is designed specifically to remove illegal guns from the streets.

RAND Report Debunked

- The city often relies on a report it commissioned in 2007 from the RAND Corporation that claims its stop-and-frisk policy is not racially biased. The Fagan report, however, takes the science and methodology of that report apart piece by piece, showing the NYPD's and RAND's claims are unscientific and clearly without merit.

- The city frequently alleges that most violent crimes are committed by black and Latino suspects; however, violent crimes comprise less than 10 percent of all reported crimes in New York City. Furthermore, almost half of violent crime complaints do not report a suspect's race at all. The city excludes 90 percent of the picture in its primary talking point.

On February 24, 2011, CCR issued the statement below in response to a summary of stop-and-frisk statistics for the year 2010 made available to the press. CCR also launched a fifteen-second spot on the Jumbotron in Times Square to raise awareness of the issue.

With more than 600,601 stops, 87 percent of which were of black and Latino New Yorkers, last year was the worst year for stop-and-frisks since the city began keeping records. For many children, being stopped by the police on their way home from school has become a normal afterschool activity, and that is a tragedy.

CCR has found significant racial disparities for stop-and-frisks over the last decade based on NYPD data turned over by court order. The preliminary numbers reported on February 23 indicate a 4 percent rise in the number of stops of New Yorkers by the police over the previous year—an additional 25,000 stops.

A February 23rd NYPD press release makes the bold claim "Stops save lives," yet the department has never been able to prove that stop-and-frisk even reduces crime. Only 0.13 percent of last year's stops resulted in the discovery of a firearm, and only 7 percent of the stops resulted in arrests. The weapons and contraband yield from stop-and-frisks is the same as that from random checkpoints.

Ten years' worth of previous data show that NYPD officers use physical force at a far higher rate during stops of blacks and Latinos compared to whites, and that this disparity exists despite corresponding rates of arrest and weapons or contraband yield across racial lines, which further supports our legal claims that the NYPD is engaged in a pattern of racial profiling in its stop-and-frisk practices.

The NYPD now presents its statistics on stop-and-frisks by race paired with its statistics for violent crime suspects by race in a way meant to imply that the disproportionate stops of black and Latino New Yorkers is justified, when in fact it proves the police are racially profiling the people they stop. The data up until the last quarter of 2010 (all that is currently available for this statistic) reveal that "fits relevant description" is the reason for actual stops only 15 percent of the time. Far and away the most often cited reason for a stop by the police is the vague and undefined "furtive movements" (nearly 50 percent of all stops); second is when the police deem someone to appear to be "casing a victim or location" (nearly 30 percent of all stops). Also listed are "inappropriate attire for season," "wearing clothes commonly used in a crime," and "suspicious bulge," among other boxes an officer can check off on the form.

Despite the overwhelming evidence of racial disparities and stops of questionable legality, in February 2011 the City of New York moved for summary judgment in the *Floyd* case, arguing that, as a matter of law, the plaintiffs cannot prove Fourth or Fourteenth Amendment violations and that their claims should therefore be dismissed without even reaching a jury. All the briefs are in, and the parties are awaiting the Court's decision on the motion.

Police stops-and-frisks without reasonable suspicion violate the Fourth Amendment, and racial profiling is a violation of fundamental rights and protections of the Fourteenth Amendment and the Civil Rights Act of 1964. This kind of heavy-handed policing promotes mistrust and fear of police officers in communities of color, and only serves to make the police's job more difficult. Stop-and-frisk is bad public policy.

6

The Shame of New York City

Bob Herbert

The whole notion of the rule of law, critical to a democracy, is sabotaged when the guardians of the law—in this case the officers of the New York City Police Department—are permitted to violate the law with impunity.

The police in New York City are not just permitted, they are encouraged to trample on the rights of black and Hispanic New Yorkers by relentlessly enforcing the city's degrading, unlawful, and outright racist stop-and-frisk policy. Hundreds of thousands of wholly innocent individuals, most of them young, are routinely humiliated by the police, day in and day out, year after shameful year.

Jeffrey Fagan, a professor of law and public health at Columbia University and a widely recognized scholar on the subject of police and citizen interactions, has filed a report in support of a federal class-action lawsuit challenging the stop-and-frisk policy as unconstitutional. Based on analyses of the department's own statistics, he found, as the plaintiffs and other observers have argued all along, that seizures of weapons or contraband as a result of the stops "is extremely rare."

The rate of gun seizures is near zero—0.15 guns seized for every 100 stops. "The N.Y.P.D. stop-and-frisk tactics," wrote Professor Fagan, "produce rates of seizures of guns or other contraband that are no greater than would be produced simply by chance."

More important, after studying six years' worth of data, the professor concluded that many of the millions of stops are violations of the Constitution. One of a number of constitutional problems, according to Professor Fagan, is that the police frequently use race or national origin rather than reasonable suspicion as the basis for the stops.

From the *New York Times*, October 30, 2010.

"I provide evidence that the N.Y.P.D. has engaged in patterns of unconstitutional stops of city residents that are more likely to affect black and Latino citizens," he wrote.

From 2004 through 2009, city police officers stopped people on the street and checked them out nearly three million times. Many were patted down, frisked, made to sprawl face down on the ground, or spread-eagle themselves against a wall or over the hood of a car. Nearly 90 percent of the people stopped were completely innocent of any wrongdoing.

An overwhelming majority of the people stopped were black or Hispanic. Blacks were nine times more likely than whites to be stopped by the police, but no more likely than whites to be arrested as a result of the stops.

While crime has been going down, the number of people getting stopped has been going up. More than 575,000 stops were made last year [2009]—a record. But 504,594 of those stops were of people who had committed no crime, were issued no summonses and were carrying no weapons or illegal substances.

If the stops go up when crime goes down, it's fair to wonder what might happen if there was no crime in the city. Mayor Michael Bloomberg and Police Commissioner Ray Kelly might decide that it is necessary to frisk everybody. The use of such stops has more than quintupled on their watch.

The Center for Constitutional Rights, which filed the class-action suit, wants the Police Department barred from engaging in what the center describes as race-based and "suspicionless stops and frisks."

Professor Fagan, in his report filed in connection with the suit, found that nearly 150,000 stops over the six-year period that he studied lacked any legal justification at all. An additional 544,252 stops lacked sufficiently detailed information from the officers involved to determine their legality.

I've no doubt that the professor's findings are, in fact, conservative. But even his figures show the police to be violating the Constitution on a scandalously vast scale. The police use such specious justifications as "furtive movements" or an alleged "bulge" in someone's pocket as the basis for stopping people. If you believe all those furtive-movement and bulging-pocket stories, I've got some antiques spanning the East River that you might be interested in.

It's important to keep in mind that what we are talking about here, in the overwhelming number of cases, are innocent people, not criminals. No one wants to stop the police from going after the bad guys. But what keeps happening with this lousy policy is that the cops target skin color, not the likelihood that a crime might be in progress, or have taken place. As

Professor Fagan found, "Blacks and Latinos are more likely to be stopped than whites, even in areas where there are low crime rates and where residential populations are racially heterogeneous or predominantly white."

It doesn't matter if innocent black or Hispanic kids are in a high-crime area or low, a minority area or white, they stand a good chance of being harassed by New York City cops.

Part III

The War on Drugs: Who Is the Real Enemy?

What is the Rorschach reaction when we think of crime? Blood or broken glass? Police tape? A hospital bed or a morgue? Certainly we think of violence, whether to person or property, and a victim, not to mention an evil or crazed perpetrator. However, the fact is that more than a third of the people held in our prisons stand convicted of nonviolent victimless crimes. They are the prisoners of the War on Drugs.

In the gruesome competition to be the nation's longest war, this one, now in its fortieth year, wins hands down. Launched for specific reasons and circumstances that no longer apply, it is now taken for granted as the standard state of affairs. Though the longest-lasting crime-fighting strategy, it has proved to be a great failure. By all accounts, the availability of illegal drugs for purchase in the United States has suffered no downturn from this war, but rather has increased. An estimated $1 trillion in interdiction, investigation, and prosecution has failed to keep the price of drugs from falling, because the supply has not gone down, but gone up.

In the process, many Americans have become collateral consequences of this war, imprisoned in huge numbers in a quest to defeat the drug trade. That is the apparent logic of waging a war on drugs: the drugs are the enemy. Yet realistically, people have become the enemy, and rhetoric is used conveniently to hide this fact.

Who are these people? Disproportionately, they are poor—not the drug lords who reap mythical fortunes from the trade but the low-level dealers and users. They are also disproportionately black and Latino. While black Americans use drugs no more (and arguably less) than white Americans, they are ten times more likely to go to prison for drug activity.[1] The explosion of the U.S. prison population in the last thirty years, with

65

its appalling racially skewed character, is largely the result of the War on Drugs.

This policing strategy surely deserves special mention in any account of race and justice. However, it is not just the numbers that stand out. This strategy has been about more than fighting crime. The War on Drugs has been a political strategy to win votes, primarily those of white Americans in the South, by demonizing black Americans. In this way, it also has been part of a governing strategy to shift spending priorities from cities to sub-urbs, from public benefits to tax cuts. The War on Drugs in fact has been a war on the poor, in particular poor people of color.

Race to Incarcerate by Marc Mauer provides a historical and statistical overview of the racial skewing of U.S. criminal justice. In the chapter excerpted here, Mauer demonstrates that this racial disparity is best characterized and explained by the War on Drugs. Where the police choose to enforce the drug laws seems key to this disparity. Mauer is the executive director of The Sentencing Project, which tracks developments in U.S. criminal justice and advocates for reform. One long-standing issue has been the enormous discrepancy between federal sentencing rules for crack and powder cocaine, the former used more often by blacks and the latter by whites. In 2010, Congress reduced but failed to eliminate this discrepancy.[2]

Decades of Disparity: Drug Arrests and Race in the United States is a 2009 report by Human Rights Watch (www.hrw.org) that provides a handy break-down of how black and white Americans experience the War on Drugs differently. The summary and tables excerpted here offer some key statistics and also debunk some of the myths about this war. Drug possession is the main battleground, not big-time drug sales. The states that specifically target drug users are also the ones that particularly target their black citizens. It is not just that they get arrested more; they also get prosecuted and sent to prison more often.

Further Reading: "The Lockdown" is a chapter from Michelle Alexander's *The New Jim Crow*, described in the introduction to Part I. It vividly describes how federal legislation and funding have fueled the War on Drugs. The politicians who aroused and exploited the public's fear of drug addicts and dealers—inevitably assumed to be black—subsequently launched programs with training, equipment, and money for states, cities, and localities willing to join the war effort. These warriors had to show results—and where would it be easier to fight than in poor neighborhoods, and whom could be easier to combat than poor people? This monetary motivation helps Alexander explain how the nation could turn on its own citizens and effectively lock them down.

7

The War on Drugs and the African American Community

Marc Mauer

Drug Use and Drug Arrests

With nondrug street crimes, such as burglary or larceny, the police operate in a reactive mode: citizens report a crime and the police investigate. With drug selling or possession, though, there is no direct "victim"; consequently, no reports are made to the police (except possibly those made by complaining neighbors). Drug law enforcement is far more discretionary than for other offenses. The police decide when and where they will seek to make drug arrests, and most important, what priority they will place on enforcing drug laws.

The drug war's impact on the African American community can be mapped by looking at two overlapping trends. First, there has been an enormous increase in the number of drug arrests overall; second, African Americans have constituted an increasing proportion of those arrests.

As seen in Figure 1, in 1980 there were 581,000 arrests for drug offenses, a number that nearly doubled to 1,090,000 by 1990. Although it appeared for a while that these trends might be leveling off in the early 1990s with a decline in arrests, that trend was quickly reversed: a record 1,579,566 drug arrests were made by 2000.[1]

Did these arrests reflect rising rates of drug abuse nationally? No. In fact, the best data available show that the number of people using drugs had been declining since 1979, when 14.1 percent of the population reported using drugs in the past month. This proportion had halved to 6.7 percent by 1990, and it declined to 6.3 percent by 2000.[2] Since fewer people were using drugs, and presumably fewer selling as well, then all things being equal, one would have thought that drug arrests would have declined as well.

From *Race to Incarcerate*, revised and updated (New York: The New Press, 2006), 158–76.

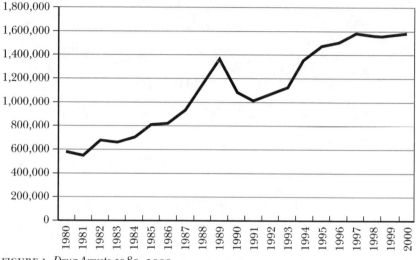

FIGURE 1 *Drug Arrests 1980–2000*
Source: FBI data provided to the author.

But all things are not equal when it comes to crime and politics. Instead, heightened political and media attention and increased budgets for law enforcement all contributed to a greater use of police resources to target drug offenders. At the same time, police increasingly began to target low-income minority communities for drug law enforcement.

We can see this most clearly by analyzing arrest data prepared annually by the FBI. As seen in Figure 2, in 1980, African Americans, who constitute 13 percent of the U.S. population, accounted for 21 percent of drug possession arrests nationally. This number rose to a high of 36 percent in 1992 before dropping somewhat to 32 percent by 2000. For juveniles, the figures are even more stark: although blacks represented 13 percent of juvenile drug possession arrests in 1980, this proportion climbed to 40 percent by 1991, before declining to 23 percent in 2000. In looking at these statistics, we might conclude that blacks began using drugs in greater numbers during the decade of the 1980s, thereby leading to their being arrested more frequently. Certainly, a glance at television newscasts or weekly newsmagazines would have given us this impression.

In fact, no such dramatic rise can be detected. The best data available on drug use is compiled by the Substance Abuse and Mental Health Services Administration (SAMHSA) of the Department of Health and Human Services, which conducts a household survey annually to prepare estimates on the extent of drug use. Although these data cover 98 percent of the population, they have some limitations. Since this is by definition a household survey, anyone not living in a household will not be incorporated in the findings. Thus, prisoners, homeless persons not living in a shelter, and military personnel are not covered. Since minorities are disproportionately represented among these groups, they will therefore be underrepresented in the household survey. Nevertheless, the survey is generally regarded as the best portrait of the nation's drug-using population.

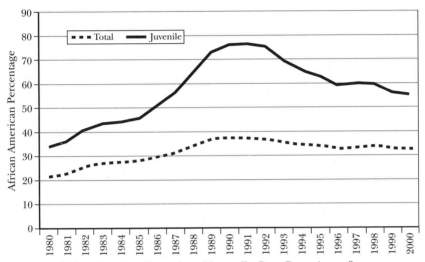

FIGURE 2 *African American Proportion of Arrests For Drug Possession 1980–2000*
Source: FBI data provided to the author.

The SAMHSA surveys question individuals regarding drug use during the past month, past year, or ever in their lifetime. For our purposes, drug use during the past month is the most relevant piece of information, since frequent users are more likely to be arrested than infrequent ones.

Looking at the data for 2000, we find that African Americans were no more likely to be monthly drug users than whites and only slightly more likely than Hispanics (6.4 percent vs. 6.4 percent and 5.3 percent respectively).[3] But the much greater number of whites in the overall population resulted in their constituting the vast majority of drug users. Thus, the SAMHSA data indicate that whites represented 75 percent of current drug users, with African Americans constituting 12 percent of users and Hispanics, 9 percent. Even assuming that blacks may be somewhat undercounted in the household surveys, it is difficult to imagine that African American drug use is of a magnitude that could explain blacks representing 12 percent of current drug users yet 32 percent of arrests for drug possession.

Some observers have speculated that the higher arrest rates for drug possession may reflect the type of drug that is being used—in essence, law enforcement is more likely to target cocaine users or crack cocaine users. Unfortunately, FBI arrest data do not distinguish between powder cocaine and crack cocaine. Arrest data for all cocaine possession offenses for 2000 show that African Americans constituted 45 percent of all such arrests. Looking at data on cocaine use, though, we find that there are no dramatic differences in cocaine use by race or ethnicity. In 2000, 0.7 percent of blacks reported that they had used cocaine in the past month, compared to 0.8 percent of Hispanics and 0.5 percent of whites.[4] Overall, this translates into African Americans representing 16 percent of all recent cocaine users.

For users of crack cocaine, the disproportionate use among blacks is considerably higher than for cocaine overall, but it doesn't explain the arrest disparities. Because relatively few people use crack compared to most other illicit drugs, demographic estimates of use rates are subject to a significant amount of variation. In 2002, for example, blacks reported using crack in the past month at a rate eleven times that of whites or Hispanics, but in 2003, the differential was just 4.5 times as much.[5] Given the relatively modest proportion of blacks in the overall population, though, these rates translate into blacks constituting 35 percent of users in 2002 and 46 percent in 2003. In either case, these proportions are well below arrest rates for crack offenses. In the federal court system, blacks have consistently represented about 85 percent of crack defendants for more than a decade.

Are police arresting crack and cocaine users in general or preferentially going into black neighborhoods where some people are using these drugs? Conducting drug arrests in inner-city neighborhoods does have advantages for law enforcement. First, it is far easier to make arrests in such areas, since drug dealing is more likely to take place in open-air drug markets. In contrast, drug dealing in suburban neighborhoods almost invariably takes place behind closed doors and is therefore not readily identifiable to passing police. Second, because both drug use and dealing are more likely to take place openly, residents of African American neighborhoods are more likely to complain about these behaviors and to ask for police intervention. Since law enforcement has long been accused of failing to respond to problems of minority neighborhoods in a timely manner, many police departments are now more focused on attempting to remedy this problem—so they are likely to respond to complaints emanating from these neighborhoods.

Racial targeting by police may also have an effect on black neighborhoods that are not inner-city. Criminologists James Lynch and William Sabol analyzed data on incarceration rates, race, and class during the period 1979–91.[6] They identified inmates as either being "underclass" or "non-underclass" ([non-underclass includes] working-class or middle class) based on educational levels, employment history, and income. They concluded that the most significant increase in incarceration rates was for working class black drug offenders, whose rates increased sixfold, from 1.5 per 1,000 in 1979 to match that of underclass blacks at 9 per 1,000 by 1991. The trend for whites, on the other hand, was just the opposite; the underclass drug incarceration rate was double that of the non-underclass by 1991.

Lynch and Sabol suggest that two factors may explain these trends. First, law enforcement targeting of inner-city neighborhoods may initially sweep many underclass blacks into the criminal justice system. Second, due to residential racial segregation patterns, there may be a "spillover" effect whereby police increase the number of arrests in the working-class black neighborhoods that border underclass communities. They conclude that there has been

> an increased targeting of black working and middle class areas for discretionary drug enforcement and ultimately increased incarceration for drug offenses. The immunity that working and middle class status used to bring in the black community (and still does among whites) may have been lost. While the processes that produced these outcomes may not have been racially motivated in intent, they have resulted in racially disparate outcomes.[7]

Drug Sales and Arrests

Similar disproportionate arrest patterns can be seen for drug selling. In this area, the African American proportion rose from 35 percent in 1980 to 47 percent by 2000.

It is at least theoretically possible that the proportion of black drug traffickers has risen substantially in recent years, and that the arrest percentages reflect actual law-breaking behavior. However, as we examine these disparities we find that statistics on drug users are fairly irrelevant, since one can be a drug seller without being a user.[8] One means of addressing this problem is to look at responses to parts of the SAMHSA surveys in which 12–17-year-old respondents are asked whether it is "fairly or very easy" to obtain drugs in your neighborhood. Overall, 25 percent of the population in 2003 responded affirmatively regarding cocaine and 26 percent regarding crack. These figures, which document the relative ease of obtaining drugs after massive increases in the law enforcement

resources devoted to the drug war, should give pause to those committed
to such policies.

While blacks were more likely than whites to report that it was easy to
obtain these drugs (29 percent vs. 24 percent for cocaine, and 33 percent
vs. 25 percent for crack), the differences are nowhere near the order of
magnitude that would explain the arrest disparities.[9] A report issued by
the Wisconsin Policy Research Institute, a conservative think tank, provides part of the explanation in describing differences in the white suburban drug markets and inner-city black and Hispanic neighborhoods of
Milwaukee.[10] While drug dealing was prevalent in each of the communities, the inner-city sales tended to be neighborhood-based, often taking
place on street corners. In contrast, the suburban distribution of cocaine
and other drugs took place by word of mouth through contacts at work,
bars, athletic leagues, and alternative cultural events such as "raves." Suburban sales locations were more hidden from law enforcement than were
those in the inner-city neighborhoods, but they were "not very difficult to
locate," in the words of the author.

Even when such urban-suburban distinctions are not the issue, African
Americans are disproportionately targeted for drug prosecutions. A study
of arrest practices in Seattle by sociologist Katherine Beckett examined
the validity of the popular explanations for higher arrest rates for crack
cocaine and hence, blacks.[11] These explanations generally include the
idea that outdoor arrests represent higher priorities for law enforcement
and that crack is more associated with violence than other drugs. Beckett found no confirmation for these contentions. While only about one
third of outdoor serious drug transactions (also including heroin, meth-
amphetamine, and powder cocaine) involved crack, three quarters of all
arrests were for crack. Crack was also much less associated with violence
than the other drugs; crack arrests were only one tenth as likely as heroin
arrests to involve guns. Beckett concludes that "these patterns appear to
reflect a racialized conception of who and what comprises the drug problem in Seattle."[12]

A 1997 report of the National Institute of Justice lends support to the
fact that whites are frequently involved in selling drugs. In an analysis of
drug transactions in six cities, the researchers found that "respondents
were most likely to report using a main source who was of their own racial
or ethnic background."[13]

Finally, consider the patterns of daily life in urban areas. If it were true
that the overwhelming number of drug dealers are black, we would see
large numbers of drug-seeking whites streaming into Harlem, South Central Los Angeles, and the east side of Detroit day after day. While some do
visit these neighborhoods, there are few reports of massive numbers doing

so on a regular basis. As Barry McCaffrey, former director of the White House Office of National Drug Control Policy, has stated, if your child bought drugs, "it was from a student of their own race generally." [14]

Sentencing for Drug Offenses

The overrepresentation of African Americans in the criminal justice system has been exacerbated by changes in sentencing policy that coincided with the current drug war. Since 1975, every state has passed some type of mandatory sentencing law requiring incarceration for weapons offenses, habitual offenders, or other categories. These statutes have been applied most frequently to drug offenses, with two primary effects. First, they increase the proportion of arrested drug offenders who are sentenced to prison and, second, they increase the length of time that offenders serve in prison.

Data from the Bureau of Justice Statistics show that the chances of receiving a prison term after being arrested for a drug offense increased by 447 percent between 1980 and 1992.[15] A good portion of this increase was likely related to the requirement of mandatory sentencing, although no breakdown is available. Part of the increase may have also been a result of generally harsher attitudes toward drug offenders—that is, prosecutors and judges responding to a political climate increasingly punitive in its orientation toward drugs.

The impact of mandatory drug laws can be seen most dramatically in the federal court system. Drug offenders released from prison in 1990, many of whom had not been sentenced under mandatory provisions, had served an average of thirty months in prison. But offenders sentenced to prison in 1990—most of whom were subject to mandatory penalties— were expected to serve more than twice that term, or an average of 66 months.[16] This fact, combined with a greatly increased number of federal drug prosecutions, has resulted in the proportion of federal prisoners who are drug offenders increasing from 25 percent in 1980 to 55 percent by 2004.

At the state level, the longer prison terms brought about by mandatory sentencing laws have also had a significant impact on African Americans. Between 1985 and 1995, the average time served in prison for drug offenses rose by 20 percent from twenty months to twenty-four months.[17] Overall, the number of drug offenders in prison increased by 478 percent during this period, compared to a rise of 119 percent for all offenses.

A substantial portion of this increase consists of African Americans. This can be seen in Table 1. From 1985 to 1995, drug offenders constituted

42 percent of the rise in the black state prison population. Note here that drug offenders in this case refers to individuals convicted only of a drug offense and not, for example, a drug-*related* assault or robbery. For white offenders, by contrast, drug offenders represented 26 percent of the increase and violent offenders 42 percent. Overall, the number of white drug offenders increased by 306 percent in the ten-year period, while for blacks the increase was 707 percent.

TABLE 1   State Prison Inmates by Race and Offense

		White				Black		
				% Total				% Total
Offense	1985	1995	% Increase	Increase	1985	1995	%Increase	Increase
Total	224,900	471,100	109%	100%	211,100	490,100	132%	100%
Violent	111,900	214,800	92%	42%	124,800	228,600	83%	37%
Drug	21,200	86,100	306%	26%	16,600	134,000	707%	42%
Property	75,100	130,700	74%	23%	60,600	100,200	65%	14%
Public Order	14,900	39,000	162%	10%	7,600	25,000	229%	6%
Other	1,800	500	−72%	−1%	1,400	2,300	64%	0%

Source: Christopher J. Mumola and Allen J. Beck, "Prisoners in 1996," Bureau of Justice Statistics, June 1997.

The combined impact of law enforcement and sentencing policies on minorities is even more startling in some states. A 1997 study of drug law enforcement in Massachusetts found that blacks were thirty-nine times more likely to be incarcerated for a drug offense than whites.[18] And the impact of drug policies on black women has been even more dramatic than for black men. In just the five-year period 1986–91, the number of black women incarcerated in state prison for a drug offense rose by 828 percent. Although the absolute numbers of women drug offenders in the system are considerably lower than for men, the trend is clearly disturbing.

Besides mandatory sentencing, other drug policies that may have been well intended have contributed to the alarming trends in black incarceration. One such policy is the set of drug laws that increase penalties for offenders who sell drugs near schools or public housing. Ostensibly, the goal is to establish "drug-free" zones that are safe for children and other residents. As a University of Chicago law professor reminds us:

> . . . in Illinois, a fifteen-year-old first-time offender charged with selling a controlled substance within 1,000 feet of public housing is treated as an adult. In contrast, a fifteen-year-old first-time offender

charged with selling a controlled substance from or near his home in the suburbs is treated as a juvenile. Counseling, treatment, and targeted programs are made available to the juvenile suburbanite while the inner city youth most in need of social services enters the resource starved adult criminal justice system.[19]

Bobbie Marshall, an African American who has used drugs since his teens, experienced the impact of this kind of law following his arrest for selling drugs within 1,000 feet of a school in Los Angeles. Because of his three prior convictions for selling small quantities of drugs to feed his habit, Marshall faced the possibility of life without parole under a federal statute. Marshall's attorneys documented that eighty-nine of ninety persons arrested under a joint state/federal task force in the "schoolyard program" were either African American or Hispanic.

By the time of Marshall's sentencing, he had in many ways turned his life around. He had become active in counseling gang members, helped keep the peace during the 1992 Los Angeles riots, and remained drug free. His efforts led to letters of support from ministers, a police commander, a congressman, and others. Although the prosecution eventually agreed to a nine-year term for Marshall, the sentencing judge imposed only half that term, arguing that Marshall's rehabilitation and value to the community were exceptional. Under the federal mandatory sentencing laws, though, the judge was overruled on appeal.

The most discussed reason for the racial disparity in drug sentencing in recent years has been the issue of sentencing for crack cocaine offenses. As crack made its entry into urban areas in the mid-1980s, reports began to surface about this new highly addictive and powerful drug. Cover stories appeared in *Newsweek*, *Time*, and periodicals around the country. Reports of "crack babies" born to addicted mothers were among the most frightening to surface. How could anyone fail to respond to this human tragedy? Only later did information surface that indicated that there were in fact no data on crack-addicted babies.

Testing cannot distinguish between prenatal exposure to crack cocaine and powder cocaine, so there is no way to know how many of these mothers had in fact used crack while pregnant. Further, the children of drug-abusing mothers who develop poorly may in fact be suffering from a combination of factors that often correlate with low-income drug abusing mothers, including poor nutrition, smoking, and lack of prenatal care. A study by researchers at the Albert Einstein Medical Center in Philadelphia tracked the development of more than 200 low-income inner-city children, half of whom had been exposed to cocaine in the womb and half not. The study found that both groups of children scored below average on IQ tests and other measures of cognitive development, but that there was no significant difference between the two groups.[20] Clearly, any type of substance abuse by pregnant women is unhealthy for both mother and child. In this instance, though, the image of "crack babies" had a significant impact on subsequent legislation.

Crack, of course, is a dangerous drug; its use has caused real destruction to many individuals and communities. The extent of this harm and any realistic assessment of possible responses, though, were hardly considered by Congress in its rush to adopt harsh "anti-drug" penalties in 1986 and again in 1988. The mandatory sentencing laws passed by Congress provided for far harsher punishments for crack offenses than for powder cocaine crimes. Thus, the sale of 500 grams of cocaine powder resulted in a mandatory five-year prison term, while only five grams of crack was required to trigger the same mandatory penalty.

In addition to the other racial dynamics of the drug war, these laws have had a major impact on African Americans. The vast majority of persons charged with crack cocaine offenses in the federal system—81 percent in 2001–02—have been African American.[21] Federal prosecutors contend that these figures merely reflect the proportions of large-scale traffickers in crack who qualify for federal prosecution because of their substantial role in the drug trade. Data analyzed by the U.S. Sentencing Commission, though, casts doubt on this contention. In the Commission's analysis of crack defendants in 2000, two-thirds (69 percent) were considered street-level dealers or couriers.[22]

Given the severity of crack penalties in the federal system, the prosecutorial decision regarding whether to charge a drug offense as a state or federal crime has potentially significant consequences for sentencing. The results of a *Los Angeles Times* analysis, which examined prosecutions for crack cocaine trafficking in the Los Angeles area from 1988 to 1994, are quite revealing.[23] During that period, not a single white offender was convicted of a crack offense in federal court, despite the fact that whites comprise a majority of crack users. During the same period, though, hundreds of white crack traffickers were prosecuted in state courts, often receiving sentences as much as eight years less than those received by offenders in federal courts. As is true nationally, the *Times* analysis revealed that many of the African Americans charged in federal court were not necessarily drug kingpins, but rather low-level dealers or accomplices in the drug trade.

The folly of using expensive prison space for drug offenders, even traffickers, has been documented in research conducted on the federal prison population. One study examined costs and recidivism for low-level drug traffickers in the federal prison system before and after the imposition of mandatory prison terms.[24] It found that over half of the offenders sentenced to prison in 1992 were drug traffickers. Of these, 62 percent, or 9,000 offenders, were considered low-risk as defined by their limited criminal histories. The study then examined recidivism rates for a comparable group of 236 offenders released from prison in 1987, prior to the adoption of mandatory minimums and the federal sentencing guidelines. It found that only 19 percent of the low-risk drug traffickers were re-arrested during the three years after release, and that none of those arrested were charged with serious crimes of violence.

In contrast, the low-risk traffickers sentenced to prison in 1992 were expected to serve three years longer in prison than the 1987 release group (fifty-one months vs. seventeen months). The study concluded that the additional time spent in prison for the 9,000 offenders would cost taxpayers approximately $515 million.

Similar findings have been documented regarding the relatively minor roles and criminal histories of drug offenders in state prisons. A study analyzing the 217,000 drug offenders in state prison as of 1997 found that only 4 percent reported any mid- or high-level drug operation engagement. Overall, nearly a quarter of the population had no history of violence, no gun involvement, no high-level drug trading, and no prior convictions for non-drug offenses.[25]

An analysis by the Urban Institute further documents that the increased incarceration of drug offenders has contributed to a rise in the imprisonment of what has been termed "socially integrated offenders"— in other words, there has been a rise in the proportion of inmates who have ties to legitimate institutions such as families, education, and labor markets. Between 1979 and 1991, for example, the number of state prison inmates with some college education rose from 10,000 to 44,000, and the number employed prior to their incarceration increased from 192,000 to 476,000.[26] The Urban Institute authors contend that the incarceration of socially integrated offenders "may be unnecessary because prior experience has shown that socially integrated people are less likely to re-offend. Such people can, therefore, be punished by means other than incarceration without putting the public at undue risk." Further, by reducing ties to legitimate institutions, incarceration may make these offenders "more prone to subsequent criminal involvement."[27]

Options in Drug Policy

Some political leaders and others contend that drug laws and the way they are implemented are unbiased, and that higher black rates of selling and using drugs are responsible for any discrepancies. Former Rep. Bill McCollum, Republican of Florida and the chair of the House Judiciary Committee, for example, has stated that "the [crack cocaine] mandatory sentences are the same for black and white people. More African Americans generally get caught up with crime and wind up doing things that put them in jail for longer periods of time. But that doesn't have anything to do with discrimination."[28]

A more sophisticated critique is offered by law professor Randall Kennedy, who is particularly concerned about the harmful impact of crack and other drugs on the black community and the fact that law enforcement has traditionally underserved minority communities. Kennedy states that "the most lethal danger facing African-Americans in their day-to-day lives is not white, racist officials of the state, but private, violent criminals (typically black) who attack those most vulnerable to them without regard to racial identity."[29] Kennedy contends, therefore, that what is needed is not less but more law enforcement in black communities.

While Kennedy's assessment of the historic relationship of law enforcement to the black community is well taken, his proposed remedy is rather narrow in scope. Law professor David Cole responds, "Jobs, housing, and education have also been inequitably distributed to the detriment of the African-American community. Their adequate provision would seem to be at least as likely to reduce crime as massive extended incarceration and without the negative effects on the community identified above."[30]

The issue of race and drug policy comes down to a question of choices. Yes, most police and prosecutors are not consciously racist in pursuing the drug war. Many firmly believe that they are aiding beleaguered communities caught in a vicious cycle of drug abuse and lack of opportunity. When a mother calls 911 to report a crack house in the neighborhood, it is only natural and proper for the police to respond swiftly.

But would more job and educational opportunities alleviate some of these neighborhood problems? Would more income support for low-income families be helpful? Before dismissing these notions as "hopelessly liberal" let us recall that these are exactly the tools used by middle-class communities to prevent these problems from developing or escalating.

The relatively recent development of drug courts, for example, demonstrates that practical innovations can both address problems in a constructive way and gain public acceptance. The drug court movement, originating in Miami and Oakland in the early 1990s, involves establishing specialized courts that hear only drug cases with the goal of diverting appropriate cases to treatment. Preliminary evaluations of these programs demonstrate that addicts who complete the treatment program are less likely to become engaged in drug use or crime than comparable offenders who do not go through the program.

The cost-effectiveness of a treatment approach to substance abuse has been demonstrated in a number of recent studies. A 1994 study conducted by the California Department of Alcohol and Drug Programs, for example, found that every dollar invested in substance abuse treatment generated seven dollars in savings, primarily through reductions in crime and reduced hospitalizations.[31] Similarly, the RAND Corporation analyzed the relative impact of harsher sentencing policies and expanded treatment on cocaine consumption. Their analysts concluded that spending $1 million to expand the use of mandatory sentencing to drug offenders would reduce consumption nationally by thirteen kilograms, that arresting and incarcerating more dealers would reduce consumption by twenty-seven kilograms, but that expanding treatment to more heavy drug users would result in a one hundred-kilogram reduction.[32]

These and similar programs are not difficult to implement. They also hold the potential for long-term cost savings and represent a more humane approach to the problem of substance abuse than mandatory sentencing and long-term incarceration. In recent years, such programs have been implemented successfully in many communities around the country. Despite this, the drug war becomes more entrenched each day.

8

Decades of Disparity: Drug Arrests and Race in the United States

Human Rights Watch

New national drug arrest data illuminate the persistence and extent of racial disparities in the "war on drugs" in the United States. According to Human Rights Watch's analysis of arrest data obtained from the FBI:

1. In every year from 1980 to 2007, blacks were arrested nationwide on drug charges at rates relative to population that were 2.8 to 5.5 times higher than white arrest rates.
2. State-by-state data from 2006 show that blacks were arrested for drug offenses at rates in individual states that were 2 to 11.3 times greater than the rate for whites.[1]

The data also shed light on the persistence and extent of arrests for drug possession rather than sales:

3. In every year between 1980 and 2007, arrests for drug possession have constituted 64 percent or more of all drug arrests. From 1999 through 2007, 80 percent or more of all drug arrests were for possession.

The higher rates of black drug arrests do not reflect higher rates of black drug offending. Indeed, as detailed in our May 2008 report, *Targeting Blacks: Drug Law Enforcement and Race in the United States*, blacks and whites engage in drug offenses—possession and sales—at roughly comparable rates. But because black drug offenders are the principal targets in the

From *Decades of Disparity: Drug Arrests and Race in the United States* (New York: Human Rights Watch, 2009), 1, 10–11, 15–16.

"war on drugs," the burden of drug arrests and incarceration falls disproportionately on black men and women, their families and neighborhoods.
The human as well as social, economic, and political toll is as incalculable
as it is unjust.

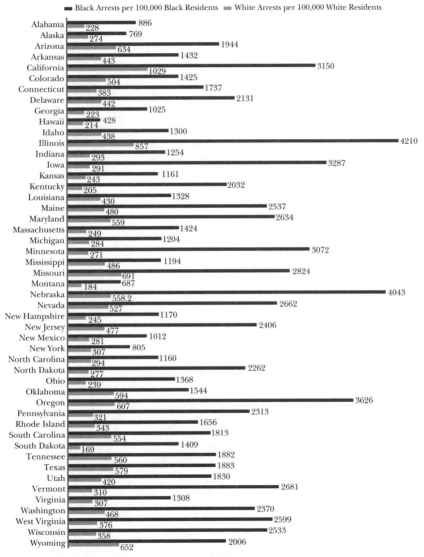

FIGURE 1 *State Rates of Adult Drug Arrests by Race, 2006*

TABLE 1   State Rates of Adult Drug Arrests by Race, 2006

State	Black Arrests	White Arrests	Ratio of Black to White Arrests
Alabama	886	228	3.9
Alaska	769	274	2.8
Arizona	1,944	634	3.1
Arkansas	1,432	443	3.2
California	3,150	1,029	3.1
Colorado	1,425	504	2.8
Connecticut	1,737	383	4.5
Delaware	2,131	442	4.8
District of Columbia	n/a	n/a	n/a
Florida	n/a	n/a	n/a
Georgia	1,025	223	4.6
Hawaii	428	214	2.0
Idaho	1,300	438	3
Illinois	4,210	857	4.9
Indiana	1,254	293	4.3
Iowa	3,287	291	11.3
Kansas	1,161	243	4.8
Kentucky	2,032	205	9.9
Louisiana	1,328	430	3.1
Maine	2,537	480	5.3
Maryland	2,634	559	4.7
Massachusetts	1,424	249	5.7
Michigan	1,204	284	4.2
Minnesota	3,072	271	11.3
Mississippi	1,194	486	2.5
Missouri	2,824	691	4.1
Montana	687	184	3.7
Nebraska	4,043	558	7.2
Nevada	2,662	527	5.1
New Hampshire	1,170	245	4.8
New Jersey	2,406	477	5
New Mexico	1,012	281	3.6
New York	805	307	2.6
North Carolina	1,160	294	3.9
North Dakota	2,262	277	8.2
Ohio	1,368	239	5.7
Oklahoma	1,544	594	2.6
Oregon	3,626	607	6
Pennsylvania	2,313	321	7.2
Rhode Island	1,656	343	4.8
South Carolina	1,813	554	3.3
South Dakota	1,409	169	8.3
Tennessee	1,882	560	3.4
Texas	1,883	579	3.3
Utah	1,830	420	4.4
Vermont	2,681	310	8.6
Virginia	1,308	307	4.3

State	Black Arrests	White Arrests	Ratio of Black to White Arrests
Washington	2,370	468	5.1
West Virginia	2,599	376	6.9
Wisconsin	2,533	358	7.1
Wyoming	2,006	653	3.1

Rates calculated per 100,000 residents of each race

TABLE 2   State Adult Drug Arrests by Offense and Race, 2006*

State	Sales as Percent of White Drug Arrests	Possession as Percent of White Drug Arrests	Sales as Percent of Black Drug Arrests	Possession as Percent of Black Drug Arrests
Alabama	7%	93%	6%	94%
Alaska	30%	70%	44%	56%
Arizona	13%	87%	16%	84%
Arkansas	16%	84%	19%	81%
California	13%	87%	25%	75%
Colorado	11%	89%	56%	44%
Connecticut	14%	86%	55%	45%
Delaware	28%	72%	45%	55%
District of Columbia	n/a	n/a	n/a	n/a
Florida	n/a	n/a	n/a	n/a
Georgia	23%	77%	22%	78%
Hawaii	22%	78%	20%	80%
Idaho	12%	88%	55%	45%
Illinois	n/a	n/a	n/a	n/a
Indiana	19%	81%	26%	74%
Iowa	10%	90%	11%	90%
Kansas	17%	83%	18%	82%
Kentucky	11%	89%	20%	80%
Louisiana	15%	85%	22%	78%
Maine	21%	79%	42%	58%
Maryland	15%	85%	27%	73%
Massachusetts	25%	75%	44%	56%
Michigan	18%	82%	29%	71%
Minnesota	37%	63%	14%	86%
Mississippi	9%	91%	14%	86%
Missouri	12%	88%	17%	83%
Montana	9%	91%	4%	96%
Nebraska	10%	90%	14%	86%
Nevada	20%	80%	25%	75%
New Hampshire	22%	78%	34%	66%
New Jersey	16%	84%	31%	69%
New Mexico	50%	50%	67%	33%
New York	8%	92%	15%	85%
North Carolina	10%	90%	21%	79%
North Dakota	19%	81%	34%	66%
Ohio	10%	90%	15%	85%
Oklahoma	14%	86%	19%	81%

State	Possession as Sales as Percent of White Drug Arrests	Percent of White Drug Arrests	Possession as Sales as Percent of Black Drug Arrests	Percent of Black Drug Arrests
Oregon	8%	92%	12%	88%
Pennsylvania	28%	72%	47%	53%
Rhode Island	16%	84%	31%	69%
South Carolina	14%	86%	27%	74%
South Dakota	7%	93%	14%	86%
Tennessee	23%	78%	32%	68%
Texas	13%	87%	12%	88%
Utah	12%	88%	13%	87%
Vermont	15%	85%	32%	68%
Virginia	17%	83%	26%	74%
Washington	14%	86%	8%	92%
West Virginia	18%	82%	32%	68%
Wisconsin	16%	84%	33%	68%
Wyoming	10%	90%	10%	90%
National	15%	85%	25%	76%

Due to rounding, some totals may not equal 100 percent.

The racial disparities in the rates of drug arrests culminate in dramatic racial disproportions among incarcerated drug offenders. At least two-thirds of drug arrests result in a criminal conviction.[2] Many convicted drug offenders are sentenced to incarceration: an estimated 67 percent of convicted felony drug defendants are sentenced to jail or prison.[3] The likelihood of incarceration increases if the defendant has a prior conviction.[4] Since blacks are more likely to be arrested than whites on drug charges, they are more likely to acquire the convictions that ultimately lead to higher rates of incarceration. Although the data in this backgrounder indicate that blacks represent about one-third of drug arrests, they constitute 46 percent of persons convicted of drug felonies in state courts.[5] Among black defendants convicted of drug offenses, 71 percent received sentences to incarceration in contrast to 63 percent of convicted white drug offenders.[6] Human Rights Watch's analysis of prison admission data for 2003 revealed that relative to population, blacks are 10.1 times more likely than whites to be sent to prison for drug offenses.[7]

Part IV

Lawyering: Whom Are the Lawyers Really Representing?

It is an American axiom that everyone charged with a crime is entitled to a defense lawyer. This is a constitutional principle arising from the Sixth Amendment guarantee of a fair trial. It also is the lawyer's convenient explanation for why it is ethical to represent someone who is obviously guilty.

Today's criminal justice system presents the lawyer with further ethical challenges. With more than 90 percent of criminal cases ending in plea bargains, the lawyer is more a negotiator than an advocate. There is often little point, not to mention time, to investigate a case in order to find out what really happened. Possible procedural violations by the police become moot, since often it does not matter whether evidence was properly obtained.

Hence it is a real question to ask whether lawyers are in fact pursuing justice or just processing people through the system. This is a matter more of poverty than of race per se, since wealthier defendants have little trouble securing all of the procedural safeguards. The poor are generally defended by court-appointed lawyers who usually have overwhelming caseloads, as do the prosecutors handling the commonplace crimes that generally ensnare the poor.

However, in the United States, race and poverty bear a substantial correlation, especially when it comes to those confronting the justice system. All too often lawyers are on the front lines of processing people through the system. Many of the policies and provisions that have led to such pronounced racial skewing—the War on Drugs, mandatory minimum sentencing, and three-strikes laws—are the typical terms of negotiation in the plea bargaining that resolves the great majority of criminal cases.

Paul Butler, author of *Let's Get Free: A Hip-Hop Theory of Justice*, is a former federal prosecutor who now teaches law at George Washington University and regularly debates current prosecutors on the subject of this selection: "Should Good People Be Prosecutors?" This is a provocative and spirited way to get at the ethical challenge of participating in a criminal justice system that claims many protections but too often comes up short. Butler shows how the system really works: how prosecutors are motivated by politics and institutional pressure, and how they can fool themselves into believing in what they are doing. Butler's reasoning cuts through standard rationalizations and leaves the worthiness of the very system in doubt.

Ordinary Injustice: How America Holds Court by Amy Bach is a lively depiction of how lawyers (and judges) struggle with fulfilling their professional roles and obligations amid overwhelming caseloads; often insufficient experience and motivation; and little, if any, support from government bodies charged with ensuring the proper functioning of the legal system. Bach, a lawyer and journalist, interviewed and observed lawyers on the front lines of criminal practice. The selection here recounts the history of the right to a defense lawyer and the various approaches that states have taken to back up that right. As described in the selection, Robert E. Surrency is a private practitioner whom officials in Greene County, Georgia, contracted to represent indigent defendants there.

9

Should Good People Be Prosecutors?

Paul Butler

W hen I stopped being a prosecutor I told my friends it was because I didn't go to law school to put poor people in prison. My friends weren't surprised that I quit; they had been shocked that I became a prosecutor in the first place. For a progressive like me—a person who believed in redemption and second chances and robust civil liberties—the work presented obvious pitfalls.

"Locking people up" was practically on the job description. Eric Holder, the first African American U.S. attorney in DC, and now President Obama's choice for attorney general, asked prospective prosecutors during interviews, "How would you feel about sending so many black men to jail?" Anyone who had a big problem with that presumably was not hired.

I began the work, however, as a liberal critic of American criminal justice—the avenging Undercover Brother who would change the system from the inside. What happened instead was that I collaborated with the system's injustice.

Thinking about the business of prosecuting crimes brings questions about the utility and morality of American criminal justice into sharp relief. If there are too many people in prison, how should we feel about the men and women who put them there?

My conclusion is that prosecutors are more part of the problem than the solution. The adversarial nature of the justice system, the culture of the prosecutor's office, and the politics of crime pose insurmountable obstacles for prosecutors who are concerned with economic and racial justice. The day-to-day work of the prosecutor is geared toward punishing people whose lives are already messed up. This does not mean that

From *Let's Get Free: A Hip-Hop Theory of Justice* (New York: The New Press, 2009), 101–14, 119–21.

criminals should be allowed to victimize others; some of the people in prison really belong there, for the protection of society. It suggests, however, that piling on is the main work of prosecutors. It is well intentioned, perhaps even necessary, but piling on nonetheless. Adding up the costs of a lifetime of deprivation and then presenting the bill to the person who suffered it seems an odd job for a humanitarian.

Also, prosecutors spend much of their time making arguments in favor of police power. They ask judges to adopt pinched interpretations of the Constitution and individual rights. When progressives bemoan the Supreme Court's approval of racial profiling, pretextual stops, widespread drug testing, camera surveillance, and police lying to suspects, they have prosecutors to thank. One of your primary functions as a prosecutor is to make the judge and jury believe the police. When the cops say that Kwame consented to the search of his backpack, and Kwame says he didn't consent, your job is to prove that Kwame is lying.

It is true that some prosecutors attempt to mitigate the harshness of the system, either openly or through the covert or subversive measures that I will discuss later in this chapter. Their principal work, however, is applying the criminal law, not ameliorating its negative effects. Becoming a prosecutor to help resolve unfairness in the criminal justice system is like enlisting in the army because you are opposed to the current war. It's like working as an oil refiner because you want to help the environment. Yes, you get to choose the toxic chemicals. True, the boss might allow you to leave one or two pristine bays untouched. Maybe, if you do really good work as a low-level polluter, they might make you the head polluter. But rather than calling yourself an "environmentalist," you should think of yourself as a polluter with a conscience.

I hope that the analysis in this chapter will be useful for any advocate for social change who ponders where she can do the most good. What is the role that our moral and political beliefs should play when we choose our work? When does compromise cross the line and become complicity? When does one do more harm than good by working within an unjust system?

A Question of Character?

Abbe Smith has zealously represented poor people accused of crimes for over two decades. She firmly believes that you cannot be both a good person and a good prosecutor.[1] She writes:

> We live in an extraordinarily harsh and punitive time, a time we will look back on in shame. The rate of incarceration in this country,

the growing length of prison terms, the conditions of confinement, and the frequency with which we put people to death have created a moral crisis. Although, arguably, all those who work in the criminal justice system have something to do with its perpetuation and legitimacy, prosecutors are the chief legal enforcers of the current regime.[2]

I would not go so far as to call prosecutors "bad people." I know prosecutors who are fair-minded, concerned about economic and racial justice, and even believe that there are too many people in prison. Unfortunately, their bodies and souls are working at cross-purposes. Especially for African American prosecutors, the job exacts a terrible toll.[3]

The Cross-Examination

I loved it when the defendant took the stand. The judge would ask, "Does the government have any questions?"

"Yes, Your Honor!" I would leap up from the government's table, stand my full six feet three inches, and stare hard at the bad guy. On the street everybody might be scared of this dude (like they were scared of me, late at night, if I wasn't wearing my suit), but at this moment, I—on behalf of the United States of America—was running the show.

I paced the entire well of the courtroom but avoided going anywhere near the defendant. Later, if my questions got the defendant too riled up and he tried to get smart-ass on me, I would get up in his face—or at least as close as the judge would allow. For now, though, I tried to convey to the jury through my movements as well as my words that the drug dealer on trial was a piece of garbage.

ME: Where were you the night of August 5?
CRETIN: Over to my baby mama's house.
ME: What is your wife's name?
CRETIN: Her name LaShonda, but she not my wife.
ME: I see. Then you left your baby mama's house and went to stand on the street corner, is that right?
CRETIN: I saw my boy and stopped to talk.
ME: What's your boy's name?
CRETIN: Lil' Boo. I mean that's what everybody calls him—I ain't know his real name.
ME: And when you and Mr. Boo saw the police, you threw your cocaine on the ground and ran away, didn't you?

CRETIN: Naw man.

ME: No further questions, your honor.

Gentle reader, could you hear the slight hint of sarcasm in my voice when I said "wife"? Did you see my eyes roll? Every time the cretin slurred his words and tripped over the conjugation of a verb, my diction became more precise.

Here's what they don't teach you in law school: As you, the black prosecutor, button your jacket and head back to the government table, you look at the jurors and then you glance back over at the defendant. You can't actually say these words, but this is what you mean: *Ladies and gentlemen of the jury, I am an African American. You are African Americans. The defendant over there—that's a nigger. Lock him up.*

I had the best conviction record in my section.

What happened to that progressive guy who joined the office? My aspirations of changing the system got shot down because I liked winning too much, and I was good at it. I wanted to be well regarded by my peers, to be successful in my career, and to serve my community. And the way to do that, I learned on the job, was to send as many people to jail as I could. I wasn't so much hoodwinked as seduced.

The Morning After

I feel a little bit used. The Supreme Court has written about the significance of African American participants in the criminal justice system.[4] It seems that we perform a symbolic function, especially in cases involving black defendants. Our presence promotes the appearance that the system is fair. The Court has stated that allowing blacks to play a role in law enforcement enhances "public respect for our criminal justice system and the rule of law." I call this the "legitimization function."

It is significant that mass incarceration, and its attendant gross racial disparities, are occurring at a time when prosecutors' offices are more diverse than ever. The United States Attorney's Office for the District of Columbia, where I worked, has the highest percentage of African American prosecutors of any U.S. Attorney's Office. The DC office also locks up a larger percentage of the city's black residents than virtually any other office. A report said that on a given day half of all the young black men in the city had a criminal case—they were either in prison, on probation or parole, or awaiting trial.[5] Remembering the "legitimization function," one doesn't have to be a conspiracy theorist to think the correlation between the number of black prosecutors and black inmates is more than a coincidence.

In DC there were many jurors who were concerned about fairness, especially about why the defendants are overwhelmingly African American. Watching the parade into arraignment court every morning, I thought of the untitled Ntozake Shange poem that begins "The suspect is always black and in his early twenties."

You had to wonder whether the 200,000 white residents of the city ever smoked pot, got into fights, or stole from their offices. The racial composition of the superior court lockup list suggests that white people in DC do not commit crimes. Does anyone who actually knows white folks believe this? So how should jurors feel about the utter blackness of the criminal court? One reason I was hired was so that people with those kinds of concerns could see my skin. It was supposed to make them feel better. To folks who had questions about racial profiling or selective prosecution, my black body answered "Everything's cool."

Everything, clearly, is not cool. Given the woes of mass incarceration and expanding police power already catalogued in this book, the shocking contention is that people who want change *should be* prosecutors. The idea that they *should not* be prosecutors seems obvious. Yet every year I entertain a parade of students who think, much as I did upon graduation from law school, that they can do the most good as an assistant district attorney. They make three claims.

Claim 1: Prosecutors Have a Lot of Power

I agree with that description absolutely; it's just that ultimately I would limit it to one prosecutor in particular. The head of a prosecution office is the most unregulated actor in the entire legal system.[6] Basically, there are no rules. There's no law, for example, that says that simply because the prosecutor knows someone is guilty of a crime, that suspect must be charged. The lead prosecutor—the district attorney or the United States attorney—can make whatever decision he wants about whether to prosecute and no judge or politician can overturn it.

The prosecutor often has more control than the judge over the outcome of a case. Sentencing guidelines and mandatory minimum sentences have reduced the discretion that judges used to have to fit the punishment to the crime.[7] The prosecutor can circumvent required sentences simply by charging a different crime, or leaving out some of the evidence. This is perfectly legal.

Federal law, for example, requires a minimum five-year sentence if someone uses a gun while engaged in drug trafficking, even if the gun is not brandished or discharged.[8] The judge who refuses to impose this sentence would almost certainly be reversed on appeal. Let's say, however, that a prosecutor doesn't want the same defendant to receive the whole five years, perhaps because she is trying to entice the defendant to snitch in another case. She can simply charge the drug case, leaving out the evidence about the firearm. No one—not the judge, not the governor, not even the president of the United States—can require the head prosecutor to add the gun charge.[9]

Line prosecutors "share" this power in the sense that they make the initial decisions about charging, plea bargains, and sentencing. As a baby prosecutor, I sometimes felt unworthy of the delegation of this much responsibility. Here I was, a kid only a few years out of law school, and cops and defense attorneys with much more experience had to suck up to me to get what they wanted. I loved it.

"Papering" was one of my favorite parts of the job. After the police arrested someone, they would bring their reports to the basement of the courthouse where we prosecutors sat in cubicles. The police would line up to talk to us, and we would make the preliminary decisions about whether or not to bring charges. We considered factors like whether the defendant had a record, if the case had "jury appeal," whether there were victims who seemed like they would be cooperative, if the statements of the police officers seemed believable, and whether there would be problems getting all of the evidence admitted in court.

I soon realized, however, that my own power was limited. Whatever a line prosecutor decides, his or her recommendation had to be approved by a supervisor. If the case was high profile or the crime grave, the review went all the way up the chain of command. Before I could proceed with my prosecution of the United States senator, for example, my co-counsel and I, along with our supervisors, had to troop to a meeting with Attorney General Janet Reno. We presented all of our evidence to her and went forward only after she blessed the case.

My concern here is not that this kind of evaluation is inappropriate; indeed, given the serious consequences of charging anyone with a crime, experienced lawyers *should* have the final say. My point is only that career prosecutors are not the people who make the decisions that have the most impact on how criminal justice works.

Here's the bottom line: rather than having "power," line prosecutors have delegated authority that is subject to several layers of review. In the federal system, the "big boss" is the attorney general, and he or she is usually not shy about reminding the legal underlings who's in charge. John Ashcroft, the first attorney general during the George W. Bush administration, reversed many decisions that lower-level prosecutors had made. He commanded federal prosecutors to appeal cases in which judges imposed lenient sentences, and, in what became known as the "Ashcroft Memorandum," he ordered his prosecutors to agree to plea bargains only when the defendant admitted the most serious charges. Bush's next attorney general, Alberto Gonzales, required prosecutors to seek the death penalty in cases in which the prosecutors had concluded it wasn't warranted.[10]

In the state system, where 90 percent of criminal cases are brought, the head prosecutor is a politician who in most cases was elected pursuant to the dysfunctional politics of criminal justice in which people get votes by promising to put more people in cages.[11] The line prosecutor has to answer to the boss, who has to answer to those politics. This limits the effectiveness of wannabe progressive prosecutors who claim that they would be more sensitive than hard-core "law and order" types. These liberal prosecutors say they would exercise their discretion to be merciful and even to not charge when that was appropriate.

The reality is that the discretion of worker bees is tightly controlled. There are certain kinds of cases that come up all the time, and for those cases there are already rules in place. A classic case of this type is that of a first-time drug offender. Virtually every prosecuting office has a procedure for dealing with those cases, and the line attorney is expected to follow the program.

In my experience, most people who work at prosecutors' offices—and especially those who reach the rank of supervisor—do not view mass incarceration and expanding police power as serious problems. To the contrary, they mistakenly believe that "tough" criminal justice makes us safer. Most will not be amenable to decisions in individual cases that are made with an eye toward locking up fewer people or limiting police power. Ultimately, the prosecutor with a social justice agenda would have to proceed more subversively than overtly.

While my experience is that line prosecutors don't have a lot of "free" discretion, there is another important limit on their power: they are stuck with the cases that the police bring. It's not as though a progressive prosecutor can say, "I don't want to try cases that are the result of selective law enforcement in poor neighborhoods" or "I want to opt out of cases that arise from racial profiling." That would be like a lawyer saying, "I want to work for a firm that pays big bucks but I don't want to represent rich people." If you are a typical prosecutor, you will spend most of your time locking up poor people. For better or worse, that's what most prosecutors do.

Claim 2: Prosecutors Help Victims

That's the goal, anyway, and it's a laudable one. It's not, however, what most prosecutors spend most of their time doing. First of all, the average urban prosecutor spends about half her time on drug cases—a crime that, at least for users, has no victim. You know people who do illegal drugs. If you saw your friend snorting cocaine, you might ask her not to do it around you. You could tell her you think that it's unhealthy and that she should seek treatment if she can't stop on her own. Here is what you would *not* do: sneak off and call 911 to have her locked up because she committed a crime. If that is not how you would treat your friend, you should not be prosecuting people for using drugs.

But, the argument continues, prosecutors, by convicting *sellers*, can help get drugs off the street. Would that it were so. I wrote part of this book in an apartment in Washington Heights, a mainly Dominican neighborhood in New York City. "Da Heights" still has open-air drug markets, which in gentrified Manhattan seems so old-fashioned it's almost quaint. In this neighborhood it's impossible to think of drug selling as victimless. I despise the dealers standing on the corner and staring at me, unsure whether I'm "5-0" (i.e., a cop) or a potential customer. Truth be told, I'm afraid of them as well. It makes the streets feel unstable, like at any moment some stuff might jump off with guns blazing and schoolkids ducking under parked cars and some innocent bystander, like me, getting hurt. It's a perfect place from which to write a book about criminal justice. My concern about how well the system is working is more than theoretical. Part of what I need my government to do is to get these guys off my corner. That's homeland security at its most urgent.[12]

But prosecutors don't seem able to rid the streets of dealers, even in New York, home of the "Rockefeller laws," one of the toughest narcotics codes in the country. The "replacement effect" is in full effect. So, to be sure, they can put away Hector and T-Bone; the next day, though, Willie, Lil' Boi, and Julio are standing there. When those guys catch their case, it's Alejandro's and Malik's turn.

So, to reiterate the point made in chapter 3, locking up buyers and sellers is a failed public policy. It simply does not work. That well-meaning prosecutor sitting right now in drug court with a hundred files on her desk? She's on the wrong side of history. It is doubtful that in fifty years we will be addressing this pressing social issue by putting users and sellers in prison.

Other crimes do, of course, have flesh-and-blood victims. Sometimes liberals seem to ignore this truth, and that has hurt the cause of criminal justice reform. Prosecutors make people pay when they have done horrible things to other people, and that is good work. Former prosecutor Lenese Herbert remembers the day she convicted a man of a brutal rape. Even though the victim, a black lesbian, had been left for dead on the street, she was still reluctant to call the police because she thought no one would care. Lenese Herbert cared. She diligently worked the case, interviewing witnesses, sending the forensic evidence to labs, and preparing the victim for the ordeal of going to trial. When the jury returned a guilty verdict, Lenese said it was the first time she had seen this woman hold her head up high.

Still, we need to be thoughtful about how and when locking someone in a cage for five or twenty years actually helps. A significant percentage of victims, in addition to defendants, are young men who are involved with gangs or drugs. In these cases, as former prosecutor Lenese Herbert puts it, "on any given Sunday, someone who is a victim today could have been a defendant yesterday and might be a witness tomorrow." This doesn't mean that their assailants get a free pass. It just means that sometimes the line between "innocent" victim and "guilty" perpetrator is not always distinct.

I am thrilled when violent offenders, especially murderers and rapists, are put away. It turns out, however, that these cases represent a small percentage of the work that prosecutors do. Fewer than 5 percent of all arrests are for violent crimes that cause injury. You would not know that from watching either *CSI* or the local news.

The most effective long-term strategy for helping victims is working to resolve the conditions that create the crime. When we address the conditions that breed antisocial conduct, we honor victims in the most meaningful way. It's not that prosecutors don't help some victims; they absolutely do. The way that they help, though, is hard medicine with major side effects. In the end, helping victims is, at best, an occasional benefit of being a prosecutor and must be balanced against the work's considerable costs.

Claim 3: We Don't Want Prosecutors' Offices to Be Too Hard-Core or All White

Some progressives worry about what would happen if prosecutors' offices were staffed exclusively with "lock 'em up" types. They also are concerned about the prospect of segregated staffs if lawyers of color opt out of this work for racial justice reasons.

As a practical matter I do not think that all-white prosecution offices are likely in cities that have a substantial minority population. Keeping in mind the "legitimization function" described earlier in this chapter, prosecutors themselves need to have some black and brown faces in the office. There is a strategic benefit in having African American prosecutors, especially in jurisdictions in which most defendants are also African American. Just as there are always blacks like Condoleezza Rice and Clarence Thomas, who, based on their own politics, are willing to serve administrations that many others feel do not promote black interests, there will always be people of color willing to be prosecutors, even if some in the community will brand them sellouts or tokens.

A more significant threat is that liberals will refuse to work as prosecutors, leaving the offices exclusively staffed with conservative law-and-order types. If that happened, would things be even worse than they are now? What is the difference that progressive prosecutors make?

I interviewed several progressive prosecutors and most thought that their presence mattered. Even if they did not change the office culture completely, they felt that people at least acted differently around them. Two prosecutors, for example, told me that others in the office had learned not to refer to defendants using pejorative names like "douche bag" when they were around.

Every progressive prosecutor indicated that he or she treated witnesses better than other prosecutors in the office. Witnesses are sometimes reluctant to testify in criminal cases; they don't want to get involved because of mistrust of the police, fear of the defendant, or not wanting to be perceived as a snitch. Some prosecutors, to induce cooperation, yell at reluctant witnesses or even threaten to lock them up until the trial. S.W., an African American former prosecutor, described her discomfort at seeing middle-class white men and women in suits shouting at the mainly poor black witnesses. She believed that her gentler tactics made her witnesses feel better about the process and ultimately helped her win more convictions.

"Win more convictions." Therein lies the rub. Many of the kind acts of progressive prosecutors are, necessarily, in the service of their work. One payoff of being nice to witnesses is that it helps you put more people in prison.

Here's a metaphor that is extreme but I hope revealing: I understand the argument that, back in the day, slave driving would have been an acceptable job for abolitionists. The drivers had a lot of power and discretion, and if abolitionists abandoned that kind of work, only hard-core racists would be available, which would make things worse for slaves. Progressive slave drivers could brandish the whip more sparingly, and perhaps on occasion cast a blind eye while an especially deserving slave escaped.

It's a harsh comparison designed to make a point. When good people work in unjust regimes—Vichy France under the control of the Nazis, for instance—they must engage in a difficult calculus of the costs and benefits

of their participation. It is difficult to contain injustice when one partici-
pates in it. Society by and large rejects the argument that collaborators
are helpful mitigators. We tend to shave their heads as soon as there is a
regime shift.

Finally, it is worth noting that many prosecutors, of all races and political ideologies, are committed to racial justice. They just have a radically
different notion of what that means. Motivated by the "law enforcement as
public good" theory, their zeal to lock up African Americans and Latinos
represents their own personal attempt at reparation to the black community, compensation for all the years when crimes against people of color
were not answered.[13] To believe that their solution is counterproductive,
and that the mass incarceration it has caused is evil, is not to say that the
prosecutors themselves are bad people. They simply don't see far enough.
We can disagree about the value of their service, but we will not condemn
them for it.

People with broader visions of justice, however, should ask themselves
whether they went to law school to put black people in jail. Or Latinos.
Or poor people. Or anyone for whom being locked in a cage will not do
any good—either for us or for them. That last category consists, conser-
vatively, of approximately 500,000 souls. For people burdened with this
truth, the shame of complicity should outweigh the misguided sense of
"serving" their community. [. . .]

Subversive Prosecutors

Harvard Law School professor Duncan Kennedy has a provocative suggestion for people who have the opportunity to work in systems that they think
foster injustice. He proposed that anticapitalist associates in corporate law
firms engage in "the politicization of corporate law practice, which means
doing things or not doing things in order to serve left purposes." Troubled
that lawyers at corporate firms "grease the wheels" of an unjust economic
system, Kennedy called on associates with leftist leanings "to think of it as
a requirement of moral hygiene that they defy the people they work for,
and do it at regular intervals. . . ."[14]

On first impression, there is a rough analogy between people working as prosecutors who want to end mass incarceration and reduce racial
disparities, and people who work at corporate law firms who believe that
wealth in the United States should be redistributed. A significant difference, however, is that many socially conscious prosecutors seem to view
their day jobs as part and parcel of their political objectives. They believe, as I did, they can do the most good on the inside. Radical corporate

lawyers, on the other hand, see their wage-earning work as being in op-position to their political leanings (hence Kennedy's prescribed cure that these lawyers should subvert their employers). Put another way, progres-sive corporate lawyers want to subvert the dominant paradigm; progres-sive prosecutors, on the other hand, want to join it. Even the most liberal prosecutor would probably be reluctant to describe herself as "radical."

Still, the progressive prosecutors I interviewed described some conduct that their employers would probably view as seditious. S.W. recalled advis-ing defense attorneys from time to time that rather than accept a plea, their clients should go to trial, because the government's evidence was not strong. D.T. remembered working harder for a defendant than his own attorney did to find him a drug treatment program. When A.F. wanted to offer a benefit to a defendant that his office wouldn't allow, he some-times would tell the defense attorney, "I can't put anything in writing," but would promise to be lenient when they got to court.

Many of the prosecutors recalled ways of missing deadlines, "forget-ting" to subpoena witnesses, leaving key sentence-enhancing facts out of indictments or pleas—all in an attempt to subvert the dominant "tough on crime" paradigm of their workplaces. It was striking that when I inter-viewed these prosecutors, in some cases years after they'd left their offices, none wanted me to use their names. They were scared. Some of their pro-gressive interventions had to remain either secret or not for attribution— an apt metaphor for the dilemma faced by liberal prosecutors.

Reform Vs. Transformation

In this and the previous two chapters we have considered three ways that progressives interact with the criminal justice system. To decide whether working as a prosecutor, cooperating with law enforcement in drug cases, or sitting as in impartial juror in those cases makes one complicit with mass incarceration and racial disparities requires a reckoning of two items. First, does working within the system contribute to the prob-lem? (As should be clear by now, I believe the answer to this question is "yes.") Second, is it possible to make a real difference from inside? If mere "reform" is required, working within the system might accomplish that change. If, on the other hand, a more substantial transformation is neces-sary, it becomes more evident that the change must come from without. Those who work inside can tinker with the punishment regime, but they probably cannot overhaul it.

Let's say that we have two goals. First, we seek to reduce incarcera-tion substantially. Our specific goal here is to return the United States to incarcerating "only" 1,750,000 people rather than the current 2.3 million. Our second objective is a major reduction in racial disparity in incarceration. The numerical goal here is to reduce the current eight-to-one black-white disparity to three-to-one, which is closer to the average black-white disparities in other measures of economic and social well-being.[15]

What level of change do these objectives require of our criminal justice system? The final chapter of this book [*Let's Get Free*] proposes seven ways that these goals might be achieved. Many of these steps demand considerably less reliance on punishment as a means of treating antisocial conduct (or conduct like drug use that is purportedly outside majoritarian constructs of morality).

At a minimum, achieving these goals requires shifting the focus away from "the deliberate infliction of pain" model that now drives American criminal justice. People who now do criminal justice (i.e., punishment) work probably would describe the changes required to achieve our goals as substantial. People now employed in the punishment regime who want to continue to serve would have to engage in what prosecutors (usually derisively) refer to as "social work." Different skill sets would be required, and I daresay different motivations.

To be a prosecutor, a snitch in drug cases, or a juror who convicts in those cases simply because someone is "guilty" of the charge is to be an active participant in a system that defines too many activities as crimes, enforces its laws selectively, and incarcerates far too many of its citizens. If the punishment response had a substantial benefit to public safety, complicity might be warranted. It does not. The punishment regime creates a level of suffering—for prisoners, their families, and their communities—that should be intolerable in a civil society. An empathetic imagination of that pain—the degradation of our fellow human beings—helps us weigh the moral cost of complicity.

10

"What's a Defense?"

Amy Bach

O f course, Greene County is not unique. The real issue here is the poor quality of defense representation throughout the nation. There are three basic systems for providing attorneys. It is difficult to rank them comparatively by quality since all three are flawed and tend to come apart when underfunded, poorly staffed, or subject to the whimsy of judges and prosecutors.[1] Still, one can quantify the differences among them. The arguably best system is called the "public defender" structure, in which full-time defense lawyers, employed by the state, are provided with central offices, secretaries, computers, investigators, and legal research tools.* A public defender system aims to put the defense on equal, or near-equal, footing with the prosecution. In the more bountiful programs, public defenders are overseen by a statewide agency that sets uniform standards and expectations for counties or circuits. A variation on this program contracts with a nonprofit program funded by public money and other sources.[2]

The second system is a panel program, in which private attorneys on a pre-approved list are appointed and paid to represent indigent defendants as needed. The idea, in theory, is for an independent agency or clerk to select lawyers from a list who want and are qualified to do the work. In many jurisdictions, however, a judge makes the assignments, which may affect

---

*In this chapter, a public defender system refers to the ideal form where the public defender works full-time with equal or near-equal resources as the prosecutor. At other times in this book, people use the term "public defender" to refer to an attorney or an office that represents the poor part-time in addition to their private practices.

From *Ordinary Injustice: How America Holds Court* (New York: Metropolitan Books, 2009), 28–37, 47–56.

the independence of the attorney, who depends on future assignments from the judge for his or her income. Lawyers who line up for assignments are paid by the case or by the hour (for which there is usually a fee cap) and can become accustomed to the quick disposal of cases. And in some places an attorney who is totally unqualified to do criminal work—an expert in real estate or matrimonial law—will be appointed unpaid as part of community service to the local bar association.

Further, private lawyers with paying clients may not want to make time for poorly funded cases. For years Virginia had the lowest fee caps in the nation for indigent representation.[3] In March of 2007, the legislature, under threat of a class-action lawsuit led by the Virginia Fair Trial Project, increased the fee cap for appointed attorneys and authorized judges to waive the caps, subject to a higher court's approval. However, the amounts are still meager and judges are unlikely to intervene. In 2007, the caps were as follows: $2,085 for clients charged with felonies that carry a sentence of twenty years to life, $600 for lesser felonies, and $240 for misdemeanors and juvenile felonies.[4] A lawyer who wants to prove his client's innocence could easily spend those amounts on the investigation alone. Prior to the fee hike, one Richmond attorney admitted that the fees were so low he reserved nearly all his time and labor for paying clients: Looking for witnesses, considering discovery, or using outside experts was impossible with so little funding. He tells court-appointed clients, who accounted for about 20 percent of his income, "to investigate the case themselves, look for witnesses and if they find them bring them to the office or to court."[5]

The third option for indigent defense is the contract system, in which one attorney or several contract with a county or circuit (group of counties) to represent a fixed or maximum number of cases for a fee, as with Robert Surrency in Georgia. Many counties prefer this method because it allows them to budget public defense for the entire year. It's also easier to administer than a panel program, which requires keeping track of many different lawyers and a complicated payroll.

There is much debate about which system is preferable, especially among county officials, who want to save money. Houston County in Georgia, for example, has employed full-time public defenders for decades. Three superior court judges, in a letter to their county commissioners, explained why the county shouldn't change to a less expensive contract system.

Having a public defender system means having a group of lawyers who are obligated to handle the county's indigent defense work full time. . . . [P]rivate attorneys under a contract system . . . would simply be operating with a lot of competing interests which a public defender does not have. . . . It is naïve to think that any private attorney in this area would, or could, completely close their private practice and handle only the indigent contract cases. Expecting that attorney to neglect "paying" clients, or to make them a lower priority so that he or she may give first priority to indigent cases is equally implausible. . . . [6]

Another problem with the contract system is the implicit power it gives judges over lawyers. In a report by a commission convened by the Georgia State Bar to assess the state's indigent defense practice, the findings were that "[s]everal court-appointed and contract attorneys expressed concern that if they were viewed by some judges as zealous advocates—e.g., if they filed several motions in one case or demanded trials—they ran the risk of being removed from the *ad hoc* counsel appointment list or denied a future contract." [7]

So for the panel and contract systems, the problem is one of incentives. If these defense attorneys are going to be paid poorly and if, for what little effort they make, the consequence might be dismissal, they have little reason to work hard on an indigent client's behalf.

The better contract systems insist on quality controls, like limited caseloads and reviews of lawyers before awarding contracts. In San Mateo County, California, a contract attorney's fee will go up in a particular case that requires more work than is covered by a lump sum or flat fee. Also, lawyers have caps on numbers of cases based on a "weighted" study of how difficult they are; additional work is paid by the hour, with a higher rate for jury trials. For example, in a misdemeanor, a lawyer is paid a case fee of $190 plus $80 for a pretrial conference; if an attorney goes to trial he receives $125 per hour plus a per diem of $260 for preparation work. "By the time you add it up you're getting pretty much what retained lawyers get," said John S. Digiacinto, the county's chief defender. "We are able to keep our staff."

The worst contract systems, like Greene County's, feature a part-time lawyer who is hired based solely on how cheaply he is prepared to do the work. By 1985, even before Surrency took over the job, such "low bid" or "fixed fee" contracts had been condemned by the American Bar Association (ABA) House of Delegates, the policy-making body of the organization, for compromising the integrity of the justice system. [8] Unfortunately, local governments are often unaware of what the ABA says or consider its rulings advisory. In 2000, a report on the status of the country's contract defense practice by the Department of Justice's Bureau of Justice Statistics "noted a decline in the number of cases taken to jury trial, an increase in guilty pleas at first-appearance hearings, a decline in the filing of motions to suppress evidence, a decline in requests for expert assistance, and an increase in complaints received by the court from defendants"—virtually all of which described what was happening in Greene County.[9] Further, the county spent only $75.38 per case, the fifth lowest cost-per-case in the state.

Beginning in 1969, when adopting a plan for Georgia, the state legislature left it up to each county to determine which of the three systems to use. A decade later the legislature created the Georgia Indigent Defense Council (GIDC), which was based in Atlanta to oversee the different systems. The GIDC issued 11 percent of the total monies used to run 152 of 159 counties statewide. Of the 152 counties, only 20 decided on full-time public defenders, seventy-three employed a panel system, and 59 used contracts as their primary method.[10]

In exchange for the money, the GIDC asked counties to adhere to a detailed set of guidelines. These guidelines fixed standards for how to determine indigence and mandated appointment of counsel within seventy-two hours of arrest or detention, among other things. The GIDC also required that a tripartite committee of three volunteers be responsible for enforcing the standards. The tripartite committee, however, lacked a staff and often included nonlawyers or local businesspeople who had no interest in meaningfully supervising the indigent defense program, other than approving vouchers. The GIDC might admonish a county based on an anecdotal complaint, but a county could ignore a reprimand at will. A report in 2002 by the Spangenberg Group, a research and consulting firm in West Newton, Massachusetts, which specializes in improving justice programs, found that in recent years, the GIDC had not refused to provide funding for any county "in part because it fears political fallout or possible complaints from judges and other local people" to the state legislature. The GIDC "has no teeth," the report stated.[11]

Traditionally, the country's legal apparatus favors the office of the district attorney. The states instinctively supported the creation of prosecutors' offices because of a political will to solve crime and punish those who commit it. By contrast, the need to provide counsel for poor people accused of crimes is a burden that the U.S. Supreme Court thrust on the states in the sixties. Thus with a more popular mandate, prosecutors tend to receive more money and resources. For instance, Congress spent $26 million building the National Advocacy Center in Columbia, South Carolina, to train prosecutors. There is a similar school in Reno, Nevada, for training state and local judges. No federally funded counterpart exists for defense lawyers. Also, the Bureau of Justice Assistance gives federal aid to state and local law-enforcement agencies (e.g. $170,433,000 through the Edward Byrne Memorial Justice Assistance Grant Program in 2008) with no equivalent moneys for the defense.[12]

Nationwide, prosecutors also receive more funding because they have a higher caseload. District attorneys (sometimes called state's attorneys or county prosecutors or county attorneys) represent the state in virtually all prosecutions, so the state foots the entire bill. But when it comes to defendants, the state pays only when they are poor and only for minimum defense. In California, for example, reports show discrepant funding between prosecutors and public defenders—for every $100 the prosecution receives, indigent defense receives an average of $60.90, which is on the high end of what most states provide.[13] A report by the Spangenberg Group in 2002 estimated that states and counties nationwide spent $3.3 billion on indigent defense;[14] whereas in 2001, the ABA reported that $5 billion was spent in prosecuting criminal cases in state and local jurisdictions—a $1.7 billion gap.[15] (Both of these statistics are dated and experts say the discrepancy is probably greater, but an absence of nationwide statistics exists.)

With such a difference in resources, even the "best" public defender offices, which have full-time professional lawyers, cannot protect attorneys from problems like high caseloads. Instead, the overload has prompted new oversight measures in several states. Broward County, Florida, for instance, with a $15 million budget, has a prestigious public defender's office, but in 2005 the head of the office announced, to the dismay of some judges, that attorneys could not plead defendants guilty at arraignment without first having some "meaningful contact" with them. "We will make every effort to meet with clients prior to any court hearings," a memo to judges stated from public defender Howard Finkelstein, according to the *Broward Daily Business Review.* "However, if such a meeting has not taken place, we are legally and ethically constrained from recommending any plea to a client."[16] What should be a baseline standard has become so hard to reach that special requirements are needed to enforce it.

If the GIDC was failing to notice the problems in Greene County, others were not. Stephen B. Bright, the president and senior counsel of the Southern Center for Human Rights in Atlanta, had decided in the mid-1990s that Georgia's indigent defense system was so bad that his organization was going to keep challenging it until it was brought into line with the ideals of American justice. Bright, in his fifties, has made a career of championing unpopular causes. He became the director of the struggling Southern Center in 1982 and has often worked without pay in defense of people facing the death penalty and on litigation to improve prison and jail conditions throughout the South. The organization has eleven attorneys, an equal number of investigators, and a stream of student interns and volunteers.

The center is fueled by a profound sense of purpose and by Bright's inspiration. One staffer wondered when Bright ate, and then, one night at around three a.m., saw him downing an energy drink at his computer. For years, Bright had set his sights on creating a state-wide public defender system in Georgia with full-time lawyers. He toured clubs and community halls to arouse the public's interest, making speeches wherever possible. He told it like it is: People charged with crimes, no matter how small, whether they are guilty or not, are treated "like hamburgers in a fast-food restaurant." He discussed the defense attorney's need for independence from the prosecutor and judiciary "so that judges would not use lawyers for the poor as clerks to process their cases." He wanted to get rid of the hodgepodge system that contracted out defense for the poor and ended up with the likes of Surrency or worse. He sought more resources from the state and counties to train both new lawyers and existing public defenders.

Until the state made proper changes, Bright planned to expose and root out bad defense systems, one by one, by observing various courts in action and filing a series of lawsuits claiming violations of the state and federal Constitutions. I had learned about Greene County's problems from a series of phone calls with advocates in Atlanta, and when I told Bright it was one of the courts I was considering looking at, he said he had never been. I asked him to join me so I could get his perspective on how this court matched up to others he had seen. Even though he had appeared on *Nightline*, on the radio, and in various newspaper articles, legal professionals knew him by name but not always by face. In Greene County, Bright slipped into Judge Hulane George's courtroom unnoticed. He sat with a yellow legal pad in his lap, at the end of the first row, near a few other lawyers who had cases that day.

Bright believes that change begins on the ground, in the courtroom, and he doesn't hesitate to speak his mind, much to the annoyance of judges, who feel like he lectures them when it should be the other way around. As the day went on, the proceedings in Greene County became harder to hear. The less people could understand, the more frustrated, bored, and restless the audience became. Spectators shifted loudly in their seats. They whispered. I sat a few people away from Bright, attempting to take notes. The people couldn't hear a thing, and Bright sensed their frustration.

He leaned over and whispered, "Why don't you go and ask the judge to speak up?" I laughed. I considered myself an observer and wanted to be as inconspicuous as possible. I was also embarrassed to make a ruckus. This was court, after all.

I went back to straining to follow.

Suddenly Bright was on his feet. "Your Honor," he said in a deep, loud voice. "This is a public hearing and there are people here who want to listen to what is going on. So if you wouldn't mind speaking up that would be much appreciated."

Judge George looked like she had been slapped. Bright didn't seem like a commanding man, more like the lanky Kentucky farm boy he had been growing up. He had a wholesome face and full red hair parted to the side. His clothes didn't match his pedigree—he teaches at Harvard and Yale law schools in his free time but prides himself on buying eighty-dollar suits on the road. A deadening, somber silence followed his interruption.

"Excuse me, could you please come before me? I would like to talk to you," Judge George said.

"No, ma'am, that's fine. I don't need to appear before you. I will stay right here. I am just an observer. And I would just appreciate it if you would speak up. Thank you, ma'am."

Bright sat down, refusing to budge.

"Sir, I order you to come stand before me," Judge George said.

Bright climbed his way over the packed row. With gravitational force, whipping himself around to play to the audience, he took control of the courtroom.

"Your Honor, my name is Steve Bright and I am a lawyer visiting court today from Atlanta. I am here to listen to this public hearing. People have a right to hear what is going on. We're all here, missing work, having left our children in the care of others. And we want to hear what is going on in court today. You are denying us our right to listen to a public hearing. So if you wouldn't mind, please speak up."

The exhausted, twitchy crowd was now focused. Someone started to clap, and soon the entire courtroom was applauding with cries of "Amen" and "That's right," and "We can't hear anything," and "Thank you, sir."

"I have this viral junk in my throat," Judge George said. She did seem tired. Alarmed, too.

For the rest of the day the judge used a microphone and would tap it regularly asking, "Can everyone hear? I just want to make sure. There seems to be a lot of interest here today."

In a court where people had grown accustomed to being ignored, merely asking the judge to speak louder was blasphemously glorious. It shook things up so that someone in the audience shouted out, "We can't hear you," at Surrency, who was now also taking the heat. Surrency, tensely flipping through his notes, had to respond to the audience, most of whom were his clients. "Can you hear me now?" he said, facing the crowd.

"No!" people shouted.

Judge George clapped her hands together. She used to teach school, she told the crowd, and couldn't stand noise.

Bright had become a celebrity. In the breaks, people patted him on the shoulder and shook his hand in gratitude.

"I got something to tell you," said a man in denim overalls, and then he launched into the complexities of his case.

"Come talk to me next," said a woman hitting Bright on the arm. [. . .]

Bright's efforts to ensure that every defendant be provided a lawyer should have been redundant. The U.S. Supreme Court has ruled that every person in state court charged with a crime who is subject to imprisonment has a right to a lawyer. Even if the person is put on probation and has his or her jail time suspended, this individual has a right to a lawyer; he cannot go to jail, otherwise.

The court based its rulings on the Sixth Amendment, which says: "In all criminal prosecutions, the accused shall enjoy the right . . . to have Assistance of Counsel for his defense."[17] It may seem obvious today that this amendment means everyone, rich or poor. After all, the adversarial system is based on a concept of symmetry: two somewhat equal sides going head to head to produce the truth. If one side can't properly challenge the accusations because of poverty, something has to be done to rectify the imbalance. The history behind the amendment, however, explains why the states enforce it so unsuccessfully.

To begin with, the colonial courts of eighteenth-century America did not permit the accused even the presence of a lawyer. Like the English courts, they permitted counsel for "petty offenses" but not for important cases like felonies and treason.[18] As Yale Law School professor John H. Langbein writes, the rationalization for having no lawyers in the big cases was that "if falsely charged, the accused would clear himself through the 'Simplicity and Innocence' of his responses, whereas the responses of guilty defendants would 'help to disclose the Truth, which probably would not so well be discovered from the artificial Defense of others speaking for them.' "[19] In general, though, the British system was not palatable to the American settlers; judges appointed by the Crown oversaw venomous prosecutions that resulted in the conviction and execution of innocent people,[20] and so, inevitably, the Americans sought to protect themselves against this kind of injustice.[21]

By 1791 when the framers adopted the Bill of Rights (containing the first ten amendments of the Constitution), virtually all of the colonies had written into their own state constitutions that defendants could use lawyers.[22] In his book *The Bill of Rights*, Akhil Reed Amar notes that the new Americans wanted "notions of basic fairness and symmetry" to exist in a criminal court. "If the prosecuting government could have a lawyer, why not the defendant?"[23] The Sixth Amendment, which provided a right to counsel in federal court, merely kept the federal government in step with what the states had already sanctioned.

Still, the Sixth Amendment was originally thought to mean that the defendant couldn't be *barred* from having a lawyer in federal court, where a minority of criminal cases were tried in revolutionary times. The framers could not have imagined that criminal procedure would become so complicated that a defendant would need a lawyer just to understand what was happening, much less that the U.S. Supreme Court would impose a burden on the states to provide lawyers. States had the authority, as they still do, to decide the rights of men and women put on trial; so long as the treatment was fair and decent, the U.S. Supreme Court or the federal government wouldn't intrude. The lack of federal involvement in state matters began to change after the Civil War with the ratification of the Fourteenth Amendment in 1868 to protect the newly freed slaves in the South from oppression by local governments. The amendment, which declared that no state would deny any person due process and equal protection of the laws, would have an enormous impact in the century to come; but few gains occurred immediately in terms of the rights of poor people accused of crime.

The status quo prevailed until 1931 when the much-publicized trial of the so-called Scottsboro Boys became a symbol of American racism and Southern injustice. Nine young black men, ages thirteen to twenty, were charged with raping two white women on a train traveling through Alabama. At the time, local citizens were incensed and threatening a lynch mob. All nine were tried in Scottsboro, the county seat. When the judge inquired whether the parties were ready for trial, the prosecutor answered yes, but no one answered for the defense. Originally, each of the members of the Scottsboro bar had been appointed as defense counsel, but each had found a reason to get out of it—except for one lawyer, Milo Moody, described as a "doddering, extremely unreliable, senile individual who is losing whatever ability he once had,"[24] and Stephen R. Roddy, from Chattanooga, Tennessee, who was unsure if he had agreed to take on the case or not. Roddy had not been employed by the boys but had come to court as an observer at the request of a black doctor, P.A. Stephens, who presided over a Tennessee church. Roddy, apparently drunk, would not clarify whether he had agreed to represent the defendants.[25] "If I was paid and employed it would be a different thing," he told the judge, "but I have not prepared this case for trial . . ." He also said he wasn't familiar with Alabama law. If he had to take the case alone, "the boys would be better off if I step entirely out of the case," he told the court.[26]

Nevertheless, the nine black youths went on trial with these two attorneys who had spent barely half an hour talking to them, had not investigated the crime or prepared a defense, and who did not seek a continuance to do so or file a motion for a change of venue despite the enormous pretrial publicity. The trials began immediately in three separate groups; each trial took one day. Three all-white juries found eight of the nine defendants guilty and imposed the death penalty (the exception was a mistrial for the thirteen-year-old, Roy Wright).[27]

The case was appealed to the U.S. Supreme Court, which reversed the lower court's decision on grounds that the lawyers did not have a chance to work on their clients' behalf. The majority opinion in *Powell v. Alabama* said that, "during perhaps the most critical period of the proceedings against these defendants, that is to say, from the time of their arraignment until the beginning of their trial, when consultation, thorough-going investigation and preparation were vitally important, the defendants did not have the aid of counsel in any real sense, although they were as much entitled to such aid during that period as at the trial itself."[28] The court referred to the Fourteenth Amendment's due process clause, citing a defendant's right to "the guiding hand of counsel at every step in the proceedings" and the "fundamental nature of that right." However, the court limited the right to "a capital case" and to a situation where the defendant is indigent and "incapable adequately of making his own defense because of ignorance, feeble-mindedness, illiteracy, or the like."[29] (After the decision, the case became a cause célèbre for the Communist Party and many appeals and re-trials followed. Eventually, one of the women later admitted that she had invented the story of the rape.[30])

Powell was groundbreaking. It recognized a right to counsel for the poor and that the representation had to be meaningful. Equally important was the court's decision to apply the Fourteenth Amendment's due process clause to the states on an issue of fundamental fairness: the trial court's failure to make an effective appointment of counsel. As Justice Pierce Butler wrote in dissent, it was "a field hitherto occupied exclusively by the several States," adding that "Nothing before the Court calls for a consideration of the point. It was not suggested below [by the lower court judges] and petitioners do not ask for its decision here."[31] So why did the Supreme Court choose to intervene when it had not been called upon even to consider the issue of effective counsel under the Fourteenth Amendment?

Perhaps the justices read the papers and wanted to step in to correct this notorious case.[32] Or maybe they felt a need to acknowledge the new unchecked power of the prosecutor. In the nineteenth century, a major power shift in courts across the country favored full-time prosecutors who were marshaled in to deal with increasing levels of crime presented by

industrialization and migration to cities.[33] Before this, the public prosecutor had been a minor actor in the criminal process, more of an adjunct to
the judge, presenting cases to grand juries or trial juries, or simply expedit-
ing prosecution on behalf of victims or their families, who at times hired
private lawyers to act as prosecutors.[34] As a bureaucracy of police arose to
manage an increasing number of arrests, prosecutors began, somewhat by
necessity, to take on the role of deciding which cases made it to court.[35] By
the early twentieth century, writers were expressing outrage at the steep
increase in prosecutorial power: prosecutors were dismissing cases, plead-
ing a high portion of them guilty, and holding fewer jury trials.[36]

No matter what the cause, the court found the Scottsboro case so disturbing that it decided to federalize the issue of representation for indigent defendants. But it did so with half-measures, leaving the states to
decide whether to appoint counsel except when the defendant was poor,
uneducated to the point of illiteracy, and charged with a capital case. Only
under these circumstances was denial of counsel considered a violation of
due process. The states still had the right, within this limit, to decide the
rest.

In the years that followed, the U.S. Supreme Court struggled to find
the perimeters of the right to counsel within the context of a fair trial.
First, the Supreme Court expanded the right, finding that a lawyer must
be provided when the defendant could not afford one, regardless of his
education or the nature of the crime—but still only in criminal cases in
federal court. In *Johnson v. Zerbst*, the court quoted *Powell* to recognize
that "without the assistance of counsel even the intelligent layman usually
lacks both the skill and knowledge adequately to prepare his defense, even
though he has a perfect one."[37] The right applied unless an accused affirmatively waived it.[38] But four years later, the court, while still recognizing
the validity of *Johnson v. Zerbst*, explicitly refused to apply the full right to
counsel to the states. In *Betts v. Brady*, it ruled that due process required
the appointment of a lawyer in state court only when the issues were difficult and the defendant inexperienced—basically broadening the due
process protection of *Powell* to other complex criminal cases where the
accused could not defend himself, case-by-case, but still maintaining a
distinction between what was mandated in federal and state court.[39] As a
result, under *Zerbst*, a defendant who was poor could always get a lawyer in
federal court; but in state courts, under *Betts*, a defendant could only get
one if the trial would be "fundamentally unfair" otherwise (depending on
the circumstances) and violated due process.

All that was needed, then, to apply the rule across the United States,
was a Supreme Court majority that regarded the right to counsel as fundamental under any circumstance. Why did the court take such incremental

steps toward establishing this right? In general, our Constitution does not frame rights in affirmative terms. It says what the government cannot do—e.g., it cannot prohibit publication of offensive statements, or prevent a religious group from practicing its faith.[40] The idea of forcing the states to give the indigent lawyers was not only unprecedented but unique in terms of the Constitution's reach.

In 1953, President Dwight D. Eisenhower appointed Earl Warren as the chief justice of the U.S. Supreme Court. Warren, the former governor of California, had spent many years as a prosecutor in Alameda County, where he had a reputation for fair-mindedness. "It was said that the DA's office in Alameda County in the years Earl Warren ran it never extracted an involuntary confession from a defendant," writes historian Richard Kluger in the classic work *Simple Justice*. "Anyone who wanted to see his lawyer before submitting to police interrogation was permitted to do so. No conviction ever won by Warren's office was thrown out on appeal by a higher court."[41] Warren and several of his associate justices, such as Hugo Black and William J. Brennan, Jr., were the driving forces in developing a body of case law that has been called a mini code of criminal procedure to prevent coerced confessions, warrantless wiretapping, and interrogation conducted in the absence of a lawyer.[42]

In 1956 in *Griffin v. Illinois*, the Supreme Court tackled the issue of poverty and inequality in the state courts. Judson Griffin, an indigent man, argued he was denied his right to appeal his conviction of armed robbery because he couldn't afford a trial transcript. The court found Griffin had been denied his right to equal protection under the Fourteenth Amendment. In a famous opinion, Justice Hugo Black wrote: "There can be no equal justice where the kind of trial a man gets depends on the amount of money he has."[43] In dissent, Justice John Harlan compared the right to counsel to a college education, commenting that it was tantamount to demanding that states provide fee waivers to students who couldn't afford a state university. "[I] think it is beyond the province of this Court to tell Illinois that it must provide such procedures," he wrote in conclusion.[44] Nevertheless, the ruling furthered protection for poor people accused of crimes.

In 1962, the Court received a letter in scrawled pencil from a prisoner named Clarence Earl Gideon who claimed he had been tried without a lawyer in Florida for breaking and entering and petty larceny. He had seemed fairly intelligent in conducting his own defense, going so far as to call a character witness and attack the credibility of the main witness against him. Still, he had been found guilty and sentenced to five years in prison.[45]

Gideon filed his handwritten petition for habeas corpus to the U.S.

Supreme Court, arguing that he had a right to counsel under the Sixth Amendment. The court appointed Abe Fortas, then a partner at Arnold, Fortas & Porter and a distinguished member of the bar, to represent him. (Fortas later became a U.S. Supreme Court justice and his name was dropped from the firm, which became Arnold & Porter.) Fortas argued that the right to counsel was indispensable for a fair hearing. In 1963, the Court found in *Gideon v. Wainwright* that what had been an "obvious truth" for federal criminal trials now applied to the states as well: "Reason and reflection require that in our adversary system of criminal justice, any person hauled into court, who is too poor to hire a lawyer, cannot be assured a fair trial unless counsel is provided for him."[46] *Gideon* overruled *Betts v. Brady* and put the burden on the states to provide the indigent with lawyers in felony cases.

Ultimately, Gideon was retried with a lawyer at his side and acquitted. But the battle to enforce the Court's ruling continues to this day, in part because *Gideon* did not prescribe standards for what passed for an effective lawyer, and many states do not want to pay for lawyers to defend the poor—a resistance that has given way to token representation.

In the decades which followed *Gideon*, the U.S. Supreme Court went to great lengths to limit the right to counsel.[47] *Strickland v. Washington* set a very low bar for what constituted effective counsel in 1984. The *Strickland* court held that "[n]o particular set of detailed rules for counsel's conduct can satisfactorily take account of the variety of circumstances faced by defense counsel or the range of legitimate decisions regarding how best to represent a criminal defendant."[48] The Court said only that a lawyer's representation must meet an "objective standard of reasonableness."[49] However, it granted counsel tremendous leeway by presuming a lawyer is competent unless a defendant can prove there was "a reasonable probability that, but for counsel's unprofessional errors, the result of the proceeding would have been different." The Court defined "reasonable probability" as "a probability sufficient to undermine confidence in the outcome."[50] Justice Thurgood Marshall dissented. He found the standard adopted by the Court so malleable as to be meaningless. He wrote, "To tell lawyers and the lower courts that counsel for a criminal defendant must behave 'reasonably' and must act like a reasonably competent attorney, is to tell them almost nothing."[51]

The benchmark for what constitutes adequate assistance is so low that in 2001 in the infamous Calvin Burdine trial, the Fifth Circuit Court of Appeals openly debated whether to affirm a death-penalty decision where the lawyer, Joe Frank Cannon, had slept through significant parts of his client's case (a three-judge panel of the Fifth Circuit had initially upheld the conviction and death sentence, 2–1). Nine judges of the Fifth Circuit

Court agreed to overturn the death penalty decision and grant Burdine a new trial, but not without five dissenters, two of whom took issue with how much of the trial it was permissible to sleep through and still be adversarial: "[O]f utmost importance . . . there is no state-finding that Cannon was 'repeatedly unconscious' during 'substantial' portions of the trial." The dissenters said information was missing about:

> When Cannon "dozed" as opposed to "slept"; How long he slept, individually and collectively; How many times he slept; How deeply he slept; What happened while he slept, including which witness(es) was (were) testifying or other evidence was being presented; and When the sleeping occurred—which day(s), or whether during the morning or afternoon.[52]

To this day it remains debatable whether a lawyer can sleep during his client's death-penalty trial.[53] So we can only imagine what is tolerated in ordinary cases that fail to attract scrutiny from the public or appellate courts.

According to an ABA report published in 2004 apropos *Gideon's* fortieth anniversary, "Indigent defense in the United States remains in a state of crisis, resulting in a system that lacks fundamental fairness and places poor persons at constant risk of wrongful conviction."[54] And while this is true at the state level, the federal system is much improved, beginning with the Criminal Justice Act of 1964 that compensated counsel at an hourly rate on a case-by-case basis; several years later Congress authorized the federal courts to establish federal defender organizations (FDOs), which today represent approximately 64 percent of the federal indigent cases and have a very good reputation. The organizations have resources similar to those of prosecutors—reasonable salaries for its staff, funds for expert services, investigators and paralegals—and they also provide regular training and supervision to full-time staff so that they develop the expertise that results from practicing federal criminal law full-time.

If it is true that the federal system is considerably better than what is in place state by state, it is still difficult actually to assess whether an indigent defense system is effective because there is no single barometer of success. The *ABA Standards for Criminal Justice* outlines how a lawyer should defend a criminal case so that an office can assess whether it has the personnel, time, and resources to do the basics to meet with clients and investigate. The guidelines are better than other attempts to set out principles, but still lack an ongoing methodology to ascertain how well an office is serving the nation's poorest defendants.[55]

When North Carolina's Indigent Defense Services (IDS) sought in

2001 to develop a set of indicators that would measure the quality and cost-effectiveness of the system, it could not find a model to emulate. "There is so little objective measurement in this business, it is astonishing," said Malcolm Ray Hunter Jr., IDS executive director until December 2008. Instead, Margaret A. Gressens, IDS research director, had to begin from scratch to establish indicators of system performance. The plan was for North Carolina's one hundred counties to report data: if a county shows below-average performance on one of many indicators, IDS will be able to get involved. The percentage of defendants who are released from jail pretrial, for example, or who promptly see their attorney, say within forty-eight hours of arrest, are both indicators of what Gressens called the "cornerstone" of good criminal defense. "It costs a state a lot of money to have people in jail who don't need to be," she said. While in jail, people can lose their jobs and homes, become welfare recipients, and have their lives ruined—considerations of vital importance to an individual, which, from a policy perspective, also entail significant costs for the state.

IDS hopes eventually to take the indicators a step further and do what no state has come close to doing: to look at the impact of indigent defense services on the criminal justice system and the community. Gressens says that governments quantify hard-to-measure things all the time, like quality of life. But the health of our courts has been left virtually unchecked. According to Gressens, part of the problem is that each entity in the adversarial system works independently, and rarely, if ever, sits down with the others to solve problems or inefficiencies. "No one steps back and says we are really one system, how is this system working." The project is still in its initial stages but IDS hopes to have an evaluation tool in place by 2010.

Part V

The Jury: Who Are Your Peers and Who Are Mine?

Jury service is the greatest official power over other people that most Americans will ever have. In the power-heavy world of law enforcement, the juror is the only outsider who can keep police, prosecutors, and even judges in check by deciding whether to convict or acquit a defendant. The double jeopardy clause of the Fifth Amendment to the U.S. Constitution means that no one can second-guess a jury acquittal. This provision also protects jurors from having to explain why they decided one way or the other (short of corruption).

As we have seen, nearly all criminal cases end with plea bargains and thus are never heard by a jury. It is the big cases that come down to a jury trial: when the defendant has a good defense (like innocence) or when the crime is so infamous that the prosecutor will not consider a plea bargain. In those instances, the lawyers hone in on selecting the ideal jury. It turns out that there are two ideal juries in every case, and they do not overlap.

The Sixth Amendment to the Constitution guarantees the defendant a jury of his peers. What this means, of course, is a matter of great debate. It does not mean, as the law has evolved, that someone facing the death penalty has the right to jurors who do not believe in that punishment. It also does not mean that someone is guaranteed jurors of his or her gender, race, or level of education.

Needless to say, race has been the main point of contention when it comes to selecting jurors, not just historically but still to this day. There is a history of court administrators devising stratagems to keep the names of black residents out of the pool of available jurors. These stratagems have evolved in sophistication alongside expanding civil rights. When Jim Crow effectively kept black Americans from registering to vote, the voting roll was a convenient jury pool. Some courts have kept two lists, but used only one.

Prosecutors also have devised methods to excuse potential jurors who are black, typically relying on the peremptory challenge—their right to excuse a certain number of proposed jurors without giving a reason. And, astonishingly, the U.S. Supreme Court has approved peremptory challenges that rejected only black jurors, as long as the prosecutor made no overt expression of discrimination.

No Equal Justice: Race and Class in the American Criminal Justice System by David Cole describes how the U.S. Supreme Court in the last thirty years or so has interpreted the Constitution to permit racial skewing of justice. With regard to jury selection, he explains how it is supposed to work and how it has been subverted by discrimination. Cole, a Georgetown University law professor and a prominent critic of the national security state and the criminal justice system, considers discrimination in jury selection to be a microcosm of the discrimination present in the overall system. He also analyzes the Supreme Court's decisions on peremptory challenges and calls for a new jurisprudence that honestly acknowledges race-based decision making and attempts to control it pragmatically.

The Equal Justice Initiative (www.eji.org) is an Alabama-based nonprofit law organization that defends indigent people facing the death penalty and advocates against criminal justice measures that disproportionately disadvantage black Americans. Its 2010 report *Illegal Racial Discrimination in Jury Selection: A Continuing Legacy* surveys ongoing widespread use of peremptory challenges by prosecutors in southern states to block black jurors from serving. State appellate courts, the report says, have failed to provide consistent guidance against this practice. This undermines the integrity of the criminal justice system and thus citizens' respect for the law.

Further Reading: Paul Butler, in *Let's Get Free* (described in the introduction to Part IV), offers a populist provocation to take on the unfairness of the criminal justice system. Jury nullification, he says, is a long-standing if infrequently used tradition in criminal trials. Juries are free to decide cases as they choose and cannot be punished for any decision, as long as it does not involve corruption. Butler claims to have witnessed nullification (acquittal of a clearly guilty person) when he was a prosecutor and proposes—not necessarily facetiously—that this would be an appropriate response to the War on Drugs in particular. His argument underscores the power and responsibility that juries have.

11

Judgment and Discrimination

David Cole

The jury is the heart of the criminal justice system. It renders judgment on the most important question in criminal law—guilt or innocence. Many lawyers believe that cases are won and lost when they pick a jury. The jury has been lauded as a bulwark against government tyranny, a repository of democratic deliberation, and a stirring example of representative government in action. Alexis de Tocqueville described it as placing "the direction of society in the hands of the governed, or of a portion of the governed, and not in that of the government." [1] The Supreme Court has characterized the jury as "an inestimable safeguard against the corrupt or overzealous prosecutor and against the compliant, biased, or eccentric judge." [2] If the state overplays its hand, the jury, reflecting community sentiment, has the freedom to acquit, to convict of lesser charges, or to reach an impasse and require a new trial.

The jury is also, according to the Supreme Court, the "criminal defendant's fundamental 'protection of life and liberty against race or color prejudice.' " [3] Virtually all the attention the Court has paid to race discrimination in criminal justice has been focused on the jury. The first law of any kind that the Supreme Court ever struck down as racially discriminatory was a statute restricting jury service to white men,[4] and the Court has addressed race discrimination in jury selection in more cases than any other form of race discrimination. Justice Lewis Powell described the Court's efforts in this area as "unceasing;" [5] and Justice Anthony Kennedy has proudly characterized the Court's record as "over a century of jurisprudence dedicated to the elimination of race prejudice within the jury selection process." [6]

From *No Equal Justice: Race and Class in the American Criminal Justice System* (New York: The New Press, 1999), 101–26.

117

Yet racial discrimination in jury selection remains a persistent reality
to this day. As it did with the right to counsel, the Court has made strong
pronouncements about equality, but has not backed them up with meaningful implementation. As with the right to counsel, achieving equality
is extremely difficult, in part for reasons beyond the Court's control. But
much of the blame for the persistence of discrimination in jury selection
must nonetheless be attributed to the Court's historic and continuing tolerance of measures that perpetuate and facilitate discrimination.

The problem of jury discrimination is a microcosm of the problem
of discrimination in criminal justice, and indeed of race discrimination
generally. The fundamental question is this: How can we ensure that juries treat defendants and victims of different races, genders, and classes
equally, when we know that race, gender, and class distinctions play a significant role in how people view the world? Whether we like it or not, race
matters in our culture. As Tanya Coke has argued,

> racial identity, though not biological race, informs cultural
> experience. . . . Racial identity, like gender identity, is an organizing
> principle of group consciousness: as long as patterns of residential
> and economic segregation continue to separate the races in differ-
> ent enclaves, blacks, whites, Latinos, and others will exhibit cultural
> differences in their perceptions of the world.[7]

If we ignore those differences in constructing the rules that govern juries, we risk denying equal justice. But if we construct a system on the
premise that race matters, we risk institutionalizing and thereby perpet-
uating racial stereotypes. This fundamental dilemma is exacerbated by
the secret character of jury deliberations. Because juries need not justify
their actions with any sort of public account, they exercise virtually un-
bridled discretion, and that discretion may invite stereotyped judgments,
including judgments predicated on race. In addition, nothing breeds
skepticism like secrecy. Thus, whether or not the jury is actually a source
of discrimination, it is likely to be viewed with distrust by those excluded
from participation.

This problem admits of no easy answers, and the Court's approach has
been deeply ambivalent. Although selection of jury pools was the first
setting in which the Court invalidated racial discrimination, in 1880, selection of trial juries through "peremptory challenges" was also the last
setting in which the Court openly tolerated racial discrimination, which
it expressly *permitted* until 1986. As it stands today, the Court's jury discrimination doctrine imposes conflicting constitutional mandates on
the jury selection process: its Sixth Amendment doctrine is predicated

on an acknowledgment that race matters, but its equal protection doctrine requires color-blind jury selection. And while the Court has long condemned jury discrimination in principle, it has consistently adopted weak enforcement mechanisms that have tolerated continuing inequality.

Over the past one hundred years, the Court has reviewed every aspect of jury selection, from the initial processes for identifying a pool, or "venire," of eligible jurors, to the use of "peremptory challenges" by the parties' lawyers to select the trial jury from the jury pool. The Court's focus has shifted over time. It initially paid attention to discrimination in jury pool composition, and only later addressed discrimination in selection of trial juries. This chronology makes sense: As long as blacks were excluded from the jury pool, the issue of discriminatory selection for trial juries was largely moot, because there were no blacks in the pool to discriminate against in selecting the trial jury. "Peremptory challenges," used in selecting trial juries, grew in importance as a mechanism for discrimination as blacks began to appear in the jury pools. This chapter therefore first reviews the Court's approach to discrimination in the selection of jury pools, and then turns to its treatment of the discriminatory use of "peremptory strikes" to obtain a trial jury.

"A Violent Presumption"

Three facts about jury discrimination are largely undisputed. First, the all-white jury has been a staple of the American criminal justice system for most of our history.[8] Second, the Supreme Court has long condemned discrimination in jury selection.[9] And third, race discrimination in jury selection remains a pervasive feature of our justice system to this day.[10] The interesting question is how all these facts can be true at the same time. A historical review of jury discrimination suggests the answer: while the Supreme Court has long condemned overt racism in jury selection, it has been reluctant to adopt measures that would make selection processes fair in practice. The Court's record has improved over the century, but its doctrine remains conflicted and compromised to this day, thereby permitting disproportionately white juries to endure.

Although procedures vary from state to state, several basic features are common to all jury selection processes. Jury commissioners start by creating a jury list or roll, which identifies all persons eligible for jury service. Voter registration lists are most commonly used as a source, in some instances supplemented by other sources, such as driver's license lists. Some southern states still rely on the "key man" system to compile their jury rolls. In Alabama, for example, jury commissioners are directed to place on the rolls persons in the community who are "generally reputed to be honest and intelligent and . . . esteemed in the community for integrity, good character and sound judgment."[11]

From the jury roll, jury commissioners then select a jury pool, or venire, which consists of those persons actually summoned to appear in court on a given day for jury service. Trial juries, or "petit juries," which judge guilt or innocence in individual cases, are then selected by a process of elimination from the jury pool. First, the court excuses those citizens who are exempt by virtue of occupation or other obligations. Then prospective jurors are asked about potential biases: are they related to any of the participants, have they been victimized by crime, do they have relatives who are in prison or in law enforcement, etc. Parties may challenge "for cause" any juror who cannot judge the facts objectively and fairly by virtue of such biases. Finally, each side ordinarily uses a number of "peremptory challenges," which permit them to strike jurors without explanation, to obtain the requisite number for the petit jury.

Each of these stages may result in the exclusion of minorities from jury service. Voter registration and even driver's license lists underrepresent poor people and racial minorities.[12] Key man lists tend to be filled with persons who belong to the same social circles as the jury commissioners, and therefore also underrepresent minorities and the poor. Because minorities and the poor move more frequently than whites and the rich, these groups are less likely to receive jury summonses. For a number of reasons, from skepticism and alienation to the inability to take time off from their jobs, minorities and the poor are also less likely to respond to those summonses they receive.[13] Finally, and most significantly today, because peremptory challenges need not be explained, they are especially fertile soil for racial discrimination.

The history of racial discrimination in jury selection is long and sordid. No black person sat on a jury in the United States until 1860.[14] During the post–Civil War Reconstruction, blacks began to serve on juries in the South for the first time.[15] Not coincidentally, integrated juries at that time began to convict whites for racially motivated violence against blacks.[16] But Democratic conservatives soon regained power in the South, Klan violence intimidated Republicans and blacks alike, and the all-white jury returned.[17] In 1875, Congress responded by making it a federal crime to exclude a juror on the basis of race, but violations of the law have rarely been prosecuted.[18]

A lawyer reading the 1880 decision in *Strauder v. West Virginia*,[19] the Supreme Court's first word on jury discrimination, might well have predicted that the all-white jury would soon go the way of slavery. At issue was a West Virginia statute that expressly reserved jury service to white males. The Court squarely held that barring blacks from serving on juries violated the recently enacted Fourteenth Amendment, which it construed as "securing to a race recently emancipated, a race that through many generations had been held in slavery, all the civil rights that the superior race enjoys."[20] It portrayed the exclusion of blacks from jury service as "practically a brand upon them, affixed by the law, an assertion of their inferiority, and a stimulant to that race prejudice which is an impediment to securing . . . equal justice."[21] The Court asked:

> how can it be maintained that compelling a colored man to submit to a trial for his life by a jury drawn from a panel from which the State has expressly excluded every man of his race, because of color alone, however well qualified in other respects, is not a denial to him of equal protection.[22]

In reaching its result, the Court in *Strauder* acknowledged what could hardly be denied in post–Civil War America: Race matters. In particular, by finding that the black *defendant's* right to equal protection was infringed by the exclusion of black *jurors*, the Court necessarily presumed that white and black jurors would react differently to prosecutions against black defendants, that is, that jurors are not color-blind. The Court expressly noted that "prejudices often exist against particular classes in the community, which sway the judgment of jurors," and asserted that "[t]he framers of the [Fourteenth A]mendment must have known full well the existence of such prejudice and its likelihood to continue against the manumitted slaves and their race, and that knowledge was doubtless a motive that led to the amendment."[23]

Notwithstanding its strong rhetoric, however, *Strauder* had virtually no impact on the practice of jury discrimination. From the end of Reconstruction through the New Deal, "the systematic exclusion of black men from Southern juries was about as plain as any legal discrimination could be short of proclamation in state statutes or confession by state officials."[24] The Supreme Court repeatedly upheld convictions of black defendants by all-white juries in situations where intentional exclusion of black jurors was self-evident. In *Smith v. Mississippi*, to cite one of many examples, the Court in 1896 upheld the conviction of a black man for murder where the defendant alleged that although there were 1,300 black and 300 white voters in Bolivar County, no black person had been summoned for jury service since the end of the Civil War.[25]

Until 1935, the only Supreme Court decision other than *Strauder* itself that invalidated a conviction on jury discrimination grounds was *Neal v. Delaware*.[26] William Neal, a black man, was indicted for the rape of a white woman, an offense punishable by death. Delaware law explicitly restricted jury service to white males, but a state court had ruled that ban inoperative in light of the Fourteenth Amendment. The state conceded, however, "that no colored citizen had ever been summoned as a juror in the courts of the State," in a county where blacks numbered more than 26,000 among a total population of less than 150,000.[27] The Delaware Supreme Court had denied Neal's equal protection challenge with the following reasoning:

> That none but white men were selected is in nowise remarkable in view of the fact—too notorious to be ignored—that the great body of black men residing in this State are utterly unqualified by want of intelligence, experience, or moral integrity to sit on juries. Exceptions there are, unquestionably, but they are rare . . . [28]

The U.S. Supreme Court reversed, noting that the state had conceded that it excluded all black jurors, and that the only explanation offered—that "the great body of black men residing in this State are utterly unqualified by want of intelligence, experience, or moral integrity"—"a violent presumption" that the Court could not sanction.[29]

The most remarkable thing about *Neal*, however, is how little distinguishes it from the legion of cases that followed in which the Supreme Court *upheld* convictions of black men by all-white juries. In case after case, the Supreme Court, much like the Delaware Supreme Court in *Neal*, discounted showings of stark disparities as insufficient, deferred to lower court findings of no discrimination, and indulged a presumption that public officials would not exclude jurors on the basis of race unless the law explicitly directed them to do so. What made *Neal* different was that the Delaware Supreme Court had made *explicit* the violent presumption that black citizens were unqualified for jury service. Apparently, so long as the presumption was left unstated, the Supreme Court in the pre–New Deal era was willing to condone discriminatory results.

Professor Benno Schmidt has sought to explain the Supreme Court's dismal record of tolerating all-white juries for so long after declaring race discrimination in jury selection unconstitutional by noting that defendants were required to develop the facts underlying their claims in often hostile state courts. In *Strauder* and a companion case, *Virginia v. Rives*,[30] the Supreme Court ruled that state defendants could not bring such claims in federal court, where judges would be more sympathetic. Instead, defendants had to litigate their race discrimination claims before state judges, who were often extremely reluctant to find their own jury commissioners guilty of the federal criminal offense of racial exclusion. Although

U.S. Supreme Court review was theoretically available on appeal from state court convictions, the Supreme Court could not possibly review every claim of jury discrimination that arose in a state criminal proceeding. When it did review such claims, it adopted a highly deferential attitude toward the trial court's fact-finding regarding discrimination. Thus, at the very moment that it declared jury discrimination unconstitutional, the Court relegated enforcement of such claims to unsympathetic state courts, where most would fail.

Schmidt attributes this result to the Court's ambivalence about the shift in federal-state relations brought about by the Civil War amendments to the Constitution.[31] Prior to the Civil War, states were seen as the prime protectors of individual rights, and the federal government's authority was sharply limited. In retrospect, historians now view the Civil War, and the Civil War amendments, as fundamentally shifting the power and responsibility for assuring equal rights from the states to the federal government. This shift, Schmidt argues, was not an easy one, and the Court was reluctant to assert its newly dominant federal role.

Schmidt also posits another motive. Had the Court actually put an end to the all-white jury, it might have encouraged widespread private vigilantism of the type practiced by the Ku Klux Klan.[32] The unstated concern—speculative at best—was that if discrimination could not be effected through judicial channels, it would be effected through extra-judicial methods, such as lynchings. In any event, the Court announced a broad principle of nondiscrimination in *Strauder*, but left its enforcement to state courts. In Schmidt's view:

> The advantages of [such an approach] are clear: shift the everyday burden of enforcement to the state courts and officialdom. At least make them say the right things about nondiscrimination. If profession of principle is to force actual effects in life, make the state courts the forcing institutions. If there is to be hypocrisy between judicial profession and judical process, let the state courts dirty their hands. Keep the federal trial judges out of the picture. Hold the Supreme Court at appellate remove, a distant keeper of the Ark of the (paper) Covenant, unembarrassed by hands-on confrontations with the frustration of federal guarantees.[33]

Of course, prudence can also be a cover for a lack of courage. And the costs of the Court's cautious approach were substantial. By tolerating official discrimination at the core of the criminal justice system as long as it was not explicit, the Court may well have done more damage to the cause of racial equality than the feared Klan violence. Such violence would have been seen for what it was—extralegal and illegitimate—and might have prompted more substantial federal intervention. By instead channeling racial subordination through a facially race-neutral judicial system that imposed official violence on blacks through imprisonment and capital punishment, the Court arguably contributed to the "normalization" and institutionalization of subordination, rendering it even more insidious and difficult to confront.

The Court's performance in these early jury discrimination cases unfortunately is consistent with its approach to discrimination in criminal justice to this day. The Court announced a constitutional right, but then implemented it in a manner that spared mainstream society the cost of realizing that right across the board. In the jury setting, the cost to mainstream society would likely have come in increased tensions and hostilities between Democrats and Republicans, between the South and the North, and between state and federal institutions, at a time when the mainstream was seeking to suppress such hostilities and achieve a renewed union. The Court's approach spared mainstream society by shifting the cost to black defendants and permitting white domination of the jury to continue under the cover of formal race neutrality, long after it could not openly be justified.

"Plain as Punch"

In 1935, the Supreme Court abruptly shifted course, invalidating a second round of convictions in the high-profile Scottsboro case on the ground that the state had discriminatorily applied a race-neutral selection scheme to exclude black citizens from the jury rolls.[34] After the Supreme Court reversed the initial convictions in the Scottsboro case for lack of effective counsel, the Communist Party hired Samuel Leibowitz, an experienced New York trial attorney, to represent the defendants on retrial. Leibowitz aggressively challenged the racial composition of the jury rolls. He put on witnesses who testified that they could not remember a black man serving on any jury in the county in their lifetimes. He interrogated jury commissioners, who admitted that they designated black citizens as "col."—for "colored"—on the lists from which they drew the jury venire. And he subpoenaed the books containing the jury roll.

Those books became a central exhibit in the case. Alabama officials pointed to the names of six black citizens on the jury roll as evidence that they had not systematically excluded black citizens. But Leibowitz called a handwriting expert, who testified that the six black names had been entered *after* the jury rolls were completed. Red lines had been drawn at the bottom of each page when the lists were initially recorded, and the black men's names appeared to have been written in later, over the red lines.

The Alabama courts nonetheless found no discrimination. Like so many courts before, they credited the jury commissioners' general denials of discriminatory intent, presumed that the commissioners had faithfully followed their obligations, and found that they had not tampered with the jury rolls. This case's conclusion was to be different, however. In part the difference may have been due to the nationwide attention that the case had achieved. But in part the difference lay in Leibowitz's marshalling of the evidence. At the Supreme Court oral argument, Leibowitz made the brute fact of discrimination dramatically visible in a way that no argument had before. Supreme Court arguments are usually exercises in technical legal discourse far removed from the facts of a case. But Leibowitz brought the jury books with him to the argument, and invited the Justices to witness the tampering for themselves. Although the Court rarely reviews evidence during argument, each Justice in turn examined the books with a magnifying glass as Leibowitz explained how the black men's names were added after the fact. When Justice Willis Van Devanter saw the books, he whispered to his colleague Chief Justice Charles Evans, in a voice loud enough to be heard by spectators, "Why it's plain as punch!"[35]

The Court reversed the convictions, finding that the Alabama jury commissioners had intentionally excluded black jurors because of their race.[36] Where the Court had in previous cases presumed good faith on the part of government officials absent a direct showing of racist motive, it now stated that a case of discrimination could be made by a sufficiently strong statistical showing that blacks were qualified for jury service but absent from juries.[37] A direct showing of intentional discrimination was no longer necessary. And the Court abandoned its previous stance of deference to lower court fact finding on the issue of whether intentional discrimination occurred, insisting now that its duty was to "analyze the facts in order that the appropriate enforcement of the federal right may be assured."[38]

After the Scottsboro case, the Court reviewed jury discrimination claims with much more care, at the rate of about one a year, and frequently reversed convictions based on statistical showings.[39] The Court's record was by no means consistent, however. In 1945, the Court rejected a race discrimination challenge to a grand jury where Dallas County had adopted a practice of placing one, and only one, black juror on each grand jury.[40] The Court upheld this practice, even though jury commissioners admitted that once they found one black juror, they "felt like that was satisfactory representation," and "had no intention of placing more than one negro on the panel."[41] In dissent, Justice Murphy argued that "clearer proof of intentional and deliberate limitation on the basis of color would be difficult to produce."[42]

In the early 1970s, the Court began to look beyond tokenism, and invalidated selection schemes where defendants showed a "substantial disparity" between the racial makeup of the community and that of the jury list, absent a specific explanation for the disparity from state officials. In 1970, for example, the Court upheld a constitutional challenge to a Georgia jury selection scheme where blacks comprised 37 percent of a jury venire, but 60 percent of the population, and the state had not adequately explained the difference.[43]

While the Court's decisions from 1935 to 1975 exhibit a relatively consistent effort to ferret out the most blatant racially exclusionary selection measures, the very persistence of the cases illustrated the limits of the Court's approach. It could review only a small number of jury selection cases each year, and many cases with strong showings of discrimination went unreviewed. In 1943, for example, the Supreme Court declined to review a lower court decision finding no discrimination where the jury roll contained only 3 percent black jurors in a county whose population was 19 percent black.[44] In 1965, the Court refused to review a case in which the lower court had upheld a death penalty for a black man accused of raping a white woman, notwithstanding evidence that the jury list had been marked with a handwritten "c" next to each potential black juror's name.[45] And in 1971 it declined to review a case finding no discrimination in New York City's grand jury list even though, in a city that was 24 percent black and 12 percent Puerto Rican, only 1.65 percent of those summoned for jury service were black and only 0.3 percent were Puerto Rican.[46] The Court's method of case-by-case review was time consuming, factually intensive, and inefficient—in short, an administrative nightmare. The Court may well have been looking for a way out. If so, it found it in an unlikely case, that of Billy Taylor, a white male defendent complaining of discrimination against women jurors.

"A Fair Cross Section"

Like many defendants before him, Billy Taylor, convicted of aggravated kidnapping in 1972, objected to the composition of the jury list from which his jury was chosen. But unlike most defendants, Taylor did not complain that persons of his own race or sex—white men—were excluded, but that women were. Under Louisiana law at the time, women were not placed on the jury roll unless they affirmatively requested in writing that they be listed. As a result, no more than 10 percent of the names on the jury roll were female. Taylor, a man, could not advance a traditional equal protection claim, because such claims were predicated on the harm that a defendant suffered when members of his own race or gender were excluded from the jury that judged him. In any event, in 1961 the Court had unanimously rejected an equal protection challenge to a similar law excusing women from jury service, reasoning that women could be presumptively excused because a "woman is still regarded as the center of home and family life."[47]

Taylor therefore relied on the Sixth Amendment, arguing that its guarantee that he be tried by an "impartial jury" included the right to have a jury selected from a representative cross section of the community. The exclusion of women, he argued, rendered the cross section unrepresentative. The Court agreed, holding that "the selection of a petit jury from a representative cross section of the community is an essential component of the Sixth Amendment right to a jury trial."[48] It found that Louisiana's rule disproportionately excluded women, and therefore violated the Sixth Amendment. The doctrine has since been extended to other "distinctive" groups, including racial and ethnic groups.

There are two significant features to the Sixth Amendment doctrine articulated in *Taylor v. Louisiana*. First, the Court expressly acknowledged, as it had in *Strauder*, that group identity matters. It insisted that although men and women do not necessarily vote as a class, a jury that includes only men is presumptively different from a jury that includes both men and women. Quoting Justice Thurgood Marshall (who was writing about racial exclusion), the Court explained, "It is not necessary to assume that the excluded group will consistently vote as a class in order to conclude, as we do, that its exclusion deprives the jury of a perspective on human events that may have unsuspected importance in any case that may be presented."[49] Thus, the Court's Sixth Amendment doctrine is predicated on race and gender consciousness.

Second, the Court ruled that a Sixth Amendment violation does not require any showing that the state *intentionally* excluded jurors because of their race or gender.[50] A selection process that underrepresents women or blacks violates the Sixth Amendment regardless of whether it was intended to have that effect. Because the doctrine focuses on easily measured effects rather than on the ever-elusive question of intent, the "fair cross section" requirement can be meaningfully enforced. As a result, the Court's Sixth Amendment doctrine has in large measure solved the problem of discrimination in jury roll and venire composition.

The solution, however, is not necessarily stable. Its premise—that race (and sex) matter—is in direct conflict with the principal lesson of the Court's Equal Protection Clause jurisprudence, which insists on

color-blindness and says the state *cannot* take race or sex into account in
selecting a jury. Since *Strauder*, intentional exclusion of jurors from jury
service because of their race or sex violates the Equal Protection Clause.
Yet because it requires a representative result rather than a color-blind
process, the Sixth Amendment creates an incentive for jury commissioners to consider race and gender in selecting jurors for the venire.[51] Thus,
the Sixth Amendment is predicated on, and practically mandates, race
consciousness, while the Fourteenth Amendment prohibits race consciousness and mandates color-blindness. Today's Supreme Court is more
committed to color-blindness than ever before, so much so that it views
race-conscious efforts to assist African Americans with practically the
same skepticism with which it views race-conscious efforts to harm them.
That approach threatens to dismantle affirmative action efforts in employment, education, and voting rights.[52] An equal protection challenge
to race-conscious jury selection measures cannot be far off.[53]

The tension between race consciousness and color-blindness can also
be found in the Court's refusal to extend the Sixth Amendment fair cross-
section principle to the trial jury. In *Taylor*, the Court stressed that the
Sixth Amendment imposes "no requirement that petit juries actually chosen [from jury venires] must mirror the community and reflect the various distinctive groups in the population. Defendants are not entitled to
a jury of any particular composition."[54] It is not obvious why this is so.
The Sixth Amendment on its face guarantees an impartial *jury*, not an
impartial *venire*. A defendant plainly cares more about the actual jury that
judges her case than about the venire from which that jury is chosen. If
representative perspectives of race and gender are important to include in
the jury venire, it would seem even more important to include them on the
actual jury that decides guilt or innocence.

The Court has justified its refusal to extend Sixth Amendment requirements to the trial jury on the ground that "it would be impossible to apply a concept of proportional representation to the petit jury in view of
the heterogeneous nature of our society."[55] But this cannot be a complete
explanation, for in many communities and for particular groups (e.g.,
women), it would probably not be so difficult to apply the fair cross-section
requirement to the trial jury. With respect to sex, for example, trial juries
would simply have to be roughly half women and half men. What makes
extension of the fair cross-section requirement to the petit jury unacceptable is not that it is unworkable, but that it would require the application
of race and gender presumptions to *individuals* rather than *groups*. It is
one thing to say that women as a class generally will offer different perspectives than men; it is another thing to say that a particular individual
juror, because she is female, will do so. Generalizations may be accurate

at a general level, but they begin to look like invidious stereotypes when translated to the specific level of identifiable individuals. The larger numbers of the jury venire permit generalizations; the smaller numbers on the petit jury and the individualized selection process make race and gender consciousness much more problematic.

The Court's ambivalent jury discrimination doctrine reflects the genuine difficulty of constructing fair rules in a world in which, descriptively, race and sex matter, but normatively, they should not. As Andrew Kull laments, "We stand caught between what we can't realistically deny and what we can't afford to admit." [56] It is only because race and sex matter that jury discrimination happens. In a truly race- and gender-blind world, jurors' race and gender would be of no more significance than their eye color, and jury discrimination would not even be a coherent concept. The Sixth Amendment fair cross-section requirement, with its focus on results and its rough requirement of proportionality, has come close to solving the problem of discrimination in jury rolls and venires, but only by effectively requiring that race and sex be consciously taken into account. What remains to be seen is whether a Court committed to the ideology of color-blindness will continue to tolerate such race consciousness.

The Peremptory Challenge

The Sixth Amendment fair cross-section requirement has largely made discrimination in the composition of jury rolls and venires a thing of the past. But that has not eliminated the all-white jury, for one reason: the peremptory challenge. The peremptory challenge allows a party to "strike" a potential juror from the trial jury without offering any explanation. It is used in virtually all jurisdictions as a way to select a trial jury from the larger pool of eligible jurors. Because this challenge requires no explanation, and because it is exercised on the basis of very limited information—often the parties know little more about a prospective juror than the juror's race, sex, age, and perhaps employment—it will almost necessarily be based on stereotyped judgments. Yet the Court expressly condoned race-based peremptory strikes as late as 1965, did not declare them unconstitutional until 1986, and to this day has failed to adopt an effective mechanism for prohibiting them. Thus, for more than a century after the Court held that it was unconstitutional to exclude jurors from a jury venire because of their race, it *permitted* parties to use peremptory challenges to exclude jurors from trial juries on the basis of race. And because it still has not solved the problem of race-based peremptories, the all-white jury endures.

The peremptory challenge serves several legitimate purposes. It gives the parties a direct role in shaping the jury, which theoretically increases their acceptance of verdicts. It allows the parties to strike jurors they believe are biased, but who won't admit their biases sufficiently to support a challenge for cause. And it offers parties a check on judges who may be reluctant to declare potential jurors biased absent extremely strong evidence. But peremptory strikes are notoriously based on stereotypes. Jury selection manuals have been quite candid about this fact. Consider, for example, the following advice from a 1973 Texas prosecutors' manual:

> You are not looking for any member of a minority group which may subject him to oppression—they almost always sympathize with the accused. . . .

> I don't like women jurors because I can't trust them. They do, however, make the best jurors in crimes against children . . .

> Extremely overweight people, especially women and young men, indicates a lack of self-discipline and often times instability. I like the lean and hungry look . . .

> People from small towns and rural areas generally make good State's jurors. People from the east or west coasts often make bad jurors . . .

> Intellectuals such as teachers, etc., generally are too liberal and contemplative to make good State's jurors . . .

> Ask if the venireman has any hobbies or interests that occupy their spare time. Active, outdoors type hobbies indicate the best State's jurors. Hunters always make good State's jurors . . .

> Jewish veniremen generally make poor State's jurors. Jews have a history of oppression and generally empathize with the accused. Lutherans and Church of Christ veniremen usually make good State's jurors.[57]

In a similar vein, the great Clarence Darrow advised defense attorneys to "[n]ever take a wealthy man on a jury. He will convict, unless the defendant is accused of violating the anti-trust law, selling worthless stocks or bonds, or something of that kind."[58] Darrow favored Irishmen, because "I never met [one] who didn't think that someday he might be in trouble himself."[59] Melvin Belli, a renowned trial attorney, advised that "generally a male juror is more sound than a woman juror," especially when the client "is a woman and has those qualities which other women envy—good looks, a handsome husband, wealth, social position," because women "are the severest judges of their own sex."[60]

The effects of the race-based peremptory challenge have long been noted. A *New York Times* reporter wrote in 1935 that "a Negro on a trial jury is as rare as ever in the deep South . . . Negroes can be—and are—easily eliminated by one or both sides through the [peremptory strike]."[61] Professor Douglas Colbert has found that all-white juries remained a staple of American justice in both the North and South from 1935 to 1965, largely because of the peremptory strike.[62] And the Alabama Supreme Court candidly admitted in 1963 that "Negroes are commonly on trial venires but are always struck by attorneys in selecting the trial jury."[63]

In Dallas County, Texas, prosecutors in 100 criminal trials in 1983 and 1984 used the peremptory challenge to strike 405 of 467 eligible black jurors, and struck five times as many black as white jurors.[64] From 1974 to 1981 in several counties in Georgia, one prosecutor used almost 90 percent of his peremptory strikes against black jurors in capital cases with black defendants, and used 94 percent of his strikes against black jurors where the defendant was black and the victim white.[65] Even after the Supreme Court declared race-based peremptory challenges unconstitutional in 1986, prosecutors have continued to strike many prospective black jurors to obtain disproportionately white juries.[66]

The persistence of this practice was confirmed in 1997 with the release of a videotape from a Philadelphia district attorney's training session for prosecutors, in which Jack McMahon, then an assistant district attorney, explicitly advocated that prosecutors strike black jurors because of their race. McMahon advised that

> . . . young black women are very bad. There's an antagonism. I guess maybe they're downtrodden in two respects. They are women and they're black. . . . So they somehow want to take it out on somebody, and you don't want it to be you.

> Let's face it, the blacks from the low-income areas are less likely to convict. I understand it. There's a resentment for law enforcement. There's a resentment for authority. And as a result, you don't want those people on your jury.

> It may appear as if you're being racist, but you're just being realistic. You're just trying to win the case.[67]

This training film was made in 1987, a year after the Supreme Court declared the use of race-based peremptory challenges unconstitutional. More significantly, when McMahon was questioned about it on national television after the videotape was disclosed in 1997, he unapologetically defended the practice as a simple recognition of reality:

> My point is, you have to recognize that people in those communities . . . have different human experiences. And they're less—they've had bad experiences with police. And if you're a prosecutor trying to have them believe police officers, they're going to be less likely to believe a police officer because of their human experience. And you have to recognize that if you're going to be a strong advocate.[68]

Three Philadelphia judges confirmed to local reporters after the McMahon story broke in 1997 that these techniques are still routinely used by both prosecutors and defense counsel.[69] Similarly, Harvard Law Professor Arthur Miller complained that "Jack McMahon is being scapegoated for something that every lawyer in the United States, including those defense lawyers . . . do[es]."[70]

Given such practices, the peremptory challenge means that a racially mixed jury venire can easily produce an all-white trial jury. A minority group will by definition constitute a minority of a representative venire, and often a few peremptory challenges will suffice to eliminate all prospective minority jurors. Yet the Supreme Court did not even take up the issue of race-based peremptory challenges until 1965, at the height of the civil rights movement, and when it did so, it expressly *approved* of them.

Robert Swain, the defendant in *Swain v. Alabama*,[71] was a nineteen-year-old black man accused of raping a seventeen-year-old white woman. He was convicted and sentenced to death by an all-white jury after the prosecutor struck all six prospective black jurors. Represented by the NAACP Legal Defense and Educational Fund's Constance Baker Motley (now a federal judge), Swain showed that no black had ever served on a trial jury in Talladega County, Alabama, where he was tried and convicted, even though blacks comprised more than one-quarter of the county's population. Blacks had been consistently underrepresented on jury venires, but more significantly, black jurors on the venire had been eliminated by peremptory challenges *in every case*.

The Supreme Court was not troubled. It reasoned that the "essential nature of the peremptory challenge is that it is one exercised without a reason stated, without inquiry, and without being subject to the court's control," and therefore the challenge "would no longer be peremptory" if it had to be explained.[72] The Court admitted that peremptory challenges are often based on "'sudden impressions and unaccountable prejudices,'" and on "grounds normally thought irrelevant to legal proceedings or official action, namely . . . race, religion, nationality, occupation or affiliations."[73] But in reasoning that echoed *Plessy v. Ferguson*[74]—which found segregation on trains to be nondiscriminatory because whites were barred from riding with blacks just as blacks were barred from riding with whites—the Court in *Swain* explained that "[i]n the quest for an impartial and qualified jury, Negro and white, Protestant and Catholic, are alike subject to being challenged without cause."[75] Thus, at the height of the civil rights movement, in a case involving the most racially charged of crimes, in a county where peremptory challenges against blacks had been used so successfully that no one could remember a black person ever sitting on a trial jury, the Court expressly approved the practice of race-based exclusion of black jurors.

That remained the law until 1986, when the Supreme Court decided *Batson v. Kentucky*.[76] In a burglary case against a black defendant, the prosecutor struck all four black jurors to obtain an all-white jury. Although the defendant invoked the Sixth Amendment, presumably to avoid the dictates of *Swain*, the Supreme Court resolved his case on equal protection grounds, overruled *Swain*, and held that race-based peremptory challenges violate the Equal Protection Clause. In *Batson*, however, the Court continued its practice, begun in *Strauder*, of pronouncing strong equal protection principles but failing to ensure their realization in practice.

Batson has by all accounts done relatively little to eliminate the use of race-based peremptory strikes for two reasons.[77] First, the Court in *Batson* made it extremely easy for attorneys to recharacterize their race-based peremptory strikes as race neutral after the fact. The essence of the peremptory strike is that it requires no explanation at all, and may be wholly arbitrary. The Court in *Batson* sought to retain as much of the peremptory challenge as possible, while surgically excising those peremptories predicated on race. But under that approach, courts must accept *any* explanation for a challenge that is not race-based, no matter how ridiculous, unless they are willing to brand the prosecutor a liar. Because peremptories need not even be rational, the most irrational reason, if deemed credible, suffices to defeat a *Batson* challenge.

Michael J. Raphael and Edward J. Ungvarsky reviewed all published decisions involving *Batson* challenges from 1986 to January 1992, and concluded that "in almost any situation a prosecutor can readily craft an acceptable neutral explanation to justify striking black jurors because of their race."[78] Courts have accepted explanations that the juror was too old, too young, was employed as a teacher or unemployed, or practiced a certain religion. They have accepted unverifiable explanations based on demeanor: the juror did not make eye contact or made too much eye contact, appeared inattentive or headstrong, nervous or too casual, grimaced or smiled. And they have accepted explanations that might often be correlated to race: the juror lacked education, was single or poor, lived or worked in the same neighborhood as the defendant or a witness, or had previously been involved with the criminal justice system.[79]

As a result of *Batson*'s underenforcement, prosecutors are not shy about continuing to use peremptory strikes against black jurors. Consider the following examples, from Alabama trials in the late 1980s and 1990s:

> the prosecutor in Jesse Morrison's case . . . remove[d] twenty of the twenty-one blacks who had qualified for jury service; twelve of thirteen black venire members were eliminated from Darrell Watkins' capital trial; Earl McGahee had to face an all-white jury after the state removed all sixteen black venire members; David Freeman was convicted and sentenced to death by an all-white panel after the state removed nine of ten prospective black jurors.[80]

The Supreme Court has, if anything, encouraged this trend of accepting any race-neutral rationale after the fact. In *Purkett v. Elem*,[81] the prosecutor offered the following rambling explanation to justify his strikes of two black jurors:

> I struck [juror] number twenty-two because of his long hair. He had long curly hair. He had the longest hair of anybody on the panel by far. He appeared to not be a good juror for that fact, the fact that he had long hair hanging down shoulder length, curly, unkempt hair. Also, he had a mustache and a goatee type beard. And juror number twenty-four also has a mustache and goatee type beard. Those are the only two people on the jury . . . with facial hair. . . . And I don't like the way they looked, with the way the hair is cut, both of them. And the mustaches and the beards look suspicious to me. And number twenty-four had been in a robbery in a supermarket with a sawed-off shotgun pointed at his face, and I didn't want him on the jury as this case does not involve a shotgun, and maybe he would feel to have a robbery you have to have a gun, and there is no gun in this case.[82]

The Court of Appeals for the Eighth Circuit held that the prosecutor's reliance on long hair and facial hair was insufficient because those factors were not plausibly related to "the person's ability to perform his or her duties as a juror." The Supreme Court reversed, holding that *any* racially neutral reason, no matter how fantastic, silly, or superstitious, is sufficient to satisfy the prosecutor's burden, provided that the trial court finds the reason genuine. Although "a trial judge *may choose to disbelieve* a silly or superstitious reason,"[83] if believed, even silly and superstitious reasons suffice to defeat a *Batson* claim.

This standard practically invites after-the-fact rationalizations. As Professor Sheri Johnson has suggested, "[i]f prosecutors exist who . . . cannot create a 'racially neutral' reason for discriminating on the basis of race, bar exams are too easy."[84] Even assuming good faith, attorneys will often exercise race-based judgments without realizing it. As Justice Thurgood Marshall explained,

> A prosecutor's own conscious or unconscious racism may lead him easily to the conclusion that a prospective black juror is 'sullen' or 'distant,' a characterization that would not have come to his mind if a white juror had acted identically. A judge's own conscious or unconscious racism may lead him to accept such an explanation as well supported.[85]

Batson does nothing to address this problem, and is generally ineffective at stopping even blatant racists, as long as they can manufacture a "neutral explanation" after the fact.

The second weakness in the *Batson* inquiry is its deference to trial judges. Because prosecutors should always be able to proffer some race-neutral reason for their strikes, the *Batson* test reduces to a question of credibility: should the prosecutor's asserted neutral reason be accepted as genuine, or is the prosecutor lying to cover up a race-based strike? It is notoriously difficult for an appellate court to second-guess a trial judge's determination on such credibility issues, as the appellate court lacks the benefit of firsthand observation of the prosecutor's demeanor. Reviewing courts therefore defer to the trial court's finding regarding the prosecutor's motive unless the finding is clearly erroneous.[86]

Trial judges are likely to be reluctant to find discrimination. It is no minor matter to find that a fellow officer of the court and representative of the state has *both* lied and acted for discriminatory reasons. In many localities, the prosecutor will have appeared quite often before the same judge, will travel in the same social circles, may well have contributed to the judge's election campaign, and may be personal friends with the judge. Not surprisingly, the vast majority of state trial courts accept prosecutors' "neutral explanations" as genuine, and such findings are only rarely overturned on appeal.[87] As with *Strauder*, the Supreme Court has left enforcement of the equal protection principle it pronounced to those least likely to enforce it effectively.

The peremptory challenge doctrine has allowed the Supreme Court to articulate and enforce a principle of nondiscrimination without incurring the social costs of actually requiring integrated juries in criminal trials. What are those costs today? One might be more hung juries and acquittals. A National Law Journal study of 800 jurors found that where a police officer's and a defendant's stories conflict, 42 percent of whites but only 25 percent of blacks believe that the police officer's version should be credited.[88] Jury studies tend to support attorneys' intuitions that jurors are in general more sympathetic to victims of their own race, and more forgiving of defendants of their own race.[89] In any event, the consistency with which prosecutors strike black jurors in cases against black defendants suggests that they believe race matters to their conviction rates. Race-based peremptory challenges, expressly tolerated until 1986 and tolerated in practice to this day, allow society to maintain the appearance of race neutrality while avoiding the costs of including blacks and other members of minority groups on juries in proportion to their representation in the general population.

Acknowledging That Race Matters

The Supreme Court has never come to terms with the fact that race matters in our culture. Nor has it been willing to confront the full costs of guaranteeing equality in this critical area of the criminal justice system. A better approach would be to acknowledge the contradiction candidly: race matters *and* racial stereotypes are pernicious. Such an approach would not require major revisions of the Court's doctrine, but would require the Court to confront the difficulties and tensions more honestly. The tension can be mediated structurally, by permitting (and even encouraging) race consciousness at the more general level of jury venire selection, and demanding true color-blindness at the petit jury selection stage. The current Sixth Amendment regime, in which significant departures from rough proportionality trigger constitutional review, effectively ensures that jury venires are representative. It often leads to race-conscious decision making on the part of jury commissioners, but taking race into account at this very general level, and for a legitimate purpose, should be permissible. It does minimal damage to the principle of individual treatment, since venires are constructed not through individualized selection but through the use of aggregate data, with respect to which generalizations are both more accurate and less offensive than when applied to individuals. Thus, the Sixth Amendment approach should be maintained, and when the Court faces the inevitable equal protection challenge to a race-conscious venire selection process, it should uphold race-conscious processes so long as they are designed to ensure a representative venire.

At the level of selecting the individuals who will serve on the trial jury, however, racial stereotypes should play no role. Unlike the construction of venires, trial jury selection is by definition an individualized process. The application of race or gender generalizations to individuals in the petit jury selection process offends basic principles of individual treatment. To say so merely restates the principle announced in *Batson*. But if that principle is to be made a reality, the Court must either impose a heightened justification requirement where a pattern of racial strikes has been shown, or eliminate peremptory challenges altogether. Until then, the peremptory strikes will be color-blind in theory only.

Once a pattern of racial strikes has been shown, the Court should require the prosecutor to defend her strikes with reasonable grounds for suspecting that the prospective juror was biased, something akin to the showing required for "for cause" strikes. This approach would retain the benefits of the peremptory challenge, so long as race and other impermissible criteria are avoided. But where a party engages in a pattern of apparently race-based strikes, she would effectively forfeit the benefits of the peremptory strike, and be required to justify her strikes on something approaching a for-cause standard.

If this system does not succeed in halting race-based strikes, the Court should eliminate peremptory strikes altogether. In that event, some adjustment of the current regime of for-cause strikes would be necessary. Under today's strict for-cause standard, judges will strike a prospective juror only if the facts strongly suggest that the juror cannot be fair; because few jurors admit their prejudices, for-cause challenges for bias are rare.[90] If peremptories were eliminated, courts would have to liberalize the for-cause standard; instead of asking whether the juror can be impartial, the judge might ask if the party objecting has reasonable grounds for suspecting that the juror might be biased—a lower standard that would exclude more marginal jurors. It is precisely because it is backed up with the peremptory challenge that the for-cause standard can afford to be so strict. A relaxed for-cause standard could be relatively deferential to the suspicions of counsel, but would nonetheless require counsel to articulate a reason for each strike. Race or sex should of course be an impermissible ground, and courts should engage in heightened scrutiny where rationales appear to be correlated with race or gender. The result would be a process in which, as now, the parties would participate in the shaping of the jury that decides their case, but all suspicious strikes would have to be justified by articulated, noninvidious reasons.

The regime proposed here openly acknowledges that race matters, but at the same time avoids the most pernicious instances of race-based decision making. It admits the tension that the Supreme Court has sought to suppress, and adopts a structural solution as a mediating mechanism. By permitting the consideration of race at the general level of venire creation, we can ensure that jury venires will generally be representative of the ethnic groups in the community. And by rigorously cleansing the trial jury selection process of racial considerations, trial juries should also, on the whole, be representative of the community. Once a representative venire has been constructed, insisting on a color-blind process of selection should not have negative consequences. Without first ensuring such a representative venire, however, insisting on color-blindness will only foster discriminatory results, and lead to still more disproportionately white juries.

One of the traditional explanations for the jury system is that it promotes the acceptability of criminal sanctions by involving the community in the process. If the criminal justice system is to be accepted by the black community, the black community must be represented on juries. The long history of excluding blacks from juries is one important reason why blacks as a class are more skeptical than whites about the fairness of the criminal justice system.[91] But the problem feeds on itself. Because African Americans are more skeptical of the criminal justice system, they are less likely to participate in jury service. And for the same reason, prosecutors are inclined to disfavor those who do volunteer to serve, as Philadelphia prosecutor Jack McMahon's comments illustrate. As long as the criminal justice system disproportionately stops, arrests, tries, and convicts blacks, that skepticism is likely to remain. Thus, even though black participation in the jury system might legitimate the results of the criminal justice system, prosecutors remain suspicious of black jurors as pro-defense, and therefore are inclined to do what they can to keep them off their juries. And so the cycle continues, with exclusion feeding skepticism, and skepticism feeding exclusion.

12

Illegal Racial Discrimination in Jury Selection: A Continuing Legacy

Equal Justice Initiative

Today, peremptory strikes are used to exclude African Americans and other racial minorities from jury service at high rates in many jurisdictions, particularly in the South. In courtrooms across the United States, people of color are dramatically underrepresented on juries as a result of racially biased use of peremptory strikes. This phenomenon is especially prevalent in capital cases and other serious felony cases. Many communities have failed to make juries inclusive and representative of all who have a right to serve.

From 2005 to 2009, in cases where the death penalty has been imposed, prosecutors in Houston County, Alabama, have used peremptory strikes to remove 80% of the African Americans qualified for jury service.[1] As a result, half of these juries were all-white and the remainder had only a single black member, despite the fact that Houston County is 27% African American.

In 2003, the Louisiana Crisis Assistance Center found that prosecutors in Jefferson Parish felony cases strike African American prospective jurors at more than three times the rate that they strike white prospective jurors.[2] Louisiana allows convictions in many cases even if only 10 of 12 jurors believe the defendant is guilty. The high rate of exclusion means that in 80% of criminal trials, there is no effective black representation on the jury because only the votes of white jurors are necessary to convict, even though Jefferson Parish is 23% black.[3]

In the years before and after *Batson*, Georgia prosecutors in the Chattahoochee Judicial Circuit used 83% of their peremptory strikes against African Americans, who make up 34% of the circuit's population.[4] As a result, six black defendants have been tried by all-white juries.[5]

From *Illegal Discrimination in Jury Selection: A Continuing Legacy* (Montgomery, AL: Equal Justice Initiative, 2010), 14–30, 35–41.

In Dallas County, Alabama, the State has used the majority of its peremptory strikes against black potential jurors in 12 reported cases since *Batson* was decided. In those cases, the prosecutor used 157 of 199 peremptory strikes (79%) to eliminate black veniremembers.[6] In cases where the death penalty was imposed, the data shows the Dallas County district attorney used peremptory strikes to exclude 76% of African Americans qualified for jury service.[7]

These extremely high rates of exclusion indicate that, even today, African Americans continue to be denied the right to sit on juries because of their race.

WHY THE PROBLEM CONTINUES

To understand why racial bias in jury selection persists, it is important to understand the framework courts use to analyze claims of discrimination. In *Batson v. Kentucky*,[8] the Supreme Court outlined a three-step process for a defendant to establish that the prosecutor removed jurors based solely on their race. If the defense suspects that the prosecutor's peremptory strikes are racially biased, it must first establish that the prosecutor's actions during jury selection, along with any other relevant circumstances, raise an inference or "prima facie" case of discrimination.[9] The defense may rely on evidence such as the prosecutor's pattern of strikes against veniremembers of color and suspicious questions or statements made by the prosecutor during voir dire.[10] To rebut the inference of discrimination, the prosecutor must then offer nonracial or "race-neutral" explanations for its challenged strikes.[11] This burden is exceedingly low. The Supreme Court has emphasized that the prosecutor's race-neutral reason need not be plausible, let alone persuasive.[12] At the final stage, the trial court must assess all relevant circumstances and determine if the defense has proven that the prosecutor intentionally discriminated against veniremembers of color.[13]

Though *Batson* recognized it is unconstitutional for a prosecutor to exclude even a single juror on the basis of race, the decision fell short of providing the tools to adequately combat racial discrimination during jury selection. Justice Thurgood Marshall, the first of only two African Americans appointed to the Supreme Court, noted in his concurring opinion in *Batson*, "Any prosecutor can easily assert facially neutral reasons for striking a juror, and trial courts are ill equipped to second-guess those reasons."[14]

Experience has borne out Justice Marshall's concerns.[15] In a number of jurisdictions across the country, district attorney's offices have trained prosecutors how to mask their efforts to exclude racial minorities from jury service. Almost immediately after the 1986 *Batson* decision, Philadelphia assistant district attorney Jack McMahon recorded a training session for Pennsylvania prosecutors on how to question African Americans during voir dire in order to later provide race-neutral reasons for their strikes.[16] Similarly, prosecutors in Dallas County, Texas, maintained a decades-long policy of systematically excluding African Americans from jury service in criminal cases and codified it in a training manual.[17] For the district attorney's office in Tuscaloosa County, Alabama, relying on peremptory strikes and other tactics to exclude black potential jurors was "standard operating procedure" and led to African Americans being underrepresented in 70% of the county's criminal trials.[18] Thus, despite *Batson*'s mandate, prosecutors continue to succeed in excluding large numbers of African Americans from jury service.

PROSECUTORS OFTEN ASSERT PRETEXTUAL "RACE-NEUTRAL" REASONS

In cases where the exclusion of African Americans from juries has been challenged, many of the reasons given by prosecutors for striking African American potential jurors obviously are a guise for race-based exclusion of potential jurors.

Sometimes these "race-neutral" reasons explicitly incorporate race. In a recent Louisiana case, the prosecutor said he removed a juror because he was a "single black male with no children."[19] An Alabama prosecutor said he struck African Americans because he wanted to avoid an all-black jury[20] and asserted in other cases that he struck African Americans because he wanted to ensure other jurors, who happened to be white, served on the jury.[21] In a Georgia case, the prosecutor stated he struck a juror because he was black and had a son in an interracial marriage.[22] Faced with such blatantly race-based reasoning, appellate courts in these cases were forced to conclude that these peremptory strikes were the result of illegal racial discrimination. Where the prosecutor's reason does not explicitly mention race, however, enforcement of anti-discrimination law has been much more difficult.

A startlingly common reason given by prosecutors for striking black prospective jurors is a juror's alleged "low intelligence" or "lack of education."[23] Courts have recognized this "is a particularly suspicious explanation given the role that the claim of 'low intelligence' has played in the history of racial discrimination from juries."[24] In several cases, appellate courts have struck down this type of reason because there is no evidence of low intelligence. A federal court reversed an Arkansas conviction where the prosecutor claimed a black juror was illiterate based solely on his statement that he had not read about the case in the newspaper, without ever asking about his reading ability.[25] In other cases, however, strikes based on "low intelligence" have been upheld, including a Louisiana case in which the prosecutor said the excluded black prospective juror was "too stupid to live much less be on a jury."[26]

Prosecutors' other reasons for striking African Americans often correlate strongly with racial stereotypes. Prosecutors frequently claim to strike African Americans because they live in a "high crime area"[27] (meaning a predominantly black neighborhood); are unemployed or receive food stamps;[28] or had a child out of wedlock.[29] These types of reasons are not always recognized as pretexts for discrimination. An Alabama court upheld as race-neutral a prosecutor's strike based on the juror's affiliation with an historically black university.[30] But other courts have struck down as illegal racial discrimination prosecutors' assertions that they struck jurors who believed police sometimes engage in racial profiling[31] and a juror who had filed a civil suit alleging racial discrimination at his job.[32]

Another stereotype-based reason given by prosecutors to justify excluding black jurors is the assumption that the potential jurors are related to other African Americans with similar but very common last names who have been prosecuted by the district attorney's office. Prosecutors chose not to simply ask prospective jurors if they knew individuals involved in other cases before striking them. This behavior has been upheld in some courts and struck down in others as a pretext for discrimination.[33]

Prosecutors frequently justify strikes by making unverifiable assertions about African American potential jurors' appearance and demeanor. In one South Carolina case, the prosecutor stated he struck a black veniremember because he "shucked and jived" as he walked.[34] A Georgia prosecutor explained his removal of a black prospective juror only by vaguely asserting he was unable to "establish a rapport"[35] with the juror.

A Louisiana court allowed the prosecutor to strike a black prospective juror because the prosecutor thought he "looked like a drug dealer."[36] An Arkansas prosecutor was permitted to rely on a "hunch" that an African American would be unfavorable to the State, without asking the juror about her actual views.[37] Courts have upheld the exclusion of black jurors for "race-neutral" reasons such as having dyed red hair[38] and wearing a large white hat and sunglasses.[39]

These thinly veiled excuses for removing qualified African Americans from juries show that many prosecutors have failed to take seriously the Constitution's requirement that every citizen has an equal right to sit on a jury.

APPELLATE COURTS HAVE NOT REVIEWED
CLAIMS OF RACIAL BIAS CONSISTENTLY

Appellate court cases from the Deep South states investigated for this report attest to the undeniable existence of racial discrimination in jury selection. Alabama provides the most disturbing example, as racially tainted jury selection required reversal of over 80 trials, nearly 98% of which were criminal cases.[40] Alabama's "struck-jury system"[41] makes racially discriminatory use of peremptory strikes much more common. In Alabama, there is no prescribed limit on peremptory strikes in criminal cases. The parties strike down to a jury from the veniremembers that remain after for-cause challenges. This process requires the parties to alternate their strikes of veniremembers until only 12 individuals remain.[42] Alabama's process maximizes the potential exposure of its citizens to discriminatory strikes.

But other states are not far behind. In Florida, 33 criminal convictions have been invalidated because the prosecutor struck jurors based on race. The highest state courts in Mississippi and Arkansas, with ten reversals each, have openly acknowledged that racial discrimination in jury selection has remained widespread since *Batson*.[43] Louisiana has seen 12 criminal verdicts reversed because prosecutors violated *Batson*, including in a recent decision from the United States Supreme Court.[44] Georgia, with eight *Batson* reversals in criminal cases, similarly has struggled to eliminate race-biased jury selection by prosecutors. The clear outlier in this analysis is Tennessee, whose appellate courts have never granted *Batson* relief in a criminal case.[45] This anomaly can be traced to defense attorneys' failure to object properly to prosecutors' racially biased strikes—making it harder for reviewing courts to review prosecutors' behavior—and a reluctance by appellate judges to find racial bias when claims are presented.[46]

Most *Batson*-related reversals came immediately following the decision. During this period, prosecutors frequently offered blatantly race-based reasons for their strikes. In *Goggins v. State*,[47] a Mississippi case decided two years after *Batson*, the prosecutor admitted he struck two African American potential jurors from serving in an armed robbery trial because he had been instructed to do so at a training course on jury selection.

Congdon v. State[48] dealt with a prosecutor in a murder case who struck all four African Americans in the venire because they lived in Ringgold, Georgia. The prosecutor based his strikes on the advice of Ringgold's sheriff, who testified he had a troubled relationship with some members of the town's African American community and was uncomfortable with any of his town's black residents serving on the jury. In the Louisiana case of *State v. Lewis*,[49] the appellate court reversed a conviction for cocaine distribution after the prosecutor acknowledged he struck an African American juror in order to seat a white juror.

Several Alabama cases display similarly unnerving expressions of racial bias. At a federal court hearing to review a capital murder conviction, a Birmingham prosecutor admitted his office followed a policy of striking African Americans because of their race.[50] A Montgomery County prosecutor confessed in response to a *Batson* motion that he struck a 23-year-old black male veniremember for fear that "he might assimilate [sic] with the [African American] defendant . . . [and] there were no other young black males that I could see on the jury venire."[51] In *McCray v. State*, a capital case in Houston County, the prosecutor used seven strikes to remove African Americans because "if I hadn't have [sic], we would have had an all black jury."[52]

Such unvarnished racial bias drove the higher rate of reversals in the few years following *Batson*, though comparably extreme cases have arisen in recent years.[53] Unfortunately, these glaring violations may have distracted courts from the necessity of policing more embedded forms of racial bias, while simultaneously suggesting to *Batson*-weary prosecutors the level of savvy necessary to avoid detection. The lower rate of reversals following this initial period can be attributed to prosecutors carefully disguising their racial bias, a practice regrettably abetted by trial and appellate courts' abdication of their duty to combat racial discrimination in the justice system.

Exacerbating this problem is that, when appellate courts find that the State has illegally excluded people of color from jury service, prosecutors face few, if any, personal consequences for their malfeasance. Prosecutors who engage in illegal racial discrimination rarely receive public scrutiny, which leaves the general public ignorant that their district attorney's office has intentionally excluded African Americans from jury service. Perhaps because of this silence, repeat violators of *Batson* remain in office—like the district attorney for Montgomery County, Alabama. The Alabama Supreme Court has criticized her office's history of racial discrimination and state and federal appellate courts have reversed her cases 13 times for *Batson* violations, but she remains in office.[54] In Houston County, Alabama, the district attorney's office continues to secure all-white or nearly all-white juries in capital cases despite five *Batson* reversals by the Alabama courts in just a seven-year period from 1991 to 1998.[55] Similarly, the district attorney in Jefferson Parish, Louisiana, has retained his position despite five *Batson* reversals since his initial election in 1996.[56]

Continued tenure by prosecutors who have demonstrated racial bias reveals an indifference to racial discrimination in jury selection that allows it to persist. Absent vigilant enforcement of *Batson* by the courts, citizens of color are left powerless to combat their deliberate exclusion from the justice system.

VARIATION AMONG STATE COURTS

The states analyzed for this report are addressing claims of racially biased jury selection in a variety of ways. Although in every state there is evidence of general indifference to the seriousness of excluding people from jury service based on race and of impunity for discriminatory actors who rarely are held accountable for bias, some states seem particularly resistant to enforcing every citizen's right to serve on a jury. Moreover, courts are inconsistent and can be skeptical about the presence of racial bias even when the history and evidence strongly suggest that relief should be granted. As techniques to avoid detection of discriminatory practices have grown more sophisticated, so has the need grown for greater accountability from prosecutors, trial judges, and appellate courts that review claims of racially discriminatory jury selection and too often tolerate racial bias.

NEAR-TOTAL DEFERENCE TO PROSECUTORS IN TENNESSEE

More than 100 criminal defendants have raised *Batson* claims on appeal in Tennessee, but this state's courts have *never* reversed a criminal conviction because of racial discrimination during jury selection. While this might seem to indicate that Tennessee is free from race discrimination, the reality is that proving discrimination in Tennessee is extraordinarily difficult because state courts tend to accept at face value prosecutors' explanations for striking jurors of color—even reasons that are implausible or not supported by the record. In the 2007 case of *State v. Hill*, the prosecutor struck all but one African American, leaving a black man to be tried by a nearly all-white jury.[57] The prosecutor claimed he struck one African American man because he was "not very bright" and "went on some diatribe" during voir dire. The appellate court found no such "diatribe" in the record, but still upheld the case.[58] In a similarly disturbing case from 2006, *State v. Tyler*, the prosecutor struck only African Americans, and both the trial and appellate courts accepted his explanation that he struck one black juror for being "tentative and timid" and another for wearing a large hat and sunglasses.[59] These cases demonstrate a failure by Tennessee courts to critically evaluate whether a prosecutor's explanations are mere pretexts for discrimination and a tendency, instead, to accept almost any reason that is not openly or concededly discriminatory.

BUILDING BLOCKS FOR MEANINGFUL REVIEW IN FLORIDA

Florida has crafted unique provisions under its own state laws to protect jurors from racial discrimination. Indeed, Florida law is more protective than federal anti-discrimination law in several respects. Once a prosecutor has given a race-neutral reason for striking a particular juror, Florida judges must assess whether the reason is "genuine" by considering factors such as whether (1) the prosecutor actually questioned the excluded juror; (2) the juror was singled out during voir dire or manipulated into providing answers that would tend to disqualify him from jury service; (3) the prosecutor's reason for the strike was related to the facts of the case, and (4) other jurors gave similar answers but were not struck. Under Florida law, the prosecutor's reason for the strike *must be supported by the record*, which makes it much harder for the prosecutor to manufacture explanations after the fact.[60] Florida's rule stands in stark contrast with states like Tennessee where prosecutors are allowed to rely on reasons that are not supported by the record.

Florida's protections effectively discourage overt discrimination in jury selection, but the state is far from perfect. In recent years, Florida courts in a fair number of cases have failed to recognize shocking examples of racial discrimination in jury selection.[61] Relative to its Southern neighbors, though, Florida's state law framework creates a much better environment for remedying racial discrimination in jury selection.

ONGOING PROBLEMS IN LOUISIANA

Historically, Louisiana has not been particularly receptive to jury discrimination claims. A recent United States Supreme Court decision criticizing the state courts' failure to carefully scrutinize a prosecutor's exclusion of African American jurors highlighted the problems of racially biased jury selection there. In 2008, the Court decided *Snyder v. Louisiana*, in which a black college student was excluded from jury service along with all other African Americans in the venire.[62] The Court found the prosecutor's asserted reason for striking the student—he "looked nervous" and was concerned the trial might interfere with his student teaching obligations—was a pretext for discrimination, and it implicitly recognized that Louisiana courts failed to appropriately scrutinize the prosecutor's explanation.[63] Since *Snyder*, the Louisiana Supreme Court has reversed a case after finding racial bias in jury selection.[64] However, that court also reinstated a conviction after an intermediate court had found illegal discrimination in jury selection.[65] While there are signs that courts in Louisiana have become slightly more attentive to discrimination claims since

Snyder, a great deal of work clearly is needed to effectively deter and eliminate racially biased jury selection in this state.

CONTINUED RACIAL DISCRIMINATION IN MISSISSIPPI, GEORGIA, AND ARKANSAS

The Mississippi Supreme Court has recognized that racial discrimination in jury selection continues to be a serious problem in Mississippi. In 2007, the court expressed frustration that "attorneys of this State persist in violating the principles of *Batson* by racially profiling jurors" and found that "racially-motivated jury selection is still prevalent twenty years after *Batson* was handed down."[66] The court threatened to change its system of peremptory challenges if things did not improve.[67] Among other remedies, it would consider limiting the number of peremptory strikes or enhancing voir dire.[68]

It is encouraging that the Mississippi Supreme Court has acknowledged the problem, admitted that *Batson* has not ended juror discrimination, and proposed other remedies. But Mississippi courts continue to credit highly dubious explanations for prosecutor's exclusion of jurors of color. In a 2008 case where the prosecutor used his first eight peremptory challenges against African Americans, Mississippi courts credited the prosecutor's claim that he struck two black jurors because they had "only" a twelfth-grade education and struck an African American engineer because she was "inattentive" and dyed her hair.[69] In another 2008 case, state courts accepted a prosecutor's explanation that he excluded an African American woman because she had lived in the county for "only" 22 months and did not make eye contact with him and that he struck a black information technology specialist because he might blame the state for the lack of audio and video evidence in the case.[70] The deference given to these prosecutors reveals that, despite the Mississippi Supreme Court's strong language regarding the need to end juror discrimination, the state's trial and appellate courts are failing to exercise meaningful oversight.

Individuals seeking to raise *Batson* claims in Georgia face even higher barriers to relief. It is particularly difficult to show that a poor person has been the victim of racial discrimination in Georgia because state courts have upheld strikes based on income-related characteristics, such as a juror's place of residence, perceived lack of education, and perceived lack of employment history. In *Smith v. State,* Georgia courts accepted the prosecutor's explanation that he struck two African American jurors because they lived in public housing projects with prevalent gang activity and might be prejudiced against state witnesses who were gang members.[71]

In the 2005 case of *Taylor v. State*, the prosecutor used all five peremptory strikes to remove African Americans from the jury, explaining that he struck people who lacked education or work experience, and that one juror also "seemed odd."[72] Georgia courts upheld this explanation as race-neutral, noting that the one African American who served on the jury was a college student, consistent with the prosecutor's stated desire for a well-educated jury. The court did not explain why jurors needed such a high level of education to sit on a straightforward case in which the defendant was accused of robbing and shooting a man he believed had raped his girlfriend.[73] Georgia courts' willingness to uphold strikes based on residence in a particular neighborhood, a perceived lack of education, or a perceived lack of employment history provides a shield for prosecutors to strike poor people and may lead to the disproportionate exclusion of people of color from juries.

Arkansas similarly is resistant to successful *Batson* claims, and Arkansas law has several features which make it particularly difficult to prove racial discrimination in jury selection. First, an Arkansas court typically will credit a prosecutor's explanation for a peremptory strike even when the strike is based on information known only to the prosecutor's office which cannot be verified by the record.[74] In *Thornton v. State*, the prosecutor claimed to have struck a juror because of a "hunch" that the juror was related to a criminal defendant in another case, and this strike was upheld as race-neutral.[75] In several other cases, Arkansas courts have accepted strikes of African American jurors based in part on a prosecutor's descriptions of the jurors' demeanor, body language, tone, or other amorphous characteristic that cannot be disproved by the record.[76] Finally, Arkansas courts repeatedly have found that the presence of any African American on a jury is strong evidence that the prosecution has not engaged in racial discrimination.[77] This overly simplistic approach ignores Supreme Court precedent holding that the presence of a single African American juror does not disprove discriminatory intent on the part of the prosecutor,[78] and that removing even a single juror on the basis of race violates the Equal Protection Clause.[79] Moreover, when coupled with the Arkansas courts' deference to prosecutors and acceptance of peremptory strikes not supported by the record, it effectively exempts prosecutors from any meaningful review of peremptory strikes.

THE ROLE OF DISPARATE TREATMENT IN ALABAMA AND SOUTH CAROLINA

Throughout the South, a common method of demonstrating racial discrimination in jury selection is to show that the prosecutor treated jurors of color differently from similarly situated white jurors.[80] When the prosecution claims it struck an African American juror for a race-neutral reason—such as the juror's industry or profession—but does not strike white jurors who share the same characteristic, this "disparate treatment" provides strong evidence of discrimination.[81] Disparate treatment may be the only sign as to whether a prosecutor's explanation for a peremptory strike is genuine.

Alabama and South Carolina take opposite approaches to *Batson* challenges based on disparate treatment. South Carolina initially refused to uphold reasons for striking black jurors that applied equally to whites,[82] but in the early 1990s the South Carolina Supreme Court retreated from enforcement of anti-discrimination laws. In *Sumpter v. State*, that court considered the prosecutor's strike of a black veniremember who had a "prior DUI involvement" in light of evidence that the prosecutor did not strike a white juror with a DUI conviction.[83] The court upheld the strike as race-neutral, noting the African American juror's case, but not the white juror's case, was handled by the same prosecutor's office.[84] In *State v. Dyar*, the prosecutor claimed he struck an African American because he had prosecuted the potential juror, but did not strike two white jurors who also had criminal charges.[85] The South Carolina Supreme Court again upheld the strike, accepting the prosecutor's explanation that, unlike the white jurors, he personally prosecuted the black juror.[86] In dissent, two justices wrote, "It does not require a deep analysis to realize that today's rule is fraught with enough practical problems to render a defendant powerless to counter invidious discrimination."[87] The dissent called this departure from South Carolina precedent "alarming."[88] Indeed, no criminal defendant has won a *Batson* challenge in the state since 1992.

Alabama courts, in contrast, have been reluctant to grant *Batson* relief in recent years *without* evidence of disparate treatment.[89] This has meant that even when a prosecutor uses all or almost all of his or her peremptory strikes to exclude people of color, Alabama courts often refuse to find a *Batson* violation unless a clear case can be made that an excluded African American veniremember was similarly situated to a white juror. In the 2008 case of *Floyd v. State*,[90] the prosecutor peremptorily struck 10 of 11 African Americans in the venire; the black defendant was tried by an all-white jury with one African American alternate juror. When asked to explain his peremptory strikes, the prosecutor asserted he struck one juror because of her body language and demeanor, struck another juror because she was quiet during voir dire, and could not fully recall the reason for a third strike.[91] Finding no disparate treatment, the Alabama courts accepted these reasons as race-neutral even though the prosecutor had excluded a shocking number of African Americans from Mr. Floyd's jury.[92]

It is clear that, without greater consistency and commitment to enforcing anti-discrimination laws, racially discriminatory use of peremptory strikes will continue. Lack of enforcement is a primary reason why exclusion of people of color from juries remains widespread in nearly all of the states studied for this report.

Race Discrimination's Other Victims: Jurors Wrongly Excluded

Racial discrimination in jury selection violates the constitutional rights of the jurors themselves. In *Powers v. Ohio*,[93] the United States Supreme Court held that jurors have a right not to be excluded based on their race, yet race-based exclusion continues to stigmatize growing numbers of Americans. EJI staff interviewed scores of people of color who had been excluded from jury service across the Southeast to document the impact of discrimination on citizens denied the right to serve. These African American citizens dutifully reported for jury service only to be turned away because their race created a false presumption that they could not be fair, could not follow the law, or are somehow unworthy for full civic life. Many had overcome the legacy of the Jim Crow South to serve in the military, own businesses, and send their children to college, only to find discrimination still as close as their county courthouse.

The sting of mistreatment can linger for years. Byron Minnieweather was wrongly struck in 2004 and has since moved away from his hometown of Columbia, Mississippi. Memories of the racially charged trial still trouble him. He told EJI, "It was my civil right to participate as a juror."

Excluded jurors and their families spoke about suffering shame and humiliation as a result of false inferences that criminal activity made them unfit to serve. In Montgomery County, Mississippi, Vickie Curry was illegally struck by a prosecutor who claimed her husband had a felony record.[94] The prosecutor mistook her husband for someone else, and the falsehood resurfaces each time the case appears in media reports. Charles Curry, retired from the National Guard after 23 years of service, is deeply disturbed that the district attorney suggested he does not respect the law. This common tactic thoughtlessly tarnishes the reputations of African Americans living lives of quiet decency. A prosecutor in Talladega County, Alabama, sought to characterize Ruth Garrett, a deeply religious woman who works as a school bus driver, as unfit for jury service because she was related to criminals.[95] In fact, Mrs. Garrett had never met the family who shared her last name, but the prosecutor never bothered to ask her.

Another common theme among illegally struck jurors is the sad recognition that their individual experiences were small pieces in the structure of racism that envelops their communities. "I'm not surprised because that's how the system is around here," said Gerald Mercer, who was struck from a Russell County, Alabama, jury because he had traffic tickets and expressed hesitation about the death penalty, while white jurors with similar circumstances remained on the jury.[96] "They do a lot of stuff around here that is unequal justice." Vickey Brown was illegally struck from a jury in Houston County, Alabama, by a prosecutor who admitted he wanted to avoid "an all-black jury."[97] Although Mrs. Brown had encountered racist treatment in job interviews, she was particularly offended at the district attorney's suggestion that she would be lenient on a black defendant because she is black. "I was shocked when I found out," she said. Alice Branham, a 31-year veteran of the Florida Department of Corrections, was illegally struck from a jury in Jefferson County, Florida. When forced to provide a race-neutral reason for excluding her, the prosecutor noted only her work for the State.[98] Ms. Branham was so accustomed to institutional racism that she had no idea this was a violation of her rights. After all, when she started working for the prison system, her supervisor informed her he did not like black people, and only grew to accept her after she started bringing homemade cookies and collard greens to the office.

For many excluded black jurors, the pretexts provided to refute claims of discrimination add another layer of injury. A Baldwin County, Alabama, prosecutor characterized potential juror Allen Mason as "not very well educated" and having "difficulty understanding the concepts that the state asked him" even though Mr. Mason answered every question, "Yes, sir" or "No, sir," and clearly explained his beliefs.[99] Nearly 20 years later, Mr. Mason grew emotional as he recalled how the prosecutor's racist actions made him feel unworthy. Elsewhere, prosecutors have countered *Batson* claims by describing African Americans in the jury pool as inattentive, unresponsive, or hostile.[100] Black men have been struck for wearing jeans or an earring.[101] A Mobile, Alabama, prosecutor claimed he struck Carolyn Hall because "she works at a retarded place" and he did not want jurors who were sympathetic to the disadvantaged.[102] While Mrs. Hall remains committed to the mentally disabled people she cares for, she told EJI staff that her work would not have affected her ability to be fair. [. . .]

Additional Barriers to Representative Juries

In addition to peremptory strikes, other mechanisms work to keep juries unlawfully homogenous. The jury in a particular case is drawn from a larger pool of potential jurors, and frequently this pool (or "jury box") does not adequately reflect the entire community. Underrepresentation in the jury pool creates yet another barrier to jury service among people of color, women, and other minorities.

UNDERREPRESENTATION OF RACIAL MINORITIES IN JURY POOLS

The Constitution requires that the jury pool be fairly representative of the community.[103] The process for selecting the jury pool must not systematically exclude any cognizable group.[104] A group is cognizable when it is sufficiently distinctive from the rest of society.[105] Women and African Americans are cognizable groups.[106] Such groups also include other racial or ethnic minorities, daily wage earners, and unregistered voters.[107] Despite the Supreme Court's long-established rule requiring the jury pool to fairly reflect the community, disparities between the racial makeup of the jury pool and the community persist.

The problem stems in part from the way courts evaluate whether a particular group is underrepresented in the jury pool. Courts generally look at the difference between the percentage of a particular group in the community and the percentage of that group in the pool, often called the "absolute disparity."[108] Historically, courts have required an absolute disparity of greater than 10% to find a group is underrepresented.[109] The absolute disparity actually reveals little about the degree of underrepresentation because it does not show how large a portion of the cognizable group is being excluded.

Given that it fails to take into account the size of the excluded group, use of the absolute disparity test may permit almost complete exclusion of small groups, while invalidating moderate underrepresentation of large groups. Indeed, if a group constitutes less than 10% of the population, the 10% absolute disparity requirement allows even the most blatant and intentional exclusion of every member of that group to go unremedied.[110] This means it is impossible for African Americans to challenge underrepresentation in 75% of counties in the United States.[111] For Latinos and Asian Americans, such challenges are impossible in more than 90% of counties, and for other people of color this constitutional protection is practically non-existent.[112]

A better method for measuring underrepresentation is to divide the absolute disparity by the percentage of the group in the broader community. This ratio is referred to as the "comparative disparity" and reveals the percentage of the cognizable group that is excluded, ranging from 0% (perfect representation) to 100% (total exclusion).[113] The comparative disparity test may overstate the significance of disparities where the total population of a cognizable group is very small, such that a difference of only a few individuals can create a large disparity.[114] But such situations are not difficult to identify, and comparative disparity remains the only method to accurately measure the degree of underrepresentation. Although the comparative disparity reveals much more than the absolute disparity about whether a jury pool fairly represents the community, few courts have embraced it and some have explicitly mandated exclusive use of the absolute disparity test.[115]

Unfortunately, the Supreme Court recently declined an opportunity to make clear that the comparative disparity should be considered in determining whether a group is underrepresented in the jury pool.[116] In *Berghuis v. Smith*, the Court rejected a challenge to a jury pool with an 18% comparative disparity in the representation of African Americans because it found the African American defendant (who had been convicted by an all-white jury) had not presented sufficient evidence that a particular practice used by the county had caused the underrepresentation.[117] In the wake of *Berghuis*, even where significant underrepresentation persists, it remains difficult to remedy.

EXCUSING JURORS "FOR CAUSE"

The composition of the jury pool also may be affected greatly by the way each jurisdiction decides whom to excuse from jury service. States set statutory qualifications for jury service and judges also excuse jurors from serving if it would be a hardship for the juror. The youngest and oldest members of the community are often excluded. In some states, the minimum age for jury service is 21, even as increasingly younger children are facing criminal jury trials.[118] Many states also exempt individuals over age 70 from jury service, even if they are able to serve.[119]

Other exemptions tend to deny people with low incomes the opportunity to serve on a jury.[120] Individuals who work for an hourly wage cannot afford to miss work because they will not get paid. Parents who are the sole caregivers for their children cannot serve unless they have access to affordable child care. People living in poverty often are unable to obtain transportation, or their addresses are not current in court files, so they do not receive a summons or appear in court unless additional efforts are made to serve them.

Only rarely do lawyers seek an order to provide accommodations to low-income prospective jurors, such as providing child care or other assistance. As a result, many poor and low-income people and parents without child care options never serve on a jury and an important perspective is excluded from civil and criminal proceedings.

The Perceived and Actual Integrity of
the Criminal Justice System

Excluding racial minorities from juries causes serious collateral consequences: the credibility, reliability, and integrity of the criminal justice system is compromised when there is even an appearance of bias and discrimination. Communities of color across the country have rejected and continue to reject criminal verdicts handed down by all- or predominantly white juries. During the 1980s, race riots twice erupted in Miami after all-white juries acquitted police officers charged with shooting African American men. In 1980, an all-white jury acquitted four white Dade County policemen in the beating death of Arthur McDuffie, a black insurance salesman.[121] The trial had been moved to Tampa in order to give the defendants "a fair trial."[122] The all-white jury's acquittal of the officers outraged people of color in Miami and triggered violent unrest. Riots lasted for three days and left 18 people dead and $200 million in property damage.[123] A biracial committee appointed by the Governor of Florida later concluded the riots resulted from "racism and the blacks' perception of racism."[124]

In 1984, another all-white jury acquitted police officer Luis Alvarez in the shooting death of Nevell Johnson, Jr., in Miami.[125] Protests began after the police shooting, and though there was less violence, unrest after the verdict led to hundreds of arrests.[126] One community leader reported, "[t]he community has gotten to the point where it expects an all-white jury when we have this kind of killing."[127]

Perhaps the best known example of racial conflict and violence after a verdict by a non-diverse jury is the 1992 Los Angeles Riots. The trial of one of the white police officers accused of beating Rodney King, a black man, was moved from Los Angeles to majority-white, rural Simi Valley.[128] No African Americans served on the jury, comprised of ten whites, one Asian American, and one Latino.[129] The jury's verdict finding police not guilty of excessive force in a beating that lasted 81 seconds and included 56 blows[130] led to three days of violent protests, 60 deaths, more than 16,000 arrests, and almost $1 billion in property damage.[131]

More recently, an all-white jury acquitted a white former Hartford, Connecticut, police detective who shot and killed Jashon Bryant, 18, and injured Brandon Henry, 21, African American youths from Hartford's predominantly black North End.[132] A police investigation revealed that Bryant and Henry were unarmed at the time of the shooting.[133] The acquittal brought shock and outrage from the victims' families and demonstrations by community members questioning the legitimacy of the verdict and the judicial process.[134] The *Hartford Courant* reported that "[t]he case stirred lingering frustration and mistrust of police and the criminal justice system among residents of the city's North End, including questions about why no minorities were selected for the jury."[135]

While acquittals might have been produced by juries that fairly represented African Americans and other racial minorities, the absence of diversity makes a questionable jury verdict unacceptable. In Long Island, New York;[136] Jena, Louisiana;[137] Powhatan, Virginia;[138] Panama City, Florida;[139] and Milwaukee, Wisconsin,[140] recent verdicts by all-white juries or by juries perceived as unrepresentative have triggered widespread unrest and outrage in poor and minority communities where serious concerns about the fairness and reliability of the justice system have emerged.

Social science research helps to explain these and other examples from around the country of community rejection of criminal verdicts handed down by unrepresentative juries. As a general matter, people are willing to accept the legitimacy of an authority and defer to the decisions made by that authority when they perceive the decision-making procedures as fair.[141] Conversely, decisions seen as the result of an unfair—biased, dishonest, or inconsistent—process are more likely to be rejected.[142] This is true of people's perceptions of jury verdicts in criminal cases.

Research has shown that observers are more likely to conclude that a trial is unfair when an all-white jury finds a defendant guilty.[143] Token representation by minorities is similarly inadequate to address the problem. African Americans serving on white-dominated juries—especially when they are in a "minority of one"—are more likely to remain quiet and give in to the pressures of the majority.[144] The few African Americans who actually manage to serve on capital juries may be "especially discontented with their own experiences" and critical of the jury's deliberative process.[145]

Beyond perceptions about the criminal trial process and the negative experience of lone minority jurors, the racial composition of juries also influences the reliability of outcomes. In death penalty cases, the absence of diversity appears to shape sentencing outcomes, making them less reliable and credible.[146] The effect is greater for nonwhite defendants, especially when the defendant is black and the victim is white.[147]

Research suggests that, compared to diverse juries, all-white juries tend to spend less time deliberating, make more errors, and consider fewer perspectives.[148] Moreover, even though bifurcated capital trials require separate deliberations regarding guilt/innocence and sentencing, it is not uncommon for all-white juries to decide on punishment during guilt/innocence deliberations, before they have heard any mitigation evidence.[149]

The nature and quality of jury deliberations is better when jury diversity is greater:[150]

By every deliberation measure . . . heterogeneous groups outper-
formed homogeneous groups. First, diverse groups spent more time
deliberating than did all-White groups . . . us[ing] their extra time
productively, discussing a wider range of case facts and personal
perspectives. . . . Even though they deliberated longer and discussed
more information, diverse groups made fewer factual errors than
all-White groups. Moreover inaccuracies were more likely to be cor-
rected in diverse groups. . . . [D]iverse groups were also more open-
minded in that they were less resistant to discussions of controversial
race-related topics.[151]

Racial diversity significantly improves a jury's ability to assess the reliability and credibility of witness testimony, evaluate the accuracy of
cross-racial identifications, avoid presumptions of guilt, and fairly judge
a criminally accused.[152] Accordingly, the reliability and accuracy of the
criminal justice system is greatly enhanced when juries represent a fair
cross-section of the community as the Constitution requires.[153]

Part VI

Sentencing: Does Time Come in Different Colors?

To paraphrase Winston Churchill, how a society punishes the guilty is the clearest measure of its morality. The difference between being locked behind prison walls or staying outside on probation is vast. The death penalty, of course, belongs to a category of its own.

When judges pass sentence, the law lets them—indeed requires them—to consider any and all information about the criminals who appear before them and the crimes they have committed. The jury, which by law must decide whether or not to impose the death penalty, likewise hears both mitigating and aggravating factors, as presented by lawyers, victims, relatives, psychologists, and the like. Sentencing eliminates the criminal justice system's separation of the case's facts from the people involved. This amounts to open season for discretion. Moreover, judges and juries sentencing criminals do not need to explain the sentences they give. Pity or hostility may not be provided in the law as reasons for a sentence, but it is almost always impossible to discern and correct an impermissible reason.

In light of these realities, race ends up making a striking difference in the sentences that people receive. While this may be no surprise, *how* race figures into sentencing is not a simple matter. To the jury condemning a defendant to death, the race of the victim is more important than the race of the defendant. Judges, as it turns out, are influenced by the facial features of the defendants they sentence even more than by their race.[1]

As we have seen, the law is always struggling with discretion, relying on it as a companion but trying to control it as a wanderer. When it comes to sentencing, the trend over recent years has been to keep judges from being too forgiving by forcing them to apply minimum terms of incarceration or, in the case of third offenses, mandatory life imprisonment. This

trend, for reasons explained in the following selections, has disproportionately affected black defendants. Sentencing is a key part of the racial
skewing of our criminal justice system.

The Sentencing Project is a twenty-five-year-old organization that describes itself as "working for a fair and effective criminal justice system
by promoting reforms in sentencing law and practice, and alternatives to
incarceration." It conducts research and issues reports on trends in criminal justice and offers a clearinghouse on race and justice at http://www
.sentencingproject.org/clearinghouse/. Its July 2009 report by Ashley Nellis and Ryan S. King, *No Exit: The Expanding Use of Life Sentences in America*,
details how racial disparity in incarceration continues and indeed height-
ens as sentences grow longer. As the report shows, young black Americans
disproportionately receive life sentences.[2]

Peculiar Institution: America's Death Penalty in an Age of Abolition by David
Garland attempts to explain why the death penalty persists in the United
States despite having been abolished in all other Western nations. A New
York University law professor and preeminent scholar of capital punishment, Garland brings history, politics, and sociology to bear on this question. He explains that the question is even more interesting, since the U.S.
Supreme Court at one point had abolished the death penalty, in its 1972
decision *Furman v. Georgia*. The infrequency and unpredictability of the
application of the ultimate sanction indicate to Garland that it is less a
criminal justice measure than a political strategy. He explains that its restoration, starting with the 1976 decision *Gregg v. Georgia*, coincided with a
backlash against the civil rights movement, signifying that race may be a
key player in the national drama of executing our own. That black Americans once again are disproportionately sentenced to death suggests that the
American sense of who exactly comprises "our own" may not be so simple.

Further Reading: David Cole, in *No Equal Justice* (described in the introduction to Part V), uses a famous death penalty case to describe how race infects
the sentencing process. In the case of *McCleskey v. Kemp*, the U.S. Supreme
Court upheld the death penalty against a challenge of widespread racial
discrimination. As Cole sees it, the decision was based on basic pragmatism:
the Supreme Court found any way it could to prevent regular challenges to
criminal sentences, based on the obvious disadvantages that black defendants experience throughout the criminal justice process. The law has now
created an ironic and bewildering standard by which a black person must
prove that he received unfair treatment because of his race, but may not rely
on the fact that such racial discrimination is widespread—as though only he
had been a victim of bias against a whole group. Cole also explains other sentencing practices that have contributed to racial disparity in incarceration.

13

No Exit: The Expanding Use of
Life Sentences in America

Ashley Nellis and Ryan S. King

Growth in Life Sentences

Every state has provisions for sentencing people to prison for the remainder of their lives for some types of crimes. While life and life without parole (LWOP) sentences have long been incorporated into sentencing policy, the frequency with which they have been used has increased dramatically during the last 20 years as sentencing statutes, prosecutorial practices, and parole policies have evolved in a more punitive direction. In particular, support for the expansion of LWOP sentences grew out of the same mistrust of the judicial process that birthed sentencing guidelines, mandatory minimums, and "truth-in-sentencing" laws to restrict parole eligibility. These policies have often been politically inspired and fueled by accounts of people sentenced to life, often for violent crimes, being released on parole within a decade. Public dissatisfaction was part of a larger movement toward more legislative control of the criminal justice process at the expense of the discretion of judges and parole boards. The expansion of LWOP sentencing in particular was intended to ensure that "life means life."

While every state provides for life sentences, there is a broad range in the severity and implementation of the statutes. In six states—Illinois, Iowa, Louisiana, Maine, Pennsylvania, and South Dakota—and the federal system, all life sentences are imposed without the possibility of parole.[1] Only Alaska provides the possibility of parole for all life sentences, while the remaining 43 states have laws that permit sentencing most defendants to life with or without parole.

In the case of life sentences with the possibility of parole, the range of time that must be served prior to eligibility for release varies greatly, from

From *No Exit: The Expanding Use of Life Sentences in America* (Washington, DC: The Sentencing Project, 2009), 5–24.

under 10 years in Utah and California to 40 and 50 years in Colorado and Kansas.[2] The median length of time served prior to parole eligibility nationally is in the range of 25 years.[3] However, eligibility does not equate to release and, owing to the reticence of review boards and governors, it has become increasingly difficult for persons serving a life sentence to be released on parole.

LIFE SENTENCES, 2008

Our national survey of departments of correction documented 140,610 persons serving a life term in 2008. One in 11 persons in a state or federal prison is now serving a life sentence. Over the last quarter-century, the number of individuals serving life sentences has more than quadrupled from 34,000 in 1984 (See Figure 1). Nearly 97% of those serving a life sentence are men, while women comprise 4,694 (3.3%) of persons serving a life sentence.

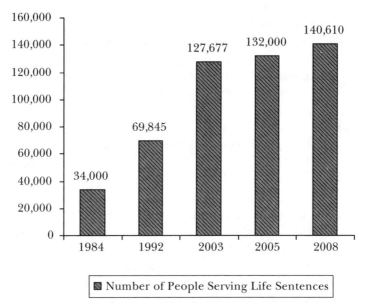

FIGURE 1 *Growth in life sentenced population, 1984–2008*
Sources: Figures for 1984 obtained from: American Correctional Association (1984).
Corrections Compendium. *Vol. 3 (9). Figures for 1992 obtained from: Maguire, K., Pastore, A. L., and Flanagan, T. J. (Eds.) (1993).* Sourcebook of Criminal Justice Statistics 1992. *Washington, D.C.: Bureau of Justice Statistics. Figures for 2003 obtained from: Mauer, M., King, R., and Young, M. (2004).* The Meaning of 'Life': Long Prison Sentences in Context. *Washington, D.C.: The Sentencing Project. Figures for 2005 obtained from: Liptak, A. (2005, October 5). Serving Life with No Chance at Redemption.* The New York Times. *Data for 2008 collected from each state's department of corrections by The Sentencing Project.*

The scope of life sentences varies greatly by state. In 16 states, at least 10% of people in prison are serving a life sentence. In Alabama, California, Massachusetts, Nevada and New York, at least 1 in 6 people in prison are serving a life sentence. On the other end of the spectrum, there are 10 states in which 5% or fewer of those in prison are serving a life sentence, including less than 1% in Indiana.

LIFE WITHOUT PAROLE

Substantially longer sentences and the restriction or abolition of parole are two key contributing factors to the rapidly expanding prison population. This is perhaps best illustrated by the use of LWOP sentences. In 2008, 41,095 people, or 1 in 36 persons in prison, were serving a sentence of life without parole. Women comprise slightly more than 3% of this group (1,333). As with the overall population of life sentences, the number of people serving LWOP has increased dramatically in recent years. In 1992, 12,453 persons—1 in 68—were serving LWOP sentences.[4] In the intervening 16 years that figure has tripled (See Figure 2).

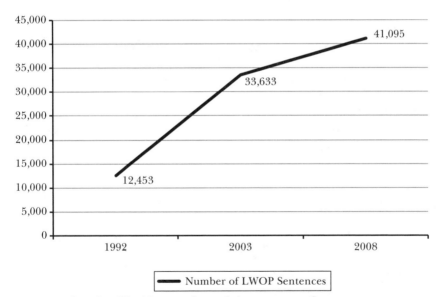

FIGURE 2 *Growth in life without parole population, 1992–2008*
Sources: Figures for 1992 obtained from: Maguire, K., Pastore, A. L., and Flanagan, T. J. (Eds.) (1993). Sourcebook of Criminal Justice Statistics 1992. *Washington, DC: Bureau of Justice Statistics. Figures from 2003 obtained from: Mauer, M., King, R.S., and Young, M. (2004).* The Meaning of 'Life': Long Prison Sentences in Context. *Washington, DC: The Sentencing Project. Figures for 2008 collected from each state's Department of Corrections by The Sentencing Project.*

As with the overall life sentenced population, the use of LWOP varies greatly among states. In Louisiana, a state in which all life sentences lack the possibility of parole, one of every nine (10.9%) people in prison is serving an LWOP sentence. Pennsylvania, another LWOP-only state, incarcerates 9.4% of its prison population for the rest of their lives. Nationally, there are nine states in which more than 5% of persons in prison are serving an LWOP sentence. On the other end of the spectrum, 15 states incarcerate less than 1% of persons in prison for LWOP.

States also vary in the relative proportions of parole-eligible life sentences and LWOP. For example, in California and New York, the states with the highest proportion of persons serving life sentences, only 2.2% and 0.3% respectively of incarcerated persons are serving a sentence of LWOP. In 16 states, 10% or more of the prison population is serving a life sentence, yet in 11 of these states, the LWOP population comprises less than 5% of the prison population. This is largely a reflection of statutory law and prosecutorial practices that deemphasize LWOP and underscores the local contours of life sentencing practices.

RACE/ETHNICITY AND LIFE SENTENCES

This study represents the first national collection of state-level life sentence data by race and ethnicity. Nationally, nearly half (48.3%) of the life-sentenced population is African American, comprising 67,918 people (See Table 3). The black proportion of persons serving a life sentence is considerably higher than the black representation in the general prison population (37.5%).

The portion of African Americans serving life sentences varies widely across states, as seen in Table 1. In 13 states and the federal system, African Americans comprise more than 60% of persons serving a life sentence.

TABLE 1   Racial and Ethnic Distribution of Life Sentenced Population

State	Life Population	Black #	Black %	White #	White %	Hispanic #	Hispanic %
Alabama	5,087	3,342	65.7%	1,732	34.0%	Unk.	Unk.
Alaska	229	24	10.5%	132	57.6%	4	1.7%
Arizona	1,433	285	19.9%	670	46.8%	392	27.4%
Arkansas	1,376	728	52.9%	630	45.8%	13	0.9%
California	34,164	12,036	35.2%	8,163	23.9%	11,182	32.7%
Colorado	2,136	432	20.2%	1,064	49.8%	569	26.6%
Connecticut	430	225	52.3%	123	28.6%	80	18.6%
Delaware	526	334	63.5%	190	36.1%	Unk.	Unk.
Florida	10,784	5,660	52.5%	4,753	44.1%	301	2.8%
Georgia	7,193	5,103	70.9%	2,051	28.5%	Unk.	Unk.

State	Life Population	Black #	Black %	White #	White %	Hispanic #	Hispanic %
Hawaii	412	25	6.1%	95	23.1%	14	3.4%
Idaho	523	11	2.1%	425	81.3%	66	12.6%
Illinois	103	74	71.8%	19	18.4%	10	9.7%
Indiana	250	86	34.4%	153	61.2%	9	3.6%
Iowa	616	156	25.3%	409	66.4%	34	5.5%
Kansas	806	338	41.9%	372	46.2%	68	8.4%
Kentucky	1,073	312	29.1%	747	69.6%	7	0.7%
Louisiana	4,161	3,049	73.3%	1,105	26.6%	Unk.	Unk.
Maine	58	2	3.4%	55	94.8%	0	0.0%
Maryland	2,311	1,773	76.7%	508	22.0%	Unk.	Unk.
Massachusetts	1,760	561	31.9%	827	47.0%	318	18.2%
Michigan	5,010	3,208	64.0%	1,655	33.0%	93	1.9%
Minnesota	496	173	34.9%	273	55.0%	Unk.	Unk.
Mississippi	1,914	1,387	72.5%	516	27.0%	7	0.4%
Missouri	2,582	1,370	53.1%	1,170	45.3%	21	0.8%
Montana	171	3	1.8%	137	80.1%	8	4.7%
Nebraska	515	165	32.0%	280	54.4%	39	7.6%
Nevada	2,217	509	23.0%	1,340	60.4%	246	11.1%
New Hampshire	177	Unk.	Unk.	Unk.	Unk.	Unk.	Unk.
New Jersey	1,257	787	62.6%	356	28.3%	46	3.7%
New Mexico	391	44	11.3%	153	39.1%	170	43.5%
New York	11,147	6,167	55.3%	1,814	16.3%	2,937	26.3%
North Carolina	2,390	1,511	63.2%	786	32.9%	23	1.0%
North Dakota	40	1	2.5%	33	82.5%	1	2.5%
Ohio	5,202	2,741	52.7%	2,304	44.3%	103	2.0%
Oklahoma	2,135	655	30.7%	1,200	56.2%	98	4.6%
Oregon	719	80	11.1%	544	75.7%	58	8.1%
Pennsylvania	4,349	2,742	63.0%	1,200	27.6%	356	8.2%
Rhode Island	182	53	29.1%	88	48.4%	36	19.8%
South Carolina	2,056	1,318	64.1%	717	34.9%	10	0.5%
South Dakota	169	11	6.5%	122	72.2%	2	1.2%
Tennessee	2,020	1,007	49.9%	975	48.3%	25	1.2%
Texas	8,558	3,721	43.5%	2,893	33.8%	1,886	22.0%
Utah	Unk.	Unk.	Unk.	Unk.	Unk.	Unk.	Unk.
Vermont	89	3	3.4%	76	85.4%	Unk.	Unk.
Virginia	2,145	1,334	62.2%	786	36.6%	12	0.6%
Washington	1,967	315	16.0%	1,303	66.2%	207	10.5%
West Virginia	612	89	14.5%	494	80.7%	2	0.3%
Wisconsin	1,072	466	43.5%	478	44.6%	97	9.0%
Wyoming	197	10	5.1%	154	78.2%	21	10.7%
FEDERAL	5,400	3,494	64.7%	962	17.8%	738	13.7%
TOTAL	140,610	67,918	48.3%	47,032	33.4%	20,309	14.4%

Notes: Individuals identified as "Other" not included in this table. Race and ethnicity were not available for all individuals. Illinois officials did not provide usable data on life sentences or LWOP sentences for 2008. In 2003, the year in which data were previously collected for our report, The Meaning of Life, *Illinois reported 1,291 individuals*

The issue of racial disparity becomes even more pronounced in examining LWOP sentences. As mentioned, African Americans comprise 48.3% of those serving life sentences; yet, as seen in Table 2, while 45% of the parole-eligible population is African American, blacks comprise 56.4% of the LWOP population.

TABLE 2   National Life Sentenced Population, By Race and Ethnicity

Race/Ethnicity	Life Sentences	LWOP #	LWOP %	Parole Eligible #	Parole Eligible %
WHITE	47,032	13,751	33.5%	33,281	33.4%
BLACK	67,918	23,181	56.4%	44,737	45.0%
HISPANIC	20,309	3,052	7.4%	17,257	17.3%
OTHER	5,174	1,048	2.6%	4,126	4.1%
TOTAL LIFE SENTENCES	140,610	41,095		99,515	

Note: Race and ethnicity were not available for all individuals. Therefore, totals do not add up to 100%.

These figures are consistent with a larger pattern in the criminal justice system in which African Americans are represented at an increasingly disproportionate rate across the continuum from arrest through incarceration. African Americans comprise 12% of the general population but represent 28% of total arrests and 38% of persons convicted of a felony in a state court and in state prison. These disparities increase with the severity of punishment.

It is more difficult to identify the involvement of Hispanics in the criminal justice system due to frequent state-level data shortcomings; often, the category of ethnicity is combined with race, resulting in a serious undercount of the national Hispanic population. Nevertheless, when counted accurately, Hispanics are usually shown to be overrepresented in various stages of the criminal justice system. For instance, even though Hispanics represent 15% of the general population, 22.3% of those in prison are Hispanic.[5] In our survey of individuals serving life sentences, we find that the 20,309 Hispanics serving life sentence comprise 14.4% of all persons serving a life sentence, a figure lower than their proportion of the general prison population.[6] Hispanics comprise only 7.4% of LWOP sentences.

(continued from page 162)

serving life sentences, all of whom were LWOP. The prison population reported at this time was 43,418. The figure of 103 juveniles serving LWOP was confirmed through an independent report in 2008 and is included in this table. The current number of adult life sentences and LWOP sentences in Illinois could not be determined. Utah officials did not provide data on life sentences. New Hampshire does not maintain race/ethnicity data for its adult population but does have this information for juveniles serving a life sentence and JLWOPs. Please see Tables 8 and 9 for this information.

Yet, these figures may be misleading, as six states do not collect ethnicity data from their prison population.

Among states that did report ethnicity information, there are five in which 25% or more of the LWOP population is Hispanic—Arizona, California, Colorado, Texas, and Wyoming. Except for Wyoming, these are states that also have a sizeable Hispanic population. Meanwhile, in 30 states, the representation of the LWOP population that is Hispanic is less than 1 in 10.

TABLE 3   Racial and Ethnic Distribution of LWOP Population

State	LWOP Population	Black LWOP #	Black LWOP %	White LWOP #	White LWOP %	Hispanic LWOP #	Hispanic LWOP %
Alabama	1,413	963	68.2%	447	31.6%	Unk.	Unk.
Alaska	0	0	0.0%	0	0.0%	0	0.0%
Arizona	208	40	19.2%	92	44.2%	68	32.7%
Arkansas	541	305	56.4%	230	42.5%	3	0.6%
California	3,679	1,332	36.2%	960	26.1%	1040	28.3%
Colorado	464	143	30.8%	167	36.0%	134	28.9%
Connecticut	334	170	50.9%	96	28.7%	66	19.8%
Delaware	318	207	65.1%	109	34.3%	Unk.	Unk.
Florida	6,424	3,615	56.3%	2,581	40.2%	196	3.1%
Georgia	486	359	73.9%	127	26.1%	Unk.	Unk.
Hawaii	47	2	4.3%	10	21.3%	4	8.5%
Idaho	102	2	2.0%	89	87.3%	6	5.9%
Illinois	103	74	71.8%	19	18.4%	10	9.7%
Indiana	96	30	31.3%	61	63.5%	4	4.2%
Iowa	616	156	25.3%	409	66.4%	34	5.5%
Kansas	2	0	0.0%	2	100.0%	0	0.0%
Kentucky	66	21	31.8%	42	63.6%	2	3.0%
Louisiana	4,161	3,049	73.3%	1,105	26.6%	Unk.	Unk.
Maine	54	2	3.7%	51	94.4%	0	0.0%
Maryland	321	224	69.8%	88	27.4%	Unk.	Unk.
Massachusetts	902	307	34.0%	424	47.0%	142	15.7%
Michigan	3,384	2,264	66.9%	1,040	30.7%	44	1.3%
Minnesota	48	17	35.4%	25	52.1%	Unk.	Unk.
Mississippi	1,230	877	71.3%	346	28.1%	4	0.3%
Missouri	938	505	53.8%	419	44.7%	3	0.3%
Montana	51	0	0.0%	38	74.5%	1	2.0%
Nebraska	213	72	33.8%	111	52.1%	18	8.5%
Nevada	450	71	15.8%	309	68.7%	35	7.8%
New Hampshire	63	Unk.	Unk.	Unk.	Unk.	Unk.	Unk.
New Jersey	46	32	69.6%	13	28.3%	1	2.2%
New Mexico	0	0	0.0%	0	0.0%	0	0.0%
New York	190	118	62.1%	32	16.8%	36	18.9%
North Carolina	1,215	761	62.6%	389	32.0%	18	1.5%
North Dakota	11	1	9.1%	7	63.6%	1	9.1%
Ohio	216	103	47.7%	105	48.6%	5	2.3%

State	LWOP Population	Black LWOP #	Black LWOP %	White LWOP #	White LWOP %	Hispanic LWOP #	Hispanic LWOP %
Oklahoma	623	187	30.0%	343	55.1%	40	6.4%
Oregon	143	17	11.9%	108	75.5%	14	9.8%
Pennsylvania	4,343	2,738	63.0%	1198	27.6%	356	8.2%
Rhode Island	32	11	34.4%	16	50.0%	5	15.6%
South Carolina	777	515	66.3%	250	32.2%	5	0.6%
South Dakota	169	11	6.5%	122	72.2%	2	1.2%
Tennessee	260	123	47.3%	130	50.0%	5	1.9%
Texas	71	27	38.0%	19	26.8%	25	35.2%
Utah	Unk.	Unk.	Unk.	Unk.	Unk.	Unk.	Unk.
Vermont	13	1	7.7%	10	76.9%	Unk.	Unk.
Virginia	774	478	61.8%	285	36.8%	8	1.0%
Washington	542	144	26.6%	319	58.9%	31	5.7%
West Virginia	251	36	14.3%	207	82.5%	1	0.4%
Wisconsin	171	58	33.9%	88	51.5%	15	8.8%
Wyoming	20	1	5.0%	9	45.0%	6	30.0%
FEDERAL	4,514	3,104	66.8%	704	15.6%	664	14.7%
TOTAL	41,095	23,181	56.4%	13,751	33.5%	3,052	7.4%

Notes: Individuals identified as "Other" not included in this table. Race and ethnicity were not available for all individuals. Illinois officials did not provide usable data on life sentences or LWOP sentences for 2008. In 2003, the year in which data were previously collected for our report, The Meaning of Life, *Illinois reported 1,291 individuals serving life sentences, all of whom were LWOP. The prison population was reported at this time was 43,418. The figure of 103 juveniles serving LWOP was confirmed through an independent report in 2008. The current number of adult life sentences and LWOP sentences in Illinois could not be determined. Utah officials did not provide data on life sentences.*

Individuals Serving Life Sentences for Crimes Committed as Juveniles[7]

Life in prison is the most severe punishment available for juveniles. This has been the case since 2005 when the U.S. Supreme Court ruled in *Roper v. Simmons* that juveniles cannot be executed. Every state allows for life sentences for juveniles, and 46 states hold juveniles serving such terms.[8] There are currently 6,807 individuals serving life sentences for crimes committed when they were a juvenile. Among these, 1,755 have a sentence of life without parole.

JUVENILES SERVING LIFE

As with persons serving life overall, there is significant statewide variation in the use of life sentences for juveniles. Juveniles serve life sentences in nearly every state, but more than 50% of the national population is located in five states: California (2,623), Texas (422), Pennsylvania (345), Florida (338), and Nevada (322).

YOUTH OF COLOR SERVING LIFE SENTENCES

Racial and ethnic disparities are pronounced at each stage of the juvenile justice system, from referral through secure confinement. Transfer to the adult system is the stage at which these disparities are most severe; African American youth represent 35% of judicial waivers to criminal court and 58% of youth sent to adult prisons.[9] Our data document that racial and ethnic disparities persist within the juvenile life sentenced population as well. Overall, nearly half (47.3%) of juveniles sentenced to life are African American (See Table 4).

Racial disparity in juvenile life sentences is quite severe in many states. In Alabama, 102 of the 121 persons serving life, or 84.3%, are black. In Maryland, 226 of the 269 (84.0%) youth serving life sentences are black. And in South Carolina, 42 of the 55 (76.4%) youth in adult prisons serving life sentences are black. Finally, in the federal system, 28 of the 52 youth serving life sentences, or 53.8%, are black. Nationally, Hispanics represent 23.7% of juvenile life sentences, considerably higher than the percentage of youth nationwide who are Hispanic (18.0%).[10]

TABLE 4   Racial and Ethnic Distribution of Juvenile Life Population

State	Juvenile Life Population	Black #	Black %	White #	White %	Hispanic #	Hispanic %
Alabama	121	102	84.3%	18	14.9%	Unk.	Unk.
Alaska	8	2	25.0%	4	50.0%	0	0.0%
Arizona	149	41	27.5%	55	36.9%	43	28.9%
Arkansas	58	38	65.5%	19	32.8%	1	1.7%
California	2,623	826	31.5%	306	11.7%	1,185	45.2%
Colorado	49	15	30.6%	17	34.7%	14	28.6%
Connecticut	18	10	55.6%	3	16.7%	5	27.8%
Delaware	31	17	54.8%	14	45.2%	Unk.	Unk.
Florida	338	226	66.9%	103	30.5%	9	2.7%
Georgia	6	4	66.7%	2	33.3%	Unk.	Unk.
Hawaii	8	0	0.0%	1	12.5%	0	0.0%
Idaho	21	1	4.8%	17	81.0%	3	14.3%
Illinois	103	74	71.8%	19	18.4%	10	9.7%
Indiana	0	0	0.0%	0	0.0%	0	0.0%
Iowa	37	8	21.6%	24	64.9%	5	13.5%
Kansas	64	35	54.7%	15	23.4%	12	18.8%
Kentucky	101	32	31.7%	68	67.3%	0	0.0%
Louisiana	133	97	72.9%	35	26.3%	Unk.	Unk.

State	Juvenile Life Population	Black #	Black %	White #	White %	Hispanic #	Hispanic %
Maine	0	0	0.0%	0	0.0%	0	0.0%
Maryland	269	226	84.0%	39	14.5%	Unk.	Unk.
Massachusetts	52	16	30.8%	19	36.5%	12	23.1%
Michigan	206	131	63.6%	68	33.0%	5	2.4%
Minnesota	9	5	55.6%	2	22.2%	Unk.	Unk.
Mississippi	63	44	69.8%	18	28.6%	0	0.0%
Missouri	87	63	72.4%	22	25.3%	1	1.1%
Montana	6	0	0.0%	4	66.7%	2	33.3%
Nebraska	68	34	50.0%	31	45.6%	0	0.0%
Nevada	322	101	31.4%	144	44.7%	56	17.4%
New Hampshire	15	2	13.3%	13	86.7%	Unk.	Unk.
New Jersey	17	9	52.9%	8	47.1%	0	0.0%
New Mexico	30	5	16.7%	6	20.0%	15	50.0%
New York	146	89	61.0%	16	11.0%	40	27.4%
North Carolina	46	30	65.2%	14	30.4%	0	0.0%
North Dakota	3	0	0.0%	1	33.3%	1	33.3%
Ohio	212	142	67.0%	66	31.1%	3	1.4%
Oklahoma	69	33	47.8%	23	33.3%	5	7.2%
Oregon	14	3	21.4%	11	78.6%	0	0.0%
Pennsylvania	345	231	67.0%	79	22.9%	33	9.6%
Rhode Island	12	3	25.0%	3	25.0%	5	41.7%
South Carolina	55	42	76.4%	11	20.0%	0	0.0%
South Dakota	4	0	0.0%	3	75.0%	0	0.0%
Tennessee	179	122	68.2%	54	30.2%	2	1.1%
Texas	422	205	48.6%	85	20.1%	130	30.8%
Utah	Unk.	Unk.	Unk.	Unk.	Unk.	Unk.	Unk.
Vermont	0	0	0.0%	0	0.0%	0	0.0%
Virginia	107	87	81.3%	20	18.7%	0	0.0%
Washington	56	10	17.9%	30	53.6%	4	7.1%
West Virginia	0	0	0.0%	0	0.0%	0	0.0%
Wisconsin	67	30	44.8%	25	37.3%	6	9.0%
Wyoming	6	0	0.0%	4	66.7%	2	33.3%
FEDERAL	52	28	53.9	8	22.9%	6	17.1%
TOTAL	6,807	3,219	47.3%	1,547	22.7%	1,615	23.7%

Notes: Individuals identified as "Other" not included in this table. JLWOP is prohibited in Alaska, Colorado, Kansas, New Mexico, and Oregon. JLWOP was eliminated in Colorado in 2005, but does not apply retroactively. Therefore, the 49 youth who were sentenced before the 2005 law was enacted continue to serve JLWOP sentences. Illinois officials did not provide data on life sentences of LWOP sentences. The figure of 103 juveniles serving LWOP was confirmed through an independent report in 2008. Utah officials did not provide data on life sentences or LWOP sentences.

Not surprisingly, racial disparity among JLWOP sentences is also very apparent. Juveniles serving life without parole are even more disproportionately African American, 56.1% (See Table 5). In 17 states, more than 60%

of the JLWOP population is African American. In Alabama, for instance, 75 of the 89 persons serving JLWOP (84.3%) are black, and in Maryland 15 of the 19 (78.9%) persons serving JLWOP are black. In South Carolina, 11 of 14 persons serving JLWOP are black. In the federal system, 19 of the 35 (54.3%) persons serving JLWOP are black.[11]

TABLE 5   Racial and Ethnic Distribution of JLWOP Population

State	JLWOP Population	Black #	Black %	White #	White %	Hispanic #	Hispanic %
Alabama	89	75	84.3%	13	14.6%	Unk.	Unk.
Alaska	0	0	0.0%	0	0.0%	0	0
Arizona	25	6	24.0%	8	32.0%	9	36.0%
Arkansas	57	38	66.7%	19	33.3%	0	0.0%
California	239	77	32.2%	36	15.1%	100	41.8%
Colorado	49	15	30.6%	17	34.7%	14	28.6%
Connecticut	14	9	64.3%	1	7.1%	4	28.6%
Delaware	19	13	68.4%	6	31.6%	Unk.	Unk.
Florida	96	59	61.5%	31	32.3%	6	6.3%
Georgia	0	0	0.0%	0	0.0%	Unk.	Unk.
Hawaii	2	0	0.0%	0	0.0%	0	0.0%
Idaho	4	0	0.0%	4	100.0%	0	0.0%
Illinois	103	74	71.8%	19	18.4%	10	9.7%
Indiana	0	0	0.0%	0	0.0%	0	0.0%
Iowa	37	8	21.6%	24	64.9%	5	13.5%
Kansas	0	0	0.0%	0	0.0%	0	0.0%
Kentucky	6	2	33.3%	3	50.0%	0	0.0%
Louisiana	133	97	72.9%	35	26.3%	Unk.	Unk.
Maine	0	0	0.0%	0	0.0%	0	0.0%
Maryland	19	15	78.9%	4	21.1%	Unk.	Unk.
Massachusetts	22	6	27.3%	11	50.0%	3	13.6%
Michigan	152	96	63.2%	50	32.9%	5	3.3%
Minnesota	1	1	100.0%	0	0.0%	Unk.	Unk.
Mississippi	42	27	64.3%	15	35.7%	0	0.0%
Missouri	35	24	68.6%	11	31.4%	0	0.0%
Montana	1	0	0.0%	1	100.0%	0	0.0%
Nebraska	29	14	48.3%	14	48.3%	0	0.0%
Nevada	69	11	15.9%	48	69.6%	5	7.2%
New Hampshire	4	1	25.0%	3	75.0%	Unk.	Unk.
New Jersey	0	0	0.0%	0	0.0%	0	0.0%
New Mexico	0	0	0.0%	0	0.0%	0	0.0%
New York	0	0	0.0%	0	0.0%	0	0.0%
North Carolina	26	17	65.4%	7	26.9%	0	0.0%
North Dakota	1	0	0.0%	0	0.0%	1	100.0%
Ohio	0	0	0.0%	0	0.0%	0	0.0%
Oklahoma	9	4	44.4%	4	44.4%	0	0.0%
Oregon	0	0	0.0%	0	0.0%	0	0.0%

State	JLWOP Population	Black #	Black %	White #	White %	Hispanic #	Hispanic %
Pennsylvania	345	231	67.0%	79	22.9%	33	9.6%
Rhode Island	1	1	100.0%	0	0.0%	0	0.0%
South Carolina	14	11	78.6%	1	7.1%	0	0.0%
South Dakota	4	0	0.0%	3	75.0%	0	0.0%
Tennessee	12	7	58.3%	5	41.7%	0	0.0%
Texas	3	2	66.7%	1	33.3%	0	0.0%
Utah	Unk.	Unk.	Unk.	Unk.	Unk.	Unk.	Unk.
Vermont	0	0	0.0%	0	0.0%	0	0.0%
Virginia	28	21	75.0%	7	25.0%	0	0.0%
Washington	28	3	10.7%	14	50.0%	3	10.7%
West Virginia	0	0	0.0%	0	0.0%	0	0.0%
Wisconsin	2	0	0.0%	0	0.0%	1	50.0%
Wyoming	0	0	0.0%	0	0.0%	0	0.0%
FEDERAL	35	19	54.3%	9	25.7%	6	17.1%
TOTAL	1,755	984	56.1%	497	28.3%	205	11.7%

Notes: Individuals identified as "Other" not included in this table. JLWOP is prohibited in Alaska, Colorado, Kansas, New Mexico, and Oregon. JLWOP was eliminated in Colorado in 2005, but does not apply retroactively. Therefore, the 49 youth who were sentenced before the 2005 law was enacted continue to serve JLWOP sentences. Utah officials did not provide data on life sentences or LWOP sentences. Illinois officials did not provide data on life sentences of LWOP sentences. The figure of 103 juveniles serving LWOP was confirmed through an independent report in 2008.

14

New Political and Cultural Meanings

David Garland

I'm sick of crime everywhere. I'm sick of riots . . . I'm sick of the U.S.
Supreme Court ruling for the good of a very small part rather than the
whole of our society.

LETTER FROM A CONSTITUENT TO
SENATOR SAM J. ERVIN, JR., OF NORTH CAROLINA, JUNE 1968

The immediate reactions to *Furman* [the U.S. Supreme Court ruling that the death penalty was unconstitutional] were mixed. In the days following the decision, newspapers reported it as a human interest story, highlighting the reaction of the men and women whose death sentences had been overturned. Photographs of prisoners standing beside unplugged electric chairs accompanied reports announcing, "Fifty-five inmates awaiting execution at the Ohio Penitentiary heard radio reports on the decision and then 'broke out with cheers, shouts and yelling' "; and "At Florida's Raiford Prison 96 men and 1 woman on death row engaged in 'considerable shouting and hilarity.' " But if the prisoners' reaction was straightforward, the political response was more conflicted. The *Washington Post*'s June 30 headline read: "Joy on Death Row; Praise, Scorn on Capitol Hill."[1]

Liberal voices greeted the decision as enthusiastically as we would expect. Senator Edward Kennedy acclaimed it as "one of the great judicial milestones in American history" and said that the Court had "ruled for life" and thereby "given new life to our democracy and to the quality of American justice." In the same vein, Pennsylvania Attorney General

From *Peculiar Institution: America's Death Penalty in an Age of Abolition* (New York: Oxford University Press, 2010), 231–34, 244–55.

J. Shane Creamer described the decision as "a triumph of reason and law over fear and anxiety."[2] The Congressional Black Caucus described itself as "relieved" by a "ruling that is of particular interest and importance to Black Americans because of the high percentage of Black prisoners who have been sentenced to death."[3]

But critical voices also formed part of that first day's story, many of them from Southern politicians and law enforcement officials. Police chiefs in Atlanta and Memphis complained that *Furman* had deprived them of an important deterrent at a time when crime was rising. Los Angeles Police Chief Edward M. Davis told a press conference that the decision was an "absurdity" and promised to lead a nationwide campaign to restore capital punishment.[4] Prison guards complained that the Court's decision took away "the only real protection we had."[5] Tennessee Governor Winfield Dunn professed "tremendous shock and disappointment," a sentiment echoed by Lieutenant Governor Jere Beasley of Alabama, who commented that the Court had evidently "lost touch with the real world." James O. Eastland, Democratic senator from Mississippi, raised the flag of states' rights when he accused the Supreme Court of "legislating" and "destroying our system of government," while Georgia's lieutenant governor, Lester Maddox—a firebrand white supremacist—called the decision "a license for anarchy, rape, and murder."[6]

It was to be expected that conservatives would push back against the Court's decision, but no one at first knew how or how hard. Initially there was some confusion about the meaning of the decision. Was the death penalty now completely unconstitutional? Would its reintroduction require a constitutional amendment? Republican leaders quickly took steps to clarify where things stood and to chart a way forward. The day after *Furman* was announced, President Nixon declared at a press conference that "the holding of the Court must not be taken . . . to rule out capital punishment," and Governor Ronald Reagan urged California voters to support an initiative on the November ballot to reinstate the death penalty.[7]

Before long, support for the death penalty was being mobilized all across the country. On July 2 the *New York Times* carried an article entitled "Banned—But for How Long?" describing the *Furman* precedent as "very vulnerable" and quoting legal experts to that effect. The article reported that a constitutional amendment had already been introduced into Congress permitting the death penalty for murder and treason and that "legislators in at least five states" had announced they would press for new state laws reintroducing capital punishment.[8] On July 6, only a week after *Furman*, Philadelphia District Attorney Arlen Specter was reported to have proposed a new bill to the Pennsylvania legislature that would provide the death penalty for eight different types of murder.[9] Within a few months activists were campaigning for reinstatement in every state in the country, supported by police chiefs, state attorneys general, local district attorneys, and assorted politicians.[10]

What this amounted to was the mobilization of pro–death penalty forces on a national scale for the first time in U.S. history. When the *Furman* case was argued in January 1972, dozens of *amicus* briefs had been attached to the LDF [Legal Defense Fund] brief, but not a single organized group joined the states in defending capital punishment, not even the federal government. There had been no active, pro–death penalty lobby. Now a nationwide movement had been brought into existence. Instead of ending the death penalty, *Furman* had roused the nation's pro–death penalty forces and mobilized them as never before.

For 200 years, the activists in death penalty politics were chiefly anti-gallows abolitionists, challenging a settled, traditional practice and the embedded preference of a majority of Americans. Now the balance had changed. The Court's surprise decision and the accompanying publicity focused the issue of capital punishment and moved it up the political agenda.[11] Even before the decision was announced, public opinion was already moving in favor of capital punishment, and the new activism served to accelerate this shift.[12] Citizens expressed outrage at what they regarded as the Court's attack on their values. This in turn energized state legislators, who seized the opportunity to provide their constituents with the laws they demanded. In nullifying the death penalty statutes of so many states, the Court had created a gap between majority voter preferences and state law—a gap to which many politicians were immediately drawn. As Lee Epstein and Joseph Kobylka remark, in the summer of 1972, state legislatures "could barely wait to reconvene to pass new laws."[13]

Within two years, thirty-five states had enacted new capital statutes.[14] Re-enactment was rapid everywhere but faster in states where murder rates had increased and fastest in the South. Florida was the first to enact a new law, successfully passing a new statute in December 1972.[15] The month before, California voters had endorsed death penalty restoration, voting two to one for Governor Reagan's Proposition 17. In September 1973 Reagan signed the new act into law.

In every death penalty state the story was the same. Even Jimmy Carter, the liberal Democratic governor of Georgia, signed a new bill into law in 1973. Only Governor Michael Dukakis of Massachusetts stood against the tide, vetoing a capital punishment bill that the state legislature had approved—an abolitionist stance that would cost Dukakis dearly when he ran for president in 1988. Capital trials were soon under way across the country. By the end of 1974, despite serious doubts about their validity, new state statutes had been used to sentence some 231 people to death.[16]

So the death penalty re-emerged, with the enhanced support of public opinion and of newly mobilized activists. But the institution that resurfaced in the 1970s bore a new set of political and cultural meanings that had been forged in the course of the battles fought in the lead-up to *Furman* and in its aftermath.

The LDF litigation of the 1960s swept the death penalty up into the civil rights movement, rendering abolition as an NAACP-sponsored civil rights reform. In the same way, the *Furman* majority embodied the spirit of the Warren Court in offering a liberal reading of the Constitution, intended to heal racial divisions and expand the reach of liberty and equality.[17] The immediate effect was to alter the death penalty's connotations, associating it in the public's mind with civil rights, with liberal attitudes toward blacks, and with countermajoritarian federal reform. Then, in the process of reaction that followed *Furman*, the death penalty was inscribed into a very different politics—the politics of backlash—which gave the institution a whole new set of associations, linking it with "law and order," with "states' rights," and with what would later become known as "culture war" conservatism. These new associations clung to the death penalty for a generation, investing it with layers of meaning and depths of feeling that it had not previously had—both for conservatives who supported the institution and for liberals who opposed it. The death penalty as penal policy gave way to the death penalty as political and cultural symbol. [. . .]

The Reinvention of Capital Punishment

In this post-liberal, post–civil rights, law and order America the death penalty would be remade. Having been almost abolished in the liberal 1960s, it would be revived and reinvented in the more conservative decades that followed. The late-modern mode of capital punishment that emerged, jointly forged by the Supreme Court and the states, became a kind of masthead symbol for a new culture of control with its harsh sentencing laws, its mass imprisonment, and its risk-averse retributivism. The LDF litigation had represented the death penalty as a civil rights violation, a kind of legal lynching that ought to be abolished along with segregation and Southern racism. Now it became a populist crime-fighting measure, an emblem of states' rights democracy, and a symbolic battleground in the emerging culture wars. In the process, death penalty discourse became infused with powerful currents of race and class resentment and with white fears of black violence.

From the late 1970s, the question of capital punishment functioned as a litmus test for law and order commitment in the same way that "abortion" tests for conservative commitment. To ascertain if a judicial nominee or an aspiring politician was sound on law and order, one asked if he or she supported the death penalty. If the answer was negative or even hesitant, his or her credentials were thereby shown to be suspect. The scene was played out on national television time and time again—most memorably when Michael Dukakis failed the test in 1988, a dramatic defining moment that marked the beginning of the end of his presidential campaign. But though this litmus test is familiar and taken for granted, it is actually quite peculiar.

The death penalty has always been a harsh punishment and a tool of law enforcement. And in its modern penal mode its function was to deter serious offenders and eliminate those who would not be deterred. But in post-1970s America it became not so much a policy or a penal sanction as a commitment, a symbolic badge that declared the wearer's position on "law and order" issues—and on much else besides. The paradox here is that, by the 1970s, the death penalty's deterrent effects had been shown to be uncertain at best, and the sanction had ceased to be used in a way that might make it an effective crime-fighting tool.

The idea of the death penalty as a key weapon in the war on crime became persuasive because conservatives chose to ignore doubts about its efficacy and endorse instead the popular attitude that favored the death penalty, either as a commonsense deterrent or as a harsh retributive response to hated criminals.[18] They did so, not because they were persuaded of capital punishment's penological efficacy, but because they were certain of its political benefits. Once they had made that political judgment, it became a shibboleth of the conservative movement that the equation between the death penalty and effective crime control be regarded as unquestionable.

These claims were helped by the fact that crime had been rising rapidly since 1963, and conservative figures made a point of blaming rising homicide rates on the death penalty moratorium that had been in place over the same years (though murder rates increased in death penalty and abolitionist states alike). As John Little McClellan, the Democratic senator from Arkansas, put it when he introduced death penalty bill S1401: "The last execution in this country took place in 1967 . . . In the five years between 1967 and 1971, the number of murders in this country rose 61%. . . . Can anyone argue that this was a mere coincidence?"[19] Southern newspapers made the same connection. The *Atlanta Constitution* carried articles tracing the supposedly negative impact of the suspension of executions: "Crimes punishable by death in the electric chair have increased 235 per cent in

Atlanta since the chair was last used in 1964, a survey of police records showed."[20] "We are threatened people. And it is either them or us," the same newspaper said in a 1973 editorial entitled "Liberals and Crime."[21]

The conservative message went this way: the liberal elites and radical civil rights activists who had done so much to undermine the nation's social order, its traditional values, and its Southern way of life had also tried to abolish the death penalty. This message was a powerful one all across the nation but it resonated especially in the South, where Republicans were now focusing their electoral efforts. In that context, abolition of the death penalty was civil rights for black murderers. *Furman* was the work of an "activist" federal judiciary operating in concert with Northern liberal elites who disdained the Southern way of life. As Lester Maddox had declared, the decision "was a license for anarchy, rape and murder." Women were left unprotected in their homes. Order was undermined and in danger of collapse. To a conservative white Southerner's way of thinking, the echoes of the hated Reconstruction were unmistakable. To demand the reintroduction of capital punishment was to do more than take a position in penal policy: it was to reassert the old order and oppose the changes wrought by liberal elites.

Republicans grasped that questions about capital punishment tended to put liberals on the wrong side of the "law and order" issue. If support for law and order was seen to require support for the death penalty—as Republicans now insisted—and the liberal establishment continued to oppose capital punishment (as it did for a decade and more), then Republicans won and liberals lost. However concerned Democrats might actually feel about crime, however tough their stance on sentencing or policing or crime-prevention might be, their opposition to capital punishment marked them as definitively soft on crime and out of touch with popular feeling. And in the 1970s, popular feeling was increasingly getting behind capital punishment. By November 1972, five months after *Furman* was announced, the *New York Times* reported that a Gallup poll had found a sharp rise in the numbers supporting a death penalty. As the *Times* article noted, "Despite the United States Supreme Court's ruling striking down the death penalty, public support for capital punishment is currently at its highest point in nearly two decades."[22]

Marked by fear of crime, racial hostility, and a growing gap between liberal elite sentiment and mass popular opinion, the death penalty came to function as the epitome of an *expressive* punishment. Loud demands for the death penalty were a kind of acting out, a means of communicating rage and resentment as well as hatred of the criminal other. The sanction's powerful capacity to convey emotion overwhelmed all doubts about its ability actually to deter murderers. In the cut and thrust of electoral politics and rhetorical debate—especially in the sound-bite age of TV journalism—the death penalty was the perfect leading edge for a harsher law and order politics.

It was these circumstances, together with the rhetorical work of conservative commentators and party operatives, that transformed the American death penalty into a powerful condensation metaphor, a synecdoche that enabled a single position to stand for a whole law and order attitude.[23] Despite the death penalty's tenuous link to real crime control, despite its narrow application and the rarity of its use, despite the utter implausibility of the idea, capital punishment became the "solution" to crime that dominated political debate. To voice unquestioning support for the death penalty was to communicate that one was for law and order. To raise doubts about its efficacy or morality was to lose credibility and popular support. A functioning litmus test had been devised, however unscientific its underlying chemistry, and it worked time after time for the conservative cause.

The death penalty operated as a wedge issue benefiting Republicans for twenty years, from the early 1970s until the early 1990s. Presidents Nixon, Reagan, and George H. W. Bush would each use it to win popular support and to disparage liberal opponents—most notably in the 1988 Willie Horton campaign and the trouncing of Michael Dukakis.[24] As late as 1995, the Republican House majority leader, Newt Gingrich, was pushing a platform of tax reductions and death penalty increases, and proposing mass executions ("27 or 30 or 35 people at one time") as a solution to the drug problem.[25] It was not until Bill Clinton embraced capital punishment and made it part of mainstream Democratic politics that the issue ceased to divide the parties.[26] In the mid-1990s congressional representatives of both parties competed to see who could introduce more new capital statutes—by 1996, Democrats were claiming credit for enacting no fewer than sixty new federal capital offenses. Historians might see, in this spree of legislative *Thanatos*, an echo of the eighteenth-century process that produced England's Bloody Code. In both cases, lawmakers enacted penalties of death to further their political interests and those of their constituents—private property in eighteenth-century England, social values and racial hierarchies in twentieth-century America. In both cases, the practical result was a death penalty reinvigorated and reasserted—though more often on the books than on the scaffold.

The call by Southern politicians for a return to the gallows often contained distinct echoes of lynching. In its insistence on the punishment of death and the suppression of black civil rights, the Southern backlash against *Furman* echoed the backlash against Reconstruction and the lynching scenes that it created. On occasion it even produced explicit invocations of lynching imagery. Here, for example, is Georgia's lieutenant governor, Lester Maddox, invoking the lynching past when he enthuses about "the noose" and "court house square" hangings, even though Georgia was an electrocution state that had long since abolished hangings and public executions: "There should be more hangings. Put some more electricity in the chair. Put more nooses on the gallows. We've got to make it safe on the street again . . . It wouldn't be too bad to hang some on the court house square, and let those who would plunder and destroy see." [27]

Maddox's evocation of public hangings outside the court house was not the only allusion to lynching voiced in these debates. Another Georgia legislator, State Representative Guy Hill of Atlanta, proposed a bill in the Georgia House Judiciary Committee that required hanging to take place "at or near the courthouse in the county in which the crime was committed." [28] The same debate included a remark from another death penalty enthusiast, Representative James H. (Sloppy) Floyd: "If people commit these crimes, they ought to burn." [29] No doubt Sloppy Floyd would insist, if asked, that he was referring to death in the electric chair. But the brutal language of "burning" offenders also evokes the worst kind of lynchings where black suspects were tortured and burned at the stake. [30] African Americans understood these coded messages. They, too, viewed the death penalty through a prism of race and saw that blacks were its chief targets. Little wonder, then, that black groups and black politicians were the main opponents of the new legislation as it swept through Southern state legislatures. [31]

States' Rights and Culture Wars

The *Furman* decision provoked bitter complaints about activist judges and overreaching federal government meddling in matters that fell within the autonomous scope of state authority. Herman E. Talmadge, the Democratic senator (and former governor) of Georgia greeted the decision by declaring, "Five of the nine members of the U.S. Supreme Court have once again amended by *judicial usurpation* the Constitution." His fellow Georgian, State Representative Sam Nunn, echoed Talmadge's sentiments by referring to a "dictatorship" of judges appointed for life. The chairman of the Senate Judiciary Committee, James O. Eastland, Democratic senator from Mississippi, accused the Court of "legislating" and, in doing so, "destroying our system of government." Robert List, the attorney general of Nevada, denounced the decision as "an insult to Nevada, to its laws, and to its people." [32] As the father of a murder victim said to the *Chicago Tribune*, "I guess it means nothing that the people of Illinois voted to keep the death penalty." [33] If elite-led countermajoritarian reform had been effective in ending the death penalty in Europe, in America it provoked only outrage and opposition.

Ironically—and by way of this outraged reaction—it was *Furman* that effectively forged the association between the death penalty and democracy that still prevails in America today. By denying "the people"—or at least the people of Georgia, Texas, and the other death penalty states— the punishment that they "willed," the *Furman* Court made capital punishment a symbol of that "will" and a token of popular democracy. Arguments for the death penalty, thereafter, became arguments for democracy.

Furman's invalidation of capital punishment was read in the South as an illegitimate attack on the region's cultural traditions by outside elites. (As one poster outside an execution responded, "Texas Justice: Don't Like It? Leave!"[34]) It was seen as a continuation of the same assault on the Southern way of life—mounted by the Supreme Court and by Northern liberals—that had first dismantled segregation and racial hierarchies and more recently invalidated laws banning abortion. As on previous such occasions, the *Furman* decision unleashed a flood of popular resentment against the Court, its "activist judges," and the Northern liberal elites who supported them. But whereas the earlier fights against *Brown v Board of Education* had necessarily been openly racist in their commitments, and hence lacked support in the rest of the nation, the South's fight to retain capital punishment could be framed as a straightforward "law and order" issue that could generate support elsewhere with no thought of race. *Furman* thus gave the states, above all the Southern states, a means to assert their autonomy and push back against civil rights reform on an issue that was popular, respectable, and could be argued on grounds that were neither racial nor sectional. That the Southern states had very high homicide rates and a public that keenly supported capital punishment gave real force to this campaign, allowing local politicians to insist that Washington elites simply didn't understand "the way things are down here."[35]

Today, nearly forty years later, the claim of "states' rights" continues to resonate as a basis for opposing the Supreme Court's death penalty reforms. In 2005, when the Court ruled in *Roper v Simmons* that states may not execute offenders who were minors at the time of their offense, the decision provoked another furor. But it was not the substance of the decision that was attacked in the dozens of outraged editorials and op-eds that followed. No one argued that executing minors makes for good policy or a higher standard of decency. That, its detractors said, wasn't the issue. The trouble with *Roper* was that in imposing its ruling the Supreme Court had usurped the power of the states and infringed their sovereign autonomy. The question was not, "what policy?" but, "who decides?"[36] A CNN commentator raged that "the majority's approach [is] anti-democratic, anti-states' rights, and anti-jury . . . A power that once belonged to state legislatures and local juries, now rests in the hands of the U.S. Supreme Court."[37] The decision "reeks of judicial arrogance," said the *Greenville News*, and showed what the *Omaha World Herald* called "an unhealthy disregard for the sovereignty of [our] homeland."[38] The following year a state judge in Alabama ran his election campaign on a platform of rejecting *Roper* and defying the Supreme Court on the grounds of states' rights.[39]

The same outpouring of states' rights outrage greeted *Kennedy v Louisiana* in June 2008, when the Supreme Court invalidated the capital child rape statutes of Louisiana and five other states.[40] As the *Chattanooga Times* insisted to its readers, "The basic issue is not whether there should or should not be a death penalty law for child rapists. The basic question is who should decide."[41] A Texas prosecutor, Robert Etinger, accused the Court of seeking to "overthrow the will of the people."[42] Even Democratic presidential candidate Barack Obama was moved to take issue with the *Kennedy* Court, declaring that when it comes to the crime of child rape, "states have the right to consider for capital punishment."[43] The conservative culture warrior and one-time Nixon speechwriter Pat Buchanan responded to the decision by insisting that its chief author, Justice Stevens, "should be impeached." In his opinion Stevens had suggested that it was time to reconsider the "justification of the death penalty itself"—a remark that had Buchanan fulminating about democracy, states' rights, and the culture wars. "Stevens is not, or should not be, the decider," Buchanan wrote in his syndicated column. "In a democratic republic, that is the prerogative of the majority . . . It is just such usurpations of power by the Supreme Court justices that loosed the culture war that has torn us apart."[44]

When capital punishment was abolished in other Western nations, death penalty supporters often put up fierce opposition. But none of the reports of these struggles suggests that specific groups or regions felt that in being denied the use of capital punishment they had been deprived of their heritage, that their way of life, their ethnic identity had somehow been degraded. People objected strongly to abolition, but they did not regard it as a status slight. In America, following *Furman*, many Southerners did.

If Southern legislatures had proposed banning capital punishment, as the legislatures of a dozen non-Southern states had done before 1972, those objecting to abolition would have marshaled many arguments for rejecting the proposal. But it is unlikely that they would have claimed that the death penalty was an essential part of a Southern heritage that ought to be retained on that basis. The reason that many Southerners saw the *Furman* decision as an attack on their culture had less to do with the institution's cultural belonging and more to do with perceptions of the process that brought *Furman* about.

Furman "abolished" the states' death penalty, temporarily at least, at the prompting of the same NAACP civil rights litigators, in the same federal Court, in the same countermajoritarian fashion that segregation in schools had been abolished in 1954. (Southerners and others would later see school prayer, antiabortion laws, and antisodomy laws struck down in the same way, and have much the same reaction.) The LDF litigators—who specially targeted the capital punishment practices of the Southern states—viewed death penalty abolition as the abolition of modern-day lynching and an extension of the same civil rights movement that had abolished racial segregation, black disfranchisement, and Jim Crow. This attack on capital punishment more than anything else forged the institution's identity as part of "Southern culture." In the course of the litigation against capital punishment many white Southerners saw their culture and institutions being attacked by familiar enemies, and they determined to defend them accordingly. The death penalty was more Southern after *Furman* than it had been before.

Although the "culture wars" description did not become standard journalistic parlance until the 1990s, the underlying conflict between affluent, secular, liberal elites—located on the two coasts and especially in the Northeast—and religious, traditional conservatives, centered in the South and the Midwest, began much earlier, having been brought into focus by the Southern strategy and its emphasis on traditional, populist values.[45] Sparked into action by issues such as abortion, school prayer, flag burning, gun control, women's liberation, gay rights, and same-sex marriage, the "religious right" emerged as a potent political force in the 1980s and 1990s, using its influence to promote "faith, family, and country" and push back against what it saw as "permissiveness" and "secular progressivism" in public life.

The emergence of these cultural and religious divisions polarized death penalty debates still further. Support for capital punishment came to be seen as an integral part of the "traditionalist" worldview, just as opposition to it became standard for liberal "progressives." Depriving people of the right to impose capital punishment—like depriving them of their guns, or their right to school prayer, or their right to ban abortion—came to be viewed as a kind of elite contempt for common people, for their faith, and for their way of life. Alabama judge Tom Parker captured this sentiment when he protested that the Supreme Court's decision in *Roper v Simmons* had "usurped" Alabama's power to impose the death penalty on juveniles if it so chose. He noted that "the liberals on the U.S. Supreme Court already look down on the pro-family policies, Southern heritage, evangelical Christianity and other blessings of our great state. We Alabamians will never be able to sufficiently appease such establishment liberals, so we should stop trying and instead stand up for what we believe without apology."[46] Among groups primed by their class, their beliefs, or their regional identities to feel such slights, this contempt generated bitter opposition.

Christian fundamentalists and conservative evangelicals have a strong presence in the Southwest and the Midwest, too, but the culture wars mentality found its greatest resonance in the South. Why should this be? "Much of the dynamic in America's current culture war," one author suggests, comes from the fact that American liberalism destroyed "the culture of official racism in the South."[47] Not only did the South contain large numbers of religious and social conservatives but from Reconstruction on many white Southerners developed a sense of victimization, feeling themselves disdained by Northern liberal elites and discriminated against by a federal government intent on undermining the Southern way of life and destroying its cultural heritage.

The abolition of capital punishment did, of course, raise genuine questions of religious faith. And Christian leaders were among the political and cultural figures to whom the press turned for comment when *Furman* was first announced. On June 30, 1972, the *Los Angeles Times* quoted fundamentalist preacher Dr. Carl McIntire as saying, "The Supreme Court is taking the country further away from the moral law and the teachings of God."[48]

A week later, the letters column of the same paper carried five submissions about the Court's decision.[49] One said that it was characteristic of the four Nixon-appointed justices that they had all voted for the death penalty. Another remarked that the majority justices lacked wisdom. But each of the three others raised religious, "culture war" issues which, until that point, had been relatively absent from *Furman* debate. A letter from a reader in Long Beach objected that the death penalty was being abolished while abortion was still being permitted: "it staggers the imagination," the letter said, "that a vicious murderer will be spared while totally innocent potential human beings are being flushed into eternity via abortions." Keith Kearl of Los Angeles complained, "Without the death penalty we are changing our society from Christian to atheist," a sentiment echoed by Robert McConnell, who wrote, "The death penalty may no longer be man's law but it still is God's law . . . Let's get capital punishment into our Constitution."

So conservative religious objections emerged again, just as they had whenever abolition had been debated in the nineteenth century. But in the context of post-1970s America, the language of "tradition" and "faith"—like "law and order" and "states' rights"—could also be used to express racial and cultural attitudes that had become otherwise unsayable in respectable public settings. In these conflicts over culture, fundamentalist religion came to function less as a political theology than as a vehicle for lower-class resentments and the defense of traditional ways of life. In its insistence on literal readings of biblical texts and fundamentalist commitments unleavened by modernity and liberal tolerance, this old-time religion served as an affirmation of the worth of white Southern lower-class groups in the face of perceived condescension from secular progressives and liberal elites.

The biblical texts are ambivalent on the death penalty, and the various Christian churches are similarly divided on the issue. But cultural attitudes and a chain of historical events have made capital punishment a salient issue for religious conservatives. That the death penalty is seen as "traditional" rather than "modern," that it is viewed as an integral part of a valued way of life in which masculine honor codes, revenge, and Old Testament values remain strong—are part of the motivation. So is stern dislike of those who have offended against the laws of God and of man—righteous moralizing being a familiar trait of fundamentalists. To put a murderer to death—or merely to insist on the right to do so—is thus to uphold morality and deny solidarity in the most dramatic, profound way. The culture wars made it possible to express support for capital punishment in a way that conveyed a surface moral righteousness and a subterranean social animosity.

Today's death penalty is deeply embedded in American political culture and casts a long shadow. The dramatic clash between federal courts and state legislatures—and, beyond that, the conflict between elite Northern liberalism and Southern popular conservatism—reshaped the meaning of American capital punishment and repositioned the issue in a new political and cultural context. *Furman*'s unintended effect was to mobilize a pro–death penalty backlash, give new salience to the issue of capital punishment, and transform its political connotations. After 1972, the death penalty ceased to be a matter of penal policy and became instead a symbolic battlefield—first in the "law and order" backlash against civil rights and later in the culture wars, functioning alongside issues like abortion, welfare rights, defendants' rights, and affirmative action as a litmus test of political affiliation and cultural belonging. Support for the death penalty became a marker of respect for states' rights and traditional authority; a respectable (that is to say, not openly racist) means of asserting that the civil rights movement had gone too far; and a vehicle for Southern resentment about interference by Northern liberals. It came to mean opposition to "moral decay," to the decline of personal responsibility, and to the erosion of traditional authority that was widely believed to be the social legacy of the 1960s.[50] Above all, support for the death penalty came to be a shorthand for a political position that was "tough on crime" and assumed to be in tune with popular attitudes.

After *Furman*, the death penalty became more than ever a Southern issue, first symbolically and then practically. After 1972, Northern states such as New York, Pennsylvania, and Ohio would no longer be among the leading executioners. Instead, the nation's executions would come to be concentrated in the South of the old Confederacy and Jim Crow. In the four decades since executions resumed in 1977, the Southern states have accounted for more than 80 percent of all executions.[51]

The reaction against *Furman* and America's subsequent shift to a "culture of control"—with its retributive revolution in sentencing law, the buildup of mass imprisonment, and the new politics of law and order—emerged out of the same political conflicts.[52] Indeed, the shift away from the progressive penal policy of the 1960s to the law and order politics of the 1990s began precisely at that moment, with the increase in prison population beginning in 1975 and continuing each year for more than thirty years thereafter. As retributivism and incapacitation displaced correctionalism as the core aims of penal policy, the death penalty ceased to stand in contradiction to general penal policy and became its symbolic leading edge. By politicizing the issue at a moment of rising anxiety about crime and disorder, and by mobilizing a wave of pro–death penalty activism, the *Furman* decision marked a watershed in public opinion trend lines. The steady erosion of public support for the institution that had been recorded throughout the 1950s and 1960s was reversed overnight, and majority opposition of the mid-1960s was transformed into majority support. This new pattern would continue for decades thereafter, peaking in the high-crime decade of the 1990s, when as many as 80 percent of Americans sometimes professed support for capital punishment.[53]

The decline of American liberalism in the late 1960s and 1970s is the fundamental cause of the failure of American "final-stage" abolition. That much is clear. It is also clear that the *Furman* episode was critical in transforming the political and cultural meaning of the American death penalty. The institution's new meanings were contingent—the product of a specific sequence of events, in a specific historical context. They were created by groups of actors who employed specific political rhetorics and strategies to forge semantic associations that resonated with parts of the public and eventually became embedded in the culture. But though they were contingent and event-driven, these new meanings also bear the marks of America's institutional structure. To that extent, they were overdetermined rather than chance outcomes. For this reason an analysis of

America's institutions and social structures is vital to any explanation of America's peculiar institution.

These shifts in the death penalty's meaning were an emergent outcome of interaction sequences, not a fully controlled, deliberate recoding. That is how the political process works. Contingent, historical events, specific to a time and place, give rise to a sequence of actions and reactions. In that process, contingency counts, context counts, history counts. No one fully controlled what happened—not the LDF litigants, nor the Supreme Court justices, nor the right-wing commentators, nor the onlooking audience. The death penalty's meaning escaped the grasp of all who sought to control it. Instead, the underlying conflicts and fault lines of American society structured patterns of action and helped shape the eventual outcomes. The death penalty's new meanings were grounded in the raw materials of preexisting conflicts and shaped by the structuring presence of an institutional landscape.

Part VII

Prison: What Are the Walls Hiding?

Some decades after President Dwight D. Eisenhower warned of a military-industrial complex installing itself in perpetuity, the U.S. incarceration system has attracted similar concern.[1] The 2.3 million inmates who occupy it at any one time (and outnumber the populations of all but three U.S. cities) are watched over by more than 600,000 guards and related staff.[2] The carceral state, as it has been named,[3] is thus one of the nation's largest employers. The monetary cost of this activity is overwhelming. Maintaining more than 2,000 prisons and jails alone costs approximately $74 billion annually, and the rest of the system, including police, lawyers, and judges, has an additional $154 billion price tag.

This system perpetuates itself in several ways, and one is through failure. That two-thirds of those released end up back behind bars within three years is an unintended but self-sustaining feature of the prison system. Another device is politicking; the California prison guard union is notorious for promoting tougher sentencing laws in order to preserve jobs, despite the overcrowding in the state's prison system, which this year the U.S. Supreme Court condemned in a split decision. Similarly, legislators representing upstate New York districts fight to keep open nearly empty prisons for their role in local "economic development."

Geography is a significant factor in most prison systems, and race and geography all too often go hand in hand. Many prisons end up in rural areas with low-density populations and few black or Latino residents. With black and Latino Americans overrepresented among inmates, often the result is a color clash between inmates and guards.

In addition, many inmates come from urban communities and thus are a long way from home when they are behind bars. This phenomenon is not just an inconvenience to them and their families. Most states continue to consider inmates as residents of the legislative districts where they are incarcerated, rather than their home districts. Thus, relatively conservative rural areas have larger populations, while relatively liberal urban areas have smaller ones, and legislative seats reflect this rebalancing. Compounding this dynamic is the fact that in all but two states, people in prison or jail cannot vote; in many states, disenfranchisement continues after release.

What happens inside prisons and jails gets a lot of sensationalized attention these days from television. Even the theories of what is supposed to happen have gotten muddled; there is hardly a pretense of rehabilitation anymore, but no one is quite willing to state officially that pure punishment is the point. There is little outside monitoring or investigation, partly because inmates have lost most of their legal rights to challenge prison conditions under the U.S. Constitution. The provocative question is whether the increased punitiveness and lack of legal protections that prisoners face have anything to do with the racial skewing of the prison population.

Texas Tough: The Rise of America's Prison Empire by Robert Perkinson is a 2010 history of the Texas prison system that explains much about changing penological theories and practices throughout the United States, not just in Texas. Perkinson describes the smooth transition from slavery to convict leasing that kept so many black Texans working for free but without freedom. As this system of exploitation gave way to criticisms of cruelty and corruption, pure punitiveness, managed with bureaucratic efficiency, took over. From Texas and other southern states, this modern system spread throughout the country. Perkinson's account, beautifully written, relies on diverse and detailed research, including interviews with prison officials and prisoner leaders. He demonstrates a continuous relationship between race relations and prison practices and provocatively argues that, in some sense, the South may have won the Civil War.

In a blog post on the *Huffington Post*, Eric Lotke describes the gerrymandering behind incarceration. Whether prisoners are counted as residents of their place of incarceration or their previous homes turns out to make a big difference in many states. More or fewer rural residents often means more or fewer Republican representatives. Lotke, the research director at the Campaign for America's Future, is an expert on this topic. In addition, the Prison Policy Initiative (www.prisonpolicy.org) runs a program devoted to the topic, Prisoners of the Census (www.prisonersofthe census.org). The trend seems to favor counting prisoners at their previous addresses, but the politicking around this issue is fierce.

Further Reading: Michael B. Mushlin and Naomi Roslyn Galtz, a Pace University law professor and a Pace law fellow, offer another provocative argument in "Getting Real About Race and Prisoner Rights," published in the *Fordham Urban Law Journal* in January 2009. They describe the erosion of civil rights protections for prisoners that has transpired since the 1980s. (Mushlin is a preeminent prison law scholar who writes a regularly updated compendium on this subject.) They argue that this erosion is not just coincidental with the increasingly disproportionate incarceration of poor black Americans that occurred over the same period of time. Rather, these prisoners lacked social and political resources to defend against the erosion of their rights, which also resulted from discrimination.

15

Texas Tough

Robert Perkinson

Distrust all in whom the impulse to punish is strong.[1]

—FRIEDRICH NIETZSCHE

Freedom is the United States' founding creed. "Every spot of the old world is overrun with oppression," cried Thomas Paine, but America promises "asylum for the persecuted lovers of civil and religious liberty." Andrew Jackson later told his countrymen, "Providence has showered on this favored land blessings without number, and has chosen you as the guardians of freedom, to preserve it for the benefit of the human race." Subsequent presidents, in wartime and peace, have renewed this sacred charge, proclaiming freedom as America's supranational mission, its unifying cause. In his inaugural address, Barack Obama cast the tradition forward. "Let it be said by our children's children," he said, that "we carried forth that great gift of freedom and delivered it safely to future generations."[2]

America is "the land of the free," yet by one vital measure, it is less free than any other country on earth: it incarcerates a greater portion of its citizenry than any other, about 1 out of every 100 adults. With some 2.4 million persons under lock and key, the United States manages the largest penal system in the world, the grandest ever conceived by a democratic government.[3] Just as slavery once stood as a glaring exception to the American promise, so does imprisonment more than two centuries after the birth of the republic.

The stated purpose of the U.S. prison colossus, which now outstrips

From *Texas Tough: The Rise of America's Prison Empire* (New York: Metropolitan Books, 2010), 1–11, 361–74.

the combined populations of Boston, Washington, and San Francisco, is to keep the public safe. Yet the majority of criminologists agree that the phenomenal expansion of incarceration has only modestly reduced crime, accounting for perhaps a quarter of the crime drop since the early 1990s.[4] Even as the experts increasingly doubt the utility of incarceration, however, our society has come to rely on it as never before.

Imprisonment in the United States has achieved unprecedented scale. Combining law enforcement, courts, and prisons, the U.S. criminal justice system consumes $212 billion a year and employs 2.4 million people, more than Wal-Mart and McDonald's combined, the nation's two largest private employers. There are more than eighteen hundred separate prisons in operation across the country—not counting local jails, juvenile lockups, and immigration facilities. Concrete and concertina wire have become integral features of the American landscape.[5]

Even as the use of incarceration has expanded exponentially, however, many Americans still don't know anyone who has been to prison. In middle- and upper-income, predominantly white neighborhoods, imprisonment remains a rare and shocking experience. According to the federal Bureau of Justice Statistics, only one in thirty-nine white men has ever been to prison, with the odds plummeting in the higher income brackets. Along the margins of American society, however—in poverty-blighted rural areas and struggling urban cores—imprisonment has become commonplace. One out of every six African American men has spent time in prison, one out of every thirteen Hispanics. If one takes a snapshot of those currently incarcerated, the socioeconomic indicators read more like a fact sheet from Afghanistan than the first world. Roughly half of today's prison inmates are functionally illiterate. Four out of five criminal defendants qualify as indigent before the courts.[6]

That prisons concentrate poverty and ignorance—in addition to rough and shady personalities—is nothing new. "It is well known that most of these individuals on whom the criminal law inflicts punishments, have been unfortunate before they became guilty," noted Gustave de Beaumont and Alexis de Tocqueville in 1833. More surprising is that measurable inequities in criminal justice have widened over the past few decades, particularly across the barrier that has always divided Americans most intractably—race. A half century ago—before the Montgomery bus boycott, before the War on Poverty, and before the conservative reaction against the social experimentation of the 1960s—blacks in the United States were imprisoned at roughly four times the rate of whites. Today, a generation after the triumphs of the civil rights movement, African Americans are incarcerated at seven times the rate of whites, nearly double the disparity measured before desegregation.[7] Although two generations have passed since *Brown v. Board of Education*, African American men today go to prison at twice the rate they go to college.[8]

Almost no one would have predicted this dire state of affairs two generations ago. Had you proposed in 1965 to increase the U.S. prison expenditures forty-four-fold and widen racial disparities over the next forty years, even the hardest hard-liners would have scoffed. Toward the end of the civil rights era, in fact, most observers believed the country was moving in the opposite direction. Although "there is a long way to go," concluded the authors of a 1969 primer on constitutional rights, we are making "orderly progress" toward the day when "the poor man, the Negro, the suspect, and the defender of unpopular causes truly enjoy . . . equal protection under the law." Conventional prisons, many experts believed, were destined for obsolescence. As counseling and community corrections came to the fore, one of the country's leading criminologists, Norval Morris, advised criminal justice professions to begin "conscious planning" for "the decline and likely fall of the 'prison' as that term is now understood."[9]

We now know that Professor Morris and his colleagues were not just off the mark but off the map. But why? What, indeed, propelled a resurgence of the prison precisely at the moment of its predicted demise? When I began researching criminal justice in the 1990s, analysts of all stripes were struggling with this question. Law-and-order conservatives had the simplest answers. They argued that cultural hedonism and welfare dependency had gradually eroded family values, unleashing a frightful crime wave in the 1960s that was finally brought under control only by decisive government action.[10] Critics of the crackdown, by contrast, have floated a raft of alternate explanations, from media-driven panic to a reduced tolerance for risk in late modernity.[11] Some have suggested that America's titanic penal system has reached the point of self-sustaining profitability, that a "prison-industrial complex" has emerged as a rival to the military-industrial complex first assailed by President Dwight Eisenhower in 1961.[12]

In graduate school at Yale, I learned a great deal from this growing body of literature, but I felt increasingly dissatisfied. Many commentators agreed that race plays an important role in the justice system, but relatively few were making the entwined histories of criminal punishment and racial subjugation a central category of analysis.[13] Fewer still carried the story further back than Barry Goldwater's 1964 presidential campaign, one of the first to make law and order a polarizing partisan issue.[14] Almost no one was grappling seriously with the role of the American South, despite the region's leadership in extending sentences, building new prisons, and resurrecting bygone punishments like chain gangs and striped uniforms.[15]

I suspected that vital insights lay buried in these neglected areas, so

I focused my research on the history of crime and punishment in the South. I traveled to Florida, where venerable traditions like electrocution survived into the twenty-first century, then to Georgia, where I studied the rise and fall of the chain gang. In my mother's home state of Mississippi, I surveyed the legendary penal farm at Parchman. Next door in Louisiana, I conducted a round of interviews with inmates and guards at the Angola prison plantation. The more I read and the more people I spoke with, however, the more I realized that in the realm of punishment, all roads lead to Texas.

Why Texas? Because just as New York dominates finance and California the film industry, Texas reigns supreme in the punishment business. With 173,000 inmates and more than twice as many paid employees as Google, Texas's prison system is the largest in the United States, outstripping even California, which has an overall population 50 percent larger.[16] By almost any measure, Texas stands out. The state's per capita imprisonment rate (691 per 100,000 residents) is second only to Louisiana's and three times higher than the Islamic Republic of Iran's.[17] Although Texas ranks fiftieth among states in the amount of money it spends on indigent criminal defense, it ranks first in prison growth, first in for-profit imprisonment, first in supermax lockdown, first in total number of adults under criminal justice supervision, and a resounding first in executions. When it comes to imprisonment, writes Joseph Hallinan, a reporter for the *Wall Street Journal*, Texas is "where it's happening."[18]

Texas casts a long shadow in politics as well. Since World War II, the state has produced more presidents than any other, with the differences among them providing a measure of the nation's postwar journey. Born in Denison, Eisenhower embodied the cold war consensus. In the 1960s, Lyndon Johnson championed civil rights, social democracy, and preventative criminal justice, even as he shipwrecked his Great Society in Vietnam. LBJ's two Texas successors then led the country rightward: George H. W. Bush, who rode the specter of Willie Horton, a black rapist, to the White House and widened the war on drugs when he got there, and his son George W. Bush, who funneled more money into law enforcement and incarceration, both foreign and domestic, than any chief executive before him. By the early twenty-first century, Texas had come to exercise unrivaled leadership in the political arena, especially in criminal justice, where it pioneered all manner of punitive policies, from lethal injection to prison privatization. With political conservatism ascendant, Texas became the country's new bellwether state.[19]

To a large extent, Texas stands for the country as a whole. With its mythic history, multiracial population, and immense territory that stretches from the South to the Southwest, Texas brings together vital threads of the American fabric. Its hardscrabble folk and wide-open spaces symbolize in-dividual liberty. Yet this freedom has always traveled with a wrathful twin. Torn by social divisions and wracked by violent conflict—dramatized by the lynching of James Bird in 1998—Texas also signifies for many Ameri-cans intolerance, bigotry, and sanguinary justice.[20] In the film *Thelma and Louise*, when Susan Sarandon makes Geena Davis drive hundreds of miles out of the way to avoid the state, audiences are meant to understand that Texas is no place for free spirits on the run.

For both its punitive singularity and historical contradictions, Texas is a fruitful site to study criminal justice over the *longue durée*, from one pe-riod of pervasive unfreedom to another, from the age of slavery to the age of incarceration. From its inception, the state has served as a contentious testing ground for rival styles of penal discipline: corporal punishment versus Christian charity, exploitative field labor versus penitentiary-based confinement, retribution versus rehabilitation. A populist strain in Texas politics has inspired the most spirited penal reform movements in the South, from agrarian radicals who railed against forced labor to civil rights activists who assailed prison segregation. But an even stronger tradition of racial demagoguery and penny-pinching conservatism, combined with the intransigence of the state's prison guard establishment, has managed to beat back each of these challenges. In Texas justice, as in politics, left has always battled right, but the right has usually won. "It was one of the clichés . . . that we were dragging our state, kicking and screaming, into the twentieth century," recalls Ronnie Dugger, the founding editor of the *Texas Observer*, the state's liberal standard-bearer. "But lo and behold . . . Texas has dragged the United States back into the nineteenth."[21]

The product of this mismatched historical struggle is a uniquely harsh model of criminal justice, a regime of state-sanctioned punishment based on roughshod legal proceedings, racial subjugation, corporal punish-ment, and unpaid field labor that has persevered into the twenty-first century. Texas's plantations are "probably the best example of slavery re-maining in the country," reported a national corrections expert in 1978.[22] Twenty years later, when I first started visiting southern prisons, I reached the same conclusion. Nowhere else in turn-of-the-millennium America could one witness gangs of African American men filling cotton sacks un-der the watchful eyes of armed whites on horseback. Plantation prisons at Sugar Land, Huntsville, and elsewhere have preserved the lifeways of slavery in carceral amber.

For most of American history, Texas's implacable punishment traditions relegated it to the margins of penology, a field devoted—in theory if not practice—to the "moral regeneration . . . of criminals." In the late civil rights era, however, as rehabilitation programs faltered, crime rates soared, and a new breed of politician discovered that crime, especially black crime, galvanized white voters, Texas's Lone Star became a guiding light. State after state began copying elements of what prison experts called the "Texas control model," while politicians looked with new fondness on the state's severe sentencing statutes. Once dismissed as a "disgrace of Christian civilization," Texas became the template for a more fearful and vengeful society.[23]

Nationwide, tough new crime policies—far more than rising crime rates—fueled prodigious prison growth. Between 1965 and 2000, the U.S. prison population swelled by 600 percent, in Texas by 1,200 percent. Over the same period, sentences grew longer and early releases rarer. Prison education and counseling programs withered, while supermaxes and death rows sprang up from coast to coast. "We were building prisons so fast we couldn't find wardens to run them," a criminal justice professor at Sam Houston State University told me. "It was like mobilizing for world war."[24] By the end of the century, the United States had embarked on an unprecedented experiment in mass incarceration, one that not only is changing the country's approach to crime and punishment but is reworking the fabric of American society.

This book tells the story of this punitive revolution with Texas at its epicenter. Examining the interplay of race, crime, and politics over almost two centuries, it explains how a proud frontier republic forged in democratic revolt came to build one of the roughest penal regimes in American history. It shows how a uniquely calloused, racialized, and profit-driven style of punishment that developed on slavery's frontier became a model for the nation in the post–civil rights era.

By analyzing the life and times of America's harshest, largest penal system, *Texas Tough* proposes fresh ways of thinking about imprisonment and society. First it argues that the history of punishment in the United States is more of a southern story than has generally been realized. By the numbers, the South has long been the dominant player in criminal justice.[25] Open almost any book on the subject, however, and the states of the former Confederacy are scarcely mentioned—except perhaps to underline their particularity.[26] In the historiography of imprisonment scholars have hewed to a remarkably unitary story line, with the first northeastern penitentiaries—foreboding public institutions that were meant to restore wayward citizens to virtue through penitent solitude—imperfectly evolving into modern correctional bureaucracies, complete with psychological counseling and parole. Although historians vary widely in their approaches and viewpoints, they have overwhelmingly replicated narratives of halting progress in pursuit of the rehabilitative ideal.[27]

Until recently, this progressive, regionally restrictive version of history possessed a certain logic. Because prison managers, whatever their shortcomings, steadfastly claimed reformation as their goal, and because most rehabilitative innovations originated in the North, it seemed only logical for historians to thus focus their efforts.[28] Alas, now that the country's prison establishment has largely abandoned the cause of "moral regeneration," it is easier for us to detect southern roots. Over the last few decades, prisons have not become more humane, less racially divisive, less authoritarian, or even more supple in their exercise of power, as the dominant literature had led us to expect. Rather, American lockups have become harsher, more regimented, more racially divisive, and markedly less rehabilitative. They no longer aim to repair and redeem but to warehouse, avenge, and permanently differentiate convicted criminals from law-abiding citizens. Today's prisons operate less in the tradition of what the founding penologist Enoch Wines called "the reformatory idea" than in a retributive mode that has long been practiced and promoted in the South.[29]

To piece together a more complete genealogy of the modern prison, therefore, this book redirects the spotlight from the North, the birthplace of rehabilitative penology, to the South, the fountainhead of subjugationist discipline. In addition to tracing the evolution of social welfare and the gospel of redemption, it examines the development of labor control, racial division, and corporal debasement. The result is that two ancestral lines come into view: one reformatory, one retributive; one integrative, one exclusionary; one conceived in northern churches and the other on southern work farms. Over the course of American history, these rival traditions have contended for influence, and in the closing decades of the twentieth century, exclusion and revenge gained the upper hand. In short, this book posits that most historians have studied only half of the family tree. American prisons trace their lineage not only back to Pennsylvania penitentiaries but to Texas slave plantations.

This historical reorientation leads to the book's second principal argument: the evolution of the prison has had surprisingly little to do with crime and a great deal to do with America's troubled history of racial conflict and social stratification. Decoupling punishment from crime defies conventional wisdom; most citizens like to think that prisons keep predatory villains off the streets—and to a certain extent they do. Yet an examination of the historical record, as well as present-day statistics, reveals that state punishment has consistently served purposes beyond crime control.

Indeed, the strong arm of the law has been regularly deployed not only to protect public safety but to preserve privilege, bolster political fortunes, and, most of all, to discipline those on the social margins, especially African Americans.

The notion that the law serves the powerful is probably as old as the law itself. A character in Plato's *Republic* asserted, "In every case the laws are made by the ruling party in its own interest."[30] Yet in the United States, where the highest court bears the inscription "Equal Justice Under Law," this basic critique is too often ignored. We tend to see justice even where dominion resides.

The history of Texas brings dominion into sharp focus. Although the Lone Star Republic was founded on the lofty principles of liberty and independence, its 1836 constitution codified an inviolable hierarchy of rights, barring all "Africans, the descendants of Africans, and Indians" from citizenship.[31] After abolition, these rigid distinctions blurred, but a two-tiered legal framework persisted. During the protracted epoch of formal segregation, a variety of de jure and de facto controls ensured that African Americans, and to a significant extent Mexican Americans, rarely interacted with the legal system in any capacity other than defendant. For more than two-thirds of Texas history, the state's criminal justice institutions—from the Texas Rangers to the jury box to the prison farms—remained legally and rigidly stratified, guided more by the exigencies of white supremacy than equal justice.

Despite the historic victories of the civil rights movement—culminating with the election of the country's first black president in 2008—the criminal justice patterns set during slavery and segregation have not faded away. Rather, according to key statistical indicators on crime, arrest, conviction, imprisonment, and release, the United States is dispensing less equitable justice today than it was a generation ago. Even as segregationist barriers to equal opportunity and achievement have crumbled in the free world, we have fortified the racial divide in criminal justice. Denied a place in society at large, Jim Crow has moved behind bars.

This paradoxical resurgence of racial injustice in the face of racial progress has a troubling precedent. In the aftermath of the Civil War and Reconstruction, white conservatives regrouped and regained power in the states of the former Confederacy, largely through violence and intimidation. The result was a restoration of white supremacy, combined with peonage, convict leasing, and lynching, practices that delayed emancipation's promise of equal rights for a century. In the wake of the modern civil rights movement—or the "Second Reconstruction"—an analogous historic turn took place.[32] In reaction against court-ordered integration, rising crime rates, and urban unrest, white conservatives, most effectively in the South, again regrouped and returned to power, often by campaigning on the issue of law and order. The consequence, this book contends, was an explosion of racialized imprisonment and a retreat, once again, from liberty.

In addition to reexamining the dynamic between imprisonment and society, *Texas Tough* examines the prison itself as a peculiar species of "total institution."[33] The book wrestles with a question that has long puzzled students of the law and public policy: Why has the penitentiary failed so spectacularly to fulfill its founding objectives—to rehabilitate criminals and prevent crime—yet persisted so tenaciously as our primary sanction for serious lawbreaking? Why have prisons resisted every effort at reformation? After analyzing the trials and tribulations of northern and especially southern penal institutions over two centuries, I believe the answer resides both inside and outside the prison walls.

In the first place, it is important to recognize that the rehabilitative prison has failed, in part, because it was never allowed to succeed. Although politicians and prison managers have perennially trumpeted the cause of inmate reclamation, in practice they have more often prioritized cost savings, control, and political maneuvering. This is particularly true in Texas. Just as promising reform efforts got under way in the 1880s, 1910s, and 1920s, state leaders slashed the prison budget and demanded that convicts return to the fields, thus squashing innovations in their infancy. Prison reforms have repeatedly disappointed, therefore—in Texas and to a substantial extent in other states—largely because they haven't really been tried. Or even desired. Prisons have persisted, conversely, despite their putative failures, not because they effectively protect the public but because they excel in other, generally unspoken ways, at dispensing patronage, fortifying social hierarchies, enacting public vengeance, and symbolizing government resolve.

But this is only part of the story. By stepping into the shrouded world of the prison itself, this book will also show how convicts and staff—not just policy makers—have sabotaged efforts at reform and reconciliation, and how, in the process, they have extended penitential discipline. On the prisoner side, even cooperative inmates determined to "do their own time" find the daily deprivations and petty humiliations of prison life maddening. Many turn to scamming, smuggling, and, when opportunities arise, escaping and rioting—acts of defiance that occasionally jump-start reforms but more often infuriate prison managers and lawmakers.[34] In this way, insurgent convict politics has often undermined inmate welfare, inspiring not innovation but backlash. More subtly, by chafing against the depersonalizing regimentation of prison life—as almost all convicts do—prisoners inadvertently validate the justice of their convictions. By breaking rules and lashing out, they mark themselves as criminal and further legitimate their incarceration.

The flip side of this corrosive dynamic plays out among the guards. Over time, even the most high-minded officers find the daily grind of prison work hardening. Charged to manage inmates who always seem to be working an angle, they come to think of their wards as untrustworthy and treacherous, as generic criminals rather than troubled individuals. Vested with near absolute authority over inmates, they come to wield power with confidence and sometimes capriciousness. Just as the kept inexorably slip into the role of contumacious convict, the keepers morph into hardhearted screws. "It gets to where there's not a whole lot of difference between the prisoners and the bosses," recalls an officer at the Ramsey farm, one of the state's oldest plantations. "See, [the Texas Department of Corrections] alters your mind. You live TDC. You work TDC. Your friends work at TDC. You were a bad ass and that's all there was to it." [35]

Over time, this guard-prisoner dialectic has played a critical role in destabilizing prison environments and discrediting reform efforts. By herding together edgy individuals against their will and enacting daily rituals of subjection, even the best prisons tend to foster more conflict than cooperation. They tend to drive forward cycles of reform, rebellion, and retrenchment that have characterized prison history in Texas and beyond. Conceived to enforce the law and impose order on chaos, prisons, by their very nature, tend to become bastions of lawlessness. This is not to say that no prisons are better than others. Yet by assessing the wreckage of prison reform movements, we may conclude that the prison itself is more irredeemable than most of its inmates. [. . .]

To be sure, there is evidence of advancing technology and gradually improved living conditions within Texas's prisons. In the early days, convicts lived in fetid firetraps and labored through every daylight hour under the gun. Today, they are kept in comparably hygienic concrete structures with electric lighting and indoor plumbing. They have access—albeit restricted and contested access—to relatively modern medical facilities. [36] Although hoe squads still turn out at the older units, prisoners these days are as plagued by tedium as by toil. Perhaps the most reliable index of prison amelioration is the inmate death rate, which has dropped from 2 to 7 percent annually under leasing to 0.3 percent today—this despite longer sentences and a surge in executions. [37]

Even in areas of obvious betterment, however, ambiguities remain. Take internal prison sanctions, which have become less physically painful but more prolonged. From the 1850s through the mid-1980s, prisoners writhed under the whip or got smacked upside the head, but they rarely spent more than thirty days in the hole; now, they might spend years there, even decades. As prison management has become more bureaucratic, another paradox has emerged. Inmates are less likely to be treated capriciously by staff, but they are also commensurably less likely to get treated favorably, less likely to exercise anything like personal autonomy. In the old days, even at the height of the exacting control model, strong, hardworking convicts could hunt, make spirits, gamble, and have sex with some impunity; the toughest or wiliest could jockey for BT or bookkeeper positions. These days, prisoners are more apt to be treated equally: as bodies to contain and count. "Sure, they . . . worked you till you dropped, but when you got back to the building you could do whatever you wanted," recalls one prisoner a bit too fondly. Now "the guards perceive us as animals . . . and view the pods as livestock pens."[38] The most notable difference of all is that there are so many more pens.

This conflicted assessment of historical change runs against the American grain. Since John Winthrop proclaimed his Puritan settlement a "city on a hill," Americans have treated progress as a covenant. The notion that each generation will be richer than the last, that each adversity will be overcome by pluck and hard work is a national creed. Prisons, though, present a stark challenge to this manifest destiny. They are built in progress's name; their architects have promised to cure crime, to reclaim fallen citizens, and to supplant barbarism with humanitarian correction. But more often they have delivered everything they were built to overcome: lawlessness, cruelty, abomination. "Penal history is littered with unfulfilled promises, abandoned hopes, and discarded institutions," observes one historian.[39]

This legacy of disappointment is most pronounced in the North, where the prison's virtues were promoted most rapturously. Benjamin Rush set the tone when he predicted that his "house of repentance" would unite "humanity, philosophy, and Christianity . . . to teach men that they are brethren; and to prevent their preying any longer upon each other." Southerners were always suspicious of such Panglossianism. They built prisons hesitantly in the nineteenth century and avidly in the twentieth but charged them with a more modest purpose: to punish criminals. In prison management, they emphasized subjection over salvation and, until recently, hard labor and white supremacy above all. From the beginning, southern progressives recoiled at this rejection of institutional idealism. They denounced southern penal institutions as "sources of disgrace" and tried to remake them in a northern image. When forward-thinking Texans built the Walls, for instance, they spoke of Auburn. When they opened the Gatesville reformatory, they invoked Elmira. When they dreamed up

the Austin penal colony, they referenced Thomas Mott Osborne at Sing
Sing and Katherine Bement Davis at Bedford Hills. In bringing the *Ruiz*
case to trial, civil rights activists believed they were nudging the state toward "community supervision," which Ramsey Clark called "the future of
corrections."[40]

To almost everyone's surprise, the opposite sort of geographic diffusion has taken place. After 180 years of failing to fulfill its founding
promise—as crime rates reversed their historic decline and as the New
Right clawed its way to power over the wounded body of civil rights—
the northern prison became more southern rather than the other way
around. In this unforeseen punitive turn, race has played a pivotal role.
During the extended epoch of American penal innovation from the Revolution through the Great Society, northern penitentiaries overwhelmingly
imprisoned whites. But as migration transformed these Yankee prisons
into demographic facsimiles of their southern counterparts, Dixie-style
management migrated north as well. Programs oriented toward social re-
integration, like counseling and parole, remain on the books, but they
have been eclipsed in recent years by sanctions that permanently differentiate criminals from free citizens: "real life" sentences, adult penalties for
juveniles, and lifelong restrictions on exfelons.[41] If northern prisons once
gestured toward freedom and southern penal farms toward bondage, the
whole Union is in alignment now, pointing back toward the eternal bifur-
cations of slavery.

About the only northern penological innovation that has truly flour-
ished in recent years is what Charles Dickens once called "rigid, strict,
and hopeless solitary confinement," the brainchild of Benjamin Rush.
Modern-day supermaxes have achieved a technical mastery of isolation
that Cherry Hill's warders could only have dreamed of but with none of
the founders' idealism. Today, the country's most regimented lockups—
high-tech überprisons like Pelican Bay in California, ADX Florence in
Colorado, and Estelle High Security Unit in Texas—aspire not to "cure . . .
the diseases of the mind," as Dr. Rush once dubiously envisioned, but to
secure perfect discipline by excluding troublesome inmates from all human contact, by exiling them from the land of the living without actually
extinguishing their breath.[42]

This resurgence of hard-edged, permanently debasing punishment coincided with a renewal of southern political potency in the latter third of
the twentieth century. Before secession, the South dominated American
politics from the presidencies of George Washington to Zachary Taylor.
Northerners and midwesterners commanded for a century thereafter, but
since the mid-1960s a majority of presidents have been southerners,
and the exceptions mostly southern-strategy sunbelters. Each of these

late-twentieth-century presidents, in his own way, pushed the country further away from the New Deal consensus. After the unlikely reign of Texas's most famous liberal, Lyndon Johnson, the social safety net frayed while the policeman's net widened; Keynesianism gave way to trickle down economics; the helping hand of government closed into a fist. Although regional distinctiveness is generally on the wane—with homogenization driven by interstates and the Internet—the North has become more southern over the past generation than the South has become northern. As we approach the sesquicentennial of the Civil War, it's not always clear which side came out on top.

One of the symptoms of "Dixie rising" is an uneven hardening of American race relations. Even with the disappearance of formal segregation and the election of an African American president, the United States by some measures, like family income and unemployment, is more separate and unequal today than it was at the end of the civil rights era. According to other indicators, there has been progress, but at an agonizing creep. At the present rate of convergence, for instance, the white-black poverty gap is expected to close in 2152.[43]

Nowhere is the persistence of inequality more visible than in the criminal justice system, where the "color line" has widened into a moat.[44] Why this is and how it came about becomes clear over the long march of Texas history. From the very beginning, the territory's legal and criminal justice institutions were bound up with racial subjugation. According to the first constitution, basic rights were allocated by race. According to the first penal codes, so were criminal sanctions, with wayward whites sent to the penitentiary and blacks to the whipping post or gallows. In law enforcement, racial and labor repression took precedence over traditional crime fighting. The consequence was that nonwhite Texans between the 1830s and the 1960s had little say in crafting or enforcing the laws. They were nonetheless readily punished for disobeying them.

Within the penal system itself, Texas started out by copying from Auburn but soon fell back on a more familiar mode of forced labor. Every effort was made to extract wealth from convict bodies, most mercilessly from black ones. At times, Texas made concerted efforts to break with this "penology for profit": in the 1910s after the abolition of leasing and in the 1920s under the progressives. In each case, however, lawmakers failed to appropriate the necessary funds, largely because they could conceive of no other fate for Negro convicts than picking cotton or cutting cane. From 1867, when the governor signed the first convict lease, through 1983, when the *Ruiz* rulings began taking effect, Texas's prison plantations thus carried forth the lifeways of chattel slavery. They served as racially segregated bastions of a seemingly bygone era, one that, in the distorted mirror of late-twentieth-century conservatism, started to look not backward but ominously modern.

The civil rights movement—and its offshoot the prisoners' rights movement—presented a serious challenge to this divisive racial order. Despite significant victories in court and in the political arena, however, Texas's legal institutions continued dispensing unequal justice. As Jim Crow finally collapsed, criminal justice emerged as a final bulwark of "white man's government." Under assault from Washington, the judiciary, and the streets, Texas and other southern polities eventually yielded on integration. But as they did so, they set a higher premium on public order and law enforcement and began assembling an incarceration apparatus of unprecedented scale. Although such talk was no longer polite, tough-on-crime politicians at the end of the century started institutionalizing the viewpoint of Texas's antediluvian, arch-segregationist U.S. senator Joseph Bailey, who once remarked, "I want to treat the negro justly and generously as long as he behaves himself, and when he doesn't I want to drive him out of this country."[45]

Prison proliferated in response to myriad variables, of course, among them crime, demographic shifts, and economic restructuring, especially at the bottom of the labor market. In Texas and the wider South, however (and subsequently elsewhere), prison growth proceeded according to a time line governed significantly by race relations. As Jim Crow acted out its death throes, imprisonment rallied. Between Redemption and the triumph of civil rights—that is to say, for ten decades of de jure segregation—Texas's imprisonment rate remained remarkably stable, never exceeding 200 per 100,000 residents. Between 1968 and 2005, however, the rate septupled. Over the same period—even as civil rights organizations and convict plaintiffs scored innumerable victories—Texas's prison population grew by 1,300 percent; its prison budget ballooned from $20 million to $2.6 billion.[46]

This astounding growth has put people of all sorts behind bars—but not equally. While the white prisoner population has increased eightfold since 1968, the African American prisoner population has grown fourteenfold; the Mexican American prisoner population has jumped even faster, increasing twenty-five-fold.[47] The sobering consequence is that young African Americans and Latinos today are more likely to spend time in prison—and less likely to get out—than their parents or grandparents were before the civil rights movement. A black baby boy born just after World War II faced roughly a 10 percent chance of ending up in prison by his midthirties. If he were born in the late 1960s, by contrast, the odds had increased to 20 percent, with the likelihood climbing still higher from the 1980s.[48] By the turn of the century, black Texans were being incarcerated at five times the rate of whites—a degree of racial disparity not seen since the early 1920s, when the KKK was the most powerful political force in the state.[49]

Since Stephen Austin first cleared his domain of its native inhabitants and proclaimed it a "slave country," almost everything about Texas has changed. Once dominated by subsistence farmers, the state became a cotton and then an oil kingdom. Today, it boasts the Texas Technology Corridor. Once overwhelmingly rural, it now hosts two of the five largest metropolitan areas in the United States; many Texans still don cowboy boots but rarely to ride horses.[50] Through it all—from the Texian Revolution to the Confederate insurrection to the first and second incarnations of the Klan to Massive Resistance and beyond—white supremacy has served as a mainstay of Texas politics. Over time, the language and methods have changed. But to an astonishing extent, the historic black-white divide (and to a somewhat lesser extent, the Anglo-Mexican divide) has stood fast, nowhere with greater prominence than in the prison system. Although the ghosts of the Confederacy have been, to a considerable extent, chased out of schools, lunch counters, and city buses, they continue to prowl Texas's cell blocks with relentless fury.

While racism has laid down one disheartening line of continuity in Texas's criminal justice history, crisis has another. Drop into the official archives at the start of any new management regime, and you will find uplifting reports of wrongs righted, problems fixed, and prisoners well treated. "The efficiency of the Superintendent . . . cannot be too highly appreciated," beamed prison directors in 1855, as Huntsville's textile mill went up. Thanks to "wholesome changes in management," officials trumpeted at the start of the Cunningham lease, "the convicts [are] comfortably clad, well fed, . . . and well treated." Even as the Texas control model flew off a cliff in the early 1980s, the attorney general and future governor Mark White was touting TDC as "one of the best in the nation."[51]

Such is the ebullience of official reporting. Drop into the same archives a few months or years later, however, and you find promises broken, scandals erupting, and officials scurrying for the exits. At the Walls, it turned out, obstreperous prisoners in the 1850s were being branded and maimed. Under the Sugar King, independent investigators soon agreed, prisoners received "devilish treatment" and were driven to the point of death, as one newspaper put it, like "the galley slaves of Southern Europe."[52] Not long after Mark White heaped praise upon TDC, a vicious gang war broke out in the cell blocks. At every turn, Texas officials claimed they saw the light only to descend into darkness. The state's prisons were constantly on the mend but needed ever more mending.

Like their national counterparts—if less ecstatically—Texas prison officials always claimed they were nudging their institutions forward, that they were participants in a steady if frequently rough-going march from the pillory to the modern penitentiary, from savagery to civilization. In reality, however, prison history has been characterized less by advancement than corrosive cycle. From the birth of the penitentiary forward, prisons over the long haul have followed a distressingly predictable sequence: crisis begets reform; reform (plus cutbacks) unleashes unrest; unrest bleeds into disappointment; failure leads to rollback; retrenchment gives way to neglect, or worse, which finally generates crisis anew. Like a spin on the treadmill—an invention, incidentally, of the English penitentiary that was meant to underscore the futility of dishonorable labor—these historical loops have developed over and over again in Texas's prisons and elsewhere. What Nathaniel Hawthorne called the "black flower of civilized society," it turns out, is a hearty perennial.[53] It resists every effort at beautification even as its ugliness inspires another.

Cycles of reform, rebellion, and retrenchment generate their own circles of blame—and there is plenty to go around. Corrupt administrators and guards, who gave themselves over to graft, sadism, or sexual predation, share some of it, as do irascible convicts, who responded to openness by filing a shank or running for the river. Texas's political leadership shoulders a greater share of responsibility for strangulating reform efforts in the 1880s, 1910s, 1920s, and 1980s. Such failings go a long way toward explaining the perpetual rupture and reinvention of the penitentiary, but history over the *longue durée* suggests that an incarnate agent is implicated as well—the prison itself.

Prisons are peculiar institutions. In all their forms, they lend themselves readily, almost inexorably, to trouble. This has partly to do with their purpose: to hold individuals involuntarily, to coerce them in confined spaces. It has partly to do with their demographic composition. Overwhelmingly, prisons herd together quick-tempered young men and contain them not just with walls but with haphazardly trained, inexperienced, and poorly paid personnel. These factors, combined with generally shoddy oversight, make prisons intrinsically difficult to manage, even for a day, even under the best of circumstances. Over time, they tend to get worse. In pursuit of order, they set in motion dialectical tensions between the kept and their keepers that often produce disorder.

One vital reason that prison environments tend toward deterioration is that they not only hold people but transform them. Most completely metamorphosed are their involuntary residents. Inmate initiates show up at the gates in all flavors, but over the course of depersonalizing initiation processes, they tend to develop characteristics institutionally selected for survival: circumspection, canniness, coldness, and cruelty. On the surface, they become masters of sycophancy; underneath, they seethe. Although both retributive and rehabilitative prisons aspire to convert criminals into law-abiding subjects, they most successfully manufacture convicts. "The prison may have its monks," advises one, "but it breeds no penitents."[54]

Although less completely, prison employees are remade by the prison experience as well. This was especially true in the old days, when officers hailed from similar backgrounds and more often lived on the units. But even today the unique qualities of the job—the rigid hierarchies, the geographic isolation, the forced intimacy mixed with contempt, the undercurrents of violence, the social stigma associated with prison work—foster staff insularity and individual transformation. During training, new boots learn to keep their distance from "offenders"—to use the currently favored nomenclature—to remain constantly vigilant, and to regard every interaction as potentially treacherous. Over time, as convicts test them, most guards develop a self-preserving callousness toward their charges, whom they come to regard as duplicitous, potentially dangerous, and deserving of their fate. "I'd rather work at a dog kennel," one veteran says, "they mind better."[55]

Symbiotically, convicts react by hardening further; they come to view their keepers not as honorable gray-collar stiffs struggling to make their truck payments but as "a species of humanity coated with moral filth." On both sides of the bars, then, prisons nurture the sort of personality traits that forensic psychologists associate with one of the most dangerous diagnoses, psychopathy.[56] Prisons punish empathy and reward cold calculation. On most days, the resulting mistrust and mutual hostility floats through the tiers like a toxic miasma. At flash points—often during transitions from one management regime to another—it can easily ignite, as the history of prisons in Texas and almost everywhere else makes clear. Predicated on violent containment, to violence prisons regularly return.

From the earliest days, prison managers grappled with the Manichaean tensions that took root in their shrouded domains. Many of penology's most vaunted innovations—from indeterminate sentencing to the Mutual Welfare League to group counseling—were attempts to mitigate prison polarization, to win the grudging consent of the damned. When those, too, failed to produce docile inmates, prison professionals, as well as a growing cadre of prison sociologists, surrendered to a deeper skepticism. "In spite of the many ingenious programs to bring about modification of attitudes or reform," wrote Donald Clemmer, one of the leery forerunners, "the unseen environment in the prisoner's world, with few exceptions, continues to be charged with ideational content inimical to reform."[57]

Such world weariness later undergirded the community corrections and decarceration movements, but prison boosters like John DiIulio rejected such institutional pessimism. In his influential paean to the Texas control model, *Governing Prisons,* DiIulio ridiculed what he called the "sociological understanding" of prisons, and argued that stern, consistent, Texas-style discipline could make prisons "safe" and "civilized," "no more likely to fail than . . . schools, armies, state hospitals, [or] regulatory agencies."[58] History, though, contradicts the political scientist. Although certain well-honed management regimes, including the authoritarian control model, have demonstrated above-average stability and staying power, most prisons in most places have proven remarkably entropic, incubators of not just misery but mayhem. Even in the most effective administrations—those managed by Zebulon Brockway, Joseph Ragen, and George Beto—subsequent investigations and lawsuits revealed that much villainy was going on behind closed doors.

Not all prisons are alike, of course. Some are much safer, for both inmates and staff, as DiIulio rightly points out. Some are more restrictive, others less. In the highest-security lockups, danger virtually disappears, as does human contact. At the other end of the spectrum, some minimum-security, treatment-oriented facilities bear a striking resemblance to outside life; they can seem almost pleasant. The very best prisons may help some residents turn their lives around and prepare for successful reentry to free society. By and large and over the long haul, however, the prison as an institutional form has fostered more criminogenesis than moral regeneration, more debasement than redemption, more scandal than success. Were the prison, with its lengthy record, judged by the same standard as its inhabitants, it would surely be classified as a repeat offender, perhaps a candidate for the death penalty.

For most of American history, this recurrent bankruptcy of the prison— its unremitting racism, its soul-scarring cultural dynamics, its limitless capacity for depravity, its stunning inability, despite repeated overhauls, to reclaim criminals—had, for all its horrors, a comparably minimal impact. Reformers and their rivals designed and redesigned penitentiaries, entrusting them with utopian hopes or sealing within them their darkest fears. For all their philosophical portent, however, prisons touched few lives directly. In the early twentieth century, when Osborne shook up the field, the total U.S. prisoner population stood at 69,000, about the size of Wilkes-Barre, Pennsylvania, then the nation's eighty-third largest city. By O. B. Ellis and Richard McGee's day, the prison head count had grown to 178,000, but that still amounted to just one-tenth of one percent of the larger population.[59] From the invention of penal rehabilitation to the beginnings of its demise, prisons were peripheral institutions.

Not so today. In 2008, the U.S. prison and jail population exceeded 2.4 million, equivalent to the nation's fourth largest city, outdone only by New York, Los Angeles, and Chicago. In per capita terms, the incarceration rate has reached 788 per 100,000 residents, seven times above the historic norm; in Texas, the rate is 991 per 100,000. Across the country, one out of nine young African American men is currently in prison or jail, with a greater portion on parole or probation.[60] Once marginal, prisons have emerged as pillars of American government, core institutions in the management of an increasingly diverse society.

Even as prisons have extended their reach, however, most people have lost faith in their ability to promote public good. Once erected in grand architectural style and imbued with grand hopes, prisons today are spare concrete boxes with confused missions. The most compelling contemporary argument for their large-scale deployment is that they keep crime-prone individuals off the streets. This incapacitation effect, most criminologists agree, has contributed to perhaps a quarter of the decline in U.S. crime rates over the past decade. Because this sort of postconviction preventative detention costs so much and deprives so many of their liberty, however, few want to acknowledge incapacitation as the primary objective of incarceration; to do so seems too utilitarian, too contrary to the principle of individuated justice. Instead, alternative explanations continue bouncing around in the popcorn popper of public ideas, no matter how weakly buttered by evidence. There is the moral, frequently biblical, injunction to punish wrongdoing, although no one agrees on how much or for how long. There is the old canard, deterrence, which remains as unverifiable as ever (in truth, burglars rarely stop to consult sentencing statutes before breaking a window in search of the next score). There is the victims' rights rationale, an update of the ancient eye-for-an-eye credo. Even rehabilitation still gets invoked, although robustly funded, well-designed programs are fewer and further between. At TDCJ, the agency mission statement pledges to "promote positive change in offender behavior," though the administration makes no more effort than it ever did.[61] The sum total of these cacophonous, often contradictory rationales for mass incarceration is incoherence. Prisons are among the country's most structurally solid and historically resilient institutions, but they operate on a shaky philosophical foundation.

With the mission uncertain, the results dubious, the headaches chronic, and the costs mounting, many policy makers at the start of a new century are beginning to ask themselves, Is there a better way?

This book doesn't detail specific alternatives but, as we come to the end of this rather sorrowful tale, it's worth pausing for a moment to consider where we've been and where we might go from here. We have traveled far in these pages, from the Indian wars of Stephen Austin to the terror wars of George W. Bush, from the slave plantation to the supermax. Along the way, my hope is that readers have tucked away a few lessons. We have seen that inequitable societies produce unequal justice, that criminal justice has as much to do with subjection as safety, that good intentions can easily go awry (though not so quickly as bad ones), and that the modern prison owes as much to slave masters as to Quaker reformers. My hope is that these insights will help us contend with the challenges ahead.

As we peer into the fog at the end of this extended prison journey, it seems to me that three possible pathways present themselves. One option is to stay the retributive course. America's criminal justice juggernaut currently consumes more than $200 billion a year and employs 2.4 million individuals to keep 7.3 million others under formal state supervision. Such might be the limit, but the United States is a rich country, and there's no reason to think that prosecutors and lawmakers can't keep filling new prisons as they've been doing for almost forty years.[62]

Because of the incapacitation effect, further expansion would most likely continue to curtail crime, especially if greater numbers of young repeat offenders were kept locked up into middle age. To provide space for, say, much of the country's unemployed (assuming this as a natural stopping point) would require at least quadrupling the size of our current incarceration infrastructure. This might sound outlandish, but it's precisely what the United States did between 1985 and 2000.[63]

There would be costs, of course, fundamental ones. Criminal justice expenditures would close in on the trillion-dollar mark, devouring money for schools, health care, and free-world infrastructure. America's tattered promise of equal citizenship would give way as incarceration rates for young African American men crept into majority territory. If the Confederacy at its peak held almost 4 million Americans in bondage, this new carceral Union would imprison twice as many; it would represent the Rebels' final vengeance. Increasingly, the United States would come to resemble not the social democracies it once defended in western Europe but their foes. Somewhere on this road toward an American gulag, Leviathan will slay liberty.

A more probable course, perhaps, if America's destiny is more democratic than authoritarian, is that policy makers will rediscover the "fond hope" of criminal rehabilitation. In the face of bulging budgets and persistently high recidivism rates, lawmakers may turn, as they have before, to prisoner education, job training, drug treatment, psychological counseling, parole, and aftercare. There are signs that the Obama administration, state lawmakers, and even politicians in Texas are considering this approach, shifting resources from incarceration to research-based prevention and treatment programs.[64]

But there is promise as well as peril along this well-trodden thoroughfare. Another round of penological innovation will alleviate suffering and may enhance public safety. On the other hand, if retooling proceeds without scaling back, if the criminal justice net widens rather than retracts, we may unleash further cycles of reform and reaction. On the backside of another reformatory romp, we could end up with a prison establishment even larger and more entrenched than the one we have now. Leviathan lurks down this path as well.

Finally, Americans may consider taking a road less traveled. More than four decades ago, in the closing days of the Great Society, Lyndon Johnson's crime commission suggested that the nation shift its mighty resources from punishing crime to preventing crime. "A country's most enduring protection against crime is to right the wrongs and cure the illnesses that tempt men to harm their neighbors," offered the final report.[65] In the political arena, the Katzenbach Commission's unwieldy policy recommendations were mocked by the rising right and soon forgotten. As we grapple with the formidable consequences of that mockery, however, we would do well to take another look.

Continuously fighting the "war against crime" in late-twentieth-century style—an approach that circles the wagons and opens fire against criminal enemies—is not the only way to deal with lawbreaking and seemingly intractable social problems. Instead, we could reinvigorate a rival, equally misnamed campaign of the same vintage, the War on Poverty. Its methods and even its goals are strangely foreign to us now—after four decades of the New Right counterrevolution—but they are worth rekindling, especially now that we know what their antitheses have wrought. Amid a broad democratic renewal of the sort that has swept through American society from time to time—during Reconstruction and the New Deal, for instance—we could embark on a long-neglected pursuit of justice, defined in social as well as individual terms. Rather than demanding order above all, we might prioritize hope and economic opportunity, especially in downtrodden neighborhoods that lack all three. In addition to securing the rights of crime victims, we might make amends for historic wrongs and finally, at long last, make good on the promise of equal citizenship. Rather than crafting a more punitive response to every infraction, we might provide a richer set of choices to the refractory. Rather than getting even, we might endeavor to minimize harm. Rather than clamping down, we might lift up. Such a redirection of public policy may not lead us to a "nation without prisons," as the most far-reaching reformers of the late civil rights era hoped, but it would almost certainly lead toward a nation with many fewer.

Such an optimistic trajectory might seem unlikely. Lest we consign ourselves to overly modest dreams, however, let us remember that slavery and segregation, too, once promised to rule forever. Even the widely unpopular convict lease system took half a century to dismantle. Yet unforeseen historical developments, along with dedicated people working together—some bonded, some free—ultimately toppled these ignominious institutions. In the century that followed, prison reformers time and again prevailed over harsh regimes. In most cases, they created flawed institutions in their stead. Rather than harvesting regret alone, however, we can learn from their missed opportunities and partial successes. Only by taking honest stock of the full history of the prison can we plot our escape from it.

16

Prisoners of the Census in New York: Democracy on the March!

Eric Lotke

New York is the most recent state to pass new rules about how people in prison are counted in the U.S. Census. The law passed on Tuesday evening [August 3, 2010] provides that for purposes of political redistricting, incarcerated persons count as residents of their places of residence prior to incarceration, not as residents at their place of incarceration.

Maryland passed a similar rule in April. Delaware passed one in June. If other states move in this direction, it will become a trend that the Census Bureau cannot ignore. The Bureau's job, after all, is to take the Census. Three states representing 8.5 percent of the U.S. population think something is wrong. As the votes of no confidence continue, the Census may need to change its practice.

First, some history. The Census Bureau's general rule is to count people at their "usual residence," the place where they live and sleep most of the time. People's usual residence need not be the same as their legal or voting address—but still, determining the usual residence for most people is as easy as filling out a form. Special categories present special challenges, however. Sailors in the merchant marine, children in joint custody and long-term commuters all require different rules, and these rules have evolved over time. People in prison are in a category called "group quarters" which includes nursing homes, college dormitories, military installations and other places where unrelated persons live together. As a rule, people in group quarters count where the group quarters are located. For people in prison, that's the prison. In cases like college dormitories, individuals are given forms and invited to fill them out, generally choosing either the college or their family home.

From "Prisoners of the Census in New York: Democracy on the March!" by Eric Lotke, *Huffington Post*, August 4, 2010, http://www.huffingtonpost.com/eric -lotke/new-york-state-and-prison_b_670066.html.

Applying the simple usual residence rule to people in prison might once have been reasonable—but no more. Nowadays, 2.4 million people are in prison or jail in America. Nowadays, more people live in prison and jail than in our three least populous states combined. Organized differently, they would have six votes in the U.S. Senate, almost votes enough to move from majority to cloture. The Census Bureau rule no longer makes sense. Demographics make it worse. White men are imprisoned at a rate of 770 per 100,000; black men at six times that rate, closer to 4,600 per 100,000. Regardless of crime, justice or just deserts, the Census Bureau gives this disparity new operational significance. People in prison generally lose the right to vote, but their bodies still count for purposes of political apportionment. The Census Bureau thus counts people out of the urban centers that they usually consider home and to which they will return long before the next census; it counts them instead in rural communities where they have little common interest, and will leave as soon as they are able.

Even more insidious, this population counts in the rural area with the prison but not in the similar adjacent rural area without the prison, which enhances the prison region's clout compared to its neighbors. Researchers (and I have long been one of them) call it "prison-based gerrymandering."

In New York State one out of every three people who moved to upstate New York in the 1990s actually "moved" into a prison. Most of them (66%) are New York City residents, but the vast majority of them (91%) are counted by the Census as residents of upstate prison towns. The new bill changes that. (The bill passed the Assembly a while ago and passed the Senate late Tuesday evening; it awaits the governor's signature wrapped in the budget bill.)

In Maryland, which changed its rule in April, 18 percent of the population credited to Maryland House of Delegates District 2B (near Hagerstown) is actually incarcerated people shipped in from other parts of the state. In Somerset County, 64 percent of the population in the First Commission District is a large prison, giving each resident in that district nearly three times as much influence as residents in other districts.

An especially charming example comes from Anamosa, Iowa. One City Council member was elected with only two votes, his neighbor and his wife. Everyone else who makes up his district is in a nearby prison. Peter Wagner of the Prison Policy Initiative tells the story, part of the *Gerrymandering* movie due out in the fall.

Yes, there is a solution. For the 2010 census, the Bureau has agreed to release micro-data early enough that jurisdictions who choose can try to correct the problem manually. It's hard work, but it's a step in the right direction. For 2020, the Census Bureau should simply give people in prison a form to fill out, just like they do for the rest of the population. Prisons are highly controlled environments where mail, food, uniforms and work orders are distributed daily. Passing out the Census form would present little problem. As a backup, official data for address at time of arrest or for supervision upon release are generally available in institutional files. The Census Bureau has ten years. Three states have already sent the signal. Changing the rule would be a victory for democracy over bureaucracy.

Part VIII

Collateral Consequences: Could It Get Any Worse?

Short of execution or a life sentence without parole, punishment presumably has an end. Society should not be a loan shark when it comes to paying off one's debts. But for young urban poor, especially those caught up in the drug war, the punishment never stops.

Getting locked up even once can have harsh socioeconomic consequences, not least recidivism. The odds of going to prison are much greater for those who have been there already than for those who have not. There is also the opportunity cost: time behind bars is time not in school or at work, not to mention getting married or having a family, activities that correlate positively with employment, income, and other beneficial developments. This all leaves aside the psychological, as well as possible physical, harm that confinement might cause. Many are subjected to the extremes of overcrowding or isolation, a disciplinary practice that increasingly is used as a preventive, and thus indefinite, measure. Separation from the outside world is particularly disruptive for those previously living in restricted environments, such as ghettos, which are frequently re-created by the demographics of prison populations.

Great harm is also being done through the willful and institutionalized stigmatizing and handicapping of the formerly incarcerated. Denial of the vote and the right to obtain licenses for such professions as barber or electrician are common and long-standing insults that add to the injury of imprisonment. More sophisticated add-ons have appeared in recent times; drug crime convictions now disqualify eligibility for public benefits, including public housing.

What does this do to individuals? What does this do to the communities that are home to many such individuals, particularly those of the wage-earning and family-rearing age? What does this do to Americans disproportionately provided with inferior education, accommodation, health care, employment opportunities, and social capital? What happens to our fellow black citizens, overrepresented in prison populations, when they return to a society whose conditions had something to do with getting them locked up in the first place? As far as their future is concerned, should it matter whether they turned to crime out of frustration or convenience, from lack of choice or lack of scruples?

In "Incarceration and Social Inequality," from the 2010 *Dædalus* issue on mass incarceration, sociologists Bruce Western of Harvard University and Becky Pettit of Washington University review the demographic effects of incarceration. They single out black men born since the mid-1970s who dropped out of high school as the group most affected and—through the exacting analysis for which Western is particularly renowned—analyze their employment, earnings, and upward mobility. Statistics also help them uncover incarceration's effects on marriage, divorce, domestic abuse, childbearing, and development and behavioral problems among children. They contend that the mass incarceration of this group of black men—68 percent have criminal records—is creating crime rather than preventing it.

Todd R. Clear, Rutgers University dean and founding editor of *Criminology & Public Policy*, confirms this contention in his book *Imprisoning Communities: How Mass Incarceration Makes Disadvantaged Neighborhoods Worse*. He broadens the focus to the communities where the over-incarcerated lead and return to their lives, and identifies social networks and social supports as the key elements to analyze. An impressive number of social scientists have studied specific aspects of the family lives of the formerly incarcerated, along with the economic and political strength of their communities, and Clear surveys this research. It seems that high rates of incarceration undermine the mechanisms—the relationships of informal control—that communities use to maintain order. As a result, crime increases where too many people get taken away and locked up.

Further Reading: In *Releasing Prisoners, Redeeming Communities: Reentry, Race, and Politics* (NYU Press, 2009), Anthony C. Thompson, NYU clinical law professor and former public defender, addresses the range of challenges facing recently released prisoners. Reentry has become an industry in itself, spawning academic research as well as social service organizations that attend specifically to the needs of ex-convicts. And it is a big industry: as many as 700,000 people annually have been leaving prison over recent years. Reentry is a time when it is possible to tally the opportunity cost incurred by their time away from society, in addition to the damages that they may well have suffered behind bars. Among other subjects, Thompson focuses on the health problems that most people bring with them when first incarcerated and all too often take home when released. While the law requires treatment for prisoners, they generally get released with exacerbated and additional maladies. Their families and communities must seek resources and services to help them, and must do so within a health care system that notoriously does not provide enough for anyone but the well-off.

17

Incarceration and Social Inequality

Bruce Western and Becky Pettit

The ubiquity of penal confinement in the lives of young African American men with little schooling is historically novel, emerging only in the last decade. However, this new reality is only half the story of understanding the significance of mass incarceration in America. The other half of the story concerns the effects of incarceration on social and economic inequality. The inequalities produced by contemporary patterns of incarceration have three characteristics: the inequalities associated with incarceration are invisible to our usual accounting of the economic well-being of the population; the inequality is cumulative, deepening the disadvantage of the most marginal men in society; and finally, the inequality is intergenerational, transmitting the penalties of a prison record from one generation to the next. Because the characteristic inequalities produced by the American prison boom are invisible, cumulative, and intergenerational, they are extremely enduring, sustained over lifetimes and passed through families.

Invisible Inequality. The inequality created by incarceration is often invisible to the mainstream of society because incarceration is concentrated and segregative. We have seen that steep racial and class disparities in incarceration have produced a generation of social outliers whose collective experience is wholly different from the rest of American society. The extreme concentration of incarceration rates is compounded by the obviously segregative function of the penal system, which often relocates people to far-flung facilities distant from their communities and families. As a result, people in prison and jail are disconnected from the basic institutions—households and the labor market—that dominate our common understanding and measurement of the population. The segregation

From "Incarceration and Social Inequality," *Dædalus*, Summer 2010, 11–16.

and social concentration of incarceration thus help conceal its effects. This fact is particularly important for public policy because in assessing the social and economic well-being of the population, the incarcerated fraction is frequently overlooked, and inequality is underestimated as a result.

The idea of invisible inequality is illustrated by considering employment rates as they are conventionally measured by the Current Population Survey, the large monthly labor force survey conducted by the Census Bureau. For groups that are weakly attached to the labor market, like young men with little education, economic status is often measured by the employment-to-population ratio. This figure, more expansive than the unemployment rate, counts as jobless those who have dropped out of the labor market altogether. The Current Population Survey is drawn on a sample of households, so those who are institutionalized are not included in the survey-based description of the population.

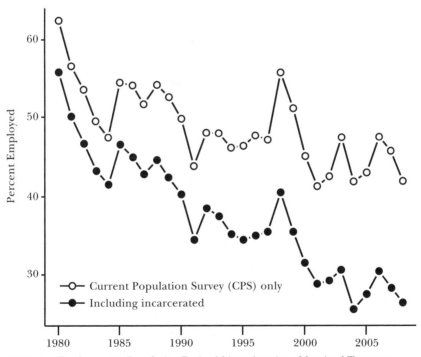

FIGURE 1 *Employment to Population Ratio, African American Men Aged Twenty to Thirty-Four with Less than Twelve Years of Schooling, 1980 to 2008*
Source: Becky Pettit, Bryan Sykes, and Bruce Western, "Technical Report on Revised Population Estimates and NLSY79 Analysis Tables for the Pew Public Safety and Mobility Project" (Harvard University, 2009).

Figure 1 shows the employment-to-population ratio for African American men under age thirty-five who have not completed high school. Conventional estimates of the employment rate show that by 2008, around 40 percent of African American male dropouts were employed. These estimates, based on the household survey, fail to count that part of the population in prison or jail. Once prison and jail inmates are included in the population count (and among the jobless), we see that employment among young African American men with little schooling fell to around 25 percent by 2008. Indeed, by 2008 these men were more likely to be locked up than employed.

Cumulative Inequality. Serving time in prison or jail diminishes social and economic opportunities. As we have seen, these diminished opportunities are found among those already most socioeconomically disadvantaged. A burgeoning research literature examining the economic effects of incarceration finds that incarceration is associated with reduced earnings and employment.[1]

We analyzed panel data from the National Longitudinal Survey of Youth (NLSY), one of the few surveys that follow respondents over a long period of time and that interview incarcerated respondents in prison. The NLSY began in 1979, when its panel of respondents was aged fourteen to twenty-one; it completed its latest round of interviews in 2006. Matching our population estimates of incarceration, one in five African American male respondents in the NLSY has been interviewed at some point between 1979 and 2006 while incarcerated, compared to 5 percent of whites and 12 percent of Latino respondents. Analysis of the NLSY showed that serving time in prison was associated with a 40 percent reduction in earnings and with reduced job tenure, reduced hourly wages, and higher unemployment.

The negative effects of incarceration, even among men with very poor economic opportunities to begin with, are related to the strong negative perceptions employers have of job seekers with criminal records. Devah Pager's experimental research has studied these employer perceptions by sending pairs of fake job seekers to apply for real jobs.[2] In each pair, one of the job applicants was randomly assigned a résumé indicating a criminal record (a parole officer is listed as a reference), and the "criminal" applicant was instructed to check the box on the job application indicating he had a criminal record. A criminal record was found to reduce callbacks from prospective employers by around 50 percent, an effect that was larger for African Americans than for whites.

Incarceration may reduce economic opportunities in several ways. The conditions of imprisonment may promote habits and behaviors that are poorly suited to the routines of regular work. Time in prison means time out of the labor force, depleting the work experience of the incarcerated compared to their non-incarcerated counterparts. The stigma of a criminal conviction may also repel employers who prefer job applicants with clean records. Pager's audit study offers clear evidence for the negative effects of criminal stigma. Employers, fearing legal liability or even just unreliability, are extremely reluctant to hire workers with criminal convictions.

A simple picture of the poor economic opportunities of the formerly incarcerated is given by the earnings mobility of men going to prison compared to other disadvantaged groups. The NLSY data can be used to study earnings mobility over several decades. We calculated the chances that a poor man in the lowest fifth of the earnings distribution in 1986 would move up and out of the lowest fifth by 2006. Among low-income men who are not incarcerated, nearly two-thirds are upwardly mobile by 2006 (Figure 2). Another group in the NLSY has very low levels of cognitive ability, scoring in the bottom quintile of the Armed Forces Qualifying Test, the standardized test used for military service. Among low-income men with low scores on the test, only 41 percent are upwardly mobile. Upward mobility is even less common among low-income high school dropouts. Still, we observe the least mobility of all among men who were incarcerated at some point between 1986 and 2006. For these men, only one in four rises out of the bottom quintile of the earnings distribution.

Intergenerational Inequality. Finally, the effects of the prison boom extend also to the families of those who are incarcerated. Through the prism of research on poverty, scholars find that the family life of the disadvantaged has become dramatically more complex and unstable over the last few decades. Divorce and nonmarital births have contributed significantly to rising rates of single parenthood, and these changes in American family structure are concentrated among low-income mothers. As a consequence, poor children regularly grow up, at least for a time, with a single mother and, at different times, with a variety of adult males in their households.

High rates of parental incarceration likely add to the instability of family life among poor children. Over half of all prisoners have children under the age of eighteen, and about 45 percent of those parents were living with their children at the time they were sent to prison. About two-thirds of prisoners stay in regular contact with their children either by phone, mail, or visitation.[3] Ethnographer Megan Comfort paints a vivid picture of the effects of men's incarceration on the women and families in their lives. She quotes a prisoner at San Quentin State Prison in California:

Nine times out of ten it's the woman [maintaining contact with prisoners]. Why? Because your homeboys, or your friends, if you're in that lifestyle, most the time they're gonna be sittin' right next to your ass in prison. . . . The males, they don't really participate like a lot of females in the lives of the incarcerated. . . . They don't deal with it, like first of all they don't like to bring to reality that you're in prison; they don't wanna think about that . . . Or some of 'em just don't care. So the male's kinda like wiped out of there, so that *puts all the burden on the woman*.[4]

Partly because of the burdens of incarceration on women who are left to raise families in free society, incarceration is strongly associated with divorce and separation. In addition to the forced separation of incarceration, the post-release effects on economic opportunities leave formerly incarcerated parents less equipped to provide financially for their children. New research also shows that the children of incarcerated parents, particularly the boys, are at greater risk of developmental delays and behavioral problems.[5]

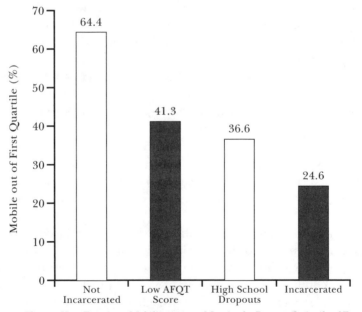

FIGURE 2 *Twenty-Year Earnings Mobility among Men in the Bottom Quintile of Earnings Distribution in 1986, National Longitudinal Survey of Youth (NLSY) Men AFQT stands for Armed Forces Qualifying Test.*
Source: Becky Pettit, Bryan Sykes, and Bruce Western, "Technical Report on Revised Population Estimates and NLSY79 Analysis Tables for the Pew Public Safety and Mobility Project" (Harvard University, 2009).

Against this evidence for the negative effects of incarceration, we should weigh the gains to public safety obtained by separating violent or otherwise antisocial men from their children and partners. Domestic violence is much more common among the formerly incarcerated compared to other disadvantaged men. Survey data indicate that formerly incarcerated men are about four times more likely to assault their domestic partners than men who have never been incarcerated. Though the relative risk is very high, around 90 percent of the partners of formerly incarcerated report no domestic violence at all.

The scale of the effects of parental incarceration on children can be revealed simply by statistics showing the number of children with a parent in prison or jail. Among white children in 1980, only 0.4 of 1 percent had an incarcerated parent; by 2008 this figure had increased to 1.75 percent. Rates of parental incarceration are roughly double among Latino children, with 3.5 percent of children having a parent locked up by 2008. Among African American children, 1.2 million, or about 11 percent, had a parent incarcerated by 2008.

18

Death by a Thousand Little Cuts:
Studies of the Impact of Incarceration

Todd R. Clear

The preceding chapter offered the conceptual case that high levels of incarceration would be damaging to impoverished communities. It turns out that from what we *already know* about social networks and social supports, especially in impoverished places, high rates of imprisonment ought to create challenges for those places. It is obvious that going to prison creates problems for the people who go there; after all, one of the reasons we use prison is to impose a deficit on the lawbreaker's life. We do not use prison in order to diminish the prospects for those who remain behind, however; to the contrary, we justify prison in part because it is expected to ameliorate the problems faced by those who live in high-crime communities. Yet cycling a large number of young men from a particular place through imprisonment, and then returning them to that place, is not healthy for the people who live in that place. There are sound theoretical reasons to expect high incarceration rates to make many of these places worse, not better. This is, to many, a surprising, even counterintuitive, conclusion. It certainly demands empirical support.

This chapter provides that support. In it, I review dozens of studies showing that different aspects of incarceration make life harder for those who live in places that experience high rates of incarceration. The chapter is organized around the three domains identified at the close of chapter 4. It begins with a review of studies of the impact of incarceration on families and children. Incarceration, it turns out, affects marriage prospects, parenting capacity, family functioning, and even sexual behavior. These effects add up to alter the way a community functions. The result of this collective impact on child, family, and community functioning is

From *Imprisoning Communities: How Mass Incarceration Makes Disadvantaged Neighborhoods Worse* (New York: Oxford University Press, 2009), 93–117.

a reduction in the capacity for informal social control. (I explore studies of the public safety consequences of reduced informal social controls in chapter 7.) Compared to the large number of studies of families and children, there are few exploring the impact of incarceration on economic activity. But here again, the way imprisonment diminishes the individual's economic viability translates into substantially reduced economic viability at the community level. Finally, I summarize the small number of studies of the political consequences of incarceration. These effects are profound for poor places; through the way disenfranchisement has affected electoral politics, the impact has reached all Americans.

None of these effects is particularly large by itself. But each effect, no matter how small, cannot be considered in isolation from the others. It is not just a single effect, like reduced rates of marriage, that is important, but rather the sum of reduced marriage rates, more teen-age motherhood, diminished parental supervision, and so on in those communities where incarceration is so concentrated. The review of these studies reads like a nonstop monologue of difficulties, one after another, building a sense that incarceration slices its way into almost every aspect of community life. The studies help us see how various negative effects of incarceration, many of them small, are cumulative; taken together, they are like suffering death by a thousand little cuts.

Children and Families

We were walking around the South City neighborhood of Tallahassee, the summer of 2001. As summers always are in the Florida Panhandle, it was steamy hot. People stay inside; there may be a threesome of pre-teens playing basketball in the schoolyard, or a couple of pre-schoolers yelling exuberantly, playing in the shade of a tree. But for the most part, the out-of-doors is empty. School's out, so it would be natural to wonder where the kids are. We enter a two-story housing project, go upstairs to knock on a door in the door of a household in our sample, and explain why we are there. We are invited in. It is dark inside, the television is blaring. Four children at various ages, maybe ranging from 4 to 9, are sitting— no, bouncing—on the couch. That is where the children are, we realize, inside. Hidden or hiding. Watching TV. It becomes a theme in almost every house we visit. Mothers, children, television, noise . . . and no fathers.

Families are the building blocks of a healthy society, and family functioning is the key ingredient in child development. Adults in the family socialize their children about the normative rules and behavioral expectations of society. Family members connect one another—especially children—to networks of social supports that become the foundation for later social capital as adults. Families are the central mechanism of informal social controls, bolstering the limited capacity of formal social controls to shape behavior. And the interpersonal dynamics of families are the source of later psychological and emotional health (or maladjustment). There is no single institution that carries more importance in the well-being of children than the family, and the prospects for healthy social relations in adulthood rely heavily on the existence of a vibrant family life.

There are indications that family life in America is changing, especially among people who are poor. In this group, changes over the last 40 years have been devastating: divorce rates are one-third higher and births to unmarried mothers have doubled, as has the rate of households headed by single mothers (see Western, Lopoo, and McLanahan 2004). Small wonder that so much attention has recently been given to strengthening and sustaining the family life of poor families in America.

Incarceration policy has been a fellow traveler in the deterioration of poor American families. For example, almost three out of five African American high-school dropouts will spend some time in prison, a rate five times higher than for equivalent whites (Pettit and Western 2004). Two-fifths of those African American high-school dropouts are fathers who were living with their children before they entered prison (Western, Patillo, and Weiman 2004). One-fourth of *juveniles* convicted of crime have children (Nurse 2004); locking up these fathers increases the chances of divorce and damages their bonds with their children. Counting both adult and juvenile parents, there are probably close to 2 million children in the United States with a parent currently behind prison bars (extrapolating from Western, Pattillo, and Weiman 2004). Between 1991 and 1999, according to Murray and Farrington (forthcoming), the number of children with a mother in prison was up 98 percent, and the number with a father in prison rose by 58 percent. Half of these children are black, almost one-tenth of all black children (Western 2005: fig. 6.2).

That incarceration affects families and children in deleterious ways should be obvious. There is a long and rich literature showing that removal of a parent from the home has, on the average, negative consequences for the partner and the children who remain (see, for example, Bloom 1995 and Hairston 1998). This is the average picture, of course, which masks considerable variation in outcomes. Some families do well in the face of loss; others fare disastrously. What is not clear is the nature and extent of the disruption that follows an adult's incarceration, though numerous negative and positive effects can be posited from the literature (see Hagan and Donovitzer 1999). Phillips et al. (2006) point out that:

There is evidence . . . that the arrest of parents disrupts marital relationships, separates children and parents, and may contribute to
the permanent legal dissolution of these relationships. It may also
contribute to the establishment of grandparent-headed households
and, upon parents' return home from prison, to three-generation
households. (103)

They go on to say that, "One must be careful . . . in attributing these family risks to parents' involvement with the [criminal justice system] because
these same situations (e.g., divorce, parent-child separation, economic
strain, instability, large households, and so forth) also occur when parents have problems such as substance abuse, mental illness, or inadequate
education" (104). Thus, while it is known that the incarceration of a parent (especially the mother) increases the chances of foster care or other
substitute-care placement, and that substitute (i.e., foster) care is associated with poorer long-term life outcomes, "we know remarkably little
about whether children placed in substitute care fare better or worse than
similar children remaining with their own parent or parents" (Johnson
and Waldfogel 2004:100). And while there is a host of behavioral and
emotional problems associated with being a child of an incarcerated parent (see Hagan and Dinovitzer 1999), there are but a few studies showing
that the parent's incarceration *causes* this kind of distress.

Having an adult family member go to prison has been shown as a source
of problems, not the least of which is increased risk of juvenile delinquency
(Widom 1994). Myriad studies show that children and partners of incarcerated adults tend to experience other difficulties, as well, compared
to children of nonincarcerated parents. These include school-related
performance problems, depression and anxiety, low self-esteem, and ag-
gressiveness (see Hagan and Dinovitzer 1999). The studies show that the
negative psychological, behavioral, and circumstantial impact on children
from the removal of a parent for incarceration is similar in form, though
not always in degree, to that produced by removal owing to divorce or
death.

It might be argued that removal of a criminally active parent *improves*
the environment of the remaining children. This is clearly not true. Studies (Nurse 2004) have found that substantial positive parental activity has
often preceded incarceration. Garfinkel, McLanahan, and Hanson concluded that even though young fathers may have trouble holding a job and
may even spend time in jail, most of them have something to offer their
children (1998).

A brief review of studies of incarceration and family life helps illustrate
the array of problems that arise.

MARRIAGE

There is consistent evidence that poor neighborhoods in which there is a large ratio of adult women to men are places where female-headed, single-parent families are common, and that incarceration is one of several dynamics that have removed black males from their neighborhoods, producing this ratio (Darity and Myers 1994). This may be a race-specific effect; in a county-level analysis for 1980 and 1990, Sabol and Lynch (2003) found that *both* removals to and returns from prison increased the rate of female-headed households in the county.

Being incarcerated reduces marriage prospects for young men. Analyzing the National Longitudinal Survey of Youth (NLSY), Harvard economist Adam Thomas (2005) found that going to prison substantially reduces the likelihood of being married. The effects hold across all racial and ethnic groups, but are strongest for black males over 23 years old, whose likelihood of getting married drops by 50 percent following incarceration. Thomas concluded that "past imprisonment is associated with a lower probability of marrying not only in the near term but also over the long run . . . [and] it is certainly the case that, among blacks, the relationship cannot easily be explained away by casually controlling for economic, family background characteristics, and neighborhood effects" (2005:26–27). He does find, however, that men with past incidents of incarceration who do become involved with women are more likely instead to cohabit without marriage. These unconventional living arrangements contribute to intergenerational family dysfunction. Cohabitation is associated with previous parental divorce, suggesting an intergenerational pattern, and it carries the risk for future abuse or neglect (called "troubled home"). Western's (2006) analysis of the NYSL confirms these patterns, and his analysis of the Fragile Families Survey of Child Well-Being estimates that going to prison cuts the rate of marriage within a year of the birth of a child by at least one-half and about doubles the chance of separating in that same year (figs. 6.8, 6.9). It is thus not surprising that Lynch and Sabol (2004b) have estimated that 46 percent of the prison population are currently divorced, compared to 17 percent of nonimprisoned adults.

The reduction in the rate of marriage is important in several respects. Families formed by marriage have more longevity than those defined by cohabitation, on average. Mothers in marriages expect and receive more support from their male partners than those in cohabitation relationships (Gibson, Edin, and McLanahan 2003, cited in Western, Lopoo and McLanahan 2004). With increases in family disruption and reduced male involvement in the home there are increased risks of poor school performance by children, of domestic violence, and of contact with the juvenile justice system (Western 2006, esp. figs. 6.10, 6.11).

For the men, there are also consequences of incarceration on marriage. Laub, Nagin, and Sampson (1998) have shown that stable marriages promote lifestyle changes in adults who were previously criminally active; marriage can thus serve as a turning point in their criminal careers (see also Sampson and Laub 1993). Men who do not get married tend to find it harder to form pro-social relationships and identify the positive social bonds that promote an end to criminal activity. It follows that reduced marriage prospects resulting from a term in prison are a risk factor in recidivism.

PARENTING

While they are locked up, many men maintain contact with their children; about half receive mail and/or phone calls, and one-fifth receive visits while in prison (U.S. Department of Justice 1997, cited in Western, Pattillo and Weiman 2004: table 1.5). But the rate at which mothers dissolve their relationships with their children's father during the latter's imprisonment is very high, even for fathers who were active in their children's lives prior to being arrested (Edin, Nelson, and Paranal 2004). In general, incarceration has "a deleterious effect on relationships between former inmate fathers and their children" (Nurse 2004:90). In their longitudinal study of the Fragile Families Survey and Child Well-Being Study data, Western, Lopoo, and McLanahan show that "men who have been incarcerated are much less likely to be married to or cohabiting with the mother of their children twelve months after the birth of their children than men who have not been incarcerated" (2004:39–40). There are several reasons for this. For women who live in poor communities, "the decision to marry or remarry depends in part on the economic prospects, social respectability and trustworthiness of their potential partners" (Western, Lopoo, and McLanahan 2004:23). Against these criteria, many (or most) ex-prisoners do not fare well.

Even when mothers retain their relationships with the incarcerated father of their children, incarceration diminishes the capacity for effective parent-child relationships. Edin, Nelson, and Paranal point out that "incarceration often means that fathers miss out on . . . key events that serve to build parental bonds and to signal . . . that they intend to support their children both financially and emotionally. . . . The father's absence at these crucial moments . . . can weaken his commitment to the child years later, and the child's own commitment to his or her father" (2004:57).

Researchers point out that this general pattern has to be understood in the context of two caveats. First, as a group, young fathers who are poor and have marginal human capital typically struggle to maintain good relationships with their children and their young mothers, and incarceration may not be a cause of further difficulties so much as a correlate of the personality and situational factors that produce these difficulties. Under the best of circumstances, the bonds between criminally active fathers and their children are often quite fragile. As a result, sometimes young mothers who made progress when their male partners went to prison suffer setbacks when they return (Cohen 1992). Second, for some fathers who have had little contact with their children before imprisonment, the descent into prison is a life-changing moment that opens a door to renewal of those bonds in ways that are not only beneficial for the child but for the father as well (Edin, Nelson, and Paranal 2004).

There are, after all, over 600,000 men who enter prison in a year, and the range of parental interests and patterns for such a group must run the gamut. On the average, however, having one's parent go to prison is not a positive life experience. It disrupts the family and damages parenting capacity.

FAMILY FUNCTIONING

Lynch and Sabol (2004) have estimated that between one-fourth and one-half of all prisoners disrupt a family when they are removed for incarceration. Joseph Murray's (2005) excellent review lists a dozen studies of the way incarceration of a male parent/spouse (or partner) affects the functioning of the family unit he left behind. The most prominent impact is economic—spouses and partners report various forms of financial hardship, sometimes extreme, that result from the loss of income after the male partner's incarceration. This "loss of income is compounded by additional expenses of prison visits, mail, telephone calls . . . and sending money to [the person] imprisoned" (2005:445). Because most families of prisoners start out with limited financial prospects, even a small financial impact can be devastating. Phillips et al. (2006) longitudinal study of poor, rural children in North Carolina found that having a parent get arrested led to family break-up and family economic strain, both of which, they point out, are risk factors of later delinquency.

After the male's imprisonment, the family responds to his incarceration in a variety of ways. In order to deal with changed financial circumstances, prisoners' families often move, leading to family disruptions that may include the arrival of replacement males in the family, reduced time for maternal parenting owing to secondary employment, and so on (Edin, Nelson, and Paranal 2004). Moves may also result in more crowded living conditions (especially when the prisoner's family moves in with relatives) and changes in educational districts that may produce disruptions in schooling.

There are also relationship problems. Female partners who find a male replacement for the man who has gone to prison often face the psychological strains that accompany the arrival of a new male in the household. Prisoners' spouses and partners report strains in relationships with other family members and neighbors. Carlson and Carvera (1992) showed that women often have to rely on family and friends to fill the hole left by the incarcerated husband, providing money, companionship, and babysitting and generally straining those ties. Strains in the relationships with children are also reported, often resulting from emotional and functional difficulties that spouses and partners encounter when a male partner goes to prison.

Residents of high-incarceration communities see imprisonment as one cause of weakened family functioning. St. Jean calls this "amputation without repair" (personal communication, 2006); in his ethnographic study of crime and neighborhood life in Buffalo, New York, he quotes one of the respondents as saying, "I say amputate, because when you take a son from his mother or from his father, you have amputated. . . . It is like someone cutting off your arm or cutting off your head. It is an unnatural extraction, that puts you in an unnatural place." St. Jean concludes:

> I observed through 4.5 years of intense ethnography that incarceration was the major strategy used to address high crime problems in Wentworth (a poor neighborhood of Buffalo) and when men and women went to jail or prison, they often . . . became more angry and desperate than [when] they entered . . . had more hopelessness . . . and they were less employable. They also became part of a cultural attitude which seemed to treat incarceration as a right of passage.

CHILD FUNCTIONING

Incarceration has an effect on the child that is both direct and indirect (Murray 2005). The mother's incarceration has been shown to produce "a significant worsening of both reading scores and behavioral problems" (Moore and Shierholz 2005:2). Likewise, male parent incarceration has been shown to lead to later antisocial behavior by children in an English sample (Murray and Farrington 2005). This latter study compared children whose parents were incarcerated during their early childhoods to children without parental separation, children for whom parental separation was due to other factors (i.e., death), and children whose parents went to prison and returned before they were born. Outcomes included delinquency, antisocial personality measures, and life successes. The children of incarcerated parents were between 2 and 13 times more likely to have had various negative outcomes than any of the comparison groups. These effects appear to be direct, in part because they survive in the face of statistical controls for social class and other family demographics.

Indirect effects stem from the way incarceration undermines family stability. Changes in parental working conditions and family circumstances often result from incarceration and are known to affect children's social adjustment and norm transmission across generations (Parcel and Menaghan, 1993). Among the problems suffered by children during a parent's incarceration are: "depression, hyperactivity, aggressive behavior, withdrawal, regression, clinging behavior, sleep problems, eating problems, running away, truancy and poor school grades" (Murray 2005:466). Studies have also shown that parental incarceration is a risk factor in delinquency (Gabel and Shindledecker 1993), emotional maladjustment (Kampfner 1995), and academic performance problems (Phillips and Bloom 1998). In her summary of the literature on childhood loss of a parent, including parental incarceration, Marcy Viboch (2005) points to a range of common reactions to the trauma, including depression, aggression, drug abuse, and running away. Murray and Farrington's (forthcoming) systematic review of studies of parental incarceration on children find evidence of both direct and mediated effects on anti-social behavior, school performance, mental health, drug abuse, and adult unemployment. They conclude that "parental imprisonment may cause adverse child outcomes because of traumatic separation, stigma, or social and economic strain." (1)

The potential negative impact of incarceration on school performance is particularly important. School success is linked to family structure, which has an effect independent of social class and parenting style in impoverished families (Vacha and McLaughlin 1992). Behavioral problems in school are also correlated with problems in parental relationships, including child abuse—an early family dynamic that contributes to later delinquency. Psychologist Cathy Spatz Widom (1989, 1994), following a cohort of children from early school years to adulthood, has observed that victims of early childhood abuse had earlier criminal activity, increased risk of an arrest during adolescence (by more than 50%), and, when they became adults, twice as many arrests as controls.

The impact of incarceration on children may become stronger with higher incarceration rates. A study of the impact of incarceration on a

Swedish sample of children (Murray, Janson, and Farrington 2005) found the same kind of higher rate of delinquency for those children, but unlike the other studies cited above, it washed out when statistical controls were introduced. The authors conclude that sparing use of prison stays in Sweden—almost always for very short terms—tends to ameliorate the negative effects of parental incarceration. If that is the case, then the U.S. effects would be even greater than those found in European studies.

COMMUNITY DYNAMICS

At a most basic level, the absence of males restricts the number of adults available to supervise young people in the neighborhood. The presence of large numbers of unsupervised youth is predictive of various aspects of community-level disorder, including serious crime (Sampson and Groves 1989). It is also known that the existence of "adverse neighborhood conditions" as rated by mothers, tended to be associated with a decrease in the self-control of youth who live in disadvantage (Pratt, Turner, and Piquero 2004). Under these conditions, the informal social control over youths that might have been exercised by family members or neighbors often fails to materialize. These attenuated informal social controls are the springboard for crime, and the effects can be felt in adjacent neighborhoods as well (Mears and Bhati 2006).

In the face of community disruptions, some families isolate themselves from neighbors. In a series of interviews in the South Bronx, Andres Rengifo (2006) has observed that many residents seek to withdraw from their impoverished surroundings. One housing project resident, a single mother with four children (one of whom was attending Yale University and two of whom were in the prestigious Bronx High School of Science public school) said that although she had lived in the projects for seven years, "this place is a dump. I don't talk to anyone, I don't know anyone. That's how we made it here."

While it is commonly assumed that criminally active adults are less capable or less willing guardians, there is no evidence to support this. In fact, Venkatesh (1997) reports that although many problems within the housing project he studied were gang related, gang members involved in criminal activity tended to be accepted because they contributed to the well-being of the community in a variety of ways. For instance, they acted as escorts or protectors, renovated basketball courts, and discouraged truancy. These factors eroded perceptions of them as social deviants, partly because their roles as sons and brothers helped residents view them as "only temporarily" bad, and partly because the gang helped the community in tangible ways.

INTIMATE (SEXUAL) RELATIONS

The incarceration of large numbers of parent-age males restricts the number of male partners available in the neighborhood. This means that mothers find more competition for intimate partners and to serve as parents for their children. In the context of more competition for male support, mothers may feel reluctant to end relationships that are unsuitable for children, partly because prospects for suitable replacements are perceived as poor. Thus, even when men who have been sent to prison were abusers, if they are replaced by men who are also abusive, the trade-off is negative. Likewise, men living with advantageous gender ratios may feel less incentive to remain committed in their parenting partnerships. When the remaining family unit is forced to choose from a thinning stock of males, the options may not be attractive. For those women who end abusive relationships and live alone, the neighborhood implications may also be problematic.

Citing these dynamics, epidemiologists James Thomas and Elizabeth Torrone (2006) investigated the role of high rates of incarceration on sexual behavior in poor neighborhoods. They argued that the pressures on men for safe sex and monogamy are reduced as the ratio of women to marriageable men gets very high. Analyzing North Carolina counties and communities, they found that incarceration rates in one year predicted later increases in rates of gonorrhea, syphilis, and chlamydia among women. They also found that a doubling of incarceration rates increased in the incidence of childbirth by teenage women by 71.61 births per 100,000 teenage women. They conclude that "high rates of incarceration can have the unintended consequence of destabilizing communities and contributing to adverse health outcomes" (2006:1).

This latter finding is notable because teenage births are associated with numerous problematic outcomes for both the mothers and their children. For mothers, teenage births are more likely to lead to a life plagued with lower wages, underemployment, reliance upon welfare, and single parenthood. For *all* children of mothers who have their first child at a very early age, there is an increased likelihood that those children will be arrested for delinquency and violent crime (Pogarsky, Lizotte, and Thornberry 2003). Not surprisingly, rates of out-of-wedlock births also predict higher levels of incarceration across time in the United States (Jacobs and Helms 1996).

Incarceration also seems to explain at least part of the higher rate of HIV among African American men and women. Johnson and Raphael (2005) analyzed data on AIDS infection rates, provided by the U.S. Centers for Disease Control and Prevention, from 1982 to 2001, combined with national incarceration data for the same period. As did Thomas, they posit that "male incarceration lowers the sex ratio (male to female), abruptly disrupts the continuity of heterosexual relationships, and increases the exposure to homosexual activity for incarcerated males—all of which may have far-reaching implications for an individual or group's AIDS infection risk" (2005:2). What is important about their perspective is that they assume *both* removal and reentry as potential destabilizing factors in sexual relations. They find "very strong effects of male incarceration rates on both male and female AIDS infection rates [and] that the higher incarceration rates among black males over this period explain a large share of the racial disparity in AIDS between black women and women of other racial and ethnic groups" (3).

INCARCERATION AND FAMILIES: A SUMMARY

Available studies, listed above, show that incarceration imposes a long list of costs on families and children. Children experience developmental and emotional strains, have less parental supervision, are at greater risk of parental abuse, and face an increased risk of having their own problems with the justice system. Mothers find it harder to sustain stable intimate relationships with men who have gone to prison, and they have an increased risk of contracting sexually transmitted diseases. Families are more likely to break up, and they encounter economic strains. Girls raised in these high-imprisonment places are more likely to become pregnant in their teen years; boys are more likely to become involved in delinquency. Residents feel less positively about their neighbors, and they may tend to isolate themselves from them. The descriptions of these challenges to family life in impoverished places are not surprising, as we have long known that poor neighborhoods are problem settings for family life. What is new is to see, demonstrated in the data, the role incarceration plays in creating these challenges by disrupting social networks and distorting social relationships.

To be sure, incarceration is not the sole cause of these situations. Studies find that parental problems such as drug abuse and mental illness also contribute directly and separately to these situations (Phillips et al. 2006). Addressing the problem of incarceration alone will not be sufficient to ameliorate these problems. By the same token, trying to overcome the many family deficits experienced by these at-risk children without considering the effect of incarceration is not likely to work.

The Economics of Community Life

Mrs. Anderson is a 60-year-old, retired Florida state worker with a decidedly tired demeanor. One of the reasons she is tired is that she has eight children living with her. Five are hers and three are her grandchildren, living with her because both the father (her son) and the mother are currently back in prison. Mrs. Anderson is keeping them until the son gets released, due in another six months. Her pension barely stretches to cover the cost of keeping this hungry, active crew fed and dressed. She explains that she cannot afford to take the kids to visit their father, send him money for the commissary, and pay for the collect long-distance phone calls he sometimes makes. Instead, she has to choose only one way to help, whatever she can afford and whatever seems most pressing at the time. Usually, she sends canteen money. The children rarely visit or talk to their parents. Mrs. Anderson also says she is beginning to delve into her savings and has no plan to turn to when that money is gone.

Wealth is created by the production of goods and services that people want to pay money to acquire. It is sustained through the value of property. Incarceration, when present in large concentration, affects both the markets for goods and services in a neighborhood and the value of its property.

When money changes hands multiple times in a neighborhood, it creates income for each person who receives it. Even impoverished places have this kind of economic activity. Often, it is a cash economy comprising of legal economic activity related to marginal—sometimes off-the-books—employment and state welfare. Sometimes the work takes place in illegal markets. Illegal markets, such as drug trade, are one of the main ways money is brought into the neighborhood. This money can be a substantial source of funds when it changes hands multiple times in the same neighborhood. Much more typically, in other forms of commerce, the meager funds that poor people have quickly leave their neighborhoods to pay for rent, food, health care, and other services.

Of course, impoverished places are poor because people there do not make much money, from work or otherwise. People who get into trouble with the law are characterized by poor work records before they get arrested. Only 42 percent of mothers and 55 percent of fathers who are incarcerated were working full time at the time of their arrest; 32 percent of mothers and 18 percent of fathers were unemployed and not even looking for work (Uggen, Wakefield, and Western 2005).

On top of this poor starting place, going to prison is not good for long-term employment prospects. There is some evidence that during their initial period of release from incarceration, both women and men are slightly *more* likely to be employed, perhaps because they are required to get jobs as a condition of many community supervision agencies (see LaLonde and George 2003 and Cho and LaLonde 2005 for women; Western, Kling, and Weiman 2001 for men). Yet these short-term effects rapidly wear off, as participation in the labor market by people who have been to prison diminishes over time. Regardless of *rates* of participation, various economists have documented how going to prison has a serious, long-term negative impact on lifetime earnings. Jeffrey Grogger (1995) demonstrates that merely being arrested has a short-term, negative impact on earnings, while Richard Freeman (1992) shows that suffering a conviction and imprisonment has a permanent impact on earning potential. Jeffrey Kling (1999) finds small effects on the earnings of people convicted of federal crimes, mostly concentrated among those convicted of white-collar crimes. Western (2005: fig. 5.1) estimates that going to prison reduces annual earnings by about one-third among people sent to state prison.

We know, then, that most of these former residents of a neighborhood do not return there from prison better prepared to participate in the labor force. Uggen and his colleagues (Uggen, Wakefield, and Western 2005) argue that incarceration impedes the capacity for work by stigmatizing people convicted of crimes, damaging the social networks they might use to find jobs, undermining job skills, exacerbating mental and physical illnesses that impede work, and teaching bad work habits. In short, prison takes ill-prepared labor-market participants and reduces their work prospects. Western's analysis of the National Longitudinal Survey of Youth offers "strong evidence that incarceration carries not just an economic penalty on the labor market; it also confines ex-prisoners to bad jobs that are characterized by high turnover and little chance of moving up the ladder" (2006:128). This economic marginality explains some of the problems families encounter in high-incarceration neighborhoods, since men who are "stuck in low-wage or unstable jobs [find] that their opportunities for marriage will be limited . . . [and] the stigma of incarceration makes single mothers reluctant to marry or live with the fathers of their children" (Uggen, Wakefield, and Western 2005:221), with the result that *both* work and marriage prospects are degraded (Huebner 2005).

THE PRODUCTION OF LOCAL LABOR MARKETS

The economic prospects of people who live in poor communities are linked. Family members earning money contribute to the welfare of their families, and this is true even when some of those earnings are from criminal activity such as drug sales. Edin and Lein (1997) show that, in an effort to sustain their families, mothers rely on regular, substantial financial help from people in their personal networks, because neither welfare nor low-paying jobs provide sufficient income to cover expenses. In their study, up to 91 percent of the respondents reported that they had received money from members in their networks; 55 percent had received cash from their families, 32 percent received cash from their boyfriends, 41 percent from their child's father. Incarceration removes from the neighborhood many of the men who provide support to these women.

The concentration of formerly incarcerated men in poor neighborhoods not only affects them but may also damage the labor-market prospects of others in the community. Roberts (2004) points out that "the spatial concentration of incarceration . . . impedes access to jobs for youth in those communities because it decreases the pool of men who can serve as their mentors and their links to the working world . . . generating employment discrimination against entire neighborhoods (1294). Sabol and Lynch (2003) have shown that, as county-level incarceration rates grow, so do unemployment rates for blacks who live in those counties.

To the extent that incarceration primarily removes young men from the neighborhood, it also increases the likelihood of single-parent families being headed by women, with welfare as a consequence. Browne (1997) has shown that long-term exposure to welfare, lack of work experience, and having never been married are factors that disconnect poor women from mainstream society, a condition contributing to earning differences between black and white women. Thus, large-scale incarceration of men may influence the earning power of the women they leave behind. Communities with strong concentrations of families on welfare do not support a vibrant private labor market.

Sullivan's work (1989) suggests that, in impoverished neighborhoods, a work-age male generates economic activity that translates into purchases at the local deli, child support, and so forth. This economic value is generated in a variety of endeavors, including off-the-books work, intermittent illicit drug trade, theft, welfare, and part-time employment. Fagan's (1997) review of legal and illegal work confirms that it is simplistic to view these workers as solely oriented toward illicit income (see also Fagan and Freeman 1999). Research shows that many, if not most, of those who engage in crime also have legal employment, so that their removal from the neighborhood removes a worker from the local economy. Fagan recognizes the argument that sending a single person who held a legal job to prison frees that position for another (potentially law-abiding) resident. However, in local areas where a high proportion of residents engage in both legal and illegal work, Fagan notes that removing many individuals may injure the local economy. Even if sending someone to prison does free the legitimate job for someone else, at best this simply shifts the economic benefit of the job from one community household to another, with no net benefit to the neighborhood. In large numbers, however, it raids supplies of local human capital and leaves a gap in employable residents. The result is that numerous household units suffer specific losses and the community suffers a net loss. Even families that reap the individual benefit of newly available employment suffer the indirect costs of depleted neighborhood economic strength.

The erosion of local labor markets is a precursor to higher rates of crime. Economic hardship is one of the strongest geographic predictors of crime rates. The socially imbedded nature of crime and unemployment suggests that those communities suffering deprivation experience greater criminal involvement among residents (Hagan 1993). Therefore, it is reasonable to assume that a neighborhood experiencing economic loss as a result of incarceration will experience an increase in crime (Wilson 1987). In fact, studies have documented the impact of a community's economic well-being on its level of criminality. Taylor and Covington (1988) show that shifts in the rate of community violent crimes are linked to changes in relative deprivation, and Block (1979) finds a link between a community's crime rate and its ratio of wealthy to impoverished residents. Crutchfield and Pitchford (1997) show that the level of community-wide labor-force participation may be even more important than an individual's employment in shaping individual criminality. These studies confirm that social processes damaging a neighborhood's economic viability may also tend to make it less safe.

THE VALUE OF PROPERTY

When it comes to the value of real estate, the saying goes, three aspects matter: location, location, location. Of the many factors that go into determining the value of residential property (square footage, amenities, age, and the nature of nearby structures), generalized community safety is by far one of the most important. Economists David Rasmussen and Allen Lynch (2001) have shown that nearby crimes reported in well-functioning neighborhoods have virtually no impact on the value of property for residential use. High-crime areas are another matter; in such neighborhoods crime substantially lowers the value of residential property.

Extensions of this work have analyzed the impact of incarceration on housing values in Jacksonville, Florida. Rasmussen and his colleagues developed a "hedonic model," a statistical representation of the contribution of each of the main characteristics of property in relation to its sale price in the year 1995. This work shows that localized (neighborhood) incarceration rates are correlated with hedonic values of housing, but that the correlation disappears when crime rates are taken into account. Thus, crime has a direct impact on the value of a home, reducing its sale price in high-crime areas by at least 37 percent. Incarceration has no direct effect on the sale value of a residential property.

That is not to say that incarceration is irrelevant to the value of property. To the extent that incarceration reduces crime in high-crime areas, it tends to improve the value of private property for housing. But if the effect of incarceration rates at the high end do not reduce crime, but rather increase it, the net effect is to reduce housing values if increased crime is the result of incarceration's effect on neighborhood stability. Rasmussen concludes that "the worst neighborhoods are characterized by crime and social instability that has a devastating effect on house prices. To the extent that excessive incarceration exacerbates this instability, we can be sure that house prices will reflect the accompanying increase in crime" (2004).

The Politics of Community Life

It has been estimated that nearly 1 million of Florida's citizens are banned from voting for life because of a previous felony conviction, 50 percent of them black. The Florida laws are so strict that their enforcement formed the basis for a campaign warning people in black neighborhoods that ineligible residents who tried to vote would be subject to imprisonment. At least one set of form letters, sent out to tell black people they were ineligible to vote, had hundreds of inaccuracies. There is no telling how many legal voters assumed they were ineligible and how many more were intimidated from voting. Ironically, had Florida's felony disenfranchisement laws enabled even just the nonimprisoned to vote, most people believe the 2000 presidential election would have resulted in an Al Gore presidency.

In minority communities where incarceration is concentrated, prison is a part of life. The overwhelming presence of the American criminal justice system in high-incarceration communities goes a long way toward defining the meaning of the state for this segment of society. The state is more likely to be encountered as a coercive agent of control than as a fair agent of justice. Research now reliably shows that when people think the law is unfair, they are less likely to conform their behavior to its requirements (Tyler 1990). They may also fear it less. A black 10-year-old living in an impoverished place is likely to have at least one (and likely more) excons among his fathers, uncles, brothers, and neighbors. There are many potential lessons to be learned from this. One is that state power can be used to harm family members and family interests. Another is that prison is not an unusual experience—not awesome, easily survivable. Widespread use of imprisonment becomes a kind of reassurance that the experience is "normal." Thus, the politics of imprisonment may be a combination of increasing resentment and decreasing marginal gain. Turning dominant cultural symbols upside down, there is even a claim that inner-city residents accrue street status from surviving prison.

ATTITUDES TOWARD AUTHORITY AND THE STATE

In high-incarceration neighborhoods, many residents do not believe that the state's justice agencies work on their behalf. Most minority children can tell stories of racism in the criminal-justice system, and the validation of these tales is apparent to the eye. One in three African American males in his twenties is under some form of formal justice-system control (Mauer and Huling 1995); in large cities, as many as half are subjects of the system (Miller 1992). Many are casualties of the war on drugs.

Peter St. Jean (2006) has gathered extensive crime and community data on Buffalo, New York's, neighborhoods, including interviews of "old heads" in poor, primarily black areas. He concludes that "preexisting socio-economic and other conditions [combined with] preexisting law enforcement factors—profiling, discrimination, different responses to crime committed by blacks and Hispanics as opposed to whites" has led to a pervasive sense of cynicism among those he has interviewed. They describe the conundrum they face, choosing between cooperation with the police and support for their family members—a "darned if you do and darned if you don't" situation. For some youth, it is perceived that incarceration has become "cool," and this counter-normativity makes the older residents distrust the prospects for many young men who come back, while at the same time distrusting the police presence in their communities.

The alienation of residents who no longer feel part of a society that is so hostile to the drug economy leaves them less likely to participate in local political organizations or to submit to the authority of more formal ones. Stewart and Simons (2006) analyzed two waves of data from the Family and Community Health Study and found that experiencing racial discrimination and living in an impoverished neighborhood, combined with poor family discipline, promoted the adoption by young black males of what Anderson (1999) has referred to as "the code of the street." High concentrations of youth who adopted "the code" were in turn associated with higher levels of crime and violence in the neighborhood.

Sociologist Robert Crutchfield has been interested in the way social conditions, such as labor markets, affect attitudes toward society and

community, especially social cohesion and trust as building blocks for social capital (see Crutchfield and Pitchford 1997). Recently Crutchfield
(2005) investigated the impact of concentrated levels of young men in reentry on the attitudes of neighbors who had not been to prison. In a survey
of residents of Seattle, Washington, Crutchfield asked respondents a series of questions regarding their attitudes toward the legitimacy of the law
and the belief in authority—questions tapping social cohesion and trust.
He found that in neighborhoods where there are high rates of young men
returning from prison, overall social cohesion and trust are affected: in
"neighborhoods with relatively large concentrations of former prisoners
and, by extension . . . communities with more churning of people into
and out of the prison system . . . [the negative attitude] in those places
that we ordinarily attribute to economic disadvantage is due in part to
sentencing patterns and correctional policies" (2004). This disrespect of
formal institutions portends badly for community safety, as earlier work
has shown that individuals whose jobs hold no future have less of a stake
in conformity and are more likely to engage in criminal activity (Crutchfield and Pitchford 1997). In similar research in New York City, Tyler and
Fagan (2005) show that people in the neighborhoods where incarceration
rates are highest tend to view the police as unfair and disrespectful, cor-
roding their views of the legitimacy of policing and broader governmental
authority, and in turn signaling their withdrawal from social regulation
and political life.

VOTING

Alienation and negativity toward authority tend to suppress political participation, further alienating people in these areas from influence on law
and policy. But the effects of intangible attitudes on the exercise of political power are augmented by laws that restrict voting by people with criminal records.

All states impose voting limitations on people who go to prison—some
states impose very broad restrictions, others much less so. It has been estimated that more than 5.3 million people in the United States are prohibited from voting as a consequence of their criminal records (Uggen and
Manza 2006). These disenfranchised Americans mirror the prison population in their socio-demographics: one in seven black males is disenfranchised (Mauer and Huling 1995). They also tend to concentrate in poor
neighborhoods, as we would expect, so that mass incarceration "translates
the denial of individual felon's voting rights into disenfranchisement of
entire communities" (Roberts 2004). A study of voter disenfranchisement patterns in Atlanta (King and Mauer 2004), for example, finds an

extremely high correlation between the portion of voters who are disenfranchised and the racial composition of the local area. Areas that are predominantly black have a voter disenfranchisement rate three to four times higher than the rate in areas that are predominantly white. They conclude:

> The disenfranchisement effect contributes to a vicious cycle . . . that further disadvantages low-income communities of color. The first means by which this occurs is through decisions of resource allocation. . . . At a state level, beleaguered communities are affected through a diminished impact on public policy. (15)

Places with residents who do not vote carry limited potential for influencing the politics of resource acquisition and dissemination. In poor places that have so many ex-prisoners, voting rates are very low in part because of the laws, but also because of generally low rates of voting. People with felony arrests who may legally vote are 18 percent less likely to vote than those who have not been arrested; people in prison who are allowed to vote are 27 percent less likely to do so than their non-incarcerated counterparts (Uggen and Manza 2005).

Do high incarceration rates in poor neighborhoods suppress *legal* voting in those places? Jeffrey Fagan (2006) and his colleagues studied the impact of rates of incarceration on voting practices in New York City neighborhoods from 1985 to 1996. They found that poor neighborhoods had very low rates of voter participation in elections, but that the non-participation was not directly affected by the rate of incarceration. Voter registration and participation rates were lower in neighborhoods with high rates of incarceration, and especially in neighborhoods where drug enforcement was the primary engine fueling the incarceration rate. They concluded that the same factors that produce elevated crime rates, invite close police surveillance, and promote drug-law enforcement also encourage lower voter participation. The withdrawal of citizens from this most basic function of civil society may be another way in which citizens signal a perception that laws are applied unfairly, disproportionately, and in a manner that is disrespectful of citizens' rights and dignity (see also Tyler and Fagan 2005).

The result is that, in these places, political clout is diminished and the people struggle to influence the policy decisions that affect their interests. Tax policy, social welfare practices, and political priorities do not reflect the interests of these (non)voters. The macroeconomics of crime policy also damage inner-city communities by shifting government funding away from those communities and toward penal institutions. The harsh

budgetary politics of the 1990s have corresponded to equally harsh punitive politics in which correctional expenditures have grown by billions
of dollars annually while money to support schools, supplement tuition,
provide summer jobs for teens, and so forth were diminished. The latter
funding provided meager supports for communities already hard hit by
crime and justice, and the funding has become even more meager. Whatever role these social programs play in propping up informal networks of
social control is eliminated with the depletion of their funding.

COLLECTIVE ACTION

Communities vary in the means they use to deal with problems. While it is
generally perceived that poor communities do not organize, some clearly
do (Henig 1982). Researchers have found collective activity, covering a
broad range of approaches, in all types of neighborhoods (Podolefsky and
DuBow 1980). Variations in collective action can be attributed to several
factors. For instance, the extent to which communities rely on authority structures or formal social controls varies according to differences in
the racial and class composition of the community (Bennett 1995). The
degree to which residents perceive that they receive inadequate police services is also related to their propensity to organize locally (Henig 1982).
The political capacity of the community may be a critical factor, too, particularly for communities that have fewer internal resources and need to
increase their external resources (Bennett 1995). In other words, communities vary in their desire and their capacity to organize. The extent
to which a neighborhood has developed a network of political and social
institutions prior to the occurrence of a specific threat helps to determine
whether the community will be able to mobilize collective action against
the threat (Henig 1982).

Podolefsky and DuBow (1980) found that residents who define the
crime problem as stemming from within the neighborhood advocate different control tactics than do residents who see crime as coming from
outside. To the extent that this is true, residents are inclined to develop
a social-problems approach to crime reduction; to the extent that they
define the problem as coming from outside the neighborhood, they are
likely to ask for an approach that emphasizes victimization and calls for
law enforcement. A social-problems approach focuses on improving social
conditions thought to be the root of crime, such as youth behavior, lack
of job opportunities, and neighborhood environmental hazards. Policy
makers who may not understand that residents make this distinction often
implement victimization-approach strategies when the community would
prefer a social-problems approach.

Collective efficacy is the term coined by Robert Sampson and his colleagues to refer to the "social cohesion among neighbors combined with their willingness to intervene on behalf of the common good" (Sampson, Raudenbush, and Earls 1997:918). Places that are collectively effective are capable of coming together to attain their common good. People organize politically, form social groups that advance collective interests, and assist one another in exerting informal social control.

Lynch and Sabol (2004) investigated the incarceration-affected community-level variables, including collective efficacy, in Baltimore neighborhoods. They explain their conceptualization as follows:

> If residents have expectations that norms will be observed, invoking norms . . . is likely to bring about compliance because the belief is shared. . . . Without the . . . shared beliefs about norms (or community solidarity), invoking norms can be unproductive or even dangerous. (140)

They found that "incarceration reduces community solidarity and attachment to communities," though it improves the level of collective efficacy as measured by normative consensus (157). Their results are mixed—an issue to which we will turn our attention again in detail in chapter 7. But for our purposes here, they find that incarceration is associated with a reduction in "the social processes on which social controls depend" (157).

ECONOMICS AND POLITICS: A SUMMARY

A string of studies show that workers face labor-market problems as a result of their imprisonment. When they go to prison, they put financial pressures on those who remain. When they come back out, they struggle to participate in legal labor markets. When their numbers are quite large, they make it difficult for a legitimate employment market to flourish in the places they live. Adding to these economic strains are the ways that high incarceration rates impede a place's ability to exert influence on politics. Because people disenfranchised as a result of felony convictions are often concentrated in a small number of communities, the political influence of poor communities is diminished. Because many who live in these impoverished areas are alienated from participation in political life regardless of their legal records, these places can have a dominant ethic of distrust of authority and disrespect for the state.

Part IX

Solutions: Can Anything Be Done About This?

At key moments in his first campaign and presidency, Barack Obama evoked Martin Luther King Jr.'s poetic optimism: "the arc of the moral universe is long, but it bends towards justice." When it comes to America's criminal justice system, the arc seems bent in the opposite direction. As we have seen, history, politics, and economics have contributed to a shocking racial skewing of justice over the last few decades. That so much of the impetus for the over-incarceration of poor black Americans was a reaction against the civil rights movement is the irony expressed in Langston Hughes's poem "Blind Goddess." That America's first black president has said and done so little about it is heartbreaking.

Needless to say, there have been many distractions, as well as strong resistance. Upon making a single off-the-cuff comment that the police officer who had arrested Professor Henry Louis Gates Jr. was "stupid," Obama had to backtrack in the face of public outcry.[1] It is not clear which topic is further out of bounds, racism or police error. Public discourse does not welcome criticism of criminal justice policy, and strongly discourages critiques of the shocking and pervasive racial inequalities of the system.

To accuse America—or any part of it—of structural racism is too often and too easily seen as unpatriotic. Many people will say that we already fought that war in the nineteenth century, recognized civil rights in the twentieth century, and in this century elected President Obama. It seems we agreed long ago that what matters is what we say, not what we really think. Racism in the heart is just like Jimmy Carter's lust in the heart: it doesn't mean that he or we are bad.

The myths that Americans choose to define our national identity

247

reveal much about our moral sentiments toward one another. The stories of Horatio Alger Jr. symbolize how every American can rise from rags to riches and suggest that, if someone does not manage such a transformation, the fault lies with that individual. The cowboy and his horse express our sense of being on our own against a hostile world. There is an underlying threat of violence that the totemic gun serves to protect against. There is also the enemy: the savage, who cannot be dealt with except through violence.

One of our strongest cultural myths concerns the founding of the nation and the establishment of our system of laws with the world's first—and, of course, best—written constitution. The Bill of Rights serves to reinforce individualism by offering protection against government intrusion. Implicit is an assurance that government will do the right thing, as long as (and because) it is properly constrained. There is no need to revisit or improve our Constitution, but only to make sure it is followed. The ageless wisdom of the Founding Fathers is apparently our best guide.

To doubt the goodness of our legal system challenges our national identity. Instead we believe, sure, there are occasional instances of unfairness, but nearly all get remedied by litigation. We treasure our courts for their independence, objectivity, and competence. Mistakes happen, but they get fixed on appeal.

The severe racial skewing of our system of criminal justice described throughout this book defies recognition, because it is so at odds with how we think of our nation. We cannot explain or justify this phenomenon, since it confounds our myths, our categories, and our perceptions of reality. If forced to confront it, we must question much about how we think and how we live. After all, for many of us, it is a phenomenon that we can avoid and ignore simply by not listening or learning about it. We can pretend that it is not happening to us, even though it is part of the society we live in and plays an integral role in how that society functions.

On the other hand, there are many reasons to confront the over-incarceration and general criminalization of poor black Americans beyond moral fairness. Even for people not directly implicated, self-interest compels undoing this distortion and perversion of our system of justice. First, it does not serve its supposed purpose: crime prevention. Instead, it worsens many of the conditions that contribute to criminality by undermining the integrity of the system and the functioning of afflicted communities. Second, it costs an enormous amount of money: sending someone to prison for a year costs more than sending someone to college for a year.

The selections in this final part tackle the task of imagining how to bring balance and efficiency to our criminal justice system. The obstacles are not only ideological; they are temporal. We must undo past events, as well as avoid future mistakes. Even beyond the taboos of racism and police error, so many people have so many years of prison sentences to serve that reducing them would be a monumental bureaucratic challenge.

Our system insists on treating everyone as an individual, even while it manages them as a group. This is not just a matter of the law's protections and provisions. Public discourse also alternates easily between the individual and the masses, complicating appropriate attention to either with the interests of the other. Any attempt at systematic reform, such as eliminating three-strikes sentencing, must overcome the inevitable example of a person who seems to deserve the life sentence that his third, but only first violent, crime brought him. Similarly, the case for an individual to get out of prison early must confront the argument that it will set a bad precedent for the many others like him.

Punishing Race: A Continuing American Dilemma is a 2010 work of social and political science by Michael Tonry, a University of Minnesota law professor. He presents and parses the statistics of incarceration as they relate to black Americans, including updating and clarifying pioneering studies of crime rates. He dismisses standard criminological rationales for the racial skewing of U.S. justice and considers historical, sociological, and political explanations for the enormous imbalances in the numbers. In the chapter excerpted here, Tonry explains that reducing racial disparity requires significant changes to key features of the criminal justice system, which contribute to excessive incarceration.

Michelle Alexander in *The New Jim Crow* (described in the introduction to Part I) and Lani Guinier, a Harvard law professor and scholar on race in America, in her introduction to *12 Angry Men*, a recently published collection of first-person narratives of racial profiling experiences, focus first on changing how we think about race and justice. They insist on recognizing race as a key feature of our system of criminal justice and our society as a whole. How we consider—or, in Guinier's terms, "read"—race is vital to progress. Alexander pushes for solidarity, first among black Americans, and ultimately across racial lines to include all people who suffer from systemic injustice. She argues that law enforcement is a matter of civil rights, and that challenging the War on Drugs is essential. This would constitute a new civil rights movement in the interest of all Americans, advocating for racial justice in our prisons, courts, police stations, streets, and communities.

Further Reading: Todd R. Clear in *Imprisoning Communities* (described in the introduction to Part VIII) takes a harsh view of the status quo, including reform measures like alternatives to incarceration and reentry programs. He emphasizes the current lack of any coherent penological philosophy, with default punitiveness leading to mandatory and lengthy sentencing. As an alternative vision, Clear offers a philosophy of community justice, where police and courts enforce community solidarity as the ultimate value of justice. There is genuine hope in this far-sighted vision.

19

Doing Less Harm

Michael Tonry

Contemporary public opinion cannot be invoked as justification for the injustices of the American justice system. Crime and drugs no longer rank high as matters of public concern. Between 2002 and 2008 only 1 to 3 percent of Americans named crime or drugs the most important problem facing the nation. In the twenty-first century concerns about crime or drugs rank far below the economy, unemployment, terrorism, health care, and education.

Crime has not featured prominently in an American presidential election since 1988, and in recent years has only occasionally been a major element in state and local elections. The flurry of adoptions of unprecedentedly severe sentencing laws ended in the mid-1990s. Many states have since enacted amendments mitigating some effects of these laws.

If policy making were animated primarily by rational and humane values, the second decade of the twenty-first century would be an auspicious time to remake American criminal justice and drug policies. Racial justice in the American criminal justice system can be improved, though it will not be easy. Americans continue to be influenced by unconscious associations of blackness with crime. The cynicism that underlay the Republican Southern Strategy, and the related willingness to deal unjustly with black offenders in order to appeal to white voters, have not disappeared. Nor has the risk averseness of many Democratic politicians to any action that might be characterized by Republicans as soft on crime. The Clinton administration notoriously supported a federal three-strikes law, new mandatory sentencing laws, and fifty-eight new death penalty provisions in the mid-1990s, and did only by stealth such few good things as it did in

From *Punishing Race: A Continuing American Dilemma* (New York: Oxford University Press, 2011), 148–52, 164–74.

251

relation to crime policy. At the time of this writing the Obama administration and Congress have done nothing significant to roll back the policy excesses of the 1980s and 1990s, so it is not clear whether the Democratic Party even now has set aside its unwillingness to stand up for what is right.

Nonetheless if counsels of despair are allowed to dominate our thinking, nothing will change, and there are many historical examples of successful against-all-odds social and political changes concerning other subjects. Franklin Roosevelt's New Deal, which created the Social Security System, the Tennessee Valley Authority, and many other still surviving governmental programs and institutions, and revived the American economy after the Great Depression, is one. The civil rights movement is another. Lyndon Johnson's Great Society, which in the aftermath of John F. Kennedy's assassination produced Medicare and Medicaid and much of the major civil rights legislation, is yet another. Barack Obama's successful effort to create a national system of medical insurance and medical care is a historical accomplishment. Compared with changes of those magnitudes, the criminal justice system is small potatoes. Here is what needs to be done.

Radically Reduce the Use of Imprisonment

Efforts to reduce the influence of bias and stereotyping in official decision making are being made throughout the United States and should continue. Unfortunately, even if they were completely successful they could have only modest effects. Table 1 shows why. Prison disparities do not result primarily from biased or unconsciously stereotyped decisions. The top row of Part A shows black and white non-Hispanic imprisonment rates per 100,000 population for jail and prison combined in 2006. The second row shows what would happen if black rates were decreased by 10 percent—a high estimate of the degree to which bias and stereotyping enhance disparities—while white rates were left unchanged. The black imprisonment rate would fall from approximately 2,661 per 100,000 to 2,395, and the ratio of black-to-white imprisonment rates would fall from 5.5:1 to 5.0:1. The number of black people locked up would fall by about 100,000.

If instead, as Part B shows, the prison population were cut by half across the board, disparities would not be reduced, but the black imprisonment rate would fall from 2,661 to 1,330. Or if, as Part C shows, imprisonment rates were cut to 1980 levels, disparities would not be reduced and the black imprisonment rate would be 827 per 100,000.

TABLE 1 HYPOTHETICAL REDUCTION IN INCARCERATION RATES

	Black	White	Ratio
	A. Disparity Reduced 10%		
Imprisonment rate, 2006	2,661	483	5.5:1
10% less disparity	2,395	483	5.0:1
Reduction in prison per 100,000	266	0	
Reduction in black prisoners	101,000		
	B. Use of Imprisonment Halved		
Imprisonment rate, 2006	2,661	483	5.5:1
Imprisonment halved	1,330	241	5.5:1
Reduction in prison per 100,000	1,330	241	
Reduction in black prisoners	505,400		
	C. Return to 1980 Imprisonment Rates		
Imprisonment rate, 1980	827	134	6.2:1
Reduction in prison per 100,000	1,834	349	
Reduction in black prisoners	697,000		

Source: Tonry and Melewski (2008, table 5).

The differences in the projected effects of these alternative approaches are enormous. The U.S. Census Bureau estimated that 38.34 million U.S. residents in 2006 were black. If the number of people in prison were halved, but nothing else changed, the black imprisonment rate would fall from 26,613 per million to 13,306. More than 500,000 fewer black Americans would be in prison or jail. Returning to the 1980 level would mean 700,000 fewer black Americans behind bars.

Of course every effort should be made to eliminate bias and stereotyping. Their diminution will reduce injustices, disparities, and the absolute size of the bite prisons take out of the black population. In absolute terms, though, that will only nibble at the problem. Only radical reduction in the scale of imprisonment can make a big difference. To attempt to limit damage done to people now entangled in the arms of the criminal justice system, devices need to be created for reducing the lengths of prison sentences and releasing hundreds of thousands of people serving unnecessarily long terms. Sentencing laws and guidelines need to be changed to reduce the emphasis on imprisonment, and new programs need to be created to divert many people from prison or jail into community correctional programs. New systems of parole, pardon, and commutation need to be developed, as do programs of social welfare and support to ease people's transitions back into the free community.

None of these changes need be focused on black offenders or on black prisoners. Although disparities are largely the result of contemporary drug and sentencing policies, black imprisonment rates are so absolutely high because American imprisonment rates are so absolutely high.

The prison population cannot be substantially reduced overnight or in a year, but it can be reduced relatively quickly and in ways that do not significantly impair public safety. The imprisonment rate in 1980, after all, was 221 per 100,000, and the violent crime rate was a third higher than it was in 2008. The imprisonment rate in 1970, when violent crime rates were not much lower than in 2010, was 161 per 100,000. All of these rates are significantly higher than those of any other country with which American citizens would ordinarily want their country to be compared. To return to 1980 rates would mean that U.S. rates would continue to be three times those of the Scandinavian countries, twice those in Canada, Germany, and France, and significantly higher than those in England and Wales, Spain, and New Zealand.

There is no good reason to believe that ambitious reduction in the scale of imprisonment would worsen American drug and crime problems. Much of what is done now is counterproductive. The mistaken belief that current drug and crime policies can achieve their aims has impoverished searches for other, more effective approaches.

REPEAL INEFFECTIVE CRIME AND DRUG CONTROL POLICIES

Repeal or fundamental alteration of ineffective crime control and drug policies will benefit Americans of every race. The 100-to-1 federal law for sentencing crack cocaine offenses and its 18-to-1 successor are classic—and extreme—examples. No one has ever made a credible case for that law's effectiveness at reducing drug use or trafficking. However, there are other laws and policies that do as great damage and that also cannot be shown to produce more than offsetting benefits. Three-strikes, mandatory minimum sentence, and truth-in-sentencing laws and the drug war's emphasis on inner-city drug dealing are examples. [. . .]

Targeting the Causes of Racial Disparities

A wide range of contemporary criminal justice policies do unnecessary damage to black Americans. Some can be addressed by the police; others require administrative or legislative changes.

Years ago Alfred Blumstein (1993) showed that American practitioners and policy makers can respond quickly to racial disparity problems when they are motivated to do so. He observed that from 1965 to 1969 white and nonwhite arrest rates for young offenders were indistinguishable, that during the 1970s white rates exceeded nonwhite rates, and that thereafter until 1989 nonwhite rates nearly tripled and white rates halved, leaving nonwhite rates nearly four times higher. Figure 1 tells the story. Here is what Blumstein surmises happened:

> The decline [in white arrest rates] after the 1974 peak was undoubtedly a consequence of the general trend toward decriminalization of marijuana in the United States. A major factor contributing to that decriminalization was probably a realization that the arrestees were much too often the children of individuals, usually white, in positions of power and influence. These parents certainly did not want the consequences of a drug arrest to be visited on their children, and so they used their leverage to achieve a significant degree of decriminalization. Following the peak, arrest rates for both racial groups declined, and continued to decline for whites. On the other hand, for non-whites, the decline leveled out in the early 1980s and then began to accelerate at a rate of between twenty and twenty-five percent per year, until the peak in 1989. This clearly reflects the fact that drug enforcement is a result of policy choices. (758)

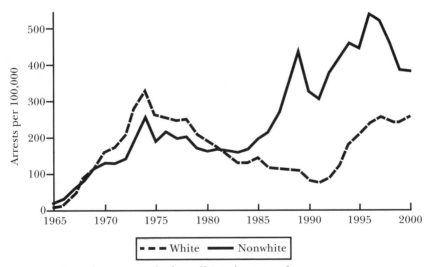

FIGURE 1 *Juvenile arrest rates for drug offenses, by race, 1965–2000.*
Source: Blumstein (1993); Blumstein and Wallman (2006).

It is not completely cynical to wonder why soaring arrest rates for non-white kids in the 1980s and 1990s did not provoke the kinds of reactions that Blumstein attributes to soaring arrest rates of white kids in the 1970s and did not lead to a comparable policy adjustment. To the contrary, as economist Glenn Loury points out, so many black kids were sent to prison in order to dissuade white kids from drug use:

> Significantly, throughout the period 1979–2000, white high school seniors reported using drugs at a significantly higher rate than black high school seniors. High drug-usage rates in white, middle-class American communities in the early 1980s account for the urgency many citizens felt to mount a national attack on the problem. But how successful has the effort been, and at what cost? Think of the cost this way: to save middle-class kids from the threat of a drug epidemic that might not have even existed by the time drug offense-fueled incarceration began its rapid increase in the 1980s, we criminalized underclass kids. (2008, 16–17)

Major policy improvements that do not require legislation could be made by police executives if they wished. These concern arrest policies for young people, police profiling, and drug arrest practices in the inner city. It has long been clear that police arrest young black people in circumstances when they do not arrest young whites, and that as a result young blacks accumulate criminal records from younger ages than whites do (Feld 1999). The earlier arrest records are stigmatizing, often unnecessarily interrupt young black people's educational careers, and reduce their chances of living conventional law-abiding lives later on. Convictions resulting from such arrests sometimes remove them from school altogether and always make it harder for them ever to get decent jobs.

RACIAL PROFILING

Racial profiling is per se unfair and puts black people at greater risk than whites of being arrested for reasons that would otherwise not come to the attention of the police. Some might say that the police should arrest people whenever there is evidence they have committed a crime, but sometimes not doing do so is a price free societies pay to protect liberty. Police could no doubt arrest many more white drug dealers if they were allowed to enter private houses without warrants, but few people believe that would be a good idea. Protection of privacy is why issuance of arrest and search warrants is tightly controlled and why they must, except in emergencies, be approved in advance by a judge. When an arrest results from an unlawful search or seizure, the criminal charges must be tossed out.

Criminal charges resulting from arrests based on racial profiling should be dealt with in the same way. Because profiling arrests generally are made in public spaces and the police claim to have legitimate grounds for the stop, warrant requirements do not apply. Police incentives to engage in profiling would change substantially if after the fact every arrest arguably resulting from profiling were subject to the same degree of judicial scrutiny that warrants before the fact require.

DRUG ARRESTS

Drug arrests are the second source of disparity that is within the power of police executives to alter. Police focus attention on inner-city drug markets for three reasons: arrests of dealers are relatively easy to make, street markets are visible so citizens complain about them, and police officials (and politicians who put pressure on them) like to be seen as "doing something" about drugs. However, we know that those policies have produced racial disparities between blacks and whites in drug arrest rates as high as 6 to 1 in some years, that arrested inner-city dealers are replaced by willing successors within days, and that wholesale arrests have no effect on the price or availability of drugs. Police forces that retargeted their efforts to focus equally on white drug dealers would make an important symbolic statement about racial fairness, reduce racial disparities, and pursue the aims of drug law enforcement no less effectively. They would reduce racial disparities in arrests, convictions, and imprisonment in a stroke. They would free up large amounts of police resources to be redeployed in more socially constructive ways. They would also probably greatly reduce police emphasis on arrests of drug dealers. As happened with young whites arrested and convicted of marijuana offenses in the 1970s, white citizens would probably not tolerate substantial increases in the number of low-level white dealers who would be sent to prison. People sympathetic to young black drug dealers and worried about the damage done to them by recent arrest policies have had insufficient political influence to persuade police to deemphasize arrests in the inner city. People sympathetic to the interests of low-level white drug dealers do have that kind of influence.

CRIMINAL RECORDS

At the sentencing stage the damage-doing policies include heavy reliance on prior criminal records to aggravate punishments for new crimes and the effects of mandatory minimum sentences, life-without-possibility-of-parole sentences, and truth-in-sentencing laws. Heavy reliance on prior convictions in setting sentences means that convicted offenders receive much harsher punishments and longer prison terms than they otherwise would. Reducing the weight given previous convictions in sentencing would alleviate a major contributor to racial disparities in imprisonment.

Most of us share an intuition that people who have committed a previous crime should be punished more severely for a subsequent one, and most legal systems respect that intuition. In most other countries, legal doctrines tightly limit how much a punishment can be increased because of a previous conviction (sometimes they forbid any increase). The increases allowed are usually measured in months. In the United States, however, punitive increments to a punishment for a new crime imposed in respect of a criminal record are often measured in years or decades. Because black offenders are arrested more often and at younger ages than whites, they are more often affected by prior-record increments. And because they are more often sentenced for drug and violent crimes, they receive the longest increments.

Even in states with relatively low imprisonment rates, prior criminal records are a major cause of racial disparities in prison. Richard Frase has shown that Minnesota sentencing guidelines call for prison sentences for 39 percent of black convicted offenders but only 25 percent of whites: "The principal source of the increase in racial disproportionality from conviction to sentencing appears to be racial differences in average criminal history scores, combined with the heavy weight these scores have in determining which offenders are recommended to receive [prison terms]" (2009, 254). Differences in criminal records account for "about two-thirds of the black/white difference" (250).

An argument can be made, and often is made, that the book should be closed on an offense when an offender completes his sentence: Did the crime, did the time (Fletcher 1978; Singer 1979; Tonry 2010). The basic argument parallels the logic of the double jeopardy rule that forbids retrying a defendant who was acquitted at the first trial. If you cannot be tried twice for the same crime, you should not be punished twice. Increasing the punishment for a new conviction because of an old conviction is, in effect, an additional punishment for the first crime.

A recent book of essays shows that no one has yet managed to provide a principled justification for why a person who has previously been convicted deserves a harsher punishment for a new crime (Roberts and von Hirsch 2010). Nonetheless the intuition that criminal records matter is strong, and I assume the practice will continue. But it should not result in vastly harsher punishments.

Other countries' legal systems limit the influence of criminal records. Sometimes they allow criminal records to be used to aggravate sentences only for designated crimes, as, for example, when the string of convictions shows a long-term pattern of specialization in a particular offense. In some countries criminal records are allowed to be used to justify longer sentences, but subject to a strict outer limit, often that the sentence may never be lengthened beyond what would be appropriate for the most serious version of the current offense.

American jurisdictions could also allow but limit the influence of prior convictions. One of the most important steps is to repeal three-strikes and other laws that predicate vastly longer sentences on prior convictions. A second is to establish caps, such as that a prior violent conviction can justify extension of a sentence up to but never beyond six months, and a prior nonviolent conviction can justify up to but not more than some shorter extension. Jurisdictions that operate sentencing guideline systems have an obvious and principled approach readily at hand: prior convictions could justify an aggregate sentence up to but not beyond the top of the applicable guideline range for the offense being sentenced.

The precise method used to limit the influence of prior convictions is not so important. What is important is recognition that current approaches greatly worsen racial disparities in imprisonment and that means must be found to lessen that effect.

LENGTHY PRISON SENTENCES

Mandatory minimum, LWOP, and truth-in-sentencing laws are a major contributor to racial disparities in prison. They mostly affect drug and violent crimes and so disproportionately affect black and other minority offenders. Most such laws were adopted primarily for symbolic or expressive purposes rather than, as my survey of the deterrent and incapacitative effects of severe punishments and punishment increases demonstrated, with any reasonable basis for believing they would significantly affect crime rates and patterns. They should be repealed, and no new ones should be enacted.

To address current overimprisonment, American jurisdictions need to establish principled new systems of sentencing guidelines that prescribe proportionate sentences for most crimes measured mostly in months, as in most other Western countries, and in years only for the very serious.

American jurisdictions also need to develop new mechanisms for shortening unduly, disparately, or disproportionately long prison sentences. Parole boards long performed that function. Many have been abolished. They should be reestablished. Most surviving parole boards became much more cautious. Often they do not release most eligible prisoners even though they have authority to do so, and they hold many prisoners far longer than is necessary. Half a century ago the Model Penal Code, the most influential criminal law document of the twentieth century, recommended a legal presumption that prisoners should ordinarily be released the first time they become eligible, and should be held longer only rarely and for very good reasons (American Law Institute 1962). Modern parole boards should adopt that policy.

RACIAL BIAS AND STEREOTYPING

Criminal justice executives have been working for decades to reduce racially biased and discriminatory patterns of decision making. Except at the police stage, where racial profiling remains rife and drug enforcement policy still targets inner-city drug markets, substantial progress has been made.

Many states in the 1990s and since have created racial equity task forces in their court systems. Innovative prosecutors' offices have established research programs to help them identify racial differences in case processing and to change them (Miller and Wright 2008). Continuing education programs attempt to sensitize judges and court and correctional personnel about the ubiquity and perniciousness of unconscious stereotyping and attribution. Programs such as these are as important for the normative messages they send—about the injustice of racial stereotyping, and the importance of treating people as equals—as for the improvements they produce in the quality of American justice. They need to continue and to be expanded to address subtler problems of unconscious bias against black offenders resulting from their skin tone or distinctively African American facial features. By itself, however, consciousness raising can make only a marginal contribution to the reduction of racial disparities in prison and to the damage American criminal justice does to its black citizens as a class. Larger changes are needed if major improvements are to be achieved.

PROPHYLACTIC MEASURES

U.S. governments have long used prophylactic measures to guard against unwanted effects of governmental decisions. To protect the public purse, legislatures routinely require that legislative proposals be accompanied by or trigger fiscal impact statements. Some legislatures require that the assessment show that a proposed law's effects will be revenue-neutral before it can be considered. Others require that any proposal for a new law that would increase public expenditure contain within it provisions for raising the additional money required. Federal and state laws routinely require the preparation of environmental impact statements before building and other permits may be issued, and most states require archaeological impact assessments. Projects cannot go forward until the assessment has been completed and the proposed project's effects are shown to be benign. If that cannot be shown, the project must be reconsidered and either abandoned or made subject to amelioration or mitigation requirements.

Similar laws should be enacted concerning racial and other disparities in the criminal justice system (Tonry 1995, 2004; Mauer 2007). Proposals calling for the development of racial disparity audits and impact projections should be relatively uncontroversial. When differences are documented, the next question is whether they can be justified, whether racial or ethnic disparities are a price appropriately to be paid to achieve, and are outweighed by, some greater public purpose.

If current or proposed policies create racially disparate effects, they should be considered inherently suspect. In most policy areas that proposition is self-evident. In employment law, for instance, the showing of a disparate effect of a hiring or promotion practice on minority groups or women creates a prima facie case of discrimination. The burden of showing that the practice is justifiable and that the disparity cannot be reduced is placed on the employer. Criminal justice policies should be subjected to similar scrutiny. Many would not survive.

The interests of people accused and convicted of crimes are no less important than those of people who apply for or are fired from jobs. Their interests are greater. What is at stake is not a livelihood but in the short term liberty and in the long term stigma and reduced chances of living a satisfying life. The standards for assessing racial and other disparities in the justice system should be no less demanding than those concerning disparities in employment.

Criminal justice system policy makers should be required to declare and justify disparate racial effects. Proposed new laws or policies should be accompanied by racial and ethnic impact projections that seek to identify foreseeable disparities and determine whether they can be justified. There should be strong presumptions against the law's or policy's adoption if it will disproportionately adversely affect members of minority groups. When disparities would be caused or worsened, the proposal should be abandoned or revised.

Current policies and practices should likewise be closely scrutinized by disparity audits to determine whether they operate in racially disparate ways. Clear and convincing evidence should be required that their other effects are substantially more important than the damage they do to the causes of racial neutrality in American law and racial justice in American society. When they cannot be justified, they should be revised or abandoned.

For many current policies the evidence has long been clear. Massive evidence documents the existence of racial profiling by the police, that they stop black people more often in cars and on the streets than they do whites, and for less cause. Police arrest policies in drug cases have long been known to target black and other minority drug dealers disproportionately and to place much less emphasis on white drug dealers. Sentencing laws for drug and some violent crimes have long been known to hit black offenders especially hard. Sentencing policies that make punishments much more severe for people with previous convictions are a significant contributor to racial disparities in prison. All of these policies should be reexamined.

The idea that proposed new laws affecting the criminal justice system should be accompanied by racial impact statements is no longer novel. Iowa has enacted such a law. Many criminal justice agencies now conduct disparity audits. The second edition of the *Model Penal Code* (American Law Institute 2007) requires them.

Are Meaningful Changes Possible?

Proposals for substantial reduction in America's prison population, abandonment of racially unfair practices, repeal of punitive but ineffective legislation, and the requirement of race and ethnicity impact statements may strike some readers as audacious. That is as it should be. Racial disparities and the damage they have done to millions of individual black Americans and their families, and to black Americans as a group, are pressing social problems. Audacity is called for.

There are pessimistic and optimistic ways to contemplate the future. The pessimistic way is to note the evolution of patterns of white dominance in American history and the succession of mechanisms by which it has been maintained. If slavery was succeeded by Jim Crow, which was succeeded by the racially segregated northern ghettoes, which was succeeded by mass imprisonment, it is hard not to wonder what will substitute for mass imprisonment or whether mass imprisonment will endure to keep patterns of racial hierarchy as they now are.

Likewise the psychology and history of American race relations predispose white Americans to resent the progress black Americans have made, to believe that black Americans with dark skin tone and stereotypically African American features are especially likely to be dangerous criminals, and to favor harsh crime control policies. It is hard not to wonder whether the goodwill and idealism exist to ameliorate the avoidable damage contemporary policies do.

The optimistic way forward is to focus on the good things the civil rights movement accomplished. Large numbers of black Americans have moved into the middle class and into positions of wealth and power. Some categories of black Americans—for example, young college-educated women—earn higher incomes than comparable white Americans. Sixty years ago many white Americans, and most southern white Americans, believed that blacks were inherently inferior; that is no longer true. Today most white Americans, including most southern white Americans, reject ideas about white supremacy and believe in legal equality.

Fifty years ago, and for several decades thereafter, Republicans shamelessly pursued the Southern Strategy. In 2005 Kenneth Mehlman, chairman of the Republican National Committee, speaking before an annual meeting of the National Association of Colored People, apologized for the Southern Strategy, saying, "Some Republicans gave up on winning the African American vote, looking the other way or trying to benefit politically from racial polarization. I am here today as the Republican chairman to tell you we were wrong" (quoted in Benedetto 2005).

Few Americans thirty years ago, whether liberal or conservative, Democratic or Republican, would have chosen the criminal justice system we now have. The social psychology, sociology, and politics of American race relations have brought us to a place where no one should want to be. There is no good reason to stay here.

20

The Fire This Time

Michelle Alexander

The first and arguably most important point is that criminal justice reform efforts—standing alone—are futile. Gains can be made, yes, but the new caste system will not be overthrown by isolated victories in legislatures or courtrooms. If you doubt this is the case, consider the sheer scale of mass incarceration. If we hope to return to the rate of incarceration of the 1970s—a time when many civil rights activists believed rates of imprisonment were egregiously high—*we would need to release approximately four out of five people currently behind bars today.*[1] Prisons would have to be closed across America, an event that would likely inspire panic in rural communities that have become dependent on prisons for jobs and economic growth. Hundreds of thousands of people—many of them unionized—would lose their jobs. As Marc Mauer has observed, "The more than 700,000 prison and jail guards, administrators, service workers, and other personnel represent a potentially powerful political opposition to any scaling-down of the system. One need only recall the fierce opposition to the closing of military bases in recent years to see how these forces will function over time."[2]

Arguably, Mauer underestimates the scope of the challenge by focusing narrowly on the prison system, rather than counting all of the people employed in the criminal justice bureaucracy. According to a report released by the U.S. Department of Justice's Bureau of Statistics in 2006, the U.S. spent a record $185 billion for police protection, detention, judicial, and legal activities in 2003. Adjusting for inflation, these figures reflect a tripling of justice expenditures since 1982. The justice system employed

From *The New Jim Crow: Mass Incarceration in the Age of Colorblindness* (New York: The New Press, 2010), 217–48.

almost 2.4 million people in 2003—58 percent of them at the local level and 31 percent at the state level. If four out of five people were released from prisons, far more than a million people could lose their jobs.

There is also the private-sector investment to consider. Prisons are big business and have become deeply entrenched in America's economic and political system. Rich and powerful people, including former Vice President Dick Cheney, have invested millions in private prisons.[3] They are deeply interested in expanding the market—increasing the supply of prisoners—not eliminating the pool of people who can be held captive for a profit. The 2005 annual report for the Corrections Corporation of America explained the vested interests of private prisons matter-of-factly in a filing with the Securities and Exchange Commission:

> Our growth is generally dependent upon our ability to obtain new contracts to develop and manage new correctional and detention facilities. This possible growth depends on a number of factors we cannot control, including crime rates and sentencing patterns in various jurisdictions and acceptance of privatization. The demand for our facilities and services could be adversely affected by the re-laxation of enforcement efforts, leniency in conviction and sentenc-ing practices or through the decriminalization of certain activities that are currently proscribed by our criminal laws. For instance, any changes with respect to drugs and controlled substances or illegal immigration could affect the number of persons arrested, convicted and sentenced, thereby potentially reducing demand for correc-tional facilities to house them.[4]

American Correctional Association President Gwendolyn Chunn put the matter more bluntly that same year when lamenting that the unprec-edented prison expansion boom of the 1990s seemed to be leveling off. "We'll have a hard time holding on to what we have now," she lamented.[5] As it turns out, her fears were unfounded. Although prison growth ap-peared to be slowing in 2005, the market for prisoners has continued to expand. The nation's prison population broke new records in 2008, with no end in sight. The nonprofit PEW Charitable Trusts reports that inmate populations in at least ten states are expected to increase by 25 percent or more between 2006 and 2011. In short, the market for private prisons is as good as it has ever been. Damon Hininger, the president and chief operations officer of Corrections Corporation of America, the largest private-prison operator in the United States, is thoroughly optimistic. His company boosted net income by 14 percent in 2008, and he fully expects the growth to continue. "There is going to be a larger opportunity for us in the future," he said.[6]

Even beyond private prison companies, a whole range of prison profiteers must be reckoned with if mass incarceration is to be undone, including phone companies that gouge families of prisoners by charging them exorbitant rates to communicate with their loved ones; gun manufacturers that sell Taser guns, rifles, and pistols to prison guards and police; private health care providers contracted by the state to provide (typically abysmal) health care to prisoners; the U.S. military, which relies on prison labor to provide military gear to soldiers in Iraq; corporations that use prison labor to avoid paying decent wages; and the politicians, lawyers, and bankers who structure deals to build new prisons often in predominantly white rural communities—deals that often promise far more to local communities than they deliver.[7] All of these corporate and political interests have a stake in the expansion—not the elimination—of the system of mass incarceration.

Consider also the lengthy to-do list for reformers. If we become serious about dismantling the system of mass incarceration, we must end the War on Drugs. There is no way around it. The drug war is largely responsible for the prison boom and the creation of the new undercaste, and there is no path to liberation for communities of color that includes this ongoing war. So long as people of color in ghetto communities are being rounded up by the thousands for drug offenses, carted off to prisons, and then released into a permanent undercaste, mass incarceration as a system of control will continue to function well.

Ending the drug war is no simple task, however. It cannot be accomplished through a landmark court decision, an executive order, or single stroke of the presidential pen. Since 1982, the war has raged like a forest fire set with a few matches and a gallon of gasoline. What began as an audacious federal program has spread to every state in the nation and nearly every city. It has infected law enforcement activities on roads, sidewalks, highways, train stations, airports, and the nation's border. The war has effectively shredded portions of the U.S. Constitution—eliminating Fourth Amendment protections once deemed inviolate—and it has militarized policing practices in inner cities across America. Racially targeted drug-law enforcement practices taken together with laws that specifically discriminate against drug offenders in employment, housing, and public benefits have relegated the majority of black men in urban areas across the United States to a permanent second-class status.

If we hope to end this system of control, we cannot be satisfied with a handful of reforms. All of the financial incentives granted to law enforcement to arrest poor black and brown people for drug offenses must be revoked. Federal grant money for drug enforcement must end; drug forfeiture laws must be stripped from the books; racial profiling must be eradicated; the concentration of drug busts in poor communities of color must cease; and the transfer of military equipment and aid to local law enforcement agencies waging the drug war must come to a screeching halt. And that's just for starters.

Equally important, there must be a change within the culture of law enforcement. Black and brown people in ghetto communities must no longer be viewed as the designated enemy, and ghetto communities must no longer be treated like occupied zones. Law enforcement must adopt a compassionate, humane approach to the problems of the urban poor—an approach that goes beyond the rhetoric of "community policing" to a method of engagement that promotes trust, healing, and genuine partnership. Data collection for police and prosecutors should be mandated nationwide to ensure that selective enforcement is no longer taking place. Racial impact statements that assess the racial and ethnic impact of criminal justice legislation must be adopted.[8] Public defender offices should be funded at the same level as prosecutor's offices to eliminate the unfair advantage afforded the incarceration machine. The list goes on: Mandatory drug sentencing laws must be rescinded. Marijuana ought to be legalized (and perhaps other drugs as well). Meaningful re-entry programs must be adopted—programs that provide a pathway not just to dead-end, minimum-wage jobs, but also training and education so those labeled criminals can realistically reach for high-paying jobs and viable, rewarding career paths. Prison workers should be retrained for jobs and careers that do not involve caging human beings. Drug treatment on demand must be provided for all Americans, a far better investment of taxpayer money than prison cells for drug offenders. Barriers to re-entry, specifically the myriad laws that operate to discriminate against drug offenders for the rest of their lives in every aspect of their social, economic, and political life, must be eliminated.

The list could go on, of course, but the point has been made. The central question for racial justice advocates is this: are we serious about ending this system of control, or not? If we are, there is a tremendous amount of work to be done. The notion that all of these reforms can be accomplished piecemeal—one at a time, through disconnected advocacy strategies—seems deeply misguided. All of the needed reforms have less to do with failed policies than a deeply flawed public consensus, one that is indifferent, at best, to the experience of poor people of color. As Martin Luther King Jr. explained back in 1965, when describing why it was far more important to engage in mass mobilizations than file lawsuits, "We're trying to win the right to vote and we have to focus the attention of the world on that. We can't do that making legal cases. We have to make the case in the court of public opinion."[9] King certainly appreciated the contributions of civil rights lawyers (he relied on them to get him out of jail), but he opposed the tendency of civil rights lawyers to identify a handful of individuals who could make great plaintiffs in a court of law, then file isolated cases. He believed what was necessary was to mobilize thousands to make their case in the court of public opinion. In his view, it was a flawed public consensus—not merely flawed policy—that was at the root of racial oppression.

Today, no less than fifty years later, a flawed public consensus lies at the core of the prevailing caste system. When people think about crime, especially drug crime, they do not think about suburban housewives violating laws regulating prescription drugs or white frat boys using ecstasy. Drug crime in this country is understood to be black and brown, and it is *because* drug crime is racially defined in the public consciousness that the electorate has not cared much what happens to drug criminals—at least not the way they would have cared if the criminals were understood to be white. It is this failure to care, really care across color lines, that lies at the core of this system of control and every racial caste system that has existed in the United States or anywhere else in the world.

Those who believe that advocacy challenging mass incarceration can be successful without overturning the public consensus that gave rise to it are engaging in fanciful thinking, a form of denial. Isolated victories can be won—even a string of victories—but in the absence of a fundamental shift in public consciousness, the system as a whole will remain intact. To the extent that major changes are achieved without a complete shift, the system will rebound. The caste system will reemerge in a *new form*, just as convict leasing replaced slavery, or it will be *reborn*, just as mass incarceration replaced Jim Crow.

Sociologists Michael Omi and Howard Winant make a similar point in their book *Racial Formation in the United States*. They attribute the cyclical nature of racial progress to the "unstable equilibrium" that characterizes the United States' racial order.[10] Under "normal" conditions, they argue, state institutions are able to normalize the organization and enforcement of the prevailing racial order, and the system functions relatively automatically. Challenges to the racial order during these periods are easily marginalized or suppressed, and the prevailing system of racial meanings, identity, and ideology seems "natural." These conditions clearly prevailed during slavery and Jim Crow. When the equilibrium is disrupted, however, as in Reconstruction and the Civil Rights Movement, the state initially resists, then attempts to absorb the challenge through a series of reforms "that are, if not entirely symbolic, at least not critical to the operation of the racial order." In the absence of a truly egalitarian racial consensus, these predictable cycles inevitably give rise to new, extraordinarily comprehensive systems of racialized social control.

One example of the way in which a well established racial order easily absorbs legal challenges is the infamous aftermath of the *Brown v. Board of Education* decision. After the Supreme Court declared separate schools inherently unequal in 1954, segregation persisted unabated. One commentator notes: "The statistics from the Southern states are truly amazing. For ten years, 1954–1964, virtually *nothing happened*."[11] Not a single black child attended an integrated public grade school in South Carolina, Alabama, or Mississippi as of the 1962–1963 school year. Across the South as a whole, a mere 1 percent of black school children were attending school with whites in 1964—a full decade after *Brown* was decided.[12] *Brown* did not end Jim Crow; a mass movement had to emerge first—one that aimed to create a new public consensus opposed to the evils of Jim Crow. This does not mean *Brown v. Board* was meaningless, as some commentators have claimed.[13] *Brown* gave critical legitimacy to the demands of civil rights activists who risked their lives to end Jim Crow, and it helped to inspire the movement (as well as a fierce backlash).[14] But standing alone, *Brown* accomplished for African Americans little more than Abraham Lincoln's Emancipation Proclamation. A civil war had to be waged to end slavery; a mass movement was necessary to bring a formal end to Jim Crow. Those who imagine that far less is required to dismantle mass incarceration and build a new, egalitarian racial consensus reflecting a compassionate rather than punitive impulse toward poor people of color fail to appreciate the distance between Martin Luther King Jr.'s dream and the ongoing racial nightmare for those locked up and locked out of American society.

The foregoing should not be read as a call for movement building to the exclusion of reform work. To the contrary, reform work *is* the work of movement building, provided that it is done consciously *as* movement-building work. If all the reforms mentioned above were actually adopted, a radical transformation in our society would have taken place. The relevant question is not whether to engage in reform work, but how. There is no shortage of worthy reform efforts and goals. Differences of opinion are inevitable about which reforms are most important and in what order of priority they should be pursued. These debates are worthwhile, but it is critical to keep in mind that the question of how we do reform work is even more important than the specific reforms we seek. If the way we pursue reforms does not contribute to the building of a movement to dismantle the system of mass incarceration, and if our advocacy does not upset the prevailing public consensus that supports the new caste system, none of the reforms, even if won, will successfully disrupt the nation's racial equilibrium. Challenges to the system will be easily absorbed or deflected, and the accommodations made will serve primarily to legitimate the system, not undermine it. We run the risk of winning isolated battles but losing the larger war.

Let's Talk About Race—Resisting the Temptation of Colorblind Advocacy

So how should we go about building this movement to end mass incarceration? What should be the core philosophy, the guiding principles? Another book could be written on this subject, but a few key principles stand out that can be briefly explored here. These principles are rooted in an understanding that any movement to end mass incarceration must deal with mass incarceration as a racial caste system, not as a system of crime control. This is not to say crime is unimportant; it is very important. We *need* an effective system of crime prevention and control in our communities, but that is not what the current system is. This system is better designed to *create* crime, and a perpetual class of people labeled criminals, rather than to eliminate crime or reduce the number of criminals.

It is not uncommon, however, to hear people claim that the mere fact that we have the lowest crime rates, at the same time that we have the highest incarceration rates, is all the proof needed that this system works well to control crime. But if you believe this system effectively controls crime, consider this: standard estimates of the amount of crime reduction that can be attributable to mass incarceration range from 3 to 25 percent.[15] Some scholars believe we have long since passed a tipping point where the declining marginal return on imprisonment has dipped below zero. Imprisonment, they say, now creates far more crime than it prevents, by ripping apart fragile social networks, destroying families, and creating a permanent class of unemployables.[16] Although it is common to think of poverty and joblessness as leading to crime and imprisonment, this research suggests that the War on Drugs is a major *cause* of poverty, chronic unemployment, broken families, and crime today. But even assuming 25 percent is the right figure, it still means that the overwhelming majority of incarceration—75 percent—has had absolutely no impact on crime, despite costing nearly $200 billion annually. As a crime reduction strategy, mass incarceration is an abysmal failure. It is largely ineffective and extraordinarily expensive.

Saying mass incarceration is an abysmal failure makes sense, though, only if one assumes that the criminal justice system is designed to prevent and control crime. But if mass incarceration is understood as a system of social control—specifically, racial control—then the system is a fantastic success.[17] In less than two decades, the prison population quadrupled, and large majorities of poor people of color in urban areas throughout the United States were placed under the control of the criminal justice system or saddled with criminal records for life. Almost overnight, huge segments of ghetto communities were permanently relegated to a second-class status, disenfranchised, and subjected to perpetual surveillance and monitoring by law enforcement agencies. One could argue this result is a tragic, unforeseeable mistake, and that the goal was always crime control, not the creation of a racial undercaste. But judging by the political rhetoric and the legal rules employed in the War on Drugs, this result is no freak accident.

In order to make this point, we need to talk about race openly and honestly. We must stop debating crime policy as though it were purely about crime. People must come to understand the racial history and origins of mass incarceration—the many ways our conscious and unconscious biases have distorted our judgments over the years about what is fair, appropriate, and constructive when responding to drug use and drug crime. We must come to see, too, how our economic insecurities and racial resentments have been exploited for political gain, and how this manipulation has caused suffering for people of all colors. Finally, we must admit, out loud, that it was *because of* race that we didn't care much what happened to "those people" and imagined the worst possible things about them. The fact that our lack of care and concern may have been, at times, unintentional or unconscious does not mitigate our crime—if we refuse, when given the chance, to make amends.

Admittedly, though, the temptation to ignore race in our advocacy may be overwhelming. Race makes people uncomfortable. One study found that some whites are so loath to talk about race and so fearful of violating racial etiquette that they indicate a preference for avoiding all contact with black people.[18] The striking reluctance of whites, in particular, to talk about or even acknowledge race has led many scholars and advocates to conclude that we would be better off not talking about race at all. This view is buttressed by the fact that white liberals, nearly as much as conservatives, seem to have lost patience with debates about racial equity. Barack Obama noted this phenomenon in his book, *The Audacity of Hope*: "Rightly or wrongly, white guilt has largely exhausted itself in America; even the most fair-minded of whites, those who would genuinely like to see racial inequality ended and poverty relieved, tend to push back against racial victimization—or race-specific claims based on the history of race discrimination in this country."

Adding to the temptation to avoid race is the fact that opportunities for challenging mass incarceration on purely race-neutral grounds have never been greater. With budgets busting, more than two dozen states have reduced or eliminated harsh mandatory minimum sentences, re-stored early-release programs, and offered treatment instead of incarcera-tion for some drug offenders.[19] The financial crisis engulfing states large and small has led to a conversion among some legislators who once were "get tough" true believers. Declining crime rates, coupled with a decline in public concern about crime, have also helped to create a rare opening for a productive public conversation about the War on Drugs. A promising indicator of the public's receptivity to a change in course is California's Proposition 36, which mandated drug treatment rather than jail for first-time offenders, and was approved by more than 60 percent of the elec-torate in 2000.[20] Some states have decriminalized marijuana, including Massachusetts, where 65 percent of state voters approved the measure.[21] Taken together, these factors suggest that, if a major mobilization got un-derway, impressive changes in our nation's drug laws and policies would be not only possible, but likely, without ever saying a word about race.

This is tempting bait, to put it mildly, but racial justice advocates should not take it. The prevailing caste system cannot be successfully dismantled with a purely race-neutral approach. To begin with, it is extremely un-likely that a strategy based purely on costs, crime rates, and the wisdom of drug treatment will get us back even to the troubling incarceration rates of the 1970s. As indicated earlier, any effort to downsize dramatically our nation's prisons would inspire fierce resistance by those faced with los-ing jobs, investments, and other benefits provided by the current system. The emotion and high anxiety would likely express itself in the form of a racially charged debate about values, morals, and personal responsibility rather than a debate about the prison economy. Few would openly argue that we should lock up millions of poor people just so that other people can have jobs or get a good return on their private investments. Instead, familiar arguments would likely resurface about the need to be "tough" on criminals, not coddle them or give "free passes." The public debate would inevitably turn to race, even if no one was explicitly talking about it. As history has shown, the prevalence of powerful (unchallenged) ra-cial stereotypes, together with widespread apprehension regarding major structural changes, would create a political environment in which implicit racial appeals could be employed, once again, with great success. Failure to anticipate and preempt such appeals would set the stage for the same divide-and-conquer tactics that have reliably preserved racial hierarchy in the United States for centuries.

Even if fairly dramatic changes were achieved while ignoring race, the results would be highly contingent and temporary. If and when the economy improves, the justification for a "softer" approach would no longer exist. States would likely gravitate back to their old ways if a new, more compassionate public consensus about race had not been forged. Similarly, if and when crime rates rise—which seems likely if the nation's economy continues to sour—nothing would deter politicians from making black and brown criminals, once again, their favorite whipping boys. Since the days of slavery, black men have been depicted and understood as criminals, and their criminal "nature" has been among the justifications for every caste system to date. The criminalization and demonization of black men is one habit America seems unlikely to break without addressing head-on the racial dynamics that have given rise to successive caste systems. Although colorblind approaches to addressing the problems of poor people of color often seem pragmatic in the short run, in the long run they are counterproductive. Colorblindness, though widely touted as the solution, is actually the problem.

Against Colorblindness

Saying that colorblindness is the problem may alarm some in the civil rights community, especially the pollsters and political consultants who have become increasingly influential in civil rights advocacy. For decades, civil rights leaders have been saying things like "we all want a colorblind society, we just disagree how to get there" in defense of race-conscious programs like affirmative action or racial data collection.[22] Affirmative action has been framed as a legitimate exception to the colorblindness principle—a principle now endorsed by the overwhelming majority of the American electorate. Civil rights leaders are quick to assure the public that when we reach a colorblind nirvana, race consciousness will no longer be necessary or appropriate.

Far from being a worthy goal, however, colorblindness has proved catastrophic for African Americans. It is not an overstatement to say the systematic mass incarceration of people of color in the United States would not have been possible in the post–civil rights era if the nation had not fallen under the spell of a callous colorblindness. The seemingly innocent phrase, "I don't care if he's black . . ." perfectly captures the perversion of Martin Luther King Jr.'s dream that we may, one day, be able to see beyond race to connect spiritually across racial lines. Saying that one does not care about race is offered as an exculpatory virtue, when in fact it can be a form of cruelty. It is precisely because we, as a nation, have not cared much about African Americans that we have allowed our criminal justice system to create a new racial undercaste.

The deeply flawed nature of colorblindness, as a governing principle, is evidenced by the fact that the public consensus supporting mass incarceration is officially colorblind. It purports to see black and brown men not as black and brown, but simply as men—raceless men—who have failed miserably to play by the rules the rest of us follow quite naturally. The fact that so many black and brown men are rounded up for drug crimes that go largely ignored when committed by whites is unseen. Our collective colorblindness prevents us from seeing this basic fact. Our blindness also prevents us from seeing the racial and structural divisions that persist in society: the segregated, unequal schools, the segregated, jobless ghettos, and the segregated public discourse—a public conversation that excludes the current pariah caste. Our commitment to colorblindness extends beyond individuals to institutions and social arrangements. We have become blind, not so much to race, but to the existence of racial caste in America.

More than forty-five years ago, Martin Luther King Jr. warned of this danger. He insisted that blindness and indifference to racial groups is actually more important than racial hostility to the creation and maintenance of racialized systems of control. Those who supported slavery and Jim Crow, he argued, typically were not bad or evil people; they were just blind. Even the Justices who decided the infamous *Dred Scott* case, which ruled "that the Negro has no rights which the white man is bound to respect," were not wicked men, he said. On the contrary, they were decent and dedicated men. But, he hastened to add, "They were victims of a spiritual and intellectual blindness. They knew not what they did. The whole system of slavery was largely perpetuated through spiritually ignorant persons." He continued:

> This tragic blindness is also found in racial segregation, the not-too-distant cousin of slavery. Some of the most vigorous defenders of segregation are sincere in their beliefs and earnest in their motives. Although some men are segregationists merely for reasons of political expediency and political gain, not all of the resistance to integration is the rearguard of professional bigots. Some people feel that their attempt to preserve segregation is best for themselves, their children, and their nation. Many are good church people, anchored in the religious faith of their mothers and fathers. . . . What a tragedy! Millions of Negroes have been crucified by conscientious blindness. . . . Jesus was right about those men who crucified him. They knew not what they did. They were inflicted by a terrible blindness.[23]

Could not the same speech be given about mass incarceration today? Again, African Americans have been "crucified by conscientious blindness." People of goodwill have been unwilling to see black and brown men, in their humanness, as entitled to the same care, compassion, and concern that would be extended to one's friends, neighbors, or loved ones. King recognized that it was this *indifference* to the plight of other races that supported the institutions of slavery and Jim Crow. In his words, "One of the great tragedies of man's long trek along the highway of history has been the limiting of neighborly concern to tribe, race, class or nation." The consequence of this narrow, insular attitude "is that one does not really mind what happens to the people outside his group."[24] Racial indifference and blindness—far more than racial hostility—form the sturdy foundation for all racial caste systems.

Abandoning the quest for a colorblind society is easier said than done, of course. Racial justice advocates, if they should choose this path, will be required to provide uncomfortable answers to commonly asked questions. For example, advocates are frequently asked, When will we (finally) become a colorblind society? The pursuit of colorblindness makes people impatient. With courage, we should respond: *Hopefully never.* Or if those words are too difficult to utter, then say: "Not in the foreseeable future."

More than a little patience will be needed when explaining the complete about-face. Probably around the same number of people think the Earth is flat as think race consciousness should be the rule in perpetuity, rather than the exception. It would be a mistake, though, to assume that people are incapable of embracing a permanent commitment to color consciousness. The shift may, in fact, come as something of a relief, as it moves our collective focus away from a wholly unrealistic goal to one that is within anyone's reach right now. After all, to aspire to colorblindness is to aspire to a state of being in which you are not capable of seeing racial difference—a practical impossibility for most of us. The shift also invites a more optimistic view of human capacity. The colorblindness ideal is premised on the notion that we, as a society, can never be trusted to see race and treat each other fairly or with genuine compassion. A commitment to color consciousness, by contrast, places faith in our capacity as humans to show care and concern for others, even as we are fully cognizant of race and possible racial differences.

If colorblindness is such a bad idea, though, why have people across the political spectrum become so attached to it? For conservatives, the ideal of colorblindness is linked to a commitment to individualism. In their view, society should be concerned with individuals, not groups. Gross racial disparities in health, wealth, education, and opportunity should be of no interest to our government, and racial identity should be a private

matter, something best kept to ourselves. For liberals, the ideal of color-
blindness is linked to the dream of racial equality. The hope is that one
day we will no longer see race because race will lose all of its significance.
In this fantasy, eventually race will no longer be a factor in mortality rates,
the spread of disease, educational or economic opportunity, or the distribution of wealth. Race will correlate with nothing; it will mean nothing;
we won't even notice it anymore. Those who are less idealistic embrace
colorblindness simply because they find it difficult to imagine a society in
which we see race and racial differences yet consistently act in a positive,
constructive way. It is easier to imagine a world in which we tolerate racial
differences by being blind to them.

The uncomfortable truth, however, is that racial differences will *always*
exist among us. Even if the legacies of slavery, Jim Crow, and mass incarceration were completely overcome, we would remain a nation of immigrants in a larger world divided by race and ethnicity. It is a world in which
there is extraordinary racial and ethnic inequality, and our nation has
porous boundaries. For the foreseeable future, racial and ethnic inequality will be a feature of American life.

This reality is not cause for despair. The idea that we may never reach a
state of perfect racial equality—a perfect racial equilibrium—is not cause
for alarm. What is concerning is the real possibility that we, as a society,
will choose not to care. We will choose to be blind to injustice and the suffering of others. We will look the other way and deny our public agencies
the resources, data, and tools they need to solve problems. We will refuse
to celebrate what is beautiful about our distinct cultures and histories,
even as we blend and evolve. That is cause for despair.

Seeing race is not the problem. Refusing to care for the people we see
is the problem. The fact that the meaning of race may evolve over time
or lose much of its significance is hardly a reason to be struck blind. We
should hope not for a colorblind society but instead for a world in which
we can see each other fully, learn from each other, and do what we can to
respond to each other with love. That was King's dream—a society that
is capable of seeing each of us, as we are, with love. That is a goal worth
fighting for.

The Racial Bribe—Let's Give It Back

The foregoing could be read as a ringing endorsement of affirmative action and other diversity initiatives. To a certain extent, it is. It is difficult to
imagine a time, in the foreseeable future, when the free market and partisan politics could be trusted to produce equitable inclusion in all facets of

American political, economic, and social life, without anyone giving any thought—caring at all—about race. It may always be necessary for us, as a society, to pay careful attention to the impact of our laws, policies, and practices on racial and ethnic groups and consciously strive to ensure that biases, stereotypes, and structural arrangements do not cause unnecessary harm or suffering to any individual or any group for reasons related to race.

There is, however, a major caveat. Racial justice advocates should consider, with a degree of candor that has not yet been evident, whether affirmative action—as it has been framed and defended during the past thirty years—has functioned more like a racial bribe than a tool of racial justice. One might wonder, what does affirmative action have to do with mass incarceration? Well, perhaps the two are linked more than we realize. We should ask ourselves whether efforts to achieve "cosmetic" racial diversity—that is, reform efforts that make institutions look good on the surface without the needed structural changes—have actually helped to facilitate the emergence of mass incarceration and interfered with the development of a more compassionate race consciousness. In earlier chapters, we have seen that throughout our nation's history, poor and working-class whites have been bought off by racial bribes. The question posed here is whether affirmative action has functioned similarly, offering relatively meager material advantages but significant psychological benefits to people of color, in exchange for the abandonment of a more radical movement that promised to alter the nation's economic and social structure.

To be clear: This is *not* an argument that affirmative action policies conflict with King's dream that we might one day be "judged by the content of our character, not the color of our skin." King himself would have almost certainly endorsed affirmative action as a remedy, at least under some circumstances. In fact, King specifically stated on numerous occasions that he believed special—even preferential—treatment for African Americans may be warranted in light of their unique circumstances.[25] And this is not an argument that affirmative action has made no difference in the lives of poor or working-class African Americans—as some have claimed. Fire departments, police departments, and other public agencies have been transformed, at least in part, due to affirmative action.[26] Finally, this is not an argument that affirmative action should be reconsidered simply on the grounds that it is "unfair" to white men as a group. The empirical evidence strongly supports the conclusion that declining wages, downsizing, deindustrialization, globalization, and cutbacks in government services represent much greater threats to the position of white men than so-called reverse discrimination.[27]

The argument made here is a less familiar one. It is not widely debated in the mainstream media or, for that matter, in civil rights organizations. The claim is that racial justice advocates should reconsider the traditional approach to affirmative action because (a) it has helped to render a new caste system largely invisible; (b) it has helped to perpetuate the myth that anyone can make it if they try; (c) it has encouraged the embrace of a "trickle down theory of racial justice"; (d) it has greatly facilitated the divide-and-conquer tactics that gave rise to mass incarceration; and (e) it has inspired such polarization and media attention that the general public now (wrongly) assumes that affirmative action is the main battlefront in U.S. race relations.

It may not be easy for the civil rights community to have a candid conversation about any of this. Civil rights organizations are populated with beneficiaries of affirmative action (like myself) and their friends and allies. Ending affirmative action arouses fears of annihilation. The reality that so many of us would disappear overnight from colleges and universities nationwide if affirmative action were banned, and that our children and grandchildren might not follow in our footsteps, creates a kind of panic that is difficult to describe. It may be analogous, in some respects, to the panic once experienced by poor and working-class whites faced with desegregation—the fear of a sudden demotion in the nation's racial hierarchy. Mari Matsuda and Charles Lawrence's book *We Won't Go Back* captures the determination of affirmative-action beneficiaries not to allow the clock to be turned back on racial justice, back to days of racial caste in America. The problem, of course, is that *we are already there.*

Affirmative action, particularly when it is justified on the grounds of diversity rather than equity (or remedy), masks the severity of racial inequality in America, leading to greatly exaggerated claims of racial progress and overly optimistic assessments of the future for African Americans. Seeing black people graduate from Harvard and Yale and become CEOs or corporate lawyers—not to mention president of the United States—causes us all to marvel at what a long way we have come. As recent data shows, however, much of black progress is a myth. Although some African Americans are doing very well—enrolling in universities and graduate schools at record rates thanks to affirmative action—as a group, African Americans are doing no better than they were when Martin Luther King Jr. was assassinated and riots swept inner cities across America. Nearly one-fourth of African Americans live below the poverty line today, approximately the same as in 1968. The child poverty rate is actually higher today than it was then.[28] Unemployment rates in black communities rival those in Third World countries. And that is *with* affirmative action!

When we pull back the curtain and take a look at what our so-called colorblind society creates without affirmative action, we see a familiar social, political, and economic structure—the structure of racial caste. When those behind bars are taken into account, America's institutions continue to create nearly as much racial inequality as existed during Jim Crow.[29] Our elite universities, which now look a lot like America, would whiten overnight if affirmative action suddenly disappeared. One recent study indicates that the elimination of race-based admissions policies would lead to a 63 percent decline in black matriculants at all law schools and a 90 percent decline at elite law schools.[30] Sociologist Stephen Steinberg describes the bleak reality this way: "Insofar as this black middle class is an artifact of affirmative action policy, it cannot be said to be the result of autonomous workings of market forces. In other words, the black middle class does not reflect a lowering of racist barriers in occupations so much as the opposite: racism is so entrenched that without government intervention there would be little 'progress' to boast about."[31]

In view of all this, we must ask, to what extent has affirmative action helped us remain blind to, and in denial about, the existence of a racial undercaste? And to what extent have the battles over affirmative action distracted us and diverted crucial resources and energy away from dismantling the structures of racial inequality?

The predictable response is that civil rights advocates are as committed to challenging mass incarceration and other forms of structural racism as they are to preserving affirmative action. But where is the evidence of this? Civil rights activists have created a national *movement* to save affirmative action, complete with the marches, organizing, and media campaigns, as well as incessant strategy meetings, conferences, and litigation. Where is the movement to end mass incarceration? For that matter, where is the movement for educational equity? Part of the answer is that it is far easier to create a movement when there is a sense of being under attack. It is also easier when a single policy is at issue, rather than something as enormous (and seemingly intractable) as educational inequity or mass incarceration. Those are decent explanations, but they are no excuse. Try telling a sixteen-year-old black youth in Louisiana who is facing a decade in adult prison and a lifetime of social, political, and economic exclusion that your civil rights organization is not doing much to end the War on Drugs—but would he like to hear about all the great things that are being done to save affirmative action? There is a fundamental disconnect today between the world of civil rights advocacy and the reality facing those trapped in the new racial undercaste.

There is another, more sinister consequence of affirmative action: the carefully engineered appearance of great racial progress strengthens the "colorblind" public consensus that personal and cultural traits, not

structural arrangements, are largely responsible for the fact that the majority of young black men in urban areas across the United States are currently
under the control of the criminal justice system or branded as felons for life.
In other words, affirmative action helps to make the emergence of a new
racial caste system seem implausible. It creates an environment in which
it is reasonable to ask, how can something akin to a racial caste system exist when people like Condoleezza Rice, Colin Powell, and Barack Obama
are capable of rising from next to nothing to the pinnacles of wealth and
power? How could a caste system exist, in view of the black middle class?

There are answers to these questions, but they are difficult to swallow
when millions of Americans have displayed a willingness to elect a black
man president of the United States. The truth, however, is this: far from
undermining the current system of control, the new caste system depends,
in no small part, on black exceptionalism. The colorblind public consensus that supports the new caste system insists that race no longer matters.
Now that America has officially embraced Martin Luther King Jr.'s dream
(by reducing it to the platitude "that we should be judged by the content of
our character, not the color of our skin"), the mass incarceration of people
of color can be justified only to the extent that the plight of those locked
up and locked out is understood to be their choice, not their birthright.

In short, mass incarceration is predicated on the notion that an extraordinary number of African Americans (but not all) have freely chosen
a life of crime and thus belong behind bars. A belief that all blacks belong in jail would be incompatible with the social consensus that we have
"moved beyond" race and that race is no longer relevant. But a widespread
belief that a majority of black and brown men unfortunately belong in jail
is compatible with the new American creed, provided that their imprisonment can be interpreted as their own fault. If the prison label imposed
on them can be blamed on their culture, poor work ethic, or even their
families, then society is absolved of responsibility to do anything about
their condition.

This is where black exceptionalism comes in. Highly visible examples of
black success are critical to the maintenance of a racial caste system in the
era of colorblindness. Black success stories lend credence to the notion
that anyone, no matter how poor or how black you may be, can make it to
the top, if only you try hard enough. These stories "prove" that race is no
longer relevant. Whereas black success stories undermined the logic of
Jim Crow, they actually reinforce the system of mass incarceration. Mass
incarceration depends for its legitimacy on the widespread belief that all
those who appear trapped at the bottom actually chose their fate.

Viewed from this perspective, affirmative action no longer appears entirely progressive. So long as some readily identifiable African Americans

are doing well, the system is largely immunized from racial critique. People like Barack Obama who are truly exceptional by any standards, along with others who have been granted exceptional opportunities, legitimate a system that remains fraught with racial bias—especially when they fail to challenge, or even acknowledge, the prevailing racial order. In the current era, white Americans are often eager to embrace token or exceptional African Americans, particularly when they go out of their way not to talk about race or racial inequality.

Affirmative action may be counterproductive in yet another sense: it lends credence to a trickle-down theory of racial justice. The notion that giving a relatively small number of people of color access to key positions or institutions will inevitably redound to the benefit of the larger group is belied by the evidence. It also seems to disregard Martin Luther King Jr.'s stern warnings that racial justice requires the complete transformation of social institutions and a dramatic restructuring of our economy, not superficial changes that can be purchased on the cheap. King argued in 1968, "The changes [that have occurred to date] are basically in the social and political areas; the problems we now face—providing jobs, better housing and better education for the poor throughout the country—will require money for their solution, a fact that makes those solutions all the more difficult." [32] He emphasized that "most of the gains of the past decade were obtained at bargain prices," for the desegregation of public facilities and the election and appointment of a few black officials cost close to nothing. "White America must recognize that justice for black people cannot be achieved without radical changes in the structure of our society. The comfortable, the entrenched, the privileged cannot continue to tremble at the prospect of change in the status quo." [33]

Against this backdrop, diversity-driven affirmative action programs seem to be the epitome of racial justice purchased on the cheap. They create the appearance of racial equity without the reality and do so at no great cost, without fundamentally altering any of the structures that create racial inequality in the first place. Perhaps the best illustration of this fact is that, thanks in part to affirmative action, police departments and law enforcement agencies nationwide have come to look more like America than ever, at precisely the moment that they have waged a war on the ghetto poor and played a leading role in the systematic mass incarceration of people of color. The color of police chiefs across the country has changed, but the role of the police in our society has not.

Gerald Torres and Lani Guinier offer a similar critique of affirmative action in *The Miner's Canary*. They point out that "conventional strategies for social change proceed as though a change in who administers power fundamentally affects the structure of power itself." [34] This narrow approach to social change is reflected in the justifications offered for affirmative action, most notably the claim that "previous outsiders, once given a chance, will exercise power *differently*."[35] The reality, however, is that the existing hierarchy disciplines newcomers, requiring them to exercise power in the same old ways and play by the same old rules in order to survive. The newcomers, Torres and Guinier explain, are easily co-opted, as they have much to lose but little to gain by challenging the rules of the game.

Their point is particularly relevant to the predicament of minority police officers charged with waging the drug war. Profound racial injustice occurs when minority police officers *follow the rules*. It is a scandal when the public learns they have broken the rules, but no rules need be broken for the systematic mass incarceration of people of color to proceed unabated. This uncomfortable fact creates strong incentives for minority officers to deny, to rationalize, or to be willingly blind to the role of law enforcement in creating a racial undercaste. Reports that minority officers may engage in nearly as much racial profiling as white officers have been met with some amazement, but the real surprise is that some minority police officers have been willing to speak out against the practice, given the ferocity of the drug war. A war has been declared against poor communities of color, and the police are expected to wage it. Do we expect minority officers, whose livelihood depends on the very departments charged with waging the war, to play the role of peacenik? That expectation seems unreasonable, yet the dilemma for racial justice advocates is a real one. The quiet complicity of minority officers in the War on Drugs serves to legitimate the system and insulate it from critique. In a nation still stuck in an old Jim Crow mind-set—which equates racism with white bigotry and views racial diversity as proof the problem has been solved—a racially diverse police department invites questions like: "How can you say the Oakland Police Department's drug raids are racist? There's a black police chief, and most of the officers involved in the drug raids are black." If the caste dimensions of mass incarceration were better understood and the limitations of cosmetic diversity were better appreciated, the existence of black police chiefs and black officers would be no more encouraging today than the presence of black slave drivers and black plantation owners hundreds of years ago.

When meaningful change fails to materialize following the achievement of superficial diversity, those who remain locked out can become extremely discouraged and demoralized, resulting in cynicism and resignation. Perhaps more concerning, though, is the fact that inclusion of people of color in power structures, particularly at the top, can paralyze reform efforts. People of color are often reluctant to challenge institutions led by people who look like them, as they feel a personal stake in the individual's success. After centuries of being denied access to leadership positions in key social institutions, people of color quite understandably are hesitant to create circumstances that could trigger the downfall of "one of their own." An incident of police brutality that would be understood as undeniably racist if the officers involved were white may be given a more charitable spin if the officers are black. Similarly, black community residents who might have been inspired to challenge aggressive stop-and-frisk policies of a largely white police department may worry about "hurting" a black police chief. People of color, because of the history of racial subjugation and exclusion, often experience success and failure vicariously through the few who achieve positions of power, fame, and fortune. As a result, cosmetic diversity, which focuses on providing opportunities to individual members of under-represented groups, both diminishes the possibility that unfair rules will be challenged and legitimates the entire system.

Obama—the Promise and the Peril

This dynamic poses particular risks for racial justice advocacy during an Obama presidency. On the one hand, the election of Barack Obama to the presidency creates an extraordinary opportunity for those seeking to end the system of mass incarceration in America. Obama's stated positions on criminal justice reform suggest that he is opposed to the War on Drugs and the systematic targeting of African Americans for mass incarceration.[36] Shouldn't we trust him, now that he is holding the reins of power, to do the right thing?

Trust is tempting, especially because Obama himself violated our nation's drug laws and almost certainly knows that his life would not have unfolded as it did if he had been arrested on drug charges and treated like a common criminal. As he wrote in his memoir about his wayward youth, "Pot had helped, and booze; maybe a little blow when you could afford it." Unlike Bill Clinton, who famously admitted he experimented with marijuana on occasion "but didn't inhale," Obama has never minimized his illegal drug use. As he said in a 2006 speech to the American Society of Magazine Editors, "Look, you know, when I was a kid, I inhaled. Frequently. That was the point."[37] Those "bad decisions," Obama has acknowledged, could have led him to a personal dead end. "Junkie. Pothead. That's where I'd have been headed: the final, fatal role of the young would-be black man." No doubt if Obama had been arrested and treated like a common criminal, he could have served years in prison and been labeled a drug felon for life. What are the chances he would have gone to Harvard Law School, much less become president of the United States, if that had happened? It seems reasonable to assume that Obama, who knows a little something about poverty and the temptations of drugs, would have a "there but for the grace of God go I" attitude about the millions of African and Latino men imprisoned for drug offenses comparable to his own or saddled for life with felony records.

But before we kick back, relax, and wait for racial justice to trickle down, consider this: Obama chose Joe Biden, one of the Senate's most strident drug warriors, as his vice president. The man he picked to serve as his chief of staff in the White House, Rahm Emanuel, was a major proponent of the expansion of the drug war and the slashing of welfare rolls during President Clinton's administration. And the man he tapped to lead the U.S. Department of Justice—the agency that launched and continues to oversee the federal war on drugs—is an African American former U.S. attorney for the District of Columbia who sought to ratchet up the drug war in Washington, D.C., and fought the majority black D.C. City Council in an effort to impose harsh mandatory minimums for marijuana possession. Moreover, on the campaign trail, Obama took a dramatic step back from an earlier position opposing the death penalty, announcing that he now supports the death penalty for child rapists—even if the victim is not killed—even though the U.S. Supreme Court ruled the death penalty for nonhomicides unconstitutional and international law strongly disfavors the practice. The only countries that share Obama's view are countries like Saudi Arabia, Egypt, and China, which allow the death penalty for things like adultery and tax evasion. So why did Obama, on the campaign trail, go out of his way to announce disagreement with a Supreme Court decision ruling the death penalty for child rapists unconstitutional? Clearly he was attempting to immunize himself from any attempt to portray him as "soft" on crime—a tactic reminiscent of Bill Clinton's decision to fly back to Arkansas during the 1992 presidential campaign to oversee the execution of a mentally retarded black man.

Seasoned activists may respond that all of this is "just politics," but, as we have seen in earlier chapters, they are the same politics that gave rise to the New Jim Crow. Now that crime seems to be rising again in some ghetto communities, Obama is pledging to revive President Clinton's Community Oriented Policing Services (COPS) program and increase funding for the Byrne grant program—two of the worst federal drug programs of the Clinton era.[38] These programs, despite their benign names, are responsible for the militarization of policing. SWAT teams, Pipeline drug task forces, and the laundry list of drug-war horrors described in chapter 2.

Clinton once boasted that the COPS program, which put tens of thousands of officers on the streets, was responsible for the dramatic fifteen-year drop in violent crime that began in the 1990s. Recent studies, however, have shown that is not the case. A 2005 report by the Government Accountability Office concluded the program may have contributed to a 1 percent reduction in crime—at a cost of $8 billion.[39] A peer-reviewed study in the journal *Criminology* found that the COPS program, despite the hype, "had little or no effect on crime."[40] And while Obama's drug czar, former Seattle Police Chief Gil Kerlikowske, has said the War on Drugs should no longer be *called* a war, Obama's budget for law enforcement is actually worse than the Bush administration's in terms of the ratio of dollars devoted to prevention and drug treatment as opposed to law enforcement.[41] Obama, who is celebrated as evidence of America's triumph over race, is proposing nothing less than revving up the drug war through the same failed policies and programs that have systematically locked young men of color into a permanent racial undercaste.

The unique and concerning situation racial justice advocates now face is that the very people who are most oppressed by the current caste system—African Americans—may be the least likely to want to challenge it, now that a black family is living in the White House. If Obama were white, there would be no hesitation to remind him of his youthful drug use when arguing that he should end the drug war and make good on his promises to end unjust mandatory minimums. But do African Americans want the media to talk about Obama's drug use? Do African Americans want to pressure Obama on any issue, let alone issues of race? To go one step further, could it be that many African Americans would actually prefer to ignore racial issues during Obama's presidency, to help ensure him smooth sailing and a triumphant presidency, no matter how bad things are for African Americans in the meantime?

The fact that the last question could plausibly be answered yes raises serious questions for the civil rights community. Have we unwittingly exaggerated the importance of individuals succeeding within pre-existing structures of power, and thereby undermined King's call for a "complete restructuring" of our society? Have we contributed to the disempowerment and passivity of the black community, not only by letting the lawyers take over, but also by communicating the message that the best path— perhaps the only path—to the promised land is infiltrating elite institutions and seizing power at the top, so racial justice can trickle down?

Torres and Guinier suggest the answer to these questions may be yes. They observe that, "surprisingly, strategists on both the left and right, despite their differences, converge on the individual as the unit of power."[42]

Conservatives challenge the legitimacy of group rights or race consciousness and argue that the best empowerment strategy is entrepreneurship and individual initiative. Civil rights advocates argue that individual group members "represent" the race and that hierarchies of power that lack diversity are illegitimate. The theory is, when black individuals achieve power for themselves, black people as a group benefit, as does society as a whole. "Here we see both liberals and conservatives endorsing the same meta-narrative of American individualism: When individuals get ahead, the group triumphs. When individuals succeed, American democracy prevails." [43]

The absence of a thoroughgoing structural critique of the prevailing racial order explains why so many civil rights advocates responded to Barack Obama's election with glee, combined with hasty reminders that "we still have a long way to go." The predictable response from the casual observer is: well, how much further? A black man was just elected president. How much further do black people want to go? If a black person can be elected president, can't a black person do just about anything now?

All of Us or None

At the same time that many civil rights advocates have been pursuing lawyer-driven, trickle-down strategies for racial justice, a growing number of formerly incarcerated men and women have been organizing in major cities across the United States, providing assistance to those newly released from prison and engaging in grassroots political activism in pursuit of basic civil rights. One such organization, based in Oakland, California, is named All of Us or None. The name explicitly challenges a politics that affords inclusion and acceptance for a few but guarantees exclusion for many. In spirit, it asserts solidarity with the "least of these among us."

Diversity-driven affirmative action, as described and implemented today, sends a different message. The message is that "some of us" will gain inclusion. As a policy, it is blind to those who are beyond its reach, the colored faces at the bottom of the well. One policy alone can't save the world, the skeptic might respond. True enough. But what if affirmative action, as it has been framed and debated, does more harm than good, viewed from the perspective of "all of us"?

This brings us to a critical question: who is the *us* that civil rights advocates are fighting for? Judging from the plethora of groups that have embarked on their own civil rights campaigns since Martin Luther King Jr.'s assassination—women, gays, immigrants, Latinos, Asian Americans—the answer seems to be that *us* includes everyone except white men.

This result is not illogical. When Malcolm X condemned "the white man" and declared him the enemy, he was not, of course, speaking about any particular white man, but rather the white, patriarchal order that characterized both slavery and Jim Crow. Malcolm X understood that the United States was created by and for privileged white men. It was white men who dominated politics, controlled the nation's wealth, and wrote the rules by which everyone else was forced to live. No group in the United States can be said to have experienced more privilege, and gone to greater lengths to protect it, than "the white man."

Yet the white man, it turns out, has suffered too. The fact that his suffering has been far less extreme, and has not been linked to a belief in his inherent inferiority, has not made his suffering less real. Civil rights advocates, however, have treated the white man's suffering as largely irrelevant to the pursuit of the promised land. As civil rights lawyers unveiled plans to desegregate public schools, it was poor and working-class whites who were expected to bear the burden of this profound social adjustment, even though many of them were as desperate for upward social mobility and quality education as African Americans. According to the 1950 census, among Southerners in their late twenties, the state-by-state percentages of functional illiterates (people with less than five years of schooling) for whites on farms overlapped with those for blacks in the cities. The majority of Southern whites were better off than Southern blacks, but they were not affluent or well educated by any means; they were semiliterate (with less than twelve years of schooling). Only a tiny minority of whites were affluent and well educated. They stood far apart from the rest of the whites and virtually all blacks.[44]

What lower-class whites *did* have was what W.E.B. Du Bois described as "the public and psychological wage" paid to white workers, who depended on their status and privileges as whites to compensate for low pay and harsh working conditions.[45] As described in chapter 1, time and time again, poor and working-class whites were persuaded to choose their racial status interests over their common economic interests with blacks, resulting in the emergence of new caste systems that only marginally benefited whites but were devastating for African Americans.

In retrospect, it seems clear that nothing could have been more important in the 1970s and 1980s than finding a way to create a durable, interracial, bottom-up coalition for social and economic justice to ensure that another caste system did not emerge from the ashes of Jim Crow. Priority should have been given to figuring out some way for poor and working-class whites to feel as though they had a stake—some tangible interest—in the nascent integrated racial order. As Lani Guinier points out, however, the racial liberalism expressed in the *Brown v. Board of Education* decision and endorsed by civil rights litigators "did not offer poor whites even an elementary framework for understanding what they might gain as a result of integration."[46] Nothing in the opinion or in the subsequent legal strategy made clear that segregation had afforded elites a crucial means of exercising social control over poor and working-class whites as well as blacks. The Southern white elite, whether planters or industrialists, had successfully endeavored to make all whites think in racial rather than class terms, predictably leading whites to experience desegregation, as Derrick Bell put it, as a net "loss."[47]

Given that poor and working-class whites (not white elites) were the ones who had their world rocked by desegregation, it does not take a great leap of empathy to see why affirmative action could be experienced as salt in a wound. Du Bois once observed that the psychological wage of whiteness put "an indelible black face to failure."[48] Yet with the advent of affirmative action, suddenly African Americans were leapfrogging over poor and working-class whites on their way to Harvard and Yale and taking jobs in police departments and fire departments that had once been reserved for whites. Civil rights advocates offered no balm for the wound, publicly resisting calls for *class*-based affirmative action and dismissing claims of unfairness on the grounds that whites had been enjoying racial preferences for hundreds of years. Resentment, frustration, and anger expressed by poor and working-class whites was chalked up to racism, leading to a subterranean discourse about race and to implicitly racial political appeals, but little honest dialogue.

Perhaps the time has come to give up the racial bribes and begin an honest conversation about race in America. The topic of the conversation should be how *us* can come to include *all of us*. Accomplishing this degree of unity may mean giving up fierce defense of policies and strategies that exacerbate racial tensions and produce for racially defined groups primarily psychological or cosmetic racial benefits.

Of course, if meaningful progress is to be made, whites must give up their racial bribes too, and be willing to sacrifice their racial privilege. Some might argue that in this game of chicken, whites should make the first move. Whites should demonstrate that their silence in the drug war cannot be bought by tacit assurances that their sons and daughters will not be rounded up en masse and locked away. Whites should prove their commitment to dismantling not only mass incarceration, but all of the structures of racial inequality that guarantee for whites the resilience of white privilege. After all, why should "we" give up our racial bribes if whites have been unwilling to give up theirs? In light of our nation's racial history, that seems profoundly unfair. But if your strategy for racial justice involves waiting for whites to be fair, history suggests it will be a long wait.

It's not that white people are more unjust than others. Rather it seems that an aspect of human nature is the tendency to cling tightly to one's advantages and privileges and to rationalize the suffering and exclusion of others. This tendency is what led Frederick Douglass to declare that "power concedes nothing without a demand; it never has and it never will."

So what is to be demanded in this moment in our nation's racial history? If the answer is more power, more top jobs, more slots in fancy schools for "us"—a narrow, racially defined *us* that excludes many—we will continue the same power struggles and can expect to achieve many of the same results. Yes, we may still manage to persuade mainstream voters in the midst of an economic crisis that we have relied too heavily on incarceration, that prisons are too expensive, and that drug use is a public health problem, not a crime. But if the movement that emerges to end mass incarceration does not meaningfully address the racial divisions and resentments that gave rise to mass incarceration, and if it fails to cultivate an ethic of genuine care, compassion, and concern for every human being—of every class, race, and nationality—within our nation's borders, including poor whites, who are often pitted against poor people of color, the collapse of mass incarceration will not mean the death of racial caste in America. Inevitably a new system of racialized social control will emerge—one that we cannot foresee, just as the current system of mass incarceration was not predicted by anyone thirty years ago. No task is more urgent for racial justice advocates today than ensuring that America's current racial caste system is its last.

Given what is at stake at this moment in history, bolder, more inspired action is required than we have seen to date. Piecemeal, top-down policy reform on criminal justice issues, combined with a racial justice discourse that revolves largely around the meaning of Barack Obama's election and "post-racialism," will not get us out of our nation's racial quagmire. We must flip the script. Taking our cue from the courageous civil rights advocates who brazenly refused to defend themselves, marching unarmed past white mobs that threatened to kill them, we, too, must be the change we hope to create. If we want to do more than just end mass incarceration—if we want to put an end to the history of racial caste in America—we must lay down our racial bribes, join hands with people of all colors who are not content to wait for change to trickle down, and say to those who would stand in our way: Accept all of us or none.

That is the basic message that Martin Luther King Jr. aimed to deliver through the Poor People's Movement back in 1968. He argued then that the time had come for racial justice advocates to shift from a civil rights to a human rights paradigm, and that the real work of movement building had only just begun.[49] A human rights approach, he believed, would offer far greater hope for those of us determined to create a thriving, multiracial, multiethnic democracy free from racial hierarchy than the civil rights model had provided to date. It would offer a positive vision of what we can strive *for*—a society in which all human beings of all races are treated with dignity, and have the right to food, shelter, health care, education, and security.[50] This expansive vision could open the door to meaningful alliances between poor and working-class people of all colors, who could begin to see their interests as aligned, rather than in conflict—no longer in competition for scarce resources in a zero-sum game.

A human rights movement, King believed, held revolutionary potential. Speaking at a Southern Christian Leadership Conference staff retreat in May 1967, he told SCLC staff, who were concerned that the Civil Rights Movement had lost its steam and its direction, "It is necessary for us to realize that we have moved from the era of civil rights to the era of human rights." Political reform efforts were no longer adequate to the task at hand, he said. "For the last 12 years, we have been in a reform movement. . . . [But] after Selma and the voting rights bill, we moved into a new era, which must be an era of revolution. We must see the great distinction between a reform movement and a revolutionary movement. We are called upon to raise certain basic questions about the whole society."[51]

More than forty years later, civil rights advocacy is stuck in a model of advocacy King was determined to leave behind. Rather than challenging the basic structure of society and doing the hard work of movement building—the work to which King was still committed at the end of his life—we have been tempted too often by the opportunity for people of color to be included within the political and economic structure as-is, even if it means alienating those who are necessary allies. We have allowed ourselves to be willfully blind to the emergence of a new caste system— a system of social excommunication that has denied millions of African Americans basic human dignity. The significance of this cannot be overstated, for the failure to acknowledge the humanity and dignity of all persons has lurked at the root of every racial caste system. This common thread explains why, in the 1780s, the British Society for the Abolition of Slavery adopted as its official seal a woodcut of a kneeling slave above a banner that read, "AM I NOT A MAN AND A BROTHER?" That symbol was followed more than a hundred years later by signs worn around the necks of black sanitation workers during the Poor People's Campaign answering the slave's question with the simple statement, I AM A MAN.

The fact that black men could wear the same sign today in protest of the new caste system suggests that the model of civil rights advocacy that has been employed for the past several decades is, as King predicted, inadequate to the task at hand. If we can agree that what is needed now, at this critical juncture, is not more tinkering or tokenism, but as King insisted forty years ago, a "radical restructuring of our society," then perhaps we can also agree that a radical restructuring of our approach to racial justice advocacy is in order as well.

All of this is easier said than done, of course. Change in civil rights organizations, like change in society as a whole, will not come easy. Fully committing to a vision of racial justice that includes grassroots, bottom-up advocacy on behalf of "all of us" will require a major reconsideration of priorities, staffing, strategies, and messages. Egos, competing agendas, career goals, and inertia may get in the way. It may be that traditional civil rights organizations simply cannot, or will not, change. To this it can only be said, without a hint of disrespect: adapt or die.

If Martin Luther King Jr. is right that the arc of history is long, but it bends toward justice, a new movement will arise; and if civil rights organizations fail to keep up with the times, they will be pushed to the side as another generation of advocates comes to the fore. Hopefully the new generation will be led by those who know best the brutality of the new caste system—a group with greater vision, courage, and determination than the old guard can muster, trapped as they may be in an outdated paradigm. This new generation of activists should not disrespect their elders or disparage their contributions or achievements; to the contrary, they should bow their heads in respect, for their forerunners have expended untold hours and made great sacrifices in an elusive quest for justice. But once respects have been paid, they should march right past them, emboldened, as King once said, by the fierce urgency of now.

Those of us who hope to be their allies should not be surprised, if and when this day comes, that when those who have been locked up and locked out finally have the chance to speak and truly be heard, what we hear is rage. The rage may frighten us; it may remind us of riots, uprisings, and buildings aflame. We may be tempted to control it, or douse it with buckets of doubt, dismay, and disbelief. But we should do no such thing. Instead, when a young man who was born in the ghetto and who knows little of life beyond the walls of his prison cell and the invisible cage that has become his life, turns to us in bewilderment and rage, we should do nothing more than look him in the eye and tell him the truth. We should tell him the same truth the great African American writer James Baldwin told his nephew in a letter published in 1962, in one of the most extraordinary books ever written, *The Fire Next Time*. With great passion and searing conviction, Baldwin had this to say to his young nephew:

This is the crime of which I accuse my country and my countrymen, and for which neither I nor time nor history will ever forgive them, that they have destroyed and are destroying hundreds of thousands of lives and do not know it and do not want to know it. . . . It is their innocence which constitutes the crime. . . . This innocent country set you down in a ghetto in which, in fact, it intended that you should perish. The limits of your ambition were, thus, expected to be set forever. You were born into a society which spelled out with brutal clarity, and in as many ways as possible, that you were a worthless human being. You were not expected to aspire to excellence: you were expected to make peace with mediocrity. . . . You have, and many of us have, defeated this intention; and, by a terrible law, a terrible paradox, those innocents who believed that your imprisonment made them safe are losing their grasp on reality. But these men are your brothers—your lost, younger brothers. And if the word integration means anything, this is what it means: that we, with love, shall force our brothers to see themselves as they are, to cease fleeing from reality and begin to change it. For this is your home, my friend, do not be driven from it; great men have done great things here, and will again, and we can make America what it must become. It will be hard, but you come from sturdy, peasant stock, men who picked cotton and dammed rivers and built railroads, and, in the teeth of the most terrifying odds, achieved an unassailable and monumental dignity. You come from a long line of great poets since Homer. One of them said, *The very time I thought I was lost, My dungeon shook and my chains fell off.* . . . We cannot be free until they are free. God bless you, and Godspeed.[52]

21

From Racial Profiling to Racial Literacy

Lani Guinier

The undisputed historical backdrop for racial profiling is two hundred and forty years of chattel slavery, a hundred years of Jim Crow, and four-hundred-plus years of intergenerational wealth transfer during which most of the time black people not only owned little property but *were* property. In roughly fifty of the first seventy-two years of our country's first century, the presidents of the United States themselves owned slaves. In the infamous Dred Scott case, in which the U.S. Supreme Court declared that a black man had no rights that a white man need respect, five of the justices were from slaveholding families.

This history may seem long ago, but it has left its thumbprint on our unconscious mental processes. Teachers, journalists, politicians, and ordinary citizens of all races find themselves unwittingly participating in a kabuki dance of racial profiling.[1] Whether we are white or black, Latino or Asian, we internalize that history's indelible impression, quickly though subconsciously pairing black faces with words like danger or with pictures of a weapon.[2] According to Dr. Mahzarin Banaji, we make these snap judgments in response to the "mindbugs" implanted by our history and our culture.

These mindbugs help explain the gaps between our words and our deeds. For example, on February 27, 2001, President George W. Bush opined that "racial profiling is wrong" and vowed to "end it in America." A little more than two years later, his Justice Department banned federal law enforcement agencies from practicing racial profiling, but with a standard exception for "national security" investigations and a just-as-typical lack of either enforcement mechanisms or data collection requirements.

From the introduction to *12 Angry Men: True Stories of Being a Black Man in America Today*, ed. Gregory S. Parks and Matthew W. Hughey (New York: The New Press, 2011), xxxv–xlii.

In August 2005, the Bush Justice Department tacked in the opposite direction, demoting the head of the Bureau of Justice Statistics for refusing to comply with a more senior official's order that he downplay in a press release the findings of a department study on racial profiling by police officers.

The Obama administration began with its own high hopes and big promises. Attorney General Eric Holder told Congress on May 7, 2009, that ending racial profiling was a "priority" and later added in a television interview that he himself had been a victim of this practice. Then, of course, came the infamous front-porch confrontation of Harvard professor Henry Louis Gates Jr., who is black, and Cambridge police sergeant James Crowley, who is white. The professor was a friend of Barack Obama, and the sergeant, a mentor of younger cops, had conducted diversity training. Both men were soon to become the president's beer buddies.

When a neighbor on Gates's tree-lined street reported what might be a prowler, the police handcuffed the fifty-eight-year-old, who walks with a cane, and arrested him for disorderly conduct on his own front porch. A June 2010 report commissioned by the city of Cambridge did not try to assess blame, but it pointed out the ways in which both Professor Gates, a prominent African American studies scholar, and Sergeant Crowley, an experienced officer, were reading and experiencing race differently. Crowley failed to "change his attitude toward Professor Gates" even after he realized that Gates posed no physical threat. In Gates's case, the commission concluded that he made the mistake of daring to talk back to the police, after taking offense that he was being mistaken for a burglary suspect in his own home. Just before he was led away in handcuffs by the police, and after he had shown his Harvard identification to the officer, Professor Gates reportedly said, "This is what happens to black men in America." Hollywood could not have asked for a more cinematic display of the many ways we each "read" race against the backdrop of history, culture, and our individual capacity to exercise power or wield authority.

Perhaps, the most important lesson of *12 Angry Men* is that Americans of all races and ethnicities need to become racially literate, not post-racially blind. Racial literacy is the capacity to "read" race, conjugate its grammar and interpret its meaning in different contexts and circumstances. All Americans, not just people of color, need to be better schooled in the subtle yet complex ways that racial profiling actually works in the twenty-first century.

For example, race is both a noun and a verb. In this sense it is like the words "profile" and "text." We read a text, but we also can text someone.

Our faces may be observed from one side in "profile" but we also can pro-file or categorize other people. Similarly, we can read race as merely a superficial or fixed thing, such as skin color. We can also "race" someone as dangerous or as competent in a particular context, using race to code what we subconsciously believe are their intentions or their capacities. We "race" other people by our actions; we can also claim a race for ourselves. Or not. Like the verb "to be," race also takes a different form when we speak about "I am" versus "you are," compared with "he is."

As with any language, the language and grammar of race influence how we see and understand the world. As a result, the multiple meanings and uses of race need to be interrogated and conjugated carefully in light of relevant local circumstances and their historic underpinnings. For ex-ample, racial literacy demands a far more nuanced approach than typi-cal charges of individual bigotry or intentional group prejudice.[3] Racial literacy, in other words, reads the grammar of racial profiling as a form of passive smoke. It reminds us that race is literally in the air we breathe and in the history that lives in our heads.

The secondhand smoke of racial profiling directly affects those in packed, close quarters defined by poverty and joblessness. It affects the young cops sent into unfamiliar neighborhoods by majors and chiefs of police focusing on statistics and quick fixes. It also insinuates its effects on those who observe the encounter replayed from a physical, though not necessarily psychic, distance on a TV watched in the privacy of a den or on a closed-circuit video from the jury box in a courtroom.

Racial literacy would help all of us understand that behind the two force fields competing for respect in the profiling moment—civil order and individual liberty—is a criminal justice system that exercises outsized power and responsibility as the major urban policy instrument for control-ling the poor. At the same time, we have too often put our police officers into the positions of legislators, prosecutors, judges, and juries—positions for which they are not qualified and that they should not be expected to fulfill—even in well-to-do neighborhoods.

Consider what might happen were we to collect—and really listen to—more survivor stories, like the racial profiling narratives featured in *12 Angry Men*. First, more of us might empathize with the pain and the stigma experienced by journalists and law professors, teenagers and black men in their sixties. Second, more of us might better understand the difference between racial literacy and post-racial blindness. Assembling these first-hand accounts also could help all Americans better understand the domi-nant roles that history and culture, race, and intergenerational poverty all play in defining how we enforce our laws. Most of all, the act of gathering these firsthand accounts can remind us of the outsized role that we give to law enforcement in running our lives. Race, in the profiling context, is a convenient, powerful, and dangerous category; it easily morphs into other categories of class and criminality. These perceptual and social constructions of ours become political and legal. Yet they are also ignored because we lack a grammar or vocabulary for talking about them. Not surprisingly then, we find ourselves trapped, looking at each other through bars fixed by our unconscious acceptance of these constructions.

If, however, we learn to "read race" through the eyes and the pain of others with experiences similar to these twelve angry men, we can begin to see through the bars. We become familiar with the grammar of racial literacy and the text and the subtext of racial profiling. We learn that the conversation on race continues in a new space. It has moved from the "colored" water fountain and the back of the bus to the profiling moment and the prison cell.

Notes

Foreword *Patricia J. Williams*

1. Christine Langdon, "Tired? Pop Your Pal's Ritalin," *New York Post*, May 28, 2000.

2. Karen Barrow, "The Ritalin Generation Goes to College," *Science Daily*, November 11, 2005.

3. Andrew Jacobs, "College Life: The Adderall Advantage," *New York Times*, July 31, 2005, http://www.nytimes.com/2005/07/31/education/edlife/jacobs31.html.

4. Henry Greely, Barbara Sahakian, John Harris, Ronald C. Kessler, Michael Gazzaniga, Philip Campbell, and Martha J. Farah "Towards Responsible Use of Cognitive-Enhancing Drugs by the Healthy," *Nature* 465, no. 7224 (December 11, 2008): 702.

5. "More and More Students are Getting High for Higher Grades," *The Sheaf*, January 5, 2011, http://thesheaf.com/news/2011/01/05/more-and-more-students-are-getting-high-for-higher-grades.

6. Timothy Williams, "Jailed Sisters Are Released for Kidney Transplant," *New York Times*, January 7, 2011, http://www.nytimes.com/2011/01/08/us/08sisters.html.

7. Naimah Jabali-Nash, "Columbia University Drug Bust: Five Students Arrested for Sale of LSD, Cocaine, Ecstasy," Crimesider, CBS News.com, December 8, 2010, http://www.cbsnews.com/8301-504083_162-20025035-504083.html.

Preface *Alexander Papachristou*

1. See Dorothy Roberts, *Fatal Invention: How Science, Politics and Big Business Re-Create Race in the Twenty-first Century* (New York: The New Press, 2011).

2. See David R. Roediger, *How Race Survived U.S. History* (New York: Verso, 2008), 5–6.

3. See Hazel Rose Markus, "Who Am I?" in *Doing Race: 21 Essays for the 21st Century*, ed. Hazel Rose Markus and Paula M.L. Moya (New York: W.W. Norton & Co., 2010), 359–89.

4. Susan Saulny, "Census Data Presents Rise in Multiracial Population of Youths," *New York Times*, March 24, 2011, http://www.nytimes.com/2011/03/25/us/25race.html.

5. Sam Roberts and Peter Baker, "Asked to Declare His Race, Obama Checks 'Black,'" *New York Times*, April 2, 2010, http://www.nytimes.com/2010/04/03/us/politics/03census.html.

1. The New Jim Crow *Michelle Alexander*

1. Michael Eric Dyson, "Obama's Rebuke of Absentee Black Fathers," *Time*, June 19, 2008.

2. Sam Roberts, "51% of Women Now Living with a Spouse, *New York Times*, Jan. 16, 2007.

3. See Jonathan Tilove, "Where Have All the Men Gone? Black Gender Gap Is Widening," *Seattle Times*, May 5, 2005; and Jonathan Tilove, "Where Have All the Black Men Gone?" *Star-Ledger* (Newark), May 8, 2005.

4. Ibid.

5. Cf., Salim Muwakkil, "Black Men: Missing," *In These Times*, June 16, 2005.

6. G. Garvin, "Where Have the Black Men Gone?," *Ebony*, Dec. 2006.

7. One in eleven black adults was under correctional supervision at year end 2007, or approximately 2.4 million people. See Pew Center on the States, *One in 31: The Long Reach of American Corrections* (Washington, DC: Pew Charitable Trusts, Mar. 2009). According to the 1850 Census, approximately 1.7 million adults (ages fifteen and older) were slaves.

8. See Andrew J. Cherlin, *Marriage, Divorce, Remarriage*, rev. ed., (Cambridge, MA: Harvard University Press, 1992), 110.

9. See Glenn C. Loury, *Race, Incarceration, and American Values* (Cambridge, MA: MIT Press, 2008), commentary by Pam Karlan.

10. See Marc Mauer and Meda Chesney-Lind, eds., *Invisible Punishment: The Collateral Consequences of Mass Imprisonment* (New York: The New Press, 2002); and Jeremy Travis, *But They All Come Back: Facing the Challenges of Prisoner Reentry* (Washington, DC: Urban Institute Press, 2005).

11. Negley K. Teeters and John D. Shearer, *The Prison at Philadelphia, Cherry Hill: The Separate System of Prison Discipline, 1829–1913* (New York: Columbia University Press, 1957), 84.

12. See David Musto, *The American Disease: Origins of Narcotics Control* (New York: Oxford University Press, 3rd ed., 1999), 4, 7, 43–44, 219–20, describing the role of racial bias in earlier drug wars; and Doris Marie Provine, *Unequal Under Law: Race in the War on Drugs* (University of Chicago Press, 2007), 37–90, describing racial bias in alcohol prohibition, as well as other drug wars.

13. Mary Pattillo, David F. Weiman, and Bruce Western, *Imprisoning America: The Social Effect of Mass Incarceration* (New York: Russell Sage Foundation, 2004), 2.

14. Paul Street, *The Vicious Circle: Race, Prison, Jobs, and Community in Chicago, Illinois, and the Nation* (Chicago Urban League, Department of Research and Planning, 2002).

15. Street, *Vicious Circle*, 3.

16. Alden Loury, "Black Offenders Face Stiffest Drug Sentences," *Chicago Reporter*, Sept. 12, 2007.

17. Ibid.

18. Street, *Vicious Circle*, 15.

19. Donald G. Lubin et al., *Chicago Metropolis 2020: 2006 Crime and Justice Index* (Washington, DC: Pew Center on the States, 2006), 5, www.pewcenteronthe states.org/report_detail.aspx?id=33022.

20. Ibid., 37.

21. Ibid., 35.

22. Ibid., 3; see also Bruce Western, *Punishment and Inequality in America* (New York: Russell Sage Foundation, 2006), 12.

23. Street, *Vicious Circle*, 3.

24. Ibid.

25. Ibid.

26. See chapter 1, page 61, which describes the view that President Ronald Reagan's appeal derived primarily from the "emotional distress of those who fear or

resent the Negro, and who expect Reagan somehow to keep him 'in his place' or at least echo their own anger and frustration."

27. For an excellent discussion of the history of felon disenfranchisement laws, as well as their modern-day impact, see Jeff Manza and Christopher Uggen, *Locked Out: Felon Disenfranchisement and American Democracy* (New York: Oxford University Press, 2006).

28. *Cotton v. Fordice*, 157 F.3d 388, 391 (5th Cir. 1998); see also Martine J. Price, Note and Comment: Addressing Ex-Felon Disenfranchisement: Legislation v. Litigation, *Brooklyn Journal of Law and Policy* 11 (2002): 369, 382–83.

29. See Jamie Fellner and Marc Mauer, *Losing the Vote: The Impact of Felony Disenfranchisement Laws in the United States* (Washington, DC: Sentencing Project, 1998).

30. Loury, *Race, Incarceration, and American Values*, 48

31. See Eric Lotke and Peter Wagner, "Prisoners of the Census: Electoral and Financial Consequences of Counting Prisoners Where They Go, Not Where They Come From," *Pace Law Review* 24 (2004): 587, available at www.prisonpolicy.org/pace.pdf.

32. See *Batson v. Kentucky* 476 U.S. 79 (1986), discussed in chapter 3, page 146.

33. See *Purkett v. Elm*, 514 U.S. 765 discussed in chapter 3, page 150.

34. Brian Kalt, "The Exclusion of Felons from Jury Service," *American University Law Review* 53 (2003): 65.

35. See *Dred Scott v. Sandford*, 60 U.S. (How. 19) 393 (1857).

36. Travis, *But They All Come Back*, 132.

37. Peter Wagner, "Prisoners of the Census"; for more information, see www.prisonersofthecensus.org.

38. Travis, *But They All Come Back*, 281, citing James Lynch and William Sabol, *Prisoner Reentry in Perspective*, Crime Policy Report, vol. 3 (Washington, DC: Urban Institute, 2001).

39. Dina Rose, Todd Clear, and Judith Ryder, *Drugs, Incarcerations, and Neighborhood Life: The Impact of Reintegrating Offenders into the Community* (Washington, DC: U.S. Department of Justice, National Institute of Justice, 2002).

40. Sudhir Alladi Venkatesh, *The Robert Taylor Homes Relocation Study* (New York: Center for Urban Research and Policy, Columbia University, 2002).

41. Street, *Vicious Circle*, 16.

42. Ibid., 17.

43. Keynote address by Paula Wolff at Annual Luncheon for Appleseed Fund for Justice and Chicago Council of Lawyers, Oct. 7, 2008, www.chicagometropolis 2020.org/10_25.htm.

44. Katherine Beckett and Theodore Sasson, *The Politics of Injustice: Crime and Punishment in America* (Thousand Oaks, CA: Sage Publications, 2004), 36, citing Mercer Sullivan, *Getting Paid: Youth Crime and Work in the Inner City* (New York: Cornell University Press, 1989).

45. Ibid.

46. Loïc Wacquant, "The New 'Peculiar Institution': On the Prison as Surrogate Ghetto," *Theoretical Criminology* 4, no. 3 (2000): 377–89.

47. See, e.g., Douglas Massey and Nancy Denton, *American Apartheid: Segregation and the Making of the Underclass* (Cambridge, MA: Harvard University Press, 1993).

48. Whites are far more likely than African Americans to complete college, and college graduates are more likely to have tried illicit drugs in their lifetime when compared to adults who have not completed high school. See U.S. Department

of Health and Human Services, Substance Abuse and Mental Health Services Administration, *Findings from the 2000 National Household Survey on Drug Abuse* (Rockville, MD: 2001). Adults who have not completed high school are disproportionately African American.

49. Devah Pager, *Marked: Race, Crime, and Finding Work in an Era of Mass Incarceration* (Chicago: University of Chicago Press, 2007), 90–91, 146–47.

50. John Edgar Wideman, "Doing Time, Marking Race," *The Nation*, Oct. 30, 1995.

51. See Julia Cass and Connie Curry, *America's Cradle to Prison Pipeline* (New York: Children's Defense Fund, 2007).

52. James Forman Jr., "Children, Cops and Citizenship: Why Conservatives Should Oppose Racial Profiling," in *Invisible Punishment*, ed. Mauer and Lind, 159.

53. Wideman, "Doing Time, Marking Race."

3. Class, Race & Hyperincarceration in Revanchist America   *Loïc Wacquant*

1. Michael B. Katz, ed., *The "Underclass" Debate: Views from History* (Princeton, NJ: Princeton University Press, 1995); Alice O'Connor, *Poverty Knowledge: Social Science, Social Policy, and the Poor in Twentieth-Century U.S. History* (Princeton, NJ: Princeton University Press, 2002).

2. See Neil Smith for a stimulating discussion of the notion of *revanche* as an extended and multiform "visceral reaction in the public discourse against the liberalism of the post-1960s period and an all-out attack on the social policy structure that emanated from the New Deal and the immediate postwar era"; Neil Smith, *The New Urban Frontier: Gentrification and the Revanchist City* (New York: Routledge, 1996), 42. See also Michael Flamm for a painstaking account of how the conflation of racial tumult, antiwar protest, civil disorder, and street crime laid the social foundation for the political demand for "law and order" in the wake of the class and racial dislocations of the 1960s; Michael W. Flamm, *Law and Order: Street Crime, Civil Unrest, and the Crisis of Liberalism in the 1960s* (New York: Columbia University Press, 2005).

3. Loïc Wacquant, *Deadly Symbiosis: Race and the Rise of the Penal State* (Cambridge: Polity Press, 2010).

4. Loïc Wacquant, *Punishing the Poor: The Neoliberal Government of Social Insecurity* (Durham, NC: Duke University Press, 2009).

5. Glenn C. Loury, "Racial Stigma, Mass Incarceration, and American Values," Tanner Lectures on Human Values, Stanford University, April 4–6, 2007. A revised version is included in Glenn C. Loury, with Pamela Karlan, Tommie Shelby, and Loïc Wacquant, *Race, Incarceration, and American Values* (Cambridge, MA: MIT Press, 2008).

6. Wacquant, *Punishing the Poor*, chap. 4–5.

7. Frieder Dünkel and Sonja Snacken, *Les Prisons en Europe* (Paris: L'Harmattan, 2005).

8. Wacquant, *Punishing the Poor*, 262–263, 121–125. The spiteful tenor of Giuliani's campaign of "class cleansing" of the streets and its strident racial overtones are captured by Neil Smith, "Giuliani Time: The Revanchist 1990s," *Social Text* 57 (Winter 1998): 1–20.

9. The sheer scale of American jails puts them in a class of their own. In 2000, the three largest custodial complexes *in the Western world* were the jails of Los Angeles (23,000 inmates), New York (18,000), and Chicago (10,000). By contrast,

the largest penitentiary center in Europe, the Fleury-Mérogis prison just south of Paris, held 3,900 and is considered grotesquely oversized by European standards.

10. The last close-up study of the daily functioning of a big-city jail and its impact on the urban poor, John Irwin's fine ethnography of San Francisco's jail, dates from thirty years ago. See John Irwin, *The Jail: Managing the Underclass in American Society* (Berkeley: University of California Press, 1985).

11. Joan Petersilia, *When Prisoners Come Home: Parole and Prisoner Reentry* (New York: Oxford University Press, 2003).

12. The national DNA database from crime scenes, persons "known to the police," and (former) convicts compiled by the FBI (under the Combined DNA Index System [CODIS] program) more than doubled over the past five years alone to reach eight million offender profiles. Its explosive expansion, fed by technological innovation and organizational imperatives, is springing a new "racialized dragnet" thrown primarily at lower-class African American men due to their massive overrepresentation among persons stopped by police; Troy Duster, "The Exponential Growth of National and State DNA Databases: 'Cold Hits' and a Newly Combustible Intersection of Genomics, Forensics and Race," paper presented to the CSSI, University of California, Berkeley, February 24, 2010.

13. Devah Pager, *Marked: Race, Crime, and Finding Work in an Era of Mass Incarceration* (Chicago: University of Chicago Press, 2007); David Thacher, "The Rise of Criminal Background Screening in Rental Housing," *Law & Social Inquiry* 31 (1) (2008): 5–30; Richard Tewksbury and Matthew B. Lees, "Sex Offenders on Campus: University-Based Sex Offender Registries and the Collateral Consequences of Registration," *Federal Probation* 70 (3) (2006): 50–57. For an extended analysis of ramifying penal disabilities outside of prison walls, see Megan L. Comfort, "Punishment Beyond the Legal Offender," *Annual Review of Law and Social Science* 3 (2007): 271–296.

14. Kathleen M. Olivares, Velmer S. Burton, Jr., and Francis T. Cullen, "Collateral Consequences of a Felony Conviction: A National Study of State Legal Codes Ten Year Later," *Federal Probation* 60 (3) (1996): 10–17.

15. Franklin E. Zimring and Gordon Hawkins, *The Scale of Imprisonment* (Chicago: University of Chicago Press, 1991); Michael Tonry, "Fragmentation of Sentencing and Corrections in America," *Alternatives to Incarceration* 6 (2): 9–13.

16. Vanessa Barker, *The Politics of Imprisonment: How the Democratic Process Shapes the Way America Punishes Offenders* (New York: Oxford University Press, 2009).

17. David F. Greenberg and Valerie West, "State Prison Populations and Their Growth, 1971–1991," *Criminology* 39 (1) (2001): 615–654; David Jacobs and Jason T. Carmichael, "Politics of Punishment across Time and Space: A Pooled Time-Series Analysis of Imprisonment Rates," *Social Forces* 80 (1) (2001): 61–89. But see Kevin B. Smith, "The Politics of Punishment: Evaluating Political Explanations of Incarceration Rates," *The Journal of Politics* 66 (3) (2004): 925–938.

18. Franklin E. Zimring and David T. Johnson, "Public Opinion and the Governance of Punishment in Democratic Political Systems," *The Annals of the American Academy of Political and Social Science* 605 (2006): 265–280.

19. Nancy E. Marion and Willard M. Oliver, "Congress, Crime, and Budgetary Responsiveness: A Study in Symbolic Politics," *Criminal Justice Policy Review* 20 (2) (2009): 115–135.

20. Lisa L. Miller, *The Perils of Federalism: Race, Poverty, and the Politics of Crime Control* (New York: Oxford University Press, 2008).

21. "The war on crime—with its constituent imagery that melded the burning cities of the 1960s urban riots with the face of [Willie] Horton as (every) black man, murderer, rapist of a white woman—remade party affiliations and then remade the parties themselves, as the war came to be embraced and stridently promoted by Republicans and Democrats alike"; Mary Louise Frampton, Ian Haney-López, and Jonathan Simon, eds., *After the War on Crime: Race, Democracy, and a New Reconstruction* (New York: New York University Press, 2008), 7.

22. See, for example, Joel Dyer, *The Perpetual Prisoner Machine: How America Profits From Crime* (New York: Basic Books, 1999); Paul Wright and Tara Herivel, eds., *Prison Nation: The Warehousing of America's Poor* (New York: Routledge, 2003); Michael Jacobson, *Downsizing Prisons: How to Reduce Crime and End Mass Incarceration* (New York: New York University Press, 2005); Marie Gottschalk, *The Prison and the Gallows: The Politics of Mass Incarceration in America* (Cambridge: Cambridge University Press, 2006); and Todd R. Clear, *Imprisoning Communities: How Mass Incarceration Makes Disadvantaged Neighborhoods Worse* (New York: Oxford University Press, 2007).

23. David Garland, ed., *Mass Imprisonment: Social Causes and Consequences* (London: Sage, 2001). Ironically, the generalized notion was first broached, not in the U.S. prison debate, but in Western Europe by the French justice official and scholar Jean-Paul Jean in a discussion of the "mass incarceration of drug addicts" in France's jails; Jean-Paul Jean, "Mettre fin à l'incarcération de masse des toxicomanes," *Esprit* 10 (1995): 130–131. (I used the term myself in several publications between 1997 and 2005, so this conceptual revision is in part a self-critique.)

24. Diane E. Bennett et al., "Prevalence of Tuberculosis Infection in the United States Population: The National Health and Nutrition Examination Survey, 1999–2000," *American Journal of Respiratory and Critical Care Medicine* 177 (2008): 348–355; Bridget F. Grant et al., "The 12-month Prevalence and Trends in DSM-IV Alcohol Abuse and Dependence: United States, 1991–1992 and 2001–2002," *Alcohol Research & Health* 74 (3) (2004): 223–234.

25. To be sure, David Garland singles out two "essential features" that define mass incarceration: "sheer numbers" (that is, "a rate of imprisonment and a size of prison population that is markedly above the historical and comparative norm for societies of this type") and "the social concentration of mass imprisonment's effects" ("when it becomes the imprisonment of whole groups of the population," in this case "young black males in large urban centers"); Garland, *Mass Imprisonment*, 5–6. But it is not clear why the first property would not suffice to characterize the phenomenon, nor what "markedly above" entails. Next, there is a logical contradiction between the two features of mass reach and concentrated impact (no other mass phenomenon "benefits" a narrow and well-bounded population). Lastly, Bernard Harcourt has pointed out that the United States had rates of forcible custody exceeding 600 per 100,000 residents from 1938 to 1962, if statistics on penal confinement and mental asylums are merged; Bernard Harcourt, "From the Asylum to the Prison: Rethinking the Incarceration Revolution," *Texas Law Review* 84 (2006): 1751–1786. These definitional troubles suggest that the *mass* characterization is an ad hoc designation crafted inductively to suit the peculiarities of U.S. incarceration trends at the twentieth century's close (as Garland observes, "a new name to describe an altogether new phenomenon").

26. The martial trope of the "war on crime" has similarly hindered the analysis of the transformation and workings of criminal policy. This belligerent

designation—espoused by advocates and critics of enlarged incarceration alike—is triply misleading: it passes civilian measures aimed at citizens for a military campaign against foreign foes; it purports to fight "crime" generically when it targets a narrow strand of illegalities (street offenses in the segregated lower-class districts of the city); and it abstracts the criminal justice wing from the broader revamping of the state entailing the simultaneous restriction of welfare and expansion of prisonfare.

27. Pieter Spierenburg, *The Prison Experience: Disciplinary Institutions and Their Inmates in Early Modern Europe* (New Brunswick, NJ: Rutgers University Press, 1991).

28. David Rothman, *The Discovery of the Asylum: Social Order and Disorder in the New Republic* (New York: Aldine, 1971); Scott Christianson, *With Liberty for Some: Five Hundred Years of Imprisonment in America* (Boston: Northeastern University Press, 1998). The only exceptions to this class rule are the periods and countries in which the prison is used extensively as an instrument of political repression; Aryeh Neier, "Confining Dissent: The Political Prison," in *The Oxford History of Prison: The Practice of Punishment in Western Society*, ed. Norval Morris and David Rothman (New York: Oxford University Press, 1995), 350–380.

29. Wacquant, *Punishing the Poor*, chap. 2.

30. William Julius Wilson, *When Work Disappears: The World of the New Urban Poor* (New York: Knopf, 1996); Loïc Wacquant, *Urban Outcasts: A Comparative Sociology of Advanced Marginality* (Cambridge: Polity Press, 2008).

31. Michael Tonry, *Malign Neglect: Race, Class, and Punishment in America* (New York: Oxford University Press, 1995), 17.

32. Michael Tonry and Matthew Melewski, "The Malign Effects of Drug and Crime Control Policies on Black Americans," *Crime & Justice* 37 (2008): 18.

33. Bruce Western, *Punishment and Inequality in America* (New York: Russell Sage Foundation, 2006), 27.

34. Cf. ibid., 17, 27.

35. Lower-class African American women come next as the category with the fastest increase in incarceration over the past two decades, leading to more African American females being under lock than there are *total women* confined in *all of Western Europe*. But their capture comes largely as a by-product of the aggressive rolling out of penal policies aimed primarily at their lovers, kin, and neighbors. (Men make up 94 percent of all convicts in the nation.) In any case, the number of female inmates pales before the ranks of the millions of girlfriends and wives of convicts who are subjected to "secondary prisonization" due to the judicial status of their partner; Megan Comfort, *Doing Time Together: Love and Family in the Shadow of the Prison* (Chicago: University of Chicago Press, 2008).

36. Wacquant, *Urban Outcasts*, 117–118.

37. The increase of this index of punitiveness is 299 percent for "violent crimes" as compared with 495 percent for "index crimes" (aggregating violent crime and the major categories of property crime), confirming that the penal state has grown especially more severe toward lesser offenses and thus confines many more marginal delinquents than in the past.

38. Georg Rusche and Otto Kirscheimer, *Punishment and Social Structure*, rev. ed. (New Brunswick, NJ: Transaction Press, 2003); Catharina Lis and Hugo Soly, *Poverty and Capitalism in Pre-Industrial Europe* (Atlantic Highlands, NJ: Humanities Press, 1979); Spierenburg, *The Prison Experience*.

39. Loïc Wacquant, "Crafting the Neoliberal State: Workfare, Prisonfare and Social Insecurity," *Sociological Forum* 25 (2) (2010): 197–220.

40. Loïc Wacquant, "Deadly Symbiosis: When Ghetto and Prison Meet and Mesh," *Punishment & Society* 3 (1) (2001): 95–133.

41. Wilson, *When Work Disappears*; Mary Patillo-McCoy, *Black Picket Fences: Privilege and Peril among the Black Middle Class* (Chicago: University of Chicago Press, 1999).

42. Smith, *The New Urban Frontier.*

43. Wacquant, *Deadly Symbiosis*, chap. 3.

44. Gresham Sykes, *The Society of Captives: A Study in a Maximum Security Prison* (Princeton, NJ: Princeton University Press, 1958).

45. Loïc Wacquant, "Race as Civic Felony," *International Social Science Journal* 181 (Spring 2005): 127–142.

46. John Irwin, *Prisons in Turmoil* (Boston: Beacon Press, 1980).

47. Martin Gilens, *Why Americans Hate Welfare* (Chicago: University of Chicago Press, 1999); Sanford F. Schram, Joe Soss, and Richard C. Fording, eds., *Race and the Politics of Welfare Reform* (Ann Arbor: University of Michigan Press, 2003).

48. In the media and policy debates leading up to the 1996 termination of welfare, three racialized figures offered lurid incarnations of "dependency": the flamboyant and wily "welfare queen," the immature and irresponsible "teenage mother," and the aimless and jobless "deadbeat dad." All three were stereotypically portrayed as African American residents of the dilapidated inner city.

49. Yeheskel Hasenfeld, "People Processing Organizations: An Exchange Approach," *American Sociological Review* 37 (3) (1972): 256–263.

50. Frances Fox Piven and Richard A. Cloward, *Regulating the Poor: The Functions of Public Welfare*, expanded edition (New York: Vintage, 1993; first published in 1971).

51. This is well illustrated by the current predicament of California, a state that employs more prison guards than it does social workers: it just slashed its higher education budgets and increased college tuition by 30 percent in response to a deficit of $20 billion in 2009, when it spends an extravagant $10 billion on corrections (more than its yearly outlay for universities for fifteen years running). The state now faces a stark choice between sending its children to college or continuing to throw masses of minor offenders behind bars for brutally long terms.

52. Dorothy E. Roberts, "Criminal Justice and Black Families: The Collateral Damage of Over-enforcement," *U.C. Davis Law Review* 34 (2000): 1005–1028.

53. Paul J. Hirschfield, "Preparing for Prison? The Criminalization of School Discipline in the USA," *Theoretical Criminology* 12 (1) (February 2008): 79–101.

54. Wacquant, *Urban Outcasts*, 69–91, 280–287.

55. Michael Tonry, ed., *Penal Reform in Overcrowded Times* (New York: Oxford University Press, 2001); Dorothy E. Roberts, "The Social and Moral Cost of Mass Incarceration in African American Communities," *Stanford Law Review* 56 (5) (2004): 1271–1305; Jacobson, *Downsizing Prisons*; Marie Gottschalk, "Dismantling the Carceral State: The Future of Penal Policy Reform," *Texas Law Review* 84 (2005): 1693–1750; Marc Mauer and the Sentencing Project, *Race to Incarcerate*, rev. ed. (New York: The New Press, 2006); James Austin and Todd R. Clear, "Reducing Mass Incarceration: Implications of the Iron Law of Prison Populations," *Harvard Law & Policy Review* 3 (2007): 307–324.

56. Contrary to the dominant public vision, research has consistently shown the superiority of rehabilitation over retribution. "Supervision and sanctions, at best, show modest mean reductions in recidivism and, in some instances, have the opposite effect and increase reoffense rates. The mean recidivism effects found in studies of rehabilitation treatment, by comparison, are consistently positive and relatively large"; Mark W. Lipsey and Francis T. Cullen, "The Effectiveness of Correctional Rehabilitation: A Review of Systematic Reviews," *Annual Review of Law and Social Science* 3 (2007): 297–320. That hardened criminals do change and turn their lives around is shown by Shadd Maruna, *Making Good: How Ex-Convicts Reform and Rebuild Their Lives* (Washington, DC: American Psychological Association, 2001); that even "lifers" imprisoned for homicide find pathways to redemption is demonstrated by John Irwin, *Lifers: Seeking Redemption in Prison* (New York: Routledge, 2009).

57. See the powerful arguments of Mary Pattillo for immediately "investing in poor black neighborhoods 'as is,' " instead of pursuing long-term strategies of dispersal or mixing that are both inefficient and detrimental to the pressing needs and distinct interests of the urban minority poor; Mary Pattillo, "Investing in Poor Black Neighborhoods 'As Is,' " in *Legacy of Racial Discrimination and Segregation in Public Housing*, ed. Margery Turner, Susan Popkin, and Lynette Rawlings (Washington, DC: Urban Institute, 2008), 31–46.

Part II: Policing: Where Are the Cops When You Need Them?

1. For a detailed and updated analysis of the law on racial profiling, see Kevin R. Johnson, "How Racial Profiling in America Became the Law of the Land: *United States v. Brignoni-Ponce* and *Whren v. United States* and the Need for Truly Rebellious Lawyering," *Georgetown Law Journal* 98, no. 4 (April 2010): 1005.

4. Profiling Unmasked: From Criminal Profiling to Racial Profiling
David A. Harris

1. Mark Hosenball, "It's Not the Act of a Few Bad Apples: A Lawsuit Shines the Spotlight on Allegations of Racial Profiling by New Jersey State Troopers," *Newsweek*, 17 May 1999, 34.

2. Report of John Lamberth (Defendant's Expert), *Revised Statistical Analysis of the Incidence of Police Stops and Arrests of Black Drivers/Travelers on the New Jersey Turnpike Between Interchanges 1 and 3 from the Years 1988 Through 1991*, at 2. Lamberth's report is relied upon and quoted at length in *State v. Pedro Soto*, 734 A. 2d 350 (N.J. Super. Ct. Law. Div. 1996).

3. *State v. Pedro Soto*, 734 A. 2d 350 (N.J. Super. Ct. Law. Div. 1996).

4. The state presented its own statistical expert, but Judge Francis found his testimony flawed and wholly unpersuasive.

5. See Lamberth report, 2–3.

6. Ibid., 3–6.

7. Ibid., 6–9.

8. Ibid., 26.

9. *Soto*, 734 A. 2d 354.

10. Gil Gallegos, interview by author, 6 September 2000.

11. Lamberth report, 20.

12. Ibid., 21.

13. Ibid., 25.

14. Ibid., 26, 28.

15. *Soto*, 734 A. 2d 359.

16. Memorandum from Sergeant Thomas Gilbert to Superintendent Carl Williams, head of state police. The memo is undated, but various news organizations have stated that it was sent in 1997. E.g., Joe Donohue, "Memos Cast New Doubts on Verniero," *Newark Star-Ledger*, 13 October 2000.

17. Kathy Barrett Carter and Michael Raphael, "State Police Reveal 75% of Arrests Along Turnpike Were of Minorities," *Newark Star-Ledger*, 10 February 1999.

18. Joe Donohue, "Trooper Boss: Race Plays a Role in Drug Crimes," *Newark Star-Ledger*, 28 February 1999.

19. Asked about profiling at a March 3 news conference at the National Press Club, Whitman said, "What proof do we have that it does exist? . . . One person makes an allegation."

20. Peter Verniero and Paul Zoubek, *Interim Report of the State Police Review Team Regarding Allegations of Racial Profiling*, 29 April 1999, 4.

21. Ibid., 26. Blacks were 27 percent, Hispanics 6.9 percent, and Asians 3.9 percent. The data represented all of the stops done by troopers from the Moorestown and Cranbury barracks—the very same units and geographic area from which John Lamberth drew his data in *Soto*. The Task Force's statistics on stops by officers from the Moorestown and Cranbury stations included more than eighty-seven thousand stops.

22. Ibid., 34.

23. Ibid., 27. Of all drivers searched by officers from the Moorestown and Cranbury barracks, those that were alleged to be profiling in the *Soto* case, 53.1 percent were black and 24.1 percent were Hispanic.

24. Ibid., 33–34.

25. Mark Pazniokas, "Discrimination Often Hard to Prove," *Hartford Courant*, 2 May 1994, A11 ("[V]ictims are reluctant to sue" and "shrug off the [racially biased] stops as an annoying fact of life").

26. Complaint, *Wilkins v. Maryland State Police et al.*, Civil No. MJG-93-468 (D. Md. 1993).

27. Michael Fletcher, "Driven to Extremes; Black Men Take Steps to Avoid Police Stops," *Washington Post*, 29 March 1996, A1.

28. Settlement Agreement, *Wilkins v. Maryland State Police*, Civil No. MJG-93-468 (D. Md. 1995).

29. Report of Dr. John Lamberth (plaintiff's expert), *Wilkins v. Maryland State Police et al.*, Civil No. MJG-93-468 (D. Md. 1996).

30. Ibid., 4–5.

31. Ibid., 4, 6.

32. Ibid., 6.

33. Ibid., 6–7.

34. Ibid., 9.

35. Ibid., 9–10.

Part III: The War on Drugs: Who Is the Real Enemy?

1. Human Rights Watch, *Decades of Disparity: Drug Arrests and Race in the United States* (New York; Human Rights Watch, 2009), 16, http://www.hrw.org/en/reports/2009/03/02/decades-disparity-0.

2. Peter Baker, "Obama Signs Drug Parity Law," *New York Times*, August 4, 2010, http://www.nytimes.com/2010/08/04/us/politics/04brfs-OBAMASIGNSDR_ BRF.html; for history and analysis of crack-powder cocaine sentencing discrepancy, see The Sentencing Project, "Federal Crack Cocaine Sentencing," October 2010, http://sentencingproject.org/doc/publications/dp_CrackBriefingSheet .pdf.

7. The War on Drugs and the African American Community   *Marc Mauer*

1. All figures on drug arrests in this chapter taken from data provided by the FBI to the author.

2. Substance Abuse and Mental Health Services Administration, *Summary of Findings from the 2000 Household Survey on Drug Abuse* (Rockville, MD: Substance Abuse and Mental Health Services Administration, 2001), Table 1.1B.

3. Ibid., Table 1.26A.

4. Ibid., Table 1.36B.

5. Substance Abuse and Mental Health Services Administration, *National Survey on Drug Use and Health, 2002 and 2003* (Washington, DC: Substance Abuse and Mental Health Services Administration, 2004), Table 1.43A.

6. James P. Lynch and William J. Sabol, "The Use of Coercive Social Control and Changes in the Race and Class Composition of U.S. Prison Populations," paper presented at the American Society of Criminology, Nov. 9, 1994.

7. Ibid., p. 30.

8. The SAMHSA surveys ask respondents if they have sold drugs, but most experts in the field do not consider these data nearly as reliable as the user figures.

9. Substance Abuse and Mental Health Services Administration. "Results from the 2003 National Survey on Drug Use and Health: National Findings" (Rockville, MD: Substance Abuse and Mental Health Services Administration, 2004), Tables 314B and 315B.

10. John M. Hagedorn, "The Business of Drug Dealing in Milwaukee," Wisconsin Policy Research Institute, June 1998.

11. Katherine Beckett, "Race and Law Enforcement in Seattle," May 3, 2004.

12. Ibid., p. 87.

13. K. Jack Riley, *Crack, Powder Cocaine, and Heroin: Drug Purchase and Use Patterns in Six U.S. Cities*, National Institute of Justice, Dec. 1997, p. 1.

14. Patricia Davis and Pierre Thomas, "In Affluent Suburbs, Young Users and Sellers Abound," *Washington Post*, Dec. 14, 1997, p. A20.

15. Allen J. Beck and Darrell K. Gilliard, *Prisoners in 1994* (Washington, DC: Bureau of Justice Statistics, August 1995), p. 13.

16. Douglas C. McDonald and Kenneth E. Carlson, *Federal Sentencing in Transition, 1986–90* (Washington, DC: Bureau of Justice Statistics, June 1992), p. 4.

17. Christopher J. Mumola and Allen J. Beck, *Prisoners in 1996* (Washington, DC: Bureau of Justice Statistics, June 1997), p. 11.

18. William N. Brownsberger, *Profile of Anti-drug Law Enforcement in Urban Poverty Areas in Massachusetts*, Harvard Medical School, 1997, p. 21. The study also documented that Hispanics were 81 times more likely than whites to be incarcerated for a drug offense.

19. Randolph N. Stone, "The Criminal Justice System: Unfair and Ineffective," paper presented at the Chicago Assembly on "Crime and Community Safety," November 19–20, 1992, pp. 2–3.

20. Susan FitzGerald, "'Crack Baby' Fears May Have Been Overstated," *Washington Post Health*, Sept. 16, 1997.

21. United States Sentencing Commission, 2002 Sourcebook of Federal Sentencing Statistics (Washington, DC: United States Sentencing Commission, 2003), p. 69.

22. Cocaine and Federal Sentencing Policy (Washington, DC: United States Sentencing Commission, May 2002), p. 38.

23. Dan Weikel, "War on Crack Targets Minorities over Whites," *Los Angeles Time*, May 21, 1995.

24. Miles D. Harer, "Do Guideline Sentences for Low-risk Traffickers Achieve Their Stated Purposes?" *Federal Sentencing Reporter 7.1* (1994).

25. Jonathan P. Caulkins and Eric L. Sevigny, "Kingpins or Mules: An Analysis of Drug Offenders Incarcerated in Federal and State Prisons," *Criminology and Public Policy* 3 (2004), pp. 401–434.

26. James P. Lynch and William J. Sabol, *Did Getting Tough on Crime Pay?* (Washington, DC: Urban Institute, 1997).

27. Ibid., p. 7.

28. Angie Cannon and Jodi Enda, "Clinton: Cut Disparity in Cocaine Laws," *Philadelphia Inquirer,* July 23, 1997, p. A13.

29. Randall Kennedy, "The State, Criminal Law, and Racial Discrimination," *Harvard Law Review* 107 (April 1994), p. 1259.

30. David Cole, "The Paradox of Race and Crime: A Comment on Randall Kennedy's Politics of Distinction," *Georgetown Law Journal* 83 (Sept. 1995), pp. 2568–69.

31. State of California Department of Alcohol and Drug Programs, *Evaluating Recovery Services: The California Drug and Alcohol Treatment Assessment* (Sacramento, CA: State of California Department of Alcohol and Drug Programs, April 1994), p. 89.

32. Jonathan P. Caulkins, et al., *Mandatory Minimum Drug Sentences: Throwing Away the Key or the Taxpayers' Money?* (Santa Monica, CA: RAND Corporation, 1997), pp. xvii–xviii.

8. Decades of Disparity: Drug Arrests and Race in the United States
Human Rights Watch

1. See Table 1.

2. Bureau of Justice Statistics (BJS), "Felony Defendants in Large Urban Counties, 2004," Statistical Tables, Table 19, http://www.ojp.usdoj.gov/bjs/pub/html/fdluc/2004/tables/fdluco4st19.htm (accessed December 2, 2008) (67 percent of drug arrests result in conviction); BJS, "Felony Sentences in State Courts, 2004," Statistical Tables, Table 1.8, http://www.ojp.gov/bjs/pub/html/scscfo4/tables/scso4108tab.htm (accessed December 2, 2008) (71 felony convictions per 100 drug arrests).

3. BJS, "Felony Defendents," Statistical Tables, Table 25, http://www.ojp.gov/bjs/pub/html/fdluc/2004/tables/fdluco4st25.htm (accessed December 2, 2008). Even absent a sentence to incarceration, felony convictions carry a host of adverse collateral consequences, including reduced access to housing, public assistance, and loans for higher education, as well as adverse impacts on employment since criminal records are easily obtained during background checks. Human Rights Watch, *United States—No Second Chance: People with Criminal Records*

Denied Access to Public Housing, November 17, 2004, http://www.hrw.org/en/ reports/2004/11/17/no-second-chance; Legal Action Center, "After Prison: Roadblocks to Re-entry," 2004, http://lac.org/roadblocks-to-reentry/upload/ lacreport/LAC_PrintReport.pdf (accessed December 2, 2008). Felony drug convictions for non-citizens frequently lead to deportation. Human Rights Watch, *Forced Apart: Families Separated and Immigrants Harmed by United States Deportation Policy*, July 2007, http://www.hrw.org/en/reports/2007/07/16/forced-apart-0.

4. For example, 42 percent of convicted drug offenders who had more than one prior felony conviction were sentenced to prison compared to 16 percent of those with no prior conviction. BJS, "Felony Defendants," Statistical Tables, Table 30, http://www.ojp.usdoj.gov/bjs/pub/html/fdluc/2004/tables/fdluc04st30.htm (accessed December 2, 2008).

5. BJS, "Felony Sentences in State Courts, 2004," Statistical Tables, Table 2.1, http://www.ojp.gov/bjs/pub/html/scscf04/tables/scs04201tab.htm (accessed December 2, 2008).

6. BJS, "Felony Sentences," Table 2.5, http://www.ojp.gov/bjs/pub/html/ scscf04/tables/scs04205tab.htm (accessed December 2, 2008).

7. In 2003, in the 34 states under analysis, the rate of prison admission on drug charges for blacks was 256.2 per 100,000 black adult residents. For whites, the rate was 25.3 per 100,000 white adults. Between 1986 and 2003, the rate of prison admission for blacks on drug charges quintupled; the white rate did not quite triple. Human Rights Watch, *Targeting Blacks: Drug Law Enforcement and Race in the United States*, May 2008, p. 16, http://www.hrw.org/en/reports/2008/05/04/ targeting-blacks-0.

9. Should Good People Be Prosecutors? *Paul Butler*

1. Abbe Smith, "Can You Be a Good Person and a Good Prosecutor?" *Georgetown Journal of Legal Ethics* 14 (2001): 355.

2. Ibid., 396.

3. Ellis Cose, ed. "The Darden Dilemma," *Black Writers on Justice, Race, and Conflicting Loyalties* (New York: HarperCollins, 2003), 12; Kenneth B. Nunn, "The 'Darden Dilemma': Should African Americans Prosecute Crimes?" *Fordham Law Review* 68 (2000): 1473; Lenese C. Herbert, "Loyalty and Criminal Justice: A Mini-Symposium: Et in Arcadia Ego: A Perspective on Black Prosecutors' Loyalty Within the American Criminal Justice System," *Howard Law Journal* 49 (2006): 495; Margaret M. Russel, "Symposium: Representing Race: Beyond 'Sellouts' and 'Race Cards': Black Attorneys and the Straightjacket of Legal Practice," *Michigan Law Review* 95 (1997): 766; David B. Wilkins, "Symposium: Representing Race: Straightjacketing Professionalism: A Comment on Russel," *Michigan Law Review* 95 (1997): 795; Felicia J. Nu'Man, "I Am Not the Enemy; I Put People in Jail Because They Break the Law, Not Because I'm a Puppet of a Racist Judicial System," *Newsweek*, April 14, 2008.

4. These cases have primarily concerned jurors. *Georgia v. McCollum*, 505 U.S. 42 (1992); *Batson v. Kentucky*, 476 U.S. 79 (1986).

5. Eric Lotke, *Hobbling a Generation: Young African American Males in Washington D.C.'s Criminal Justice System Five Years Later*, National Center on Institutions and Alternatives, 1997.

6. Angela J. Davis, *Arbitrary Justice: The Power of the American Prosecutor* (New York: Oxford University Press, 2007).

7. In *United States v. Booker*, the court held that the federal sentencing guidelines are advisory rather than binding on judges. *United States v. Booker*, 543 U.S. 220 (2005).

8. U.S.C., Crimes, Firearms, sec. 924(c)(1)(A). See also *United States v. Watson*, No. 06-571 2007.

9. In some jurisdictions the executive can fire the head prosecutor. A salient example is the "Saturday Night Massacre," in which former president Nixon triggered a series of resignations while forcing the firing of a prosecutor. See Neil A. Lewis, "Elliot Richardson Dies at 79; Stood Up to Nixon and Resigned in 'Saturday Night Massacre,'" *New York Times*, January 1, 2000.

10. Amy Goldstein, "Fired Prosecutor Says Gonzales Pushed the Death Penalty, Figures Show Attorney General Often Overrules US Attorneys' Arguments Against Capital Charges," *Washington Post*, June 28, 2007, A07.

11. William J. Stuntz, "The Pathological Politics of Criminal Law," *Michigan Law Review* 100 (2001): 505.

12. Tracey L. Meares, "Social Organization and Drug Law Enforcement," *American Criminal Law Review* 35 (1998): 191.

13. Dan M. Kahan, "A Colloquium on Community Policing: Reciprocity, Collective Action and Community Policing," *California Law Review* 90 (2002): 1513; Randall Kennedy, *Race, Crime, and the Law* (New York: Pantheon Books, 1997).

14. Duncan Kennedy, "Rebels from Principle: Changing the Corporate Law Firm from Within," *Harvard Law School Bulletin*, Fall 1981, 39.

15. It should go without saying that I wish racial disparities did not exist. A 3–1 black-white disparity is not close to ideal, in the same way that 1,500,000 people in prison is still too many. To the extent that most black-white racial disparities reflect socioeconomic deprivations suffered by African Americans, we would expect to see those deprivations reflected in criminal justice. My "goal" here—to bring disparities in criminal justice closer to the level of other racial disparities—is modest, because I intend for it to be achievable in the short term. My ultimate aspiration is for no racial disparities at all in criminal justice, but we shall not see that day until African Americans have equal access to education, health care, and capital. Those goals are not, unfortunately, likely to be achieved anytime soon.

10. "What's a Defense?"   *Amy Bach*

1. The last survey conducted by the U.S. Department of Justice Bureau of Justice Statistics on indigent defense systems was by Carol J. DeFrances, "Indigent Defense Services in Large Counties, 1999" *Bureau of Justice Statistics Bulletin* (November 2000): 1. The report details the methods by which criminal indigent defense systems are delivered in the nation's one hundred most populous counties. It found that public defenders handled about 82 percent of the 4.2 million cases received by the providers, assigned counsel 15 percent, and contract attorneys about 3 percent.

2. The three types of systems are described in Robert L. Spangenberg and Marea L. Beeman, "Indigent Defense Systems in the United States," *Law and Contemporary Problems* 58 (1995): 32–41.

3. The Spangenberg Group on behalf of the American Bar Association Standing Committee on Legal Aid and Indigent Defendants, "Indigent Defense in Virginia, Assigned Counsel," *A Comprehensive Review of Indigent Defense in Virginia* (January 2004): 40.

4. Editorial, "Overdue Relief on Attorney Fees," *Virginian-Pilot*, March 1, 2007.

5. The Spangenberg Group, *A Comprehensive View of Indigent Defense in Virginia*, 50.

6. The Spangenberg Group, *Status of Indigent Defense in Georgia: A Study for the Chief Justice's Commission on Indigent Defense—Part I* (2002), quoting Superior Court Judges George F. Nunn and Edward D. Lukemire, letter to the Houston County Board of Commissioners, January 29, 2002. This report is available at http://www.georgiacourts.org/aoc/press/idc/idc.html.

7. Ibid.

8. American Bar Association, Criminal Justice Section, Standing Committee on Legal Aid and Indigent Defendants, *Report to the House of Delegates* (February 1985). Available at http://www.abanet.org/legalservices/downloads/sclaid/110 .pdf.

9. The Spangenberg Group, *Contracting for Indigent Defense Services*, 10.

10. *Report of Chief Justice's Commission on Indigent Defense—Part I*, Georgia Supreme Court (2002): 2, http://www.georgiacourts.org/aoc/press/idc/idc.html.

11. The Spangenberg Group, *Status of Indigent Defense in Georgia*, 20.

12. American Bar Association, Standing Committee on Legal Aid and Indigent Defendants, *Gideon's Broken Promise: America's Continuing Quest for Equal Justice* (December 2004): 14. Available at http://www.abanet.org/legalservices/sclaid/ defender/brokenpromise/fullreport.pdf. The annual appropriations to state and local law enforcement, including the information cited here about the Edward Byrne Memorial Justice Assistant Grant Program in 2008, Public Law 110–161, can be found on the Library of Congress Thomas Web site: http://thomas.loc.gov.

13. American Bar Association, *Gideon's Broken Promise*, 14 (citing testimony of Gary Windom, chief public defender, Riverside County Public Defender Office, Riverside County, California).

14. The Spangenberg Group, *50 State and County Expenditures for Indigent Defense Services FY 2002* (September 2003). Available at http://www.abanet.org/ legalservices/downloads/sclaid/indigentdefense/indigentdefexpend2003.pdf.

15. American Bar Association, *Gideon's Broken Promise*, 13–14 ("The U.S. Department of Justice's *Sourcebook of Justice Statistics* reports that in 2001, nearly $5 billion was being spent in prosecuting criminal cases in state and local jurisdictions").

16. Dan Christensen, "Broward PD Says No to Instant Plea Deals," *Broward Daily Business Review*, June 6, 2005.

17. U.S. Constitution, amend. 6.

18. *Powell v. Alabama*, 287 U.S. 45, 60 (1932).

19. John H. Langbein, *The Origins of Adversary Criminal Trial*, rev. ed. (2003; repr., New York: Oxford University Press, 2005), 2–3.

20. Ibid., 76–77.

21. Lawrence M. Friedman, *Crime and Punishment in American History* (New York: Basic Books, 1993), 72.

22. *Powell v. Alabama*, 65.

23. Akhil Reed Amar, *The Bill of Rights* (New Haven: Yale University Press, 1998), 116.

24. Dan T. Carter, *Scottsboro: A Tragedy of the American South*, rev. ed. (1974; repr. Baton Rouge: Louisiana State University Press, 1994), 18.

25. Carter, *Scottsboro*, 19–22.

26. *Powell v. Alabama*, 60; Carter, *Scottsboro*, 23.

27. *Powell v. Alabama,* 65; Carter, *Scottsboro,* 48.

28. *Powell v. Alabama,* 57.

29. Ibid., 71.

30. Carter, *Scottsboro,* 249.

31. *Powell v. Alabama,* 67.

32. Historian Lawrence M. Friedman theorized as to why the U.S. Supreme Court got involved: "[The justices] read the newspapers; they must have known something about the background of this notorious case." *Crime and Punishment,* 299.

33. For a history of plea bargaining there is a plethora of material but I found two works especially helpful: Allen Steinberg, "From Private Prosecution to Plea Bargaining: Criminal Prosecution, the District Attorney, and American Legal History," *Crime and Delinquency* 30 (1984): 584, available at http://cad.sagepub .com/; and George Fisher, *Plea Bargaining's Triumph: A History of Plea Bargaining in America* (Stanford: Stanford University Press, 2003).

34. Lynn Mather, "Prosecutors," in *Encyclopedia of the American Judicial System: Studies of the Principal Institutions and Process of Law,* ed. Robert J. Janosik (New York: Charles Scribner's Sons, 1987), 671; Steinberg, "From Private Prosecution," 569.

35. Steinberg, "From Private Prosecution," 580.

36. Mather, "Prosecutors," 672.

37. *Johnson v. Zerbst,* 304 U.S. 458, 463 (1938), quoting *Powell v. Alabama,* 64.

38. Ibid., 467.

39. *Betts v. Brady,* 316 U.S. 455 (1942).

40. David Cole, *No Equal Justice: Race and Class in the American Criminal Justice System* (New York: The New Press, 1999), 66.

41. Richard Kluger, *Simple Justice: The History of Brown v. Board of Education and Black America's Struggle for Equality* (New York: Vintage Books, 1977), 660.

42. These cases include *Miranda v. Arizona,* 384 U.S. 436 (1966) (requiring that a suspect be allowed to see an attorney before being interrogated); *Mapp v. Ohio,* 367 U.S. 643 (1961) (upholding the Fourth Amendment right to be free from illegal searches and seizure and to have any illegally seized evidence excluded from criminal trials); *Malloy v. Hogan,* 378 U.S. 1 (1964) (finding a Fifth Amendment privilege against self-incrimination); and *In re Gault,* 387 U.S. 1 (1967) (guaranteeing minors the right to a lawyer).

43. *Griffin v. Illinois,* 351 U.S. 12, 19 (1956).

44. Ibid., 19.

45. Anthony Lewis, *Gideon's Trumpet,* rev. ed. (1964, repr. New York: Vintage Books, 1989).

46. *Gideon v. Wainwright,* 372 U.S. 335, 344 (1963).

47. Since *Gideon,* the U.S. Supreme Court has struggled to define the class of cases in which the Constitution mandates the appointment of counsel, including *Argersinger v. Hamlin,* 407 U.S. 25, 37 (1972), holding that "absent a knowing and intelligent waiver, no person may be imprisoned for any offense, whether classified as petty, misdemeanor, or felony, unless he was represented by counsel at his trial," and more recently, *Alabama v. Shelton,* 535 U.S. 654 (2002), in which a divided Court held that counsel must be provided for the accused in order to impose a suspended prison sentence.

48. *Strickland v. Washington,* 466 U.S. 668, 689 (1984).

49. Ibid., 669.

50. Ibid., 679.

51. Ibid., 707–8.

52. *Burdine v. Johnson*, 262 F.3d 336, 361 (5th Cir. 2001). The earlier Fifth Circuit decision can be found at *Burdine v. Johnson*, 231 F.3d 950 (5th Cir. 2000).

53. The Court of Criminal Appeals of Texas recently upheld the death penalty conviction of George McFarland, whose attorney slept during McFarland's death penalty trial. The court based its finding on the fact that a second attorney was present and an active advocate at all times. *Ex parte McFarland*, 163 S.W.3d 743 (Tex. Crim. App. 2005).

54. American Bar Association, *Gideon's Broken Promise*, 38.

55. American Bar Association, *ABA Standards for Criminal Justice: Prosecution and Defense Function* (3d ed., 1993). Available at www.abanet.org/crimjust/standards/dfunc_toc.html.

11. Judgment and Discrimination *David Cole*

1. Alexis de Tocqueville, *Democracy in America*, 282–83 (Phillips Bradley, ed. 1991) (original ed. 1835).

2. *Duncan v. Louisiana*, 391 U.S. 145, 156 (1968).

3. *McCleskey v. Kemp*, 481 U.S. 279, 310 (1987) (quoting *Strauder v. West Virginia*, 100 U.S. 303, 309 (1880)).

4. *Strauder v. West Virginia*, 100 U.S. 303 (1880).

5. *Edmonson v. Leesville Concrete Co., Inc.*, 111 S. Ct. 2077, 2081–82 (1991).

6. *Batson v. Kentucky*, 476 U.S. 79, 85 (1986).

7. Tanya E. Coke, "Lady Justice May Be Blind, But Is She a Soul Sister? Race-Neutrality and the Ideology of Representative Juries," 69 N.Y.U. L. Rev. 327, 359 (1994).

8. Randall Kennedy, *Race, Crime and the Law*, 168–230 (New York: Pantheon, 1997); Benno C. Schmidt, Jr., "Juries, Jurisdiction, and Race Discrimination: The Lost Promise of *Strauder v. West Virginia*," 61 Tex. L. Rev. 1401 (1983); Douglas L. Colbert, "Challenging the Challenge: The Thirteenth Amendment as a Prohibition Against the Racial Use of Peremptory Challenges," 76 Cornell L. Rev. 1, 13–32 (1990).

9. See, e.g., *Strauder v. West Virginia*, 100 U.S. 303 (1880); *Batson v. Kentucky*, 476 U.S. 79 (1986).

10. Bryan A. Stevenson & Ruth E. Friedman, "Deliberate Indifference: Judicial Tolerance of Racial Bias in Criminal Justice," 51 Wash. & Lee. L.Rev. 509, 519–24 (1994) ("The reality of the administration of criminal justice in the South is that a black defendant can still find himself facing a jury from which the overwhelming majority, if not all, of the prospective jurors of his race have been excluded."); Albert Alschuler & Andrew G. Deiss, "A Brief History of the Criminal Jury in the United States," 61 U. Chi.L.Rev. 867, 894–96 (1994); Stephanie Domitrovich, "Jury Source Lists and the Community's Need to Achieve Racial Balance on the Jury," 33 Duq. L. Rev. 39, 42 (1994); Tanya E. Coke, *Lady Justice*, *supra* note 7 at 345–46.

11. Ala. Code § 12-16-60(a) (1986). Georgia law similarly requires that trial jurors be "intelligent and upright," and requires that grand jurors be "among the most experienced, intelligent and upright persons of the country." O.C.G.A. § 15-12-60.

12. Hayward R. Alker, Jr., et al., "Jury Selection as a Biased Social Process," 11 L. & Soc'y Rev. 9, 31–33 (1976); Nancy J. King, "Racial Jurymandering: Cancer or Cure? A Contemporary Review of Affirmative Action in Jury Selection," 68 N.Y. U.L. Rev. 707, 712–19 (1993).

13. Hiroshi Fukurai, et al., *Race and the Jury*, 21–24, 64 (New York: Plenum Press, 1993); Kennedy, *supra* note 8 at 233; Morris B. Hoffman, "Peremptory Challenges Should Be Abolished: A Trial Judge's Perspective," 64 U.Chi. L. Rev. 809, 851 n.192 (1997) (federal judge noting that blacks, Hispanics, and the young have a "shockingly high" failure to appear rate after receiving jury summonses).

14. Leon F. Litwack, *North of Slavery: The Negro in the Free States 1790–1860*, 102 (Chicago: Univ. of Chicago Press, 1961).

15. Colbert, *Challenging the Challenge, supra* note 8 at 49–50.

16. Id. at 54–55 (noting that successful federal prosecutions for white-on-black violence increased from forty-three cases in 1870 to over 500 in 1872).

17. Id. at 62.

18. Act of March 1, 1875, ch. 114, § 4, 18 Stat. 335. See, e.g., *Cassell v. Texas*, 339 U.S. 282, 303 (1950) (Jackson, J., dissenting) (characterizing *Ex parte Virginia* as "solitary and neglected authority" for criminal prosecutions based on racially motivated jury exclusion).

19. *Strauder v. West Virginia*, 100 U.S. 303 (1880). The same day that the Court decided *Strauder*, it also upheld a conviction of a state judge for violating the 1875 jury selection statute. *Ex Parte Virginia*, 100 U.S. 339 (1880).

20. 100 U.S. at 306.

21. Id. at 308.

22. Id. at 309.

23. 100 U.S. at 309.

24. See Schmidt, *Juries, Jurisdiction, supra* note 8 at 1406. Indeed, Schmidt adds, during this time period, "virtually every embodiment of the legal process in the South, from the sheriff and police to the prosecutor, to the courtroom functionaries, to defense counsel, to the judges, was white." Id. at 1407.

25. 162 U.S. 592 (1896); see also *Gibson v. Mississippi*, 162 U.S. 565 (1896); *Brownfield v. South Carolina*, 189 U.S. 426 (1903); Schmidt, *Juries, Jurisdiction, supra* note 8 at 1463.

26. 103 U.S. 370 (1880).

27. 103 U.S. at 397.

28. 103 U.S. at 402–03 (quoting Delaware Supreme Court opinion).

29. 103 U.S. at 397.

30. 100 U.S. 313 (1880).

31. Schmidt, *Juries, Jurisdiction, supra* note 8 at 1488–99.

32. Id. at 1485–86.

33. Id. at 1486.

34. The Scottsboro case is discussed in chapter 2, at pp. 67–68.

35. Schmidt, *Juries, Jurisdiction, supra* note 8 at 1478–79 (reporting the observation of Columbia Law School Professor Herbert Wechsler, who attended the argument).

36. *Norris v. Alabama*, 294 U.S. 587 (1935).

37. 294 U.S. at 598.

38. 294 U.S. at 590.

39. Jeffrey Abramson, *We, the Jury: The Jury System and the Ideal of Democracy*, 109 (New York: Basic Books, 1994); see, e.g., *Hale v. Kentucky*, 303 U.S. 613 (1938); *Pierre v. Louisiana*, 306 U.S. 354 (1939).

40. *Akins v. Texas*, 325 U.S. 398 (1945).

41. 325 U.S. at 406.

42. 325 U.S. at 410 (Murphy, J., dissenting).

43. *Turner v. Fouche*, 396 U.S. 346, 359 (1970).

44. *United State ex rel. Jackson v. Brady*, 133 F.2d 476, 478 (4th Cir.), *cert. denied*, 319 U.S. 746 (1943).

45. *Maxwell v. Stephens*, 348 F.2d 325, 333–34 (8th Cir.), *cert. denied*, 382 U.S. 944 (1965).

46. *United States ex rel. Chestnut v. Criminal Court of City of New York*, 442 F.2d 611, 614–16 (2d Cir.), *cert. denied*, 404 U.S. 856 (1971).

47. *Hoyt v. Florida*, 368 U.S. 57, 61–62 (1961).

48. *Taylor v. Louisiana*, 419 U.S. 522, 528 (1975). The Court's constitutional interpretation followed Congress's statutory lead. In 1968, Congress had enacted the Federal Jury Selection and Service Act, which declared that "all litigants in Federal courts entitled to trial by jury shall have the right to grand and petit juries selected at random from a fair cross section of the community in the district or division wherein the court convenes." 28 U.S.C. §1861.

49. 419 US. at 532 n.12 (quoting *Peters v. Kiff*, 407 U.S. 493, 502–04 (1972) (opinion of Marshall, J., joined by Douglas and Stewart, JJ.)).

50. *Castaneda v. Partida*, 430 U.S. 482, 510 (1977) (Powell, J., dissenting).

51. The Judicial Council of Georgia's *Jury Commissioner's Handbook*, for example, directs jury commissioners to take race and gender into account because "the percentage of each distinct group in the jury box must parallel the percentage of each group in the country's population of the eligible age." Judicial Council of Georgia, Administrative Office of the Courts, *Jury Commissioner's Handbook*, 18 (1993); see generally id. at 18–27 (on "balancing the box"). In DeKalb County, Georgia, jury commissioners have programmed a computer to ensure that each jury venire reflects the race and gender proportions of the country at large, because the voter registration list from which they generate the jury roll underrepresents particular groups, and therefore venires selected at random would not be representative. Andrew Kull, "Racial Justice," *The New Republic*, 30 November 1992, 18; see generally Nancy J. King, "Racial Jurymandering: Cancer or Cure? A Contemporary Review of Affirmative Action in Jury Selection," 68 N.Y.U.L. Rev. 707, 724 (1993) (listing different techniques used to create racially proportional jury venires). The pattern is repeated across the country, as jury commissioners seek to avoid Sixth Amendment challenges by ensuring that their jury venires reflect the race and sex composition of their districts.

52. *Adarand Constructors, Inc. v. Pena*, 515 U.S. 200 (1995); *Shaw v. Reno*, 509 U.S. 630 (1993).

53. This tension exists not merely between the Sixth Amendment and the Equal Protection Clause, but is also found within the Court's interpretation of each provision. Under the Equal Protection Clause, for example, while the Court expressly bans only *intentionally* race-based selection mechanisms, the test it has developed for identifying when jury discrimination has occurred, much like the Sixth Amendment test, looks in part to *effects*. In *Castaneda v. Partida*, 430 U.S. 482

(1977), the Court ruled that a criminal defendant makes out a prima facie claim of jury discrimination under the Equal Protection Clause by demonstrating that his or her ethnic group was "a recognizable, distinct class," and that over a significant period of time that group was substantially underrepresented in the jury venire relative to its proportion of the total population. The fact that statistical underrepresentation will make out a prima facie equal protection claim adds to the incentives to construct jury venires that roughly match the ethnic and gender percentages in the population at large.

In addition, the Court's recognition—first noted in *Strauder*—that discriminatory exclusion of black jurors denies the black *defendant* equal protection of the laws is premised on the conclusion that race matters. Exclusion of jurors of the defendants' race can deny the black *defendant* equal protection only if having a black juror may make a difference in deliberations. Thus, while *Strauder*'s rule appears to require color-blindness in jury selection, the application of the rule is predicated on the recognition that race matters in jury deliberations, i.e., that jurors are not color-blind in their decisionmaking.

Sixth Amendment doctrine reflects a similar tension, although here the dominant note is race consciousness, and the minor key is color-blindness. The Court insists, for example, that the Sixth Amendment does not require proportional representation, but merely bars the exclusion of distinctive groups. In theory, this mandate is reconcilable with color-blindness; all other things being equal, a race-neutral random-selection mechanism should achieve proportional representation or something close to it. But in practice, virtually every source of jury lists seems to disproportionately underrepresent some groups, and therefore, to provide a "fair cross section," that underrepresentation needs to be offset by affirmative consideration of factors such as race and gender.

54. 419 U.S. at 538; see also *Holland v. Illinois*, 110 S. Ct. 803 (1990) (Sixth Amendment does not apply to peremptory strikes used to construct petit jury).

55. *Batson v. Kentucky*, 476 U.S. 79, 85 n.6 (1986); see also *Akins v. Texas*, 325 U.S. 398, 403 (1945) ("The number of our races and nationalities stands in the way of evolution of such a conception" under the Equal Protection Clause).

56. Andrew Kull, *Racial Justice, supra* note 51 at 21.

57. Albert W. Alschuler, "The Supreme Court and the Jury: Voir Dire, Peremptory Challenges, and the Review of Jury Verdicts," 56 U. Chi. L. Rev. 153, 210–11 (1989).

58. Pluckik & Schwarts, "Jury Selection: Folklore or Science," 1 Crim. L. Bull. 4 (May 1965) (quoting Darrow, "Attorney for the Defense," Esquire, May 1936, 211).

59. Ted Gest & Constance Johnson, "The Justice System: Getting a Fair Trial," *U.S. News and World Rep.*, 25 May 1992, 36 (quoting Darrow). William H. Arpaia, a trial attorney of less renown, went further, opining that certain nationalities—namely the Italians, French, Jews (sic), Spanish, Greeks, Slavs, and the Irish—"are emotional and react to sympathy," while others—the Germans, Swedes, Norwegians, Finns, English, and the other Nordics—"are generally less apt to be swayed emotionally and less apt to return an excessive verdict." William H. Arpaia, "Hints to a Young Lawyer on Picking a Jury," 6 J. Mar. L.Q. 344, 345 (1941).

60. Melvin M. Belli, Sr., 3 *Modern Trials*, §§ 51.6–51.68 at 446–47 (St. Paul, MN: West Pub. Co., 2d ed. 1982); see also Joseph Kelner, "Jury Selection: The Prejudice

Syndrome," 56 N.Y. St. B.J. 34, 36 (1984) ("hell may have no fury like a woman juror who is to decide the case of a young and attractive woman").

61. *N.Y. Times,* 17 November 1935, §4, at 7, col. 1 (quoted in Colbert, *Challenging the Challenge, supra* note 8 at 85 n.424).

62. Colbert, *Challenging the Challenge, supra* note 8 at 75–93.

63. *Swain v. State,* 375 Ala. 505, 515, 156 So.2d 368, 375 (1963), *aff'd,* 380 U.S. 202 (1965).

64. Steve McGonigle & Ted Timms, "Prosecutors Routinely Bar Blacks, Study Finds," *Dallas Morning News,* 9 March 1986, A1.

65. *Horton v. Zant,* 941 F.2d 1449, 1458 (11th Cir. 1991).

66. Ted Gest & Constance Johnson, "The Justice System: Getting a Fair Trial," *U.S. News & World Rep.,* 25 May 1992, 36, 38 (quoting NAACP Legal Defense Fund attorney George Kendall); see also *Georgia v. McCollum,* 112 S. Ct. 2348, 2360 n.1 (1992) (Thomas, J., concurring) (noting that the phrase "all-white jury" appeared over 200 times in the preceding five years in coverage of trials by the *New York Times, Los Angeles Times,* and *Chicago Tribune*).

67. Barry Siegel, "Storm Still Lingers Over Defense Attorney's Training Video," *L.A. Times,* 29 April 1997, A5 (quoting from Philadelphia district attorney training videotape).

68. Transcript from ABC "Good Morning America," 4 April 1997, "Do Prosecutors Try to Keep Blacks Off Juries?" (quoting Jack McMahon).

69. Barry Siegel, *L.A. Times,* 29 April 1997, *supra* note 67.

70. Tr. from ABC "Good Morning America," 4 April 1997, *supra* note 68.

71. 380 U.S. 202 (1965).

72. Id. at 220, 222.

73. Id. at 220.

74. 163 U.S. 537 (1896).

75. 380 U.S. at 221. Justice Rehnquist expressed the same view twenty years later, dissenting from the Court's ruling in *Batson v. Kentucky,* 476 U.S. 79, 137–38 (1986) (Rehnquist, J., dissenting): "In my view, there is simply nothing 'unequal' about the State's using its peremptory challenges to strike blacks from the jury in cases involving black defendants, so long as such challenges are also used to exclude whites in cases involving white defendants, Hispanics in cases involving Hispanic defendants, Asians in cases involving Asian defendants, and so on."

76. 476 U.S. 79 (1986).

77. Kenneth J. Melilli, "Batson in Practice: What We Have Learned About Batson and Peremptory Challenges," 71 Notre Dame L. Rev. 447, 503 (1996); Jere W. Morehead, "When a Peremptory Challenge Is No Longer Peremptory: Batson's Unfortunate Failure to Eradicate Invidious Discrimination from Jury Selection," 43 DePaul L. Rev. 625 (1994); Jeffrey S. Brand, "The Supreme Court, Equal Protection, and Jury Selection: Denying that Race Still Matters," 1994 Wis. L. Rev. 511, 596–613 (1994).

78. Michael J. Raphael and Edward J. Ungvarsky, "Excuses, Excuses: Neutral Explanations Under *Batson v. Kentucky,*" 27 U. Mich. J.L. Reform 229, 236 (1993).

79. Id. at 236–67; see also Brian J. Serr & Mark Maney, "Racism, Peremptory Challenges, and the Democratic Jury: The Jurisprudence of a Delicate Balance," 79 J. Crim. L. & Criminology 1, 44–47 (1988).

80. Bryan Stevenson & Ruth Friedman, *supra* note 10 at 520.

81. 115 S. Ct. 1769 (1995).

82. Id. at 1773 n. 4 (Stevens, J., dissenting) (quoting prosecutor)

83. Id. at 1771 (original emphasis).

84. Sheri Lynn Johnson, "The Language and Culture (Not to Say Race) of Peremptory Challenges," 35 Wm. & Mary L. Rev. 21, 59 (1993).

85. *Batson*, 476 U.S. at 106 (Marshall, J., concurring).

86. *Batson*, 476 U.S. at 98 n.21; *Hernandez*, 500 U.S. at 364.

87. Raphael & Ungvarsky, *supra* note 78 at 234–35.

88. "Racial Divide Affects Black, White Panelists," *Nat'l. L.F.*, 22 February 1993, 58–59.

89. See Nancy J. King, "Postconviction Review of Jury Discrimination: Measuring the Effects of Juror Race on Jury Decisions," 92 Mich. L. Rev. 63, 75–100 (1993) (reviewing jury discrimination studies and finding that race of jurors generally affects outcomes); Sheri Lynn Johnson, "Black Innocence and the White Jury," 83 Mich. L. Rev. 1611 (1983) (same); but cf. Jeffrey E. Pfeifer, "Reviewing the Empirical Evidence on Jury Racism: Findings of Discrimination or Discriminatory Findings?," 69 Neb. L. Rev. 230 (1990) (critiquing jury discrimination studies).

90. For-cause standards are set by state law, but they generally require a finding that the jurors "had such fixed opinions that they could not judge impartially the guilt of the defendant." *Mu'Min v. Virginia*, 500 U.S. 415, 430 (1991). If a juror shows some bias but says that he can render an impartial verdict nonetheless, he will not be struck for cause unless the judge finds him to lack credibility. Wayne R. LaFave & Jerold H. Israel, *Criminal Procedure*, 973 (St. Paul, MN: West Pub. Co., 2d ed. 1992); V. Hale Starr and Mark McCormick, *Jury Selection: An Attorney's Guide to Jury Law and Methods*, 303–4 (Boston: Little, Brown, 1985).

91. Randall Kennedy, "The Angry Juror," *Wall St. J.*, 30 September 1994, A12.

12. Illegal Racial Discrimination in Jury Selection: A Continuing Legacy *Equal Justice Initiative*

1. *State v. McKinnis*, CC-06-1431 (Houston County Cir. Ct.); *State v. Sale*, No. CC-06-112 (Houston County Cir. Ct.); *State v. Gobble*, No. CC-05-299 (Houston County Cir. Ct.); *State v. McCray*, No. CC-05-1532 (Houston County Cir. Ct.); *State v. Floyd*, No. CC-04-167 (Houston County Cir. Ct.); *State v. Wilson*, CC-04-112 (Houston County Cir. Ct.).

2. Richard Bourke, Joe Hingston, & Joel Devine, Louisiana Crisis Assistance Center, *Black Strikes: A Study of the Racially Disparate Use of Peremptory Challenges By the Jefferson Parish District Attorney's Office 2 (2003)*, available at http://www.black strikes.com.

3. *Id.*

4. Stephen B. Bright, *Discrimination, Death, and Denial: The Tolerance of Racial Discrimination in Infliction of the Death Penalty*, 35 Santa Clara L. Rev. 433, 455–56 (1995).

5. *Id.*

6. *See McGahee v. Allen*, 560 F.3d 1252, 1257 & nn.4, 5 (11th Cir. 2009); *Lee v. State*, 898 So. 2d 790, 812–13 (Ala. Crim. App. 2001); *Drake v. State*, 668 So. 2d 877, 878 (Ala. Crim. App. 1995); *Stokes v. State*, 648 So. 2d 1179, 1181 (Ala. Crim. App. 1994); *Ex parte Thomas*, 601 So. 2d 56, 57 (Ala. 1992); *Thomas v. State*, 611 So. 2d 416, 417 (Ala. Crim. App. 1992); *Duncan v. State*, 612 So. 2d 1304, 1307 (Ala.

Crim. App. 1992); *Johnson v. State*, 601 So. 2d 1147, 1148 (Ala. Crim. App. 1992); *Clark v. State*, 621 So. 2d 309, 311 (Ala. Crim. App. 1992); *Huff v. State*, 596 So. 2d 16, 23 (Ala. Crim. App. 1991); *Marks v. State*, 581 So. 2d 1182, 1186–87 (Ala. Crim. App. 1990); *Pollard v. State*, 549 So. 2d 593, 595 (Ala. Crim. App. 1989).

7. *McGahee*, 560 F.3d at 1257 & n.5; *State v. Lee*, No. CC-99-21 (Dallas County Cir. Ct.); *State v. Reeves*, CC-97-31 (Dallas County Cir. Ct.).

8. 476 U.S. 79, 96–98 (1986).

9. *Id.* at 96.

10. *Id.* at 97.

11. *Id.* at 97.

12. *Purkett v. Elem*, 514 U.S. 765, 768 (1995).

13. *Miller-El v. Dretke*, 545 U.S. 231, 240 (2005).

14. *Batson*, 476 U.S. at 106 (Marshall, J, concurring).

15. *Miller-El*, 545 U.S. at 268–69 (Breyer, J, concurring); *see also, e.g.*, Pamela S. Karlan, *Race, Rights, and Remedies in Criminal Adjudication*, 96 Mich. L. Rev. 2001, 2015, 2021 (1998) (noting that courts have declined to find racial discrimination under *Batson* by accepting "a sweeping scope of permissible neutral explanations for prosecutorial strikes" even though such explanations "often [were] correlated to some degree with race").

16. Nancy S. Mander, *The Jurisprudence of Justice Stevens: Justice Stevens, the Peremptory Challenge, and the Jury*, 74 Fordham L. Rev. 1683, 1726 (2006).

17. *Miller-El*, 545 U.S. at 264.

18. *Jackson v. Thigpen*, 752 F. Supp. 1551, 1554–55 (N.D. Ala. 1990).

19. *State v. Harris*, 2001-0408 (La. 6/21/02); 820 So. 2d 471, 477.

20. *McCray v. State*, 738 So. 2d 911, 912–13 (Ala. Crim. App. 1998).

21. *Id.*

22. *McCastle v. State*, 622 S.E.2d 896, 897–98 (Ga. Ct. App. 2005).

23. *McGahee v. Allen*, 560 F.3d 1252, 1265 (11th Cir. 2009); *Jackson v. State*, 5 So. 3d 1144, 1147 (Miss. Ct. App. 2008); *State v. Hill*, No. M2005-02347-CCA-R3-CD, 2007 WL 1774275, at *6 (Tenn. Crim. App. June 20, 2007); *Taylor v. State*, 620 S.E.2d 363, 366–67 (Ga. 2005); *State v. Crawford*, 03-1494 (La. App. 5 Cir. 4/27/04); 873 So. 2d 768, 784; *Ford v. Norris*, 67 F.3d 162, 168 (8th Cir. 1995); *Givens v. State*, 619 So. 2d 500, 501–02 (Fla. Dist. Ct. App. 1993); *Conerly v. State*, 544 So. 2d 1370, 1371–72 (Miss. 1989); *State v. Tomlin*, 384 S.E.2d 707, 708 (S.C. 1989).

24. *McGahee v. Allen*, 560 F.3d 1252, 1265 (11th Cir. 2009).

25. *Ford v. Norris*, 67 F.3d 162, 168 (8th Cir. 1995).

26. *State v. Crawford*, 03-1494 (La. App. 5 Cir. 4/27/04); 873 So. 2d 768, 784.

27. *Bogan v. State*, 811 So. 2d 286, 288 (Miss. Ct. App. 2001); *Robinson v. State*, 773 So. 2d 943, 948 (Miss. Ct. App. 2000); *Jessie v. State*, 659 So. 2d 167, 168 (Ala. Crim. App. 1994); *Cox v. State*, 629 So. 2d 664, 666 (Ala. Crim. App. 1992); *Bui v. State*, 627 So. 2d 849, 851 (Ala. Crim. App. 1992); *Sims v. State*, 587 So. 2d 1271, 1276–77 (Ala. Crim. App. 1991); *Ex parte State (Harrell v. State)*, 555 So. 2d 263, 265 (Ala. 1989); *Williams v. State*, 548 So. 2d 501, 505 (Ala. Crim. App. 1988).

28. *Robinson v. State*, 858 So. 2d 887, 895 (Miss. Ct. App. 2003); *Berry v. State*, 728 So. 2d 568, 572 (Miss. 1999); *Files v. State*, 613 So. 2d 1301, 1304 (Fla. 1992); *State v. Tomlin*, 384 S.E.2d 707, 708–09 (S.C. 1989).

29. *Bogan v. State*, 811 So. 2d 286, 288 (Miss. Ct. App. 2001); *Robinson v. State*, 773 So. 2d 943, 947–48 (Miss. Ct. App. 2000).

30. *Scott v. State*, 599 So. 2d 1222, 1227 (Ala. Crim. App. 1992).

31. *Turnbull v. State*, 959 So. 2d 275, 276–78 (Fla. Dist. Ct. App. 2006).

32. *State v. Coleman*, 2006-0518 (La. 11/2/07); 970 So. 2d 511, 514–15.

33. *State v. Smith*, No. E2004-02272-CCA-R3-CD, 2005 WL 1827848, at *3 (Tenn. Crim. App. Aug. 3, 2005) (upheld); *Griffin v. State*, No. CACR 97–843, 1998 WL 744261, at *2 (Ark. Ct. App. Sept. 30, 1998) (upheld); *Ridely v. State*, 510 S.E.2d 113, 116 (Ga. Ct. App. 1998) (struck down).

34. *Tomlin*, 384 S.E.2d at 708–09.

35. *George v. State*, 588 S.E.2d 312, 316 (Ga. Ct. App. 2003).

36. *State v. Crawford*, 03-1494 (La. App. 5 Cir. 4/27/04); 873 So. 2d 768, 783.

37. *Thornton v. State*, CACR 93–452, 1994 WL 114350, at *3–4 (Ark. Ct. App. Mar. 30, 1994).

38. *Jackson v. State*, 5 So. 3d 1144, 1149–50 (Miss. Ct. App. 2008).

39. *State v. Tyler*, No. M2005-00500-CCA-R3-CD, 2006 WL 264631, at *8 (Tenn. Crim. App. Feb. 1, 2006).

40. *See, e.g.*, Bryan A. Stevenson, *Pro Se Litigation Ten Years After AEDPA: Confronting Mass Imprisonment and Restoring Fairness to Collateral Review of Criminal Cases*, 41 Harv. C.R.-C.L.L. Rev. 339, 347–48 (2006) (detailing 23 Alabama death penalty cases reversed because of racially discriminatory jury selection at trial).

41. *Swain v. Alabama*, 380 U.S. 202, 210 (1965).

42. *Ex parte Branch*, 526 So. 2d 609, 617–18 (1987).

43. *Flowers v. State*, 947 So. 2d 910, 937–39 (Miss. 2007); *Ward v. State*, 733 S.W.2d 728, 731 (Ark. 1987).

44. *Snyder v. Louisiana*, 552 U.S. 472 (2008).

45. Data on the reversed cases in each state is on file with the Equal Justice Initiative.

46. *See, e.g.*, *State v. Logan*, No. W2008-00736-CCA-R3-CD, 2009 WL 782757, at *3 (Tenn. Crim. App. Mar. 25, 2009) (defendant failed to make prima facie showing of racial discrimination and did not elaborate on reasons for objections to prosecutor's strikes); *Williams v. State*, No. M2007-02070-CCA-R3-PC, 2008 WL 5272556, at *7 (Tenn. Crim. App. Dec. 19, 2008) (defendant failed to raise *Batson* objection at trial or on direct appeal, forfeiting the claim); *State v. Howard*, No. E2007-00178-CCA-R3-PC, 2008 WL 1805758, at *16 (Tenn. Crim. App. Apr. 22, 2008) (defendant failed to raise *Batson* objection at trial and only did so on motion for new trial, forfeiting issue on appeal).

47. 529 So. 2d 649 (Miss. 1988).

48. 424 S.E.2d 630 (Ga. 1993).

49. 01-155 (La. App. 5 Cir. 8/28/01); 795 So. 2d 468.

50. *Cochran v. Herring*, 43 F.3d 1404, 1410–11 (11th Cir. 1995).

51. *Carrick v. State*, 580 So. 2d 31, 31–32 (Ala. Crim. App. 1990).

52. 738 So. 2d 911, 912 (Ala. Crim. App. 1998).

53. *See, e.g.*, *Flowers v. State*, 947 So. 2d 910 (Miss. 2007); *McCastle v. State*, 622 S.E.2d 896 (Ga. Ct. App. 2005); *Lucy v. State*, 785 So. 2d 1174 (Ala. Crim. App. 2000).

54. *Bui v. Haley*, 321 F.3d 1304 (11th Cir. 2003); *Ex parte Yelder*, 630 So. 2d 107 (Ala. 1992); *Ex parte Bird*, 594 So. 2d 674 (Ala. 1991); *Pruitt v. State*, 871 So. 2d 101 (Ala. Crim. App. 2004); *Freeman v. State*, 651 So. 2d 576 (Ala. Crim. App. 1994); *Moss v. City of Montgomery*, 588 So. 2d 520 (Ala. Crim. App. 1991); *Sims v. State*, 587 So. 2d 1271 (Ala. Crim. App. 1991); *Carrick v. State*, 580 So. 2d 31 (Ala. Crim. App.

1990); *Parker v. State*, 568 So. 2d 335 (Ala. Crim. App. 1990); *Powell v. State*, 548 So. 2d 590 (Ala. Crim. App. 1988); *Williams v. State*, 548 So. 2d 501 (Ala. Crim. App. 1988); *Williams v. County of Montgomery*, 525 So. 2d 831 (Ala. Crim. App. 1987).

55. *McCrary v. State*, 738 So. 2d 911 (Ala. Crim. App. 1998); *Ashley v. State*, 651 So. 2d 1096 (Ala. Crim. App. 1994); *Andrews v. State*, 624 So. 2d 1095 (Ala. Crim. App. 1993); *Williams v. State*, 620 So. 2d 82 (Ala. Crim. App. 1992); *Bush v. State*, 615 So. 2d 137 (Ala. Crim. App. 1992); *Roger v. State*, 593 So. 2d 141 (Ala. Crim. App. 1991).

56. *Snyder v. Louisiana*, 552 U.S. 472 (2008); *State v. Harris*, 2001-0408 (La. 6/12/02); 820 So. 2d 471; *State v. Myers*, 1999-1803 (La. 4/11/00); 761 So. 2d 498; *State v. Cheatteam*, 07–272 (La. App. 5 Cir. 5/27/08); 986 So. 2d 738; *State v. Lewis*, 01–155 (La. App. 5 Cir. 08/28/01); 795 So. 2d 468.

57. *State v. Hill*, No. M2005-02437-CCA-R3-CD, 2007 WL 1774275, at *5–7 (Tenn. Ct. Crim. App. June 20, 2007).

58. *Id.* at *6.

59. No. M2005-00500-CCA-R3-CD, 2006 WL 264631, at *8 (Tenn. Crim. App. Feb. 1, 2006).

60. *See, e.g., Cobb v. State*, 825 So. 2d 1080 (Fla. Dist. Ct. App. 2002).

61. *See, e.g., Files v. State*, 613 So. 2d 1301, 1304 (Fla. 1992); *Cobb v. State*, 825 So. 2d 1080, 1085–86 (Fla. Dist. Ct. App. 2002).

62. 552 U.S. 472 (2008).

63. *Id.* at 482–85.

64. *State v. Cheatteam*, 07–272 (La. App. 5 Cir. 5/27/08); 986 So. 2d 738.

65. *State v. Jacobs*, No. 2009-K-1304, 2010 WL 1286899 (La. Apr. 5, 2010).

66. *Flowers v. State*, 947 So. 2d 910, 939 (Miss. 2007).

67. *Id.*

68. *Id.*

69. *Jackson v. State*, 5 So. 3d 1144, 1147–49 (Miss. Ct. App. 2008).

70. *Newberry v. State*, 19 So. 3d 752, 754–55 (Miss. Ct. App. 2008).

71. 448 S.E.2d 179, 181–82 (Ga. 1992).

72. 620 S.E.2d 363, 366 (Ga. 2005).

73. *Id.*

74. *See, e.g., Cleveland v. State*, 930 S.W.2d 316, 319 (Ark. 1996); *Jackson*, 954 S.W.2d 894, 895–96 (Ark. 1997); *Griffin v. State*, No. CACR 97–843, 1998 WL 744261, at *2 (Ark. Ct. App. Sept. 30, 1998).

75. No. CACR 93–452, 1994 WL 1143350, at *3 (Ark. Ct. App. Mar. 30, 1994).

76. *See, e.g., Stokes v. State*, 194 S.W.3d 762, 765 (Ark. 2004); *London v. State*, 125 S.W.3d 813, 817 (Ark. 2003); *MacKintrush v. State*, 978 S.W.2d 293, 297–98 (Ark. 1998).

77. *See, e.g., Ratliff v. State*, 199 S.W.3d 79, 83 (Ark. 2004); *Jackson v. State*, 954 S.W.2d 894, 895 (Ark. 1997); *Mitchell v. State*, 913 S.W.2d 264, 268 (Ark. 1996).

78. *See Miller-El v. Dretke*, 545 U.S. 231, 240–41 (2005).

79. *Snyder v. Louisiana*, 552 U.S. 472, 478 (2008).

80. *See, e.g., Preachers v. State*, 963 So. 2d 161, 167–70 (Ala. Crim. App. 2006); *Burnett v. State*, 27 S.W.3d 454, 458–59 (Ark. Ct. App. 2000); *Randall v. State*, 718 So. 2d 230, 232–33 (Fla. Dist. Ct. App. 1998); *Ford v. State*, 423 S.E.2d 245, 247 (Ga. 1992).

81. *See, e.g., Mayes v. State*, 550 So. 2d 496, 498–99 (Fla. Dist. Ct. App. 1989).

82. *State v. Oglesby*, 379 S.E.2d 891, 892 (S.C. 1989).

83. 439 S.E.2d 842, 844 (1994).

84. *Id.*

85. 452 S.E.2d 603, 603–04 (S.C. 1994).

86. *Id.* at 604.

87. *Id.* at 605 (Toal, J., dissenting).

88. *Id.*

89. *See, e.g., Preachers v. State*, 963 So. 2d 161, 167–70 (Ala. Crim. App. 2006); *Yancey v. State*, 813 So. 2d 1, 5 (Ala. Crim. App. 2001); McElemore v. State, 798 So. 2d 693, 700–01 (Ala. Crim. App. 2000).

90. No. CR-05-0935, 2007 WL 2811968 (Ala. Crim. App. Aug. 29, 2008) (opinion on return to remand).

91. *Id.*

92. *Id.*

93. 499 U.S. 400 (1991).

94. *Flowers v. State*, 947 So. 2d 910, 923–26 (Miss. 2007).

95. *Walker v. State*, 611 So. 2d 1133, 1136 (Ala. Crim. App. 1992). The appeals court found that the prosecutor illegally struck Mrs. Garrett and other potential jurors after presuming they were related to people involved in illegal activity because of their last names, and never asking follow-up questions to confirm or refute the presumptions.

96. *Yancey v. State*, 813 So. 2d 1, 5–7 (Ala. Crim. App. 2001).

97. *McCray v. State*, 738 So. 2d 911, 914 (Ala. Crim. App. 1998).

98. *Bellamy v. Crosby*, No. 4:05-cv-00182-MP-EMT, 2008 U.S. Dist. LEXIS 68208, at *4 (N.D. Fla. Sept. 8, 2008).

99. *Neal v. State*, 612 So. 2d 1347, 1349–50 (Ala. Crim. App. 1992).

100. *See, e.g., State v. Williams*, 89-KA-31 (La. App. 5 Cir. 6/7/89); 545 So. 2d 651, 655.

101. *See Shelley v. State*, No. 2008-KA-01284-COA, 2010 WL 702606, at *3 (Miss. Ct. App. Mar. 2, 2010); *State v. Johnson*, 00-KA-1552 (La. App. 5 Cir. 3/28/01); 783 So. 2d 520, 526.

102. *See* Transcript of Record at 81, *Jessie v. State*, 659 So. 2d 167 (Ala. Crim. App. 1994).

103. *Duren v. Missouri*, 439 U.S. 357, 363–64 (1979).

104. *Id.*

105. *Id.* at 364; *Casteneda v. Partida*, 430 U.S. 482, 494 (1977).

106. *See Strauder v. West Virginia*, 100 U.S. 303 (1880) (African Americans); *Taylor v. Louisiana*, 419 U.S. 522 (1975) (women).

107. *Hernandez v. Texas*, 347 U.S. 475, 479–80 (1954) (Mexican Americans); *United States v. Cabrera-Sarmiento*, 533 F. Supp. 799, 804 (S.D. Fla. 1982) (Latinos in Miami area); *Thiel v. Southern Pacific Co.*, 328 U.S. 217, 222 (1946) (daily wage earners); *State ex rel. Gregg v. Maples*, 239 So. 2d 198, 203 (Ala. 1970) (unregistered voters).

108. *See, e.g., Swain v. Alabama*, 380 U.S. 202, 208–09 (1965); *Floyd v. Garrison*, 996 F.2d 947, 950 (8th Cir. 1993); *United States v. Grisham*, 63 F.3d 1074, 1078–79 (11th Cir. 1995).

109. *See supra* note 108 and cases cited therein.

110. See Cynthia A. Williams, *Note: Jury Source Representativeness and the Use of Voter Registration Lists*, 65 N.Y.U.L. Rev. 590, 612 (1990).

111. See Brief for Social Scientists, Statisticians, and Law Professors, Jeffrey Fagan, et al., as Amici Curiae Supporting Respondent, at 22, Berghuis v. Smith, No. 08-1402, 2010 WL 1189555 (Mar. 30, 2010).

112. *Id.*

113. *See* Williams, *supra* note 110, at 610.

114. *See, e.g., United States v. Hafen,* 726 F.2d 21, 24 (1st Cir. 1984); *United States v. Whitley,* 491 F.2d 1248, 1249 (8th Cir. 1974). Another possible measure could be to consider whether a given level of underrepresentation is statistically significant. *See, e.g., United States v. Rioux,* 97 F.3d 648, 655 (2d Cir. 1996); *Ford v. Seabold,* 841 F.2d 677, 684 n.5 (6th Cir. 1988); *see also* Michael O. Finkelstein, *The Application of Statistical Decision Theory to the Jury Discrimination Cases,* 80 Harv. L. Rev. 338 (1996). However, as most courts to consider the issue have recognized, statistical significance does not measure the degree of underrepresentation but looks only at the probability that a given degree of underrepresentation occurred by chance. It is heavily dependant on the sample size, with even small disparities being statistically significant given a large enough sample size. *See* Brief for Social Scientists, *supra* note 111, at 27–29.

115. *See, e.g., United States v. Carmichael,* 560 F.3d 1270, 1280 (11th Cir. 2009) (requiring use of absolute disparity); *United States v. Yanez,* 136 F.3d 1329, *2 (5th Cir. 1998) (using absolute rather than comparative disparity); *Floyd,* 996 F.2d at 950 (declining to adopt comparative disparity); *United States v. Sanchez-Lopez,* 879 F.2d 541, 547–48 (9th Cir. 1989) (rejecting comparative disparity analysis).

116. *See Berghuis v. Smith,* No. 08-1402, 2010 WL 1189555, at *10 & n.4 (Mar. 30, 2010).

117. *Id.* at *5–6, 11–12.

118. *See* Miss. Code Ann. § 13-5-1 (West 2010); Mo. Rev. Stat. § 494.425(1) (West 2010).

119. *See, e.g.,* Fla. Stat. Ann. § 40.013(8) (West 2010); Md. Code Ann., Cts. & Jud. Proc. § 8-306(1) (West 2010); Okla. Stat. Ann. tit. 38, § 28(B) (West 2010).

120. *See* Mitchell S. Zuklie, *Comment: Rethinking the Fair Cross-Section Requirement,* 84 Calif. L. Rev. 101, 146–47 (1996).

121. George Volsky, *Miami Riot Report Gets Mixed Reaction,* N.Y. Times, Dec. 7, 1980, § 1, at 28.

122. Patrice Gaines-Carter, *McDuffie: The Case Behind Miami's Riots,* Southern Changes, Vol. 2, No. 7, at 21 (1980), *available at* http://beck.library.emory.edu/southernchanges/article.php?id=sco2-7_009&mdid=sco2-7_001.

123. Volsky, *supra* note 121.

124. *Id.*

125. Rick Atkinson, *Miami Jury Acquits Policeman in Fatal Shooting of Black,* Wash. Post, Mar. 15, 1984, at A2.

126. Reginald Stuart, *Police Occupy Tense Areas in Miami After 300 Arrests,* N.Y. Times, Mar. 17, 1984, § 1, at 6.

127. Atkinson, *supra* note 125.

128. John Riley, *Race, Defense Lapses Seen as Keys to Verdict,* Newsday, Apr. 30, 1992, at 4.

129. *Id.*

130. *Id.*

131. Mark Hansen, *Different Jury Different Verdict?,* 78 A.B.A. J. 54 (1992). A second, federal trial resulted in guilty verdicts for two of the police officers involved

in the beating. Michael Rezendes, *LA Relaxes in Wake of a Riot That Wasn't*, Boston Globe, Apr. 19, 1993, at 1. The jury in this case consisted of "nine whites, two blacks and one Hispanic" from Los Angeles. *Id*. The city did not riot after these verdicts were handed down. *Id*.

132. Alaine Griffin & Vanessa De La Torre, *Anger Files; After Former Cop's Acquittal, Dead Man's Family Lets Loose*, Hartford Courant, Dec. 9, 2009, at A1.

133. *Id*.

134. *Id*.

135. *Id*.

136. In New York, John White, an African American man, was found guilty of second-degree manslaughter in an incident where he and his son were threatened by a "lynch mob" outside their home in Long Island. The jury included only one black juror, who was asked by the other members to share his views on race and the use of the "N-word." The guilty verdict led Rev. Al Sharpton to plan a protest at the courthouse. Corey Kilgannon, *Jury's Deliberations May Be a Focal Point of Appeal*, N.Y. Times, Jan. 1, 2008, *available at* http://www.nytimes.com/2008/01/01/nyregion/01white.html.

137. In the highly publicized Jena 6 case, Mychal Bell was convicted by an all-white jury of assault in a climate of rising racial tension triggered when three white students hung nooses from a tree on the high school campus. Howard Witt, *Louisiana Teen Guilty in School Beating Case*, Chicago Tribune, June 29, 2007, *available at* http://www.chicagotribune.com/services/chi-jena_witt.1jun29,0,4233447.story. No African Americans were on the voir dire panel. Todd Lewan, *Black and White Becomes Gray in La. Town*, FOXNEWS.com, Sept. 22, 2007, *available at* http://www.foxnews.com/printer_friendly_wires/2007Sep22/0,4675,APlaceCalledJena,00.html. The verdict was later thrown out. *Court Overturns Conviction in Jena 6 Beating*, MSNBC, Sept. 15, 2007, *available at* http://www.msnbc.msn.com/id/20779755/.

138. Two white men were acquitted of murder in Powhatan, Virginia, outside of Richmond, in the shooting death of Tahliek Taliaferro. The jury of eleven whites and one black member found the defendants guilty of involuntary manslaughter, after they testified that they had lost control of an assault rifle. About 300 protestors marched around the Powhatan County courthouse to protest the verdict. A later news story stated that the jurors were dismayed to be accused of being racists. Bill McKelway, *About 300 Marchers in Powhatan Protest Taliaferro Verdict*, Richmond Times-Dispatch, Mar. 30, 2009, at B1, *available at* http://www2.timesdispatch.com/rtd/news/local/article/POWH30_20090329-222921/243957/; Bill McKelway, *A Look Inside the Taliaferro Jury*, Richmond Times-Dispatch, June 28, 2009, *available at* http://www2.times-dispatch.com/rtd/news/local/crime/article/POWW28_20090627-221404/276839/pa.immigrant.beating/index.html.

139. In Panama City, Florida, eight boot camp officers, including one who was African American and one Asian, were acquitted in a videotaped beating death of Martin Lee Anderson. The all-white jury decided in just 90 minutes that Anderson died of a previously undiagnosed blood disorder. About 150 protestors marched to the state capitol in protest. *Boot Camp Death Verdict Sparks Outrage*, ABCNews.com, Oct. 13, 2007, *available at* http://abcnews.go.com/GMA/story?id=3726041&page=1; Melissa Nelson, *Guards Acquitted in Boot Camp Case*, USA Today, Oct. 12, 2007, *available at* http://www.usatoday.com/news/nation/2007-10-11-3868327840_x.htm?csp=34.

140. In Milwaukee, Wisconsin three white police officers were acquitted by an all-white jury in the beating of Frank Jude, an African American man. The verdict led to a march by several thousand people. Georgia Pabst, Jesse Garza & Bob Purvis, *Thousands March to Protest Verdict*, Milwaukee Journal-Sentinel, Apr. 19, 2006, *available at* http://www3.jsonline.com/story/index.aspx?id=417026. Later federal proceedings resulted in seven officers receiving prison time. John Diedrich, *New Sentencing Ordered for Ex-Officer in Jude Beating Case*, Milwaukee Journal-Sentinel, June 8, 2009, *available at* http:/shwww.jsonline.com/news/milwaukee/47232467.html.

141. Tom R. Tyler, *Social Justice: Outcome and Procedure*, 35 Int'l J. Psychol. 117, 119–20 (2000).

142. *Id.*

143. Leslie Ellia & Shari Seidman Diamond, *Race, Diversity, and Jury Composition: Battering and Bolstering Legitimacy*, 78 Chi.-Kent L. Rev. 1033, 1048 (2003).

144. *See* Samuel R. Sommers, *On Racial Diversity and Group Decision Making: Identifying Multiple Effects of Racial Composition in Jury Deliberation*, 90 J. Personality and Soc. Psychol. 597, 600 (2006); *see also id.* at 608 ("[S]urveys have found that people often feel marginalized or threatened by minority status in a group and are therefore skeptical that their arguments will be taken seriously."); Nancy J. King, *Postconviction Review of Jury Discrimination: Measuring the Effects of Juror Race on Jury Decisions*, 92 Mich. L. Rev. 63, 98–99 (1993) (concluding that a minority of one rarely influences a jury's verdict and that "[a]dditional studies have shown that black jurors themselves believe that they have significantly less impact on deliberations than white jurors").

145. *See* William J. Bowers et al., *Death Sentencing in Black and White: An Empirical Analysis of the Role of Jurors' Race and Jury Racial Composition*, 3 U. Pa. J. Const. L. 171, 240 (2001) (concluding that blacks on white male dominated capital juries "were critical of the jury's decision-making process and especially discontented with their own experiences as capital jurors").

146. *See* David C. Baldus, et al., *The Use of Peremptory Challenges in Capital Murder Trials: A Legal and Empirical Analysis*, 3 U. Pa. J. Const. L. 3, 124 (2001) (studying capital trials in Philadelphia between 1981–1997 and concluding predominantly African American juries were less likely to impose death sentences than juries with fewer African Americans and explaining disparity due to "substantially higher death-sentencing rate in black defendant cases . . . when jury was predominantly non-black").

147. *See id.*; Bowers, *supra* note 145, at 188 (interpreting Baldus study and concluding that "tendency for Black defendants to be treated more harshly than whites ones as the number of whites on the jury increases holds especially for black-defendant/white-victim cases" (citing Baldus, *supra* note 146 at tbl. 8); *see also* Bowers, *id.* at 195 (finding that the likelihood of a death sentence in black-defendant white-victim case was "dramatically increased" with the presence of five or more white males on the jury as compared to intra racial defendant-victim cases). Like African American defendants, Latino defendants were more likely to receive harsher judgments from majority-white juries. *See* Samuel R. Sommers, *Determinants and Consequences of Jury Racial Diversity: Empirical Findings, Implications and Directions for Future Research*, 2 Soc. Issues & Policy Rev. 65, 83, 84 (2008) (citing studies of actual and mock juries with white and Latino defendants).

148. Sommers, *supra* note 144, at 609. The study consisted of mock jurors recruited from an actual jury pool while on jury duty shown trial of black defendant. *Id.* at 600. *Cf.* William J. Bowers et. al, *Crossing Racial Boundaries: A Closer Look at the Roots of Racial Bias in Capital Sentencing When the Defendant is Black and the Victim is White*, 53 DePaul L. Rev. 1497, 1531 (2004) (finding tendency of jurors on diverse juries to acknowledge how race affects their perspective and that of other jurors).

149. *See* Bowers, *supra* note 148, at 1520; *see also id.* at 1532 (finding that mitigation is voiced and considered when there are African Americans or at least one African American male on a jury as opposed to on white male dominated juries where there is a lack of serious discussion of mitigation).

150. Sommers, *supra* note 144, at 608 ("Jury representativeness can be more than a moral or Constitutional ideal; it is sometimes an ingredient for superior performance."); Neil Vidmar & Valerie P. Hans, *American Juries: The Verdict* 74 (2007) (concluding that claim that diverse juries are better fact-finders is supported by research on heterogeneous decision-making groups) *quoted in Jury Pool Diversity in New York State*, Statement of Prof. Valerie Hans to Assembly Standing Comm. on Judiciary and Codes, New York State Assembly (Apr. 30, 2009), *available at* http://juries.typepad.com/files/assembly_statement_draft_4-29-09-1 .pdf.

151. Sommers, *supra* note 144, at 608.

152. *See, e.g.,* Sommers, *supra* note 147, at 86–87 (discussing studies finding that diverse juries consider more factual information, were more likely to talk about missing evidence that they wished had been presented at trial, more willing to discuss controversial issues such as racial profiling, include more accurate information in deliberations); Justin D. Levinson, *Forgotten Racial Equality: Implicit Bias, Decisionmaking, and Misremembering*, 57 Duke L.J. 345, 414–15 (2007) (discussing studies indicating that racially diverse juries may make fewer cognitive errors than homogeneous jurors); Kim Taylor-Thompson, *Empty Votes in Jury Deliberations*, 113 Harv. L. Rev. 1261, 1285–95, 1298–1300 (2000) (discussing effects of gender and race in jury deliberation); King, *supra* note 237, at 75–100 (discussing social science studies examining influence of jury discrimination on jury decisions). Studies also suggest that cross-racial facial identification is subject to error. *See Cross-Racial Facial Identification: A Social Cognitive Integration*, 18 Personality & Soc. Psych. Bulletin 296, 296 (1992); R. Richard Banks, *Race-based Suspect Selection and Colorblind Equal Protection Doctrine and Discourse*, 48 U.C.L.A. L. Rev. 1075, 1103–04 (2001).

153. *See generally Taylor v. Louisiana*, 419 U.S. 522, 527–29 (1975).

Part VI: Sentencing: Does Time Come in Different Colors?

1. For an empirically based analysis of this subtlety, see William T. Pizzi, Irene V. Blair, and Charles M. Judd, "The Influence of Criminal Defendants' Afrocentric Features on Their Sentences," in *Critical Race Realism: Intersections of Psychology, Race, and Law*, ed. Gregory S. Parks, Shayne Jones, and W. Jonathan Cardi (New York: The New Press, 2008).

2. In 2010, the U.S. Supreme Court ruled it unconstitutional to sentence to life without parole someone who was juvenile at the time of the crime if that crime was not homicide. *Graham v. Florida*, 130 S. Ct. 2011, 2034 (2010).

13. No Exit: The Expanding Use of Life Sentences in America   *Ashley Nellis and Ryan S. King*

1. Parole is no longer an option in the federal system, as of 1987. The 886 individuals serving parole-eligible life sentences in the federal system were sentenced before parole was eliminated in 1987.

2. Advisory Committee on Geriatric and Seriously Ill Inmates (2005). *A Report of the Advisory Committee on Geriatric and Seriously Ill Inmates.* Harrisburg: Joint State Government Committee of the General Assembly of the Commonwealth of Pennsylvania.

3. Ibid.

4. LWOP data are unavailable for 1984.

5. U.S. Census Bureau (2007). *American Community Survey Demographic and Housing Estimates: 2007.* Washington, DC: U.S. Census Bureau; West, H.C. (2008). *Prisoners in 2007.* Washington, DC: Bureau of Justice Statistics.

6. Some states' department of corrections only collect and report race data but not ethnicity data. Because of this we encountered challenges in ascertaining the true representation of Hispanics among state life sentenced populations. In particular, the following states do not report life sentence data for Hispanics: Alabama, Delaware, Louisiana, Maryland, New Hampshire, and Vermont. Please see the Methodology section for more discussion of the challenges with ethnicity data.

7. In this report, we define juveniles according to each state's statutory definition of juvenile rather than the alternative definition of individuals under 18. Therefore, our estimates are frequently lower than estimates that may be found elsewhere because we exclude cases where state law automatically excludes certain youth from juvenile jurisdiction because of their age. Our use of the term "juvenile" is used deliberately instead of the term "individuals under 18," though in some states, these are synonymous.

8. Indiana, Maine, Vermont, and West Virginia do not currently have any juveniles serving life sentences though state law permits it.

9. National Council on Crime and Delinquency (2007). *And Justice for Some: Differential Treatment of Youth of Color in the Justice System.* Oakland: National Council on Crime and Delinquency.

10. Annie E. Casey Foundation (2008). *The Annie E. Casey Foundation 2008 KIDS COUNT Data Book.* Baltimore: Annie E. Casey Foundation.

11. Parole is no longer an option in the federal system, as of 1987. Seventeen of the 52 juvenile life sentences represent individuals who are serving parole-eligible life sentences, since they were sentenced before parole was eliminated in 1987.

14. New Political and Cultural Meanings   *David Garland*

1. Morton Mintz, "Joy on Death Row; Praise, Scorn on Hill," *Washington Post,* June 30, 1972, A13; "Court Spares 600: 4 Justices Named by Nixon All Dissent in Historic Decision," *New York Times,* June 30, 1972, 1; Martin Waldron, "Ruling Cheered on Florida Death Row," *New York Times,* June 30, 1972, 14; "Death Sentences Voided," *Chicago Tribune,* June 30, 1972, 1; "Ruling Hits Survivors," *Chicago Tribune,* June 30, 1972, C16; "Nixon Hopes Federal Death Penalty Stands," *Chicago Tribune,* June 30, 1972, C16; "Pall Lifts on Death Row," *Los Angeles Times,* June 30, 1972, A20; "Supreme Court Overturns Death Penalty in Nation," *Atlanta Daily World,* July 6, 1972.

2. Quoted in Mintz, "Joy on Death Row."

3. "Calls for U.S. Crime Reforms," *Chicago Daily Defender,* July 13, 1972, 17.

4. Quoted in Richard West, "Calif. Initiative in Doubt," *Los Angeles Times,* June 30, 1972, A1.

5. Douglas Watson, "Guards at Prisons Air Gripes," *Washington Post,* July 24, 1972, C1.

6. Quoted in Mintz, "Joy on Death Row."

7. William Robbins, "Nixon Backs Death Penalty for Kidnapping, Hijacking," *New York Times,* June 30, 1972, 1. Earlier in 1972 the California Supreme Court had ruled the California death penalty unconstitutional. Governor Reagan immediately proposed a public initiative, Proposition 17, to reinstate it. In November 1972 the initiative was passed by a two-to-one margin. Lee Epstein and Joseph Kobylka, *The Supreme Court and Legal Change: Abortion and the Death Penalty* (Chapel Hill: University of North Carolina Press, 1992), 85.

8. Lesley Oelsner, "Banned—But for How Long?" *New York Times,* July 2, 1972, E1.

9. "Around the Nation," *Washington Post,* July 6, 1972, A24.

10. *Los Angeles Times,* June 30, 1972, at A1, reported that Los Angeles Police Chief Edward M. Davis would lead a campaign of the Association of Chiefs of Police to restore the death penalty throughout the country. Epstein and Kobylka write, "In December 1972, the National Association of Attorneys General approved by a 32–1 margin a resolution approving capital punishment." Epstein and Kobylka, *Supreme Court and Legal Change,* 341. See also Thomas Edsall and Mary Edsall, *Chain Reaction: The Impact of Race, Rights and Taxes on American Politics* (New York: Norton, 1992), 46.

11. Christopher Mooney and Mei-Hsein Lee, "Morality Policy Reinvention: State Death Penalties," *Annals, AAPSS 566* (1999): 80–92; Epstein and Kobylka, *Supreme Court and Legal Change,* 74; Marie Gottschalk, *The Prison and the Gallows* (New York: Cambridge University Press, 2006).

12. Savelsberg reports that approval of the death penalty for persons convicted of murder increased from 42 percent in 1966 to 53 percent in 1972 to 66 percent in 1978. The proportion of Americans believing that "courts do not deal harshly enough with criminals" increased from 48 percent in 1965 to 66 percent in 1972 to 85 percent in 1978. Joachim Savelsberg, "Knowledge, Domination, and Criminal Punishment," *American Journal of Sociology 99* (1994): 929–930.

13. Epstein and Kobylka, *Abortion and the Death Penalty,* 131; Christopher Mooney and Mei-Hsein Lee, "The Temporal Diffusion of Morality Policy: The Case of the Death Penalty Legislation in the American States," *Policy Studies Journal 27* (1999): 766–780.

14. For details of the statutes and their various procedural schemes, see James Liebman and Lawrence Marshall, "Less Is Better: Justice Stevens and the Narrowed Death Penalty," *Fordham Law Review 74* (2006): 1607–1682.

15. Laura Langer and Paul Brace, "The Preemptive Power of State Supreme Courts: Adoption of Abortion and Death Penalty Legislation," *Policy Studies Journal 33* (2005): 317–340; Epstein and Kobylka, *Supreme Court and Legal Change,* 85.

16. Epstein and Kobylka, *Supreme Court and Legal Change,* 89.

17. Robert Burt, "Disorder in the Court: The Death Penalty and the Constitution," *Michigan Law Review 85* (1987): 1741–1819.

18. Gottschalk, *Prison and Gallows*. In 1975, an influential neoconservative policy expert argued that the evidence on the deterrent effects of capital punishment was inconclusive and that capital punishment ought to be viewed as a question of justice rather than of utility. James Q. Wilson, *Thinking about Crime* (New York: Basic Books, 1975).

19. Quoted in Roger Schwed, *Abolition and Capital Punishment* (New York: AMS Press, 1983), 103.

20. Keeler McCartney, "Capital Crime up 235 Pct Here," *Atlanta Constitution*, March 31, 1972, A1.

21. "Liberals and Crime," *Atlanta Constitution*, January 29, 1973, A4. Governor Ronald Reagan had responded to the California Supreme Court's 1972 decision that the state's death penalty was unconstitutional by calling it "one more step toward totally disarming society in its fight against violence and crime." Quoted in Gottschalk, *Prison and Gallows*, 219.

22. The percentage of those who answered "yes" when asked if they supported capital punishment in 1972 was 57 percent. The annual figures were: November 1972, 57 percent; March 1972, 50 percent; 1971, 49 percent; 1969, 51 percent; 1966, 42 percent; 1965, 45 percent; 1960, 51 percent; 1953, 68 percent. In 1966, more people (47 percent) had said "no" than said "yes" (42 percent).

23. As a congressional political aide remarked, "The death penalty becomes part of a complex web of issues. People think, if you agree with me on the death penalty, you probably agree with me on . . . a number of other issues." Quoted in Beth Donovan, "Congress Could Focus the Debate: Death Penalty is Reemerging as a Presidential-Level Issue," *CQ Weekly*, June 18, 1988, 1657.

24. David Anderson, *Crime and the Politics of Hysteria: How the Willie Horton Story Changed American Justice* (New York: Crown, 1995). Ellsworth and Gross note polls that report that the death penalty was a significant factor in voter choice in the 1988 election. Phoebe Ellsworth and Samuel Gross, "Hardening of Attitudes: Americans' Views on the Death Penalty," in Hugo Bedau, ed., *The Death Penalty in America: Current Controversies* (New York: Oxford University Press, 1994), 90–115.

25. Robert Singh, *Governing America: The Politics of a Divided Democracy* (New York: Oxford University Press, 2003), 385.

26. In 1972, the Democratic national platform called for "abolishing capital punishment" on the grounds that it was "recognized as an ineffective deterrent to crime, unequally applied and cruel and excessive." By 1996, the party's platform was claiming credit for adding "the death penalty to nearly 60 violent crimes" and for signing "a law to limit appeals." Naomi Murakawa, "Electing to Punish: Congress, Race and the American Criminal Justice State" (Ph.D. dissertation, Yale University, 2005), 129.

27. Maddox is reported to have shouted these remarks when a death penalty bill failed to pass the Georgia legislature. See Milo Dakin, "Angry as Death Bill Fails: Need More Hangings—Maddox," *Atlanta Constitution*, February 10, 1973, A1.

28. Celestine Sibley, "House Passes Bill to Reinstate the Death Penalty," *Atlanta Constitution*, February 14, 1973, A2. Another article in the same newspaper reports that a law-maker in the Georgia House "called for a return to public hangings 'in the courthouse square.'" This probably referred to the same incident.

29. Sibley, "House Passes Bill," 2A.

30. Another article, two years later, notes that some rural Georgians advocated "public executions in the courthouse square." Sam Hopkins, "Rural Georgians Urge Return to Public Executions," *Atlanta Constitution,* January 28, 1975, D8.

31. William Craze, "Death Penalty Stalks South," *Atlanta Constitution,* March 11, 1973, B2.

32. Both quotes from Mintz, "Joy on Death Row."

33. "Ruling Hits Survivors," *Chicago Tribune,* June 30, 1972, C16.

34. Reported in the *Fort Worth Star-Telegram,* February 25, 2000.

35. A similar response greeted federal attempts to end lynching in the 1890s and 1900s. See David Garland, "Penal Excess and Surplus Meaning: Public Torture Lynchings in 20th Century America," *Law & Society Review* 39(2005): 793–834.

36. See the *Tampa Tribune:* "the people's representatives did not make a decision. Instead, five justices imposed on the nation their moral judgment." "The Troubling Undercurrents of Court's Death Penalty Rule," *Tampa Tribune,* March 2, 2005, 10. Also see the *Baltimore Sun:* "The death penalty is a matter for state legislatures." Gregory Kane, "The Nine Divines—and the Constitution," *Baltimore Sun,* March 5, 2005, B1. The death penalty has a special significance in the context of states' rights because it is one of the few powers associated with sovereignty that the American states ever possessed. Other marks of sovereignty, such as the powers "to make war or peace, to form commercial treaties with other nations, to raise armies or navies, to control the rule of citizenship, to coin money" were never possessed by the American states. See Garry Wills, *A Necessary Evil: A History of American Mistrust of Government* (New York: Simon & Schuster, 1999).

37. Edward Lazarus, "The Supreme Court and the Juvenile Death Penalty," http://www.cnn.com/2005/LAW/03/03/lazarus.death.penalty/index.html (accessed January 27, 2010).

38. *Greenville News,* March 3, 2005, 10A; "Death Ruling Slip-Up: Foreign Views out of Place in Court Opinion Restricting U.S. Executions," *Omaha World Herald,* March 3, 2005, B6.

39. See Judge Tom Parker, "Alabama Justices Surrender to Judicial Activism," *Birmingham News,* January 1, 2006.

40. *Kennedy v Louisiana* 554 U.S. _ (2008). The other states were Georgia, Montana, Oklahoma, South Carolina, and Texas.

41. *Chattanooga Times Free Press,* "Our Busybody Judiciary," January 9, 2008, B7.

42. Quoted in the *Seguin Gazette-Enterprise* (Texas) of June 29, 2008.

43. Press conference reported by *ABC News,* June 25, 2008. See also http://www.wsws.org/articles/2008/jun2008/obam-j26.shtml (last accessed January 31, 2010).

44. Patrick Buchanan, "The (Linda) Greenhouse Effect," *Tulsa World,* April 23, 2008.

45. In a speech to the 1992 Republican Convention, Pat Buchanan invoked this idea: "My friends, this election is about much more than who gets what. It is about what we believe, what we stand for as Americans. There is a religious war going on for the soul of America. It is a culture war, as critical to the kind of nation we will one day be as was the Cold War itself." Paul Galloway, "Divided We Stand: Today's 'Cultural War' Goes Deeper Than the Political Slogans," *Chicago Tribune,* October 29, 1992, C1.

46. Tom Parker, "Alabama Justices Surrender to Judicial Activism," *Birmingham News*, January 1, 2006. Kahan highlights this subterranean status dimension of the death penalty debate. Dan Kahan, "The Secret Ambition of Deterrence," *Harvard Law Review* 113 (1999): 413–500.

47. Jeremy Rabkin, "The Supreme Court in the Culture Wars," *Public Interest* 125 (1996): 8–9.

48. "Court's Ruling Has Not Ended Controversy," *Los Angeles Times*, June 30, 1972, A24.

49. "Letters to the *Times*," *Los Angeles Times*, July 3, 1972.

50. Banner writes that Solicitor General Robert Bork, who argued the *Gregg* case for the federal government, "viewed opposition to capital punishment as a sign of moral decay." Stuart Banner, *The Death Penalty: An American History* (Cambridge, MA: Harvard University Press, 2002).

51. Death Penalty Information Center, http://www.deathpenaltyinfo.org/number-executions-state-and-region-1976.

52. David Garland, *The Culture of Control: Crime and Social Order in Contemporary Society* (Chicago: University of Chicago Press, 2001).

53. Mark Warr, "Poll Trends: Public Opinion on Crime and Punishment," *Public Opinion Quarterly* 59 (1995): 301; and Frank Newport, "In U.S., Two-Thirds Continue to Support Death Penalty," www.gallup.com, October 13, 2009, http://www.gallup.com/poll/123638/in-u.s.-two-thirds-continue-support-death-penalty.aspx (accessed January 12, 2010), 2. Public support for capital punishment has declined since the mid-1990s and has now settled at or around 65 percent in favor. McVeigh's execution in June 2001 marked the high point of the punishment's popularity but also the beginning of the displacement of "law and order" politics by new fears and concerns. In the period since, crime has become a less urgent concern as homicide rates have continued to fall and other insecurities have taken crime's place. The narratives in which the death penalty is framed by the media have shifted to include DNA doubts, stories about innocents on death row, a growing pressure of international opinion, and high-profile challenges to the protocols of lethal injection. See Frank Baumgartner, Suzanna De Boef, and Amber Boydstun, *The Decline of the Death Penalty and the Discovery of Innocence* (New York: Cambridge University Press, 2008).

Part VII: Prison: What Are the Walls Hiding?

1. "Prison-Industrial Complex," Wikipedia, http://en.wikipedia.org/wiki/Prison-industrial_complex. For a thoughtful and thorough analysis of the economic and political interests underlying mass incarceration, see Marie Gottschalk, "Cell Blocks & Red Ink: Mass Incarceration, the Great Recession & Penal Reform," *Dædalus*, Summer 2010, 62–73.

2. "Correctional Officers," *Occupational Outlook Handbook, 2010–11 Edition*, Bureau of Labor Statistics, http://www.bls.gov/oco/ocos156.htm; "Probation Officers and Correctional Treatment Specialists," *Occupational Outlook Handbook, 2010–11 Edition*, Bureau of Labor Statistics, http://www.bls.gov/oco/ocos265.htm.

3. Vesla M. Weaver and Amy E. Lerman, "Political Consequences of the Carceral State," *American Political Science Review*, November 2010, http://www.ebonterr.com/site_editor/assets/EBONTERR_69.pdf.

15. Texas Tough   *Robert Perkinson*

1. Friedrich Nietzsche, *Thus Spake Zarathustra* (London: George Allen & Unwin, 1923), 118.

2. Thomas Paine, *Common Sense* (New York: Peter Eckler, 1918), 37, 22; John S. Jenkins, ed., *Life and Public Services of Gen. Andrew Jackson* (New York: Miller, Orton, and Mulligan, 1855), 371; Barack Obama, inaugural address, January 20, 2009, http://www.nytimes.com/2009/01/20/us/politics/20text-obama.html.

3. Jennifer Warren, *One in 100: Behind Bars in America 2008* (Washington, DC: Pew Center on the States, 2008); Heather C. West and William J. Sabol, *Prison Inmates at Midyear 2008*, Statistical Tables, NCJ 225619 (Washington, DC: Bureau of Justice Statistics [BJS], March 2009), 3; Todd D. Minton and William J. Sabol, *Jail Inmates at Midyear 2008*, Statistical Tables, NCJ 225709 (Washington, DC: BJS, March 2009), 3; Roy Walmsley, World Prison Population List, 5th ed., Findings 234 (London: Research, Development, and Statistics Directorate, Home Office, 2003), 4.

4. U.S. Census Bureau, "2000 Census: US Municipalities Over 50,000," http://www.demographia.com/db-uscity98.htm; William Spelman, "The Limited Importance of Prison Expansion," in Alfred Blumstein and Joel Wallman, eds., *The Crime Drop in America* (New York: Cambridge University Press, 2000): 97–129; Franklin E. Zimring, *The Great American Crime Decline* (New York: Oxford University Press, 2007). Some economists estimate a more pronounced impact. See Steven D. Levitt, "Understanding Why Crime Fell in the 1990s: Four Factors That Explain the Decline and Six That Do Not," *Journal of Economic Perspectives* 18, no. 1 (2004): 163–90.

5. BJS, "Justice Expenditure and Employment Extracts" (2006), http://www.ojp.usdoj.gov/bjs/eande.htm#selected; "My Global Career 500," http://www.myglobalcareer.com/my-global-career-500/; James J. Stephan, *Census of State and Federal Correctional Facilities* (2005), NCJ 222182 (Washington, DC: BJS, October 2008), 1.

6. Thomas P. Bonczar, *Prevalence of Imprisonment in the U.S. Population, 1974–2001*, NCJ 197976 (Washington, DC: BJS, August 2003), 1; National Center for Education Statistics, *Literacy Behind Prison Walls*, NCES 1994-102 (Washington, DC: U.S. Department of Education, 1994), 17; Caroline Wolf Harlow, *Education and Correctional Populations*, NCJ 195670 (Washington, DC: BJS, January 2003), 1; David Cole, *No Equal Justice: Race and Class in the American Criminal Justice System* (New York: The New Press, 1999), 66. See also Bruce Western, *Punishment and Inequality in America* (New York: Russell Sage Foundation, 2006); John Hagan and Ruth D. Peterson, *Crime and Inequality* (Stanford, CA: Stanford University Press, 1995).

7. Gustave de Beaumont and Alexis de Tocqueville, *On the Penitentiary System in the United States and Its Application in France*, trans. Francis Lieber (Philadelphia: Carey, Lea & Blanchard, 1833), 44. Racial disparity estimates based on: Patrick A. Langan, *Race of Prisoners Admitted to State and Federal Institutions, 1926–1986*, NCJ-125618 (Washington, DC: BJS, May 1991); Campbell Gibson and Kay Jung, *Historical Census Statistics on Population Totals By Race, 1790 to 1990, and By Hispanic Origin, 1970 to 1990*, Working Paper Series No. 56 (Washington, DC: U.S. Census Bureau, September 2002), table 1; Allen J. Beck and Paige M. Harrison, *Prisoners in 2000*, NCJ 188207 (Washington, DC: BJS, August 2001), 10; Jesse McKinnon, *The Black Population: 2000*, Census 2000 Brief, C2KBR/01–5 (Washington, DC:

U.S. Census Bureau, August 2001), 3; Elizabeth M. Grieco, *The White Population: 2000*, Census 2000 Brief, C2KBR/01-4 (Washington, DC: U.S. Census Bureau, August 2001), 3.

8. Western, *Punishment and Inequality in America*, 29. See also Jason Ziedenberg and Vincent Schiraldi, *Cellblocks or Classrooms? The Funding of Higher Education and Corrections and Its Impact on African American Men* (Washington, DC: Justice Policy Institute [JPI], August 28, 2002).

9. BJS, "Justice Expenditure and Employment Extracts" (2005); Susan B. Carter et al., *Historical Statistics of the United States*, millennial ed., vol. 5 (Cambridge: Cambridge University Press, 2000), pt. E, 5–311; Henry W. Bragdon and John C. Pittenger, *The Pursuit of Justice* (New York: Crowell-Collier, 1969), 91, x; Norval Morris, "Prison in Evolution," in Edward Eldefonso, ed. *Issues in Corrections: A Book of Readings* (Beverly Hills, CA: Glencoe Press, 1974), 250. See also Norval Morris, *The Future of Imprisonment* (Chicago: University of Chicago Press, 1974).

10. M. Stanton Evans and Margaret Moore, *The Lawbreakers: America's Number One Domestic Problem* (New Rochelle, NY: Arlington House, 1968); William John Bennett, John J. Dilulio, and John P. Walters, *Body Count: Moral Poverty—and How to Win America's War Against Crime and Drugs* (New York: Simon & Schuster, 1996); James Q. Wilson, *Thinking About Crime*, rev. ed. (New York: Basic Books, 1983).

11. Anne-Marie Cusac, *Cruel and Unusual: The Culture of Punishment in America* (New Haven, CT: Yale University Press, 2009); Sasha Abramsky, *American Furies: Crime, Punishment, and Vengeance in the Age of Mass Imprisonment* (Boston: Beacon Press, 2007); Jonathan Simon, "Fear and Loathing in Late Modernity: Reflections on the Cultural Sources of Mass Imprisonment in the United States," *Punishment and Society* 3, no. 1 (2001): 21–34; David Garland, *The Culture of Control: Crime and Social Order in Contemporary Society* (Chicago: University of Chicago Press, 2001). For rival explanations, see Christian Parenti, *Lockdown America: Police and Prisons in the Age of Crisis* (New York: Verso, 1999); Jonathan Simon, *Governing Through Crime: How the War on Crime Transformed American Democracy and Created a Culture of Fear* (New York: Oxford University Press, 2007); Michael Tonry, *Thinking About Crime: Sense and Sensibility in American Penal Culture* (New York: Oxford University Press, 2004).

12. See Paulette Thomas, "Making Crime Pay: Triangle of Interests Creates Infrastructure to Fight Lawlessness," *Wall Street Journal*, May 12, 1995, A1, A6; J. Robert Lilly and Paul Knepper, "The Corrections-Commercial Complex," *Crime and Delinquency* 39, no. 2 (April 1993): 150–66; Joel Dyer, *The Perpetual Prisoner Machine: How America Profits from Crime* (Boulder, CO: Westview Press, 2000); Ruth Gilmore, *Golden Gulag: Prisons, Surplus, Crisis, and Opposition in Globalizing California* (Berkeley: University of California Press, 2007).

13. Notable exceptions include: Katherine Beckett, *Making Crime Pay: Law and Order in Contemporary American Politics* (New York: Oxford University Press, 1997); Marc Mauer, *Race to Incarcerate* (New York: The New Press, 1999); Loïc Wacquant, "Deadly Symbiosis: When Ghetto and Prison Meet and Mesh," *Punishment and Society* 3, no. 1 (2001): 95–134. More recently, see Glenn C. Loury, *Race, Incarceration, and American Values* (Cambridge, MA: Boston Review/MIT Press, 2008); Naomi Murakawa, "The Origins of the Carceral Crisis: Racial Order as 'Law and Order' in Postwar American Politics," in Joseph E. Lowndes, Julie Novkov, and Dorian Tod Warren, eds., *Race and American Political Development* (New York: Routledge,

2008); Loïc Wacquant, *Punishing the Poor: The Neoliberal Government of Social Insecurity* (Durham, NC: Duke University Press, 2009).

14. There are numerous long-range historical surveys of American criminal justice, of course, but these typically minimize the South and marginalize race. See James Q. Whitman, *Harsh Justice: Criminal Punishment and the Widening Divide Between America and Europe* (New York: Oxford University Press, 2003); Lawrence Friedman, *Crime and Punishment in American History* (New York: Basic Books, 1993). Exceptions include: Scott Christianson, *With Liberty for Some: 500 Years of Imprisonment in America* (Boston: Northeastern University Press, 1998); Mark Colvin, *Penitentiaries, Reformatories, and Chain Gangs: Social Theory and the History of Punishment in Nineteenth-Century America* (New York: St. Martin's Press, 1997).

15. There are numerous books that deal with the cruelties of southern justice, but they tend to move no further forward than the Progressive Era. See Edward L. Ayers, *Vengeance and Justice: Crime and Punishment in the Nineteenth-Century American South* (New York: Oxford University Press, 1984); Alex Lichtenstein, *Twice the Work of Free Labor: The Political Economy of Convict Labor in the New South* (London: Verso, 1996); David M. Oshinsky, *"Worse Than Slavery": Parchman Farm and the Ordeal of Jim Crow Justice* (New York: Free Press, 1996); Douglas A. Blackmon, *Slavery by Another Name: The Re-Enslavement of Black People in America from the Civil War to World War II* (New York: Doubleday, 2008).

16. West and Sabol, *Prison Inmates at Midyear 2008*, 3; BJS, "Justice Expenditure and Employment Extracts" (2006); Google, FY2007 results, January 31, 2008, http://investor.google.com/releases/2007Q4_google_earnings.html; U.S. Census Bureau, "State and County QuickFacts" (2008), http://quickfacts.census .gov/qfd/index.html. California and Texas both held 173,000 prisoners in July 2008, but California's numbers have decreased while Texas's are still increasing.

17. Paige M. Harrison and Allen J. Beck, *Prisoners in 2005*, NCJ 215092 (Washington, DC: BJS, November 2006), 1; Paige M. Harrison and Allen J. Beck, *Prison and Jail Inmates at Midyear 2004*, NCJ 208801 (Washington, DC: BJS, April 2005); Walmsley, *World Prison Population List*.

18. *The Fair Defense Report: Analysis of Indigent Defense Practices in Texas* (Austin: Texas Appleseed Fair Defense Project, December 2000); *Public Safety, Public Spending: Forecasting America's Prison Population 2007–2011* (Washington, DC: Pew Center on the States, 2007); West and Sabol, *Prison Inmates at Midyear 2008*, 13; Kevin Johnson, "From Extreme Isolation: Waves of Felons Are Freed," *USA Today*, December 11, 2002, http://www.usatoday.com/news/nation/2002-12-11-prison -cover-usat_x.htm; *One in 31: The Long Reach of American Corrections* (Washington, DC: Pew Center on the States, March 2009), 42; Death Penalty Information Center, "Executions in the United States, 1608–1976, by State," http://www.death penaltyinfo.org/executions-united-states-1608–1976-state; Joseph T. Hallinan, *Going Up the River: Travels in a Prison Nation* (New York: Random House, 2001); xii.

19. See Michael Lind, *Made in Texas: George W. Bush and the Southern Takeover of American Politics* (New York: Basic Books, 2003); James McEnteer, *Deep in the Heart: The Texas Tendency in American Politics* (Westport, CT: Praeger, 2004).

20. On the Byrd lynching, see Ricardo C. Ainslie, *Long Dark Road: Bill King and Murder in Jasper, Texas* (Austin: University of Texas Press, 2004); Mike Berryhill, "Prisoner's Dilemma: Did the Texas Penal System Kill James Byrd?" *New Republic*, December 27 1999; Dina Temple-Raston, *Death in Texas: A Story of Race, Murder, and a Small Town's Struggle for Redemption* (New York: Owl Books, 2003).

21. On Texas's populist tradition, see Lawrence Goodwyn, *Democratic Promise: The Populist Moment in America* (New York: Oxford University Press, 1976); V. O. Key and Alexander Heard, *Southern Politics in State and Nation*, new ed. (Knoxville: University of Tennessee Press, 1984); Chandler Davidson, *Race and Class in Texas Politics* (Princeton, NJ: Princeton University Press, 1990). Ronnie Dugger, "The Texification of the USA," *Texas Observer*, December 3, 2004, 6.

22. "Pontesso Sees State Prisons as Failing to Rehabilitate Cons," *Houston Chronicle*, September 4, 1978.

23. "Declaration of Principles Adopted and Promulgated by the Congress," in Enoch C. Wines, ed. *Transactions of the National Congress on Penitentiary and Reformatory Discipline, Held at Cincinnati, Ohio, October 12–18, 1870* (Albany, NY: Weed, Parsons & Co., 1871), 541; "Convict Camps," *Dallas Morning News*, November 2, 1909, 6.

24. Patrick A. Langan et al., *Historical Statistics on Prisoners in State and Federal Institutions, Yearend 1925–1986*, NCJ-111098 (Washington, DC: BJS, May 1988), 10; Beck and Harrison, *Prisoners in 2000*; Kathleen Maguire and Ann L. Patore, eds., *Sourcebook of Criminal Justice Statistics 2002*, NCJ 203301 (Washington, DC: BJS, 2004), 495. James Marquart, interview by author, Huntsville, Texas, March 19, 1999.

25. See Margaret Werner Cahalan, "Historical Corrections Statistics in the United States, 1850–1984" (Washington, DC: BJS, 1986); Roger Lane, *Murder in America: A History* (Columbus: Ohio State University Press, 1997).

26. See, for example, Norval Morris and David J. Rothman, eds., *The Oxford History of the Prison: The Practice of Punishment in Western Society* (New York: Oxford University Press, 1995); Thomas G. Blomberg and Karol Lucken, *American Penology: A History of Control* (New York: Aldine de Gruyter, 2000); Blake McKelvey, *American Prisons: A History of Good Intentions*, rev. ed. (Montclair, NJ: Patterson Smith, 1977).

27. Even the most critical thinkers have typically followed this forward march from sanguinary to supple discipline. See Michel Foucault, *Discipline and Punish: The Birth of the Prison*, trans. Alan Sheridan (New York: Vintage Books, 1979); Georg Rusche and Otto Kirchheimer, *Punishment and Social Structure* (New York: Columbia University Press and the Institute of Social Research, 1939).

28. Another reason that northeastern prisons have dominated the historiography is that the nation's elite universities afford ready access to their archives.

29. Enoch Wines, "Reformation of the Criminal" (1895), in Corinne Bacon, ed. *Prison Reform* (New York: H. W. Wilson Company, 1917), 1.

30. Plato, *Republic*, trans. Francis MacDonald Cornford (New York: Oxford University Press, 1951), 18.

31. Republic of Texas, *Constitution* (1836), secs. 6–10.

32. Manning Marable, *Race, Reform, and Rebellion: The Second Reconstruction in Black America, 1945–1982* (Jackson: University Press of Mississippi, 1984).

33. Erving Goffman, *Asylums: Essays on the Social Situation of Mental Patients and Other Inmates* (New York: Doubleday, 1990).

34. Here, my work is influenced by a long line of prison sociologists and anthropologists. See Donald Clemmer, *The Prison Community* (Boston: Christopher Publishing House, 1940); Gresham M. Sykes, *The Society of Captives* (Princeton, NJ: Princeton University Press, 1958); Donald R. Cressey, ed., *The Prison: Studies in Institutional Organization and Change* (New York: Holt, Rinehart and Winston, 1961);

John Irwin, *Prisons in Turmoil* (Boston: Little, Brown, 1980); Lorna Rhodes, *Total Confinement: Madness and Reason in the Maximum Security Prison* (Berkeley: University of California Press, 2004).

35. Teri Crook, "Texas Prisons—'A Bad Situation,'" *Galveston Daily News*, March 6, 1984.

36. On the problems associated with TDCJ's present-day medical system, see Mike Ward, "Sick in Secret: 'Deadly Inadequacies' Plague Inmate Wards," *Austin American-Statesman*, December 16, 2001; John E. Dannenberg, "$40.1 Million Verdict Against CSC in Texas Prisoner's Medical Neglect Death," *Prison Legal News* (February 2004): 9.

37. Christopher J. Mumola, *Suicide and Homicide in State Prisons and Local Jails*, NCJ 210036 (Washington, DC: BJS, August 2005), 3; Prison Commission, *Annual Report* (1911), 36

38. Gene Hathorn, letter to author, August 23, 2004; Gene Hathorn, "Trashcan Food and a Concrete Shithouse."

39. Christopher Lasch, *The True and Only Heaven: Progress and Its Critics* (New York: W. W. Norton, 1991), 93; Seán McConville, "The Victorian Prison, England, 1865–1965," in Norval Morris and David J. Rothman, eds., *The Oxford History of the Prison: The Practice of Punishment in Western Society* (New York: Oxford University Press, 1995), 131.

40. Benjamin Rush, "An Enquiry into the Effects of Public Punishments upon Criminals, and upon Society," Philadelphia, March 9, 1787, in Rush, *Essays: Literary, Moral, and Philosophical* (Schenectady, NY: Union College Press, 1988), 88, 90; Reverend Benjamin A. Rogers, quoted in E. C. Wines, *The State of Prisons and of Child-Saving Institutions in the Civilized World* (Cambridge, MA: John Wilson and Son, 1880), 189; Paul Lucko, "Prison Farms, Walls and Society: Punishment and Politics in Texas, 1848–1910" (PhD diss., University of Texas, 1999), 84; "Reformatory for Vicious Boys," *Dallas Morning News*, April 4, 1887, 4; CPPL, *A Summary of the Texas Prison Survey* (San Antonio, TX: Globe Publishing Co., 1924); Charles Sullivan, "Prison Reform Finally Arrives," *Texas Observer*, July 8, 1983, 6–8; Ramsey Clark, *Crime in America: Observations on Its Nature, Causes, Prevention, and Control*, 2nd ed. (New York: Pocket Books, 1971), 211.

41. Wacquant, "Deadly Symbiosis," 96; Adam Liptak, "Serving Life, with No Chance of Redemption," *New York Times*, October 5, 2005, http://www.nytimes.com/2005/10/05/national/05lifer?html?pagewanted=print; Ashley Nellis and Ryan S. King, *No Exit: The Expanding Use of Life Sentences in America* (Washington, DC: Sentencing Project, July 2009); Michele Deitch et al., *From Time Out to Hard Time: Young Children in the Adult Criminal Justice System* (Austin, TX: LBJ School of Public Affairs, 2009); Adam Liptak, "Jailed for Life After Crimes as Teenagers," *New York Times*, October 3, 2005, http://www.nytimes.com/2005/10/03/national/03lifers.html; Sentencing Project, "Felony Disenfranchisement," http://www.sentencingproject.org/template/page.cfm?id=133; Darren Wheelock, "Collateral Consequences and Racial Inequality: Felon Status Restrictions as a System of Disadvantage," *Journal of Contemporary Criminal Justice* 21, no. 1 (2005): 82–9; Monica Davey and Abby Goodnough, "Doubts Rise as States Hold Sex Offenders After Prison," *New York Times*, March 4, 2007, http://www.nytimes.com/2007/03/04/us/04civil.html; Damien Cave, "Roadside Camp for Miami Sex Offenders Leads to Lawsuit," *New York Times*, July 9, 2009, http://www.nytimes.com/2009/07/10/us/10offender.html.

42. Charles Dickens, *American Notes* (Greenwich, CT: Fawcett, 1961), 111; Rush, "An Enquiry into the Effects of Public Punishments upon Criminals, and upon Society," 88; Lorna Rhodes, *Total Confinement: Madness and Reason in the Maximum Security Prison* (Berkeley: University of California Press, 2004).

43. Peter Applebome, *Dixie Rising: How the South Is Shaping American Values, Politics, and Culture* (New York: Times Books, 1996); Dedrick Muhammad et al., "The State of the Dream: Enduring Disparities in Black and White" (Boston: United for a Fair Economy, 2004), 10. See also Lee Daniels, ed., *The State of Black America: The Complexity of Black Progress* (Washington, DC: Urban League, 2004); Orlando Patterson, *Rituals of Blood: Consequences of Slavery in Two American Centuries* (Washington, DC: Basic/Civitas, 1998); David R. Roediger, *How Race Survived U.S. History: From Settlement and Slavery to the Obama Phenomenon* (New York: Verso, 2008).

44. Frederick Douglass, "The Color Line," *North American Review* (June 1881): 567–77; W.E.B. Du Bois, *The Souls of Black Folk: Essays and Sketches*, 1953 ed. (Greenwich, CT: Fawcett Publications, 1961), 133.

45. Bruce A. Glasrud, "Child or Beast?: White Texas' View of Blacks, 1900–1910," *East Texas Historical Journal* 15 (1977): 39.

46. Michael J. Hindelang et al., *Sourcebook of Criminal Justice Statistics, 1973* (Washington, DC: U.S. Department of Justice, August 1973), 351; TSLAC, "United States and Texas Populations, 1850–2008," http://www.tsl.state.tx.us/ref/abouttx/census.html; Harrison and Beck, *Prisoners in 2005*, 3; TDC, *Annual Report* (1965); TDCJ, *Statistical Report* (FY2005), 56.

47. Simon Beardsley, "TDCJ Statistical Report Historical Breakdown, 1967–1997" (Huntsville, TX: TDCJ, 1999); TDCJ, *Statistical Report* (FY2009), 1; West and Sabol, *Prison Inmates at Midyear 2008*, 3.

48. Western, *Punishment and Inequality in America*, 20–28; Bonczar, *Prevalence of Imprisonment in the U.S. Population, 1974–2001*, 1.

49. TDCJ, Statistical Report (FY2005), 1; Paige M. Harrison and Allen J Beck, *Prison and Jail Inmates at Midyear 2005*, NCJ 213133 (Washington, DC: BJS, May 2006), 11; Census Bureau, "Texas Becomes Nation's Newest 'Majority-Minority' State," press advisory, CB05-118, August 11, 2005, table 1, http://www.census.gov/newsroom/releases/archives/population/cb05-118.html. Historical imprisonment disparities calculated by author based on TDCJ data and census estimates.

50. Austin to Wily Martin, May 30, 1833 in Eugene C. Barker, ed., *The Austin Papers*, 3 vols. (Washington, DC: U.S. Government Printing Office, 1924–1928), 2:981; Census Bureau, "Metropolitan and Micropolitan Statistical Area Estimates," July 1, 2008, table 7, http://www.census.gov/popest/metro/CBSA-est 2008-pop-chg.html.

51. Texas State Penitentiary, *Report* (1855), 15; Texas State Penitentiary, *Biennial Report* (1880), 2, 8; "White Says TDC Best in Nation," *Huntsville Item*, March 3, 1983, clipping in Pope Papers, box 4C842.

52. James Robert Reynolds, "The Administration of the Texas Prison System" (master's thesis, University of Texas, 1925), 12; "Hell on Earth," *Texas Siftings*, March 24, 1883.

53. Nathaniel Hawthorne, *The Scarlet Letter* (New York: Doubleday and McClure, 1898), 60.

54. James Burton Campbell, "The Prison Experience: Beginnings" (master's thesis, University of Texas, 1983), 2.

55. Sergeant Meduna, interview by author, July 22, 2002.

56. Hathorn, "Trashcan Food and a Concrete Shithouse." The American Psychiatric Association's *Diagnostic and Statistical Manual of Mental Disorders-IV* now uses the term "anti-social personality disorder."

57. Clemmer, *Prison Community*, xiii.

58. John J. Dilulio, *Governing Prisons: A Comparative Study of Correctional Management* (New York: Free Press, 1987), 2, 6–7.

59. Cahalan, "Historical Corrections Statistics," 29; Campbell Gibson, "Population of the 100 Largest Cities and Other Urban Places in the United States, 1790–1900," Population Division Working Paper, no. 27 (Washington, DC: Census Bureau, June 1998), table 14, http://www.census.gov/population/www/documentation/twps0027/tab14.txt.

60. West and Sabol, *Prison Inmates at Midyear 2008*, 3; "Census Bureau Announces Most Populous Cities," press advisory, CB07-91, June 28, 2007, table 1, http://www.census.gov/newsroom/releases/archives/population/cb07-91.html; *One in 31*, 42; Census Bureau, State and County QuickFacts, Texas (2008), http://quickfacts.census.gov/qfd/states/48000.html; Harrison and Beck, *Prison and Jail Inmates at Midyear 2005*, 10; Warren, *One in 100*, 3.

61. William Spelman, "The Limited Importance of Prison Expansion," in Blumstein and Wallman, *Crime Drop in America*, 97–129; TDCJ, "Mission Statement," http://www.tdcj.state.tx.us/. See also Levitt, "Understanding Why Crime Fell in the 1990s"; Zimring, *Great American Crime Decline*; Western, *Punishment and Inequality in America*, chap. 7.

62. BJS, "Justice Expenditure and Employment Extracts" (2006), http://www.ojp.usdoj.gov/bjs/eande.htm#selected; *One in 31*, 5; *Public Safety, Public Spending*.

63. Bureau of Labor Department, *News* (Washington, DC: Department of Labor, August 3, 2007), 1; Kathleen Maguire and Ann L. Pastore, eds., *Sourcebook of Criminal Justice Statistics, 2002* (Washington, DC: BJS, 2004), table 6.1, 478.

64. Sykes, *Society of Captives*, xiii; Robert Perkinson, "The Prison Dilemma," *Nation*, July 6, 2009, 35–36; Bruce Western, "Reentry: Reversing Mass Imprisonment," *Boston Review*, July-August 2008, 7–11; Jim Webb, "Why We Must Fix Our Prisons," *Parade Magazine*, March 29, 2009, http://www.parade.com/news/2009/03/why-we-must-fix-our-prisons.html; Ryan S. King, *The State of Sentencing 2007: Developments in Policy and Practice* (Washington, DC: Sentencing Project, January 2008); Grits for Breakfast, "TCJC Issues Legislative Wrapup," July 14, 2009, http://gritsforbreakfast.blogspot.com/2009/07/tcjc-issues-legislative-wrapup.html; Michele Deitch, interview by author, July 13, 2009.

65. Nicholas Katzenbach et al., *The Challenge of Crime in a Free Society* (Washington, DC: President's Commission on Law Enforcement and Administration of Justice, February 1967), 6.

17. Incarceration & Social Inequality *Bruce Western and Becky Pettit*

1. Harry J. Holzer, "Collateral Costs: Effects of Incarceration on Employment and Earnings Among Young Workers," in *Do Prisons Make Us Safer?* ed. Steven Raphael and Michael A. Stoll (New York: Russell Sage Foundation, 2009).

2. Devah Pager, *Marked: Race, Crime, and Finding Work in an Era of Mass Incarceration* (Chicago: University of Chicago Press, 2007).

3. Christopher Mumola, "Incarcerated Parents and Their Children" (Washington, DC: Bureau of Justice Statistics, 2000).

4. Megan Comfort, "In the Tube at San Quentin: The 'Secondary Prisonization' of Women Visiting Inmates," *Journal of Contemporary Ethnography* 32 (1) (2003): 82; emphasis original.

5. Christopher Wilderman, "Paternal Incarceration and Children's Physically Aggressive Behaviors: Evidence from the Fragile Families and Child Wellbeing Study," working paper 2008-02-FF (Fragile Families and Child Wellbeing, 2008).

Part IX: Solutions: Can Anything Be Done About This?

1. See Charles Ogletree, *The Presumption of Guilt: The Arrest of Henry Louis Gates, Jr. and Race, Class, and Crime in America* (New York: Palgrave MacMillan, 2010).

19. The Fire This Time   *Michelle Alexander*

1. In 1972, the total rate of incarceration (prison and jail) was approximately 160 per 100,000. Today, it is about 760 per 100,000. A reduction of 79 percent would be needed to get back to the 160 figure—itself a fairly high number when judged by international standards.

2. Marc Mauer, *Race to Incarcerate* (New York: The New Press, 1999), 11.

3. Christopher Sherman, "Cheney, Gonzales, Indicted Over Prisons," *Washington Times*, Nov. 19, 2008.

4. U.S. Securities and Exchange Commission, Corrections Corporation of America, Form 10K for the fiscal year ended Dec. 31, 2005.

5. Silja J.A. Talvi, "On the Inside with the American Correctional Association," in *Prison Profiteers: Who Makes Money from Mass Incarceration*, ed. Tara Herivel and Paul Wright (New York: The New Press, 2007).

6. Stephanie Chen, "Larger Inmate Population Is Boon to Private Prisons," *Wall Street Journal*, Nov. 28, 2008.

7. See generally Herivel and Wright, *Prison Profiteers*. For an excellent discussion of how surplus capital, labor, and land helped to birth the prison industry in rural America, see Ruth Wilson Gilmore, *Golden Gulag* (Berkeley: University of California Press, 2007).

8. For more information on racial impact statements, see Marc Mauer, "Racial Impact Statements as a Means of Reducing Unwarranted Sentencing Disparities," *Ohio State Journal of Criminal Law* 5 (2007): 19.

9. Lani Guinier, *Lift Every Voice* (New York: Simon & Schuster, 1998), 223.

10. Michael Omi and Howard Winant, *Racial Formation in the United States from the 1960s to the 1990s* (New York: Routledge, 1994), 84–88.

11. Gerald Rosenberg, *The Hollow Hope: Can Courts Bring About Social Change?* (Chicago: University of Chicago Press, 1991), 52.

12. Michael Klarman, "Brown, Racial Change, and the Civil Rights Movement," *Virginia Law Review* 80 (1994): 7, 9.

13. See ibid., arguing that Brown was "merely a ripple" with only a "negligible effect" on the South and civil rights advocacy.

14. See David Garrow, "Hopelessly Hollow History: Revisionist Devaluing of *Brown v. Board of Education*," *Virginia Law Review* 80 (1994): 151, persuasively making the case that Brown was a major inspiration to civil rights activists and provoked a fierce white backlash.

15. Bruce Western, *Punishment and Inequality in America* (New York: Russell Sage Foundation, 2006), 5, 187; William Spelman, "The Limited Importance of Prison Expansion," in *The Crime Drop in America*, ed. Alfred Blumstein and Joel Wallman

(New York: Cambridge University Press, 2000), 97–129; and Todd R. Clear, *Imprisoning Communities: How Mass Incarceration Makes Disadvantaged Neighborhoods Worse* (New York: Oxford University Press, 2007), 41–48.

16. See, e.g., Clear, *Imprisoning Communities*, 3.

17. Jeffrey Reiman makes a similar argument in *The Rich Get Richer and the Poor Get Prison*, 8th ed. (New York: Allyn & Bacon, 2006), although he mostly ignores the distinctive role of race in structuring the criminal justice system.

18. See "Study Finds Whites Anxious About Race," *Bryant Park Project*, National Public Radio, Dec. 3, 2007.

19. Fox Butterfield, "With Cash Tight, States Reassess Long Jail Terms," *New York Times*, Nov. 10, 2003.

20. Marc Mauer, "State Sentencing Reforms: Is the 'Get Tough' Era Coming to a Close?" *Federal Sentencing Reporter* 15, no. 1 (Oct. 2002).

21. Abby Goodnough, "Relaxing Marijuana Law Has Some Nervous," *New York Times*, Dec. 18, 2008, noting that eleven states have decriminalized first-time possession of marijuana.

22. For example, the ballot argument drafted by civil rights groups opposed to Proposition 54, a 2003 California ballot initiative that would have banned the collection of racial data by the state government, read: "We all want a colorblind society. But we won't get there by banning information."

23. Martin Luther King Jr., *Strength to Love* (Philadelphia: Fortress Press, 1963), 45–48.

24. Ibid., 31–32.

25. See Mary Frances Berry, "Vindicating Martin Luther King, Jr.: The Road to a Color-Blind Society," *Journal of Negro History* 81, no. 1–4 (Winter-Autumn 1996): 137, 140.

26. Stephen Steinberg, *Turning Back: The Retreat from Racial Justice in American Thought and Policy* (Boston: Beacon Press, 1995), 167.

27. Fred L. Pincus, *Reverse Discrimination: Dismantling the Myth* (Boulder, CO: Lynne Rienner, 2003).

28. Abby Rapoport, "The Work That Remains: A Forty-Year Update of the Kerner Commission Report," Economic Policy Institute, Nov. 19, 2008.

29. For an analysis of the impact of incarceration on unemployment, poverty, and education, see Western, *Punishment and Inequality in America*, 83–131.

30. Jesse Rothstein and Albert Yoon, "Affirmative Action in Law School Admissions: What Do Racial Preferences Do?" National Bureau of Economic Research, Cambridge, MA, Aug. 2008, www.nber.org/papers/w14276.

31. Steinberg, *Turning Back*, 195–96.

32. Martin Luther King Jr., "A Testament of Hope," in *A Testament of Hope: The Essential Writings and Speeches of Martin Luther King, Jr.* (New York: HarperCollins, 1986), 321.

33. Ibid., 315.

34. Lani Guinier and Gerald Torres, *The Miner's Canary: Enlisting Race, Resisting Power, Transforming Democracy* (Cambridge, MA: Harvard University Press, 2002), 114.

35. Ibid.

36. See Sentencing Project, *2008 Presidential Platforms on Criminal Justice* (Washington, DC, Mar. 2008), www.sentencingproject.org/tmp/File/Presidential CandidatesPlatforms.pdf.

37. Drew Harwell, "Obama's Drug Use Debated," CBS News, UWIRE.com, Feb. 12, 2008.

38. David Hunt, "Obama Fields Questions on Jacksonville Crime," *Florida Times-Union*, Sept. 22, 2008.

39. United States Government Accountability Office, Report to the Chairman, Committee on the Judiciary, House of Representatives, *Community Policing Grants: COPS Grants Were a Modest Contribution to Decline in Crime in 1990s*, GAO-06-104, Oct. 2005, www.gao.gov/new/items/d06104.pdf.

40. John L. Worrall and Tomislav V. Kovandzic, "COPS Grants and Crime Revisited," *Criminology* 45, no. 1 (Feb. 2007): 159–90.

41. Gary Fields, "White House Czar Calls for End of 'War on Drugs,'" *Wall Street Journal*, May 24, 2009; see also Office of National Drug Control Policy, *White House Drug Control Budget, FY2010 Funding Highlights* (May 2009).

42. Guinier and Torres, *Miner's Canary*, 118.

43. Ibid.

44. See Lani Guinier, "From Racial Liberalism to Racial Literacy: Brown v. Board of Education and the Interest-Divergence Dilemma," *Journal of American History* 92 (June 2004): 103, citing C. Arnold Anderson, "Social Class Differentials in the Schooling of Youth Within the Regions and Community-Size Groups of the United States," *Social Forces* 25 (May 1947): 440, 436; and C. Arnold Anderson, "Inequalities in Schooling in the South," *American Journal of Sociology* 60 (May 1955): 549, 553, 557.

45. W.E.B. Du Bois, *Black Reconstruction in America, 1860–1880* (New York: Free Press, 1935), 700.

46. Guinier, "Racial Liberalism," 102. See also Beth Roy, *Bitters in the Honey: Tales of Hope and Disappointment Across Divides of Race and Time* (Fayetteville: University of Arkansas Press, 1999), 318; and Pete Daniel, *Lost Revolutions: The South in the 1950s* (Chapel Hill: University of North Carolina Press, 2000), 270.

47. See Derrick Bell, "Brown v. Board of Education and the Interest-Convergence Dilemma," *Harvard Law Review* 93 (1980): 518, 525; David J. Armor, *Forced Justice: School Desegregation and the Law* (New York: Oxford University Press, 1996), 174–93, 206–7; and Robert J. Norrell, "Labor at the Ballot Box: Alabama Politics from the New Deal to the Dixiecrat Movement," *Journal of Southern History* 57 (May 1991): 201, 227, 233, 234.

48. W.E.B. Du Bois, *The Souls of Black Folk* (1903; New York: Bantam, 1989).

49. For a more detailed exploration of Martin Luther King Jr.'s journey from civil rights to human rights, see Thomas F. Jackson, *From Civil Rights to Human Rights: Martin Luther King, Jr. and the Struggle for Economic Justice* (Philadelphia: University of Pennsylvania Press, 2006); and Stewart Burns, *To the Mountaintop: Martin Luther King Jr.'s Sacred Mission to Save America* (New York: Harper One, 2005).

50. For background on the nature, structure, and history of human rights, see Cynthia Soohoo et al., eds., *Bringing Human Rights Home*, vol. 1 (New York: Praeger, 2007).

51. Stewart Burns, "America, You Must Be Born Again," *Sojourners* 33, no. 1 (Jan. 2004): 14.

52. James Baldwin, *The Fire Next Time* (New York: Vintage, 1962, 1993), 5–10.

21. From Racial Profiling to Racial Literacy   *Lani Guinier*

1. The order of the bias is highest among whites, then Asians, then Latinos, and lowest among blacks. Even though blacks deny the bias—and exhibit the lowest degree of bias—their IAT scores also show evidence of some bias. See, e.g., Mahzarin Banaji and Anthony Greenwald, *Mindbugs: The Science of Ordinary Bias* (New York: Random House, forthcoming).

2. Ibid. In the chapter "The Stealth of Stereotypes," Dr. Banaji and Dr. Greenwald analyzed the data from 85,742 race-weapon tests sampled at the Web site implicit.harvard.edu. She and her colleagues observed an extremely strong association of black faces and weapons "for all groups who took the test—white, Asian, Hispanic and even African Americans themselves." The size of the bias was largest in whites and Asians, next largest in Hispanics, and smallest in African Americans.

3. For an additional analysis of "racial literacy," please see Lani Guinier, "Race and Reality in a Front-Porch Encounter," *Chronicle of Higher Education*, July 30, 2009; Lani Guinier, "From Racial Liberalism to Racial Literacy: *Brown v. Board of Education* and the Interest-Divergence Dilemma," *Journal of American History* 91, no. 1 (June 2004): 92–118, available at http://www.law.harvard.edu/faculty/guinier/publications/racial.pdf.

Bibliography

American Law Institute. 1962. *Model Penal Code. Proposed Official Draft.* Philadelphia: American Law Institute.

———. 2007. *Model Penal Code: Sentencing.* Tentative draft no. 1 (April 9, 2007). Philadelphia: American Law Institute.

Anderson, Elijah. 1999. *Code of the Street: Decency, Violence and the Moral Life of the Inner City.* New York: W. W. Norton.

Benedetto, Richard. 2005. "GOP: 'We Were Wrong' to Play Racial Politics." *USA Today,* July 14. http://www.usatoday.com/news/washington/2005-07-14-GOP -racial-politics_x.htm (accessed July 26, 2010).

Bennett, Susan F. 1995. "Community Organizations and Crime." *Annals of the American Academy of Political and Social Science* 539 (1):72–84.

Block, Richard. 1979. "Community, Environment, and Violent Crime." *Criminology* 17 (1):46–57.

Bloom, Barbara. 1995. "Imprisoned Mothers." In Gabel and Johnston, *Children of Incarcerated Parents,* 21–30.

Blumstein, Alfred. 1993. "Racial Disproportionality of U.S. Prison Populations Revisited." *University of Colorado Law Review* 64 (3):743–60.

Blumstein, Alfred, and Joel Wallman. 2006. "The Crime Drop and Beyond." *Annual Review of Laws and Social Sciences* 2:125–46.

Browne, Irene. 1997. "The Black-White Gap in Labor Force Participation Among Women." *American Sociological Review* 62 (2):236–52.

Carlson, Bonnie, and Neil Cervera. 1992. *Inmates and Their Wives.* Westport, CT: Greenwood Press.

Cho, Rosa, and Robert LaLonde, 2005. "The Impact of Incarceration in State Prison on the Employment Prospects of Women." Unpublished paper.

Cohen, Barbara E. 1992. *Evaluation of the Teen Parents Employment Demonstration.* Washington, DC: Urban Institute.

Crutchfield, Robert D. 2005. "Neighborhoods, Collective Efficacy, and Inmate Release: A Summary of Preliminary Analyses." Unpublished paper.

Crutchfield, Robert D., and Susan R. Pitchford. 1997. "Work and Crime: The Effects of Labor Stratification." *Social Forces* 76:93–118.

Darity, William A., and Samuel L. Myers Jr. 1994. *The Black Underclass: Critical Essays on Race and Unwantedness.* New York: Garland.

Edin, Kathryn, and Laura Lein. 1997. "Work, Welfare, and Single Mothers' Economic Survival Strategies." *American Sociological Review* 62 (2):253–66.

Edin, Kathryn, Timothy Nelson, and Rechelle Paranal. 2004. "Fatherhood and Incarceration as Potential Turning Points in the Criminal Careers of Unskilled Men." In Pattillo, Weiman, and Western, *Imprisoning America,* 46–75.

Fagan, Jeffrey. 1997. "Legal and Illegal Work: Crime, Work and Unemployment." In *Dealing with Urban Crises,* edited by Burton Weisbrod and James Worthy, 33–71. Evanston, IL: Northwestern University Press.

Fagan, Jeffrey. 2006. "Incarceration and Voting." Unpublished memorandum to the Project on Concentrated Incarceration of the Open Society Institute.

Fagan, Jeffrey, and Richard B. Freeman. 1999. "Crime and Work." In *Crime and Justice: A Review of Research*, Vol. 25, edited by Michael Tonry, 225–90. Chicago: University of Chicago Press.

Feld, Barry C. 1999. *Bad Kids: Race and the Transformation of the Juvenile Court.* New York: Oxford University Press.

Fletcher, George. 1978. *Rethinking Criminal Law.* Boston: Little, Brown.

Frase, Richard. 2009. "What Explains Persistent Racial Disproportionality in Minnesota's Prison and Jail Populations?" In *Crime and Justice: A Review of Research*, vol. 38, edited by Michael Tonry. Chicago: University of Chicago Press.

Freeman, Richard B. 1992. "Crime and Unemployment of Disadvantaged Youth." In *Drugs, Crime and Social Isolation: Barriers to Urban Opportunity*, edited by Adele Harrell and George Peterson. Washington, DC: Urban Institute.

Gabel, Katherine, and Denise Johnston, eds. *Children of Incarcerated Parents.* New York: Lexington.

Gabel, Stewart, and Richard Shindledecker. 1993. "Characteristics of Children Whose Parents Have Been Incarcerated." *Hospital and Community Psychiatry* 44 (7):543–59.

Garfinkel, Irwin, Sara McLanahan, and Thomas L. Hanson. 1998. "A Patchwork Quilt of Non-Resident Fathers." Working paper no. 98–25. Princeton, NJ: Princeton University Press.

Gibson, Christina, Kathryn Edin, and Sara McLanahan. 2003. "High Hopes but Even Higher Expectations: The Retreat from Marriage Among Low-Income Couples." Working Paper 03-066-FF. Princeton, NJ: Center for Research on Child Wellbeing, Princeton University.

Grogger, Jeffrey. 1995. "The Effect of Arrests on the Employment and Earnings of Young Men." *Quarterly Journal of Economics* 110 (1):51–71.

Hagan, John. 1993. "The Social Embeddedness of Crime and Unemployment." *Criminology* 31 (4):465–92.

Hagan, John, and Ronit Dinovitzer. 1999. "Collateral Consequences of Imprisonment for Children, Communities and Prisoners." In *Prisons*, edited by Michael Tonry and Joan Petersilia, 121–62. Chicago: University of Chicago Press.

Hairston, Creasie. 1998. "The Forgotten Parent: Understanding the Forces That Influence Incarcerated Fathers' Relationships with Their Children." *Child Welfare* 77 (5):617–39.

Henig, Jeffrey R. 1982. *Neighborhood Mobilization: Redevelopment and Response.* New Brunswick, NJ: Rutgers University Press.

Huebner, Beth M. 2005. "The Effect of Incarceration on Marriage and Work in the Life Course." *Justice Quarterly* 22 (3):281–301.

Jacobs, David, and Ronald E. Helms. 1996. "Toward a Political Model of Incarceration: A Time-Series Examination of Multiple Explanations for Prison Admission Rates." *American Journal of Sociology* 102 (2):323–57.

Jacobson, Michael. 2005. *Downsizing Prisons: How to Reduce Crime and End Mass Incarceration.* New York: New York University Press.

Johnson, Elizabeth I., and Jane Waldfogel. 2004. "Children of Incarcerated Parents: Multiple Risks and Children's Living Arrangements." In Pattillo, Weiman, and Western, *Imprisoning America*, 97–134.

Johnson, Rucker C., and Steven Raphael. 2005. "The Effects of Male Incarceration on Dynamics of AIDS Infection Rates Among African-American Women and

Men." Unpublished paper presented to the incarceration study group of the Russell Sage Foundation, July.

Kampfner, Christina Jose. 1995. "Post-Traumatic Stress Reactions in Children of Imprisoned Mothers." In Gabel and Johnston, *Children of Incarcerated Parents*, 121–62.

King, Ryan S., and Marc Mauer. 2004. *The Vanishing Black Electorate: Felony Disenfranchisement in Atlanta, Georgia*. Washington, DC: Sentencing Project.

Kling, Jeffrey. 1999. "The Effect of Prison Sentence Length on Subsequent Employment and Earnings of Criminal Defendants." Woodrow Wilson School discussion paper on Economics, no. 208, Princeton University.

Lalonde, Robert, and Susan George. 2003. *Incarcerated Mothers: The Project on Female Prisoners and Their Children*. New York: Open Society Institute.

Laub, John, Daniel Nagin, and Robert Sampson. 1998. "Trajectories of Change in Criminal Offending: Good Marriages and the Desistence Process." *American Sociological Review* 63 (2):225–38.

Loury, Glenn C. "Race, Incarceration, and American Values." In Glenn Loury, Pamela S. Karlan, Tommie Shelby, and Loïc Wacquant, *Race, Incarceration, and American Values*. Cambridge, MA: MIT Press.

Lynch, Allen K., and David W. Rasmussen. 2001. "Measuring the Impact of Crime on House Prices." *Applied Economics* 33 (15):1981–89.

Lynch, James P., and William J. Sabol. 2004. "Effects of incarceration on Informal Social Control in Communities." In Pattillo, Weiman, and Western, *Imprisoning America*, 135–64.

Mauer, Marc. 2007. "Racial Impact Statements as a Means of Reducing Unwarranted Sentencing Disparities." *Ohio State Journal of Criminal Law* 5 (1): 19–46.

Mauer, Marc, and Tracy Huling. 1995. *Young Black Americans and the Criminal Justice System: Five Years Later*. Washington, DC: Sentencing Project.

Mears, Daniel P., and Avinash Bhati. 2006. "No Community Is an Island: The Effects of Resource Deprivation on Urban Violence in Spatially and Socially Proximate Communities." *Criminology* 44 (3):509–48.

Miller, Jerome G. 1992. *Hobbling a Generation: Young African American Males in the Criminal Justice System of America's Cities*. Baltimore: National Center on Institutions and Alternatives.

Miller, Marc L., and Ronald F. Wright. 2008. "The Black Box." *Iowa Law Review* 94 (1):125–96.

Moore, Quinn, and Heidi Shierholz. 2005. "Externalities of Imprisonment: Does Maternal Incarceration Affect Child Outcomes?" Paper presented at the meeting of the American Society of Criminology, Toronto.

Murray, Joseph. 2005. "The Effects of Imprisonment on the Families and Children of Prisoners." In *The Effects of Imprisonment*, edited by Allison Liebling and Shadd Maruna, 442–92. Cullompton, UK: Willan.

Murray, Joseph, and David Farrington. Forthcoming. "Effects of Parental Incarceration on Children." In *Crime and Justice: A Review of Research*, edited by Michael Tonry. Chicago: University of Chicago Press.

Murray, Joseph, and David Farrington. 2005. "Parental Imprisonment: Effects on Boys' Anti-social Behaviour and Delinquency Through the Life Course." *Journal of Child Psychology and Psychiatry* 46 (12):1269–78.

Murray, Joseph, Carl-Gunnar Janson, and David Farrington. 2007. "Crime in Adult Offspring of Prisoners: A Cross-National Comparison of Two Longitudinal Samples." *Criminal Justice & Behavior* 34 (1):133–49.

Nurse, Anne M. 2004. "Returning to Strangers: Newly Paroled Young Fathers and Their Children." In Pattillo, Weiman, and Western, *Imprisoning America*, 76–96.

Parcel, Toby L., and Elizabeth G. Menaghan. 1993. "Family Social Capital and Children's Behavior Problems." *Social Psychology Quarterly* 56 (2):120–35.

Pattillo, Mary, David Weiman, and Bruce Western, eds. *Imprisoning America: The Social Effects of Mass Incarceration.* New York: Russell Sage.

Pettit, Becky, and Bruce Western. 2004. "Mass Imprisonment and the Life Course: Race and Class Inequality in U.S. Incarceration." *American Sociological Review* 69 (2):151–69.

Phillips, Susan, and Barbara Bloom. 1998. "In Whose Best Interest? The Impact of Changing Public Policy on Relatives Caring for Children with Incarcerated Parents." *Child Welfare* 77 (5):531–41.

Phillips, Susan D., Alaatin Erkanli, Gordon P. Keeler, E. Jane Costello, and Adrian Angold. 2006. "Disentangling the Risks: Parent Criminal Justice Involvement and Child's Exposure to Family Risks." *Criminology & Public Policy* 5 (4):101–206.

Podolefsky, Aaron, and Frederik DuBow. 1980. *Strategies for Community Crime Prevention: Collective Responses to Crime in Urban America.* Reactions to Crime Project, Center for Urban Affairs. Evanston, IL: Northwestern University Press.

Pogarsky, Greg, Alan J. Lizotte, and Terence P. Thornberry. 2003. "The Delinquency of Children Born to Young Mothers: Results from the Rochester Youth Development Study." *Criminology* 41 (4):1249–86.

Pratt, Travis C., Michael G. Turner, and Alex Piquero. 2004. "Parental Socialization and Community Context: A Longitudinal Analysis of the Structural Sources of Low Self-Control." *Journal of Research in Crime & Delinquency* 41 (3): 219–43.

Rengifo, Andres, and Elin Waring. 2005. "A Network Perspective on the Impact of Incarceration on Communities." Paper presented to the annual meetings of the American Society of Criminology, Toronto, November 17.

Roberts, Dorothy. 2004. "The Social and Moral Cost of Mass Incarceration in African American Communities." *Stanford Law Review* 56 (5):1271–305.

Roberts, Julian, and Andrew von Hirsch, eds. 2010. *Previous Convictions at Sentencing: Theoretical and Applied Perspectives.* Oxford: Hart.

Sabol, William J., and James P. Lynch. 2003. "Assessing the Longer-Run Effects of Incarceration: Impact on Families and Employment." In *Crime Control and Social Justice: The Delicate Balance,* edited by Darnell Hawkins, Samuel Myers, Jr., and Randolph Stine. Westport, CT: Greenwood Press.

Sampson, Robert J., and W. Byron Groves. 1989. "Community Structure and Crime: Testing Social Disorganization Theory." *American Journal of Sociology* 94:774–802.

Sampson, Robert J., and John H. Laub. 1993. *Crime in the Making: Pathways and Turning Points Through Life.* Cambridge, MA: Harvard University Press.

Sampson, Robert J., Stephen W. Raudenbush, and Felton Earls. 1997. "Neighborhoods and Violent Crime: A Multilevel Study of Collective Efficacy." *Science* 277 (5328):918–24.

Singer, Richard. 1979. *Just Deserts: Sentencing Based on Equality and Desert.* Lexington, MA: Ballinger.

Stewart, Eric A., and Ronald Simons. 2006. "Structure and Culture in African American Adolescent Violence: A Partial Test of the Code of the Street Hypothesis." *Justice Quarterly* 23 (1):1–33.

Sullivan, Mercer L. 1989. *Getting Paid: Youth, Crime and Work in the Inner City.* Ithaca, NY: Cornell University Press.

Taylor, Ralph, and Jeanette Covington. 1988. "Neighborhood Changes in Ecology and Violence." *Criminology* 26 (4):553–89.

Thomas, Adam. 2005. "The Old Ball and Chain: Unlocking the Correlation Between Incarceration and Marriage." Unpublished manuscript.

Thomas, James C., and Elizabeth Torrone. 2006. "Incarceration as Forced Migration: Effects on Selected Community Health Outcomes." *American Journal of Public Health* 96 (10):1–5.

Tonry, Michael. 1995. *Malign Neglect: Race, Crime, and Punishment in America.* New York: Oxford University Press.

———. 2004. *Thinking about Crime: Sense and Sensibility in American Penal Culture.* New York: Oxford University Press.

———. 2010. "The Questionable Relevance of Previous Convictions to Punishments for Later Crimes." In *Previous Convictions at Sentencing: Theoretical and Applied Perspectives,* edited by Julian Roberts and Andrew von Hirsch. Oxford: Hart.

Tonry, Michael, and Matthew Melewski. 2008. "The Malign Effects of Drug and Crime Control Policies on Black Americans." In *Crime and Justice: A Review of Research,* vol. 37, edited by Michael Tonry. Chicago: University of Chicago Press.

Tyler, Tom. 1990. *Why People Obey the Law.* New Haven, CT: Yale University Press.

Tyler, Tom R., and Jeffrey Fagan. 2005. "Legitimacy and Cooperation: Why Do People Help the Police Fight Crime in Their Communities?" Columbia Public Law Research Paper No. 06-99. Available at SSRN: http://ssrn.com/abstract=887737.

Uggen, Christopher, and Jeff Manza. 2006. *Locked Out: Felon Disenfranchisement and American Democracy.* New York: Oxford University Press.

Uggen, Christopher, Sara Wakefield, and Bruce Western. 2005. "Work and Family Perspectives on Reentry." In *Prisoner Reentry and Crime in America,* edited by Jeremy Travis and Christy Visher, 209–43. New York: Cambridge University Press.

U.S. Department of Justice, Bureau of Justice Statistics. 1997. *Survey of Inmates in State and Federal Correctional Facilities.* Ann Arbor, MI: ICPSR.

Vacha, Edward F., and T.F. McLaughlin. 1992. "The Social Structural, Family, School and Personal Characteristics of At-Risk Students: Policy Recommendations for School Personnel." *Journal of Education* 174 (3):9–25.

Venkatesh, Sudhir Alladi. 1997. "The Social Organization of Street Gang Activity in an Urban Ghetto. *American Journal of Sociology* 103 (1):82–111.

Viboch, Marcy. 2005. *Childhood Loss and Behavioral Problems: Loosening the Links.* New York: Vera Institute of Justice.

Western, Bruce. 2006. *Punishment and Inequality in America.* New York: Russell Sage.

Western, Bruce, Jeffrey Kling, and David Weiman. 2001. "The Labor Market Consequences of Incarceration." *Crime and Delinquency* 47 (3):410–38.

Western, Bruce, Leonard M. Lopoo, and Sara McLanahan. 2004. "Incarceration and the Bonds Between Parents in Fragile Families." In Pattillo, Weiman, and Western, *Imprisoning America,* 21–46.

Western, Bruce, Mary Pattillo, and David Weiman. 2004. "Introduction." In Pattillo, Weiman, and Western, *Imprisoning America*, 1–18.

Whitman, James. 2003. *Harsh Justice*. New York: Oxford University Press.

Widom, Kathy Spatz. 1989. "Does Violence Beget Violence: A Critical Examination of the Literature." *Psychological Bulletin* 106 (1):3–28.

————. 1994. "Childhood Victimization and Risk for Adolescent Problem Behaviors." In *Adolescent Problem Behaviors: Issues and Research*, edited by Robert D. Ketterlinus and Michael E. Lamb, 127–64. New York: Lawrence Earlbaum.

Wilson, William Julius. 1987. *The Truly Disadvantaged: The Inner City, the Underclass, and Public Policy*. Chicago: University of Chicago Press.

Permissions

"Death by a Thousand Little Cuts: Studies of the Impact of Incarceration" by Todd R. Clear is excerpted here from *Imprisoning Communities: How Mass Incarceration Makes Disadvantaged Neighborhoods Worse* (New York: Oxford University Press, 2009), 93–117, with permission.

"Doing Less Harm" by Michael Tonry is excerpted here from *Punishing Race: A Continuing American Dilemma* (New York: Oxford University Press, 2011), 148–52, 164–74, with permission.